Fieldwork in Modern Chinese History

This book explores how fieldwork has been used to research Chinese history in the past and new ways that others might use it in the future. It introduces the previous generations of scholars who ventured out of the archive to conduct local investigations in Chinese cities, villages, farms and temples. It goes on to present the techniques of historical fieldwork, providing guidance on how to integrate oral history into research plans and archival research, conduct interviews, and locate sources in the field. Chapters by established researchers relate these techniques to specific types of fieldwork, including religion, the imperial past, natural environments and agriculture. Combining the past and the future of the craft, the book provides a rich resource for scholars coming new to fieldwork in the history of China.

Thomas David DuBois is Professor of Humanities at Beijing Normal University.

Jan Kiely is Professor and Associate Director of the Centre for China Studies and Associate Director of the Universities Service Centre for China Studies, The Chinese University of Hong Kong.

The Historical Anthropology of Chinese Society Series
Series editor: David Faure, Chinese University of Hong Kong

Historians are being increasingly attracted by the methodology of historical anthropology, an approach which combines observations in the field with documentary analysis, both of official documents and of documents collected from local society. In China, historians have been pursuing such local historical research for a generation, with very little of this work being available in English hitherto. This series makes available in English research undertaken by the Historical Anthropology of Chinese Society project based at the Chinese University of Hong Kong, and related work. The books argue that top-heavy, dynasty-centred history is incomplete without an understanding of how local communities were involved in the government process and in the creation of their own historical narratives. The books argue that Chinese social history needs to be rewritten from the bottom up.

1 **The Fisher Folk of Later Imperial and Modern China**
   An Historical Anthropology of Boat-and-Shed Living
   Edited by Xi He and David Faure

2 **Colonial Administration and Land Reform in East Asia**
   Edited by Sui-Wai Cheung

3 **Fieldwork in Modern Chinese History**
   A Research Guide
   Edited by Thomas David DuBois and Jan Kiely

For more information about this series, please visit: https://www.routledge.com/The-Historical-Anthropology-of-Chinese-Society-Series/book-series/HISTANTHCHINSOC

Fieldwork in Modern Chinese History
A Research Guide

**Edited by
Thomas David DuBois and
Jan Kiely**

LONDON AND NEW YORK

First published 2020
by Routledge
2 Park Square, Milton Park, Abingdon, Oxon OX14 4RN

and by Routledge
52 Vanderbilt Avenue, New York, NY 10017

Routledge is an imprint of the Taylor & Francis Group, an informa business

© 2020 selection and editorial matter, Thomas David DuBois and Jan Kiely; individual chapters, the contributors

The right of Thomas David DuBois and Jan Kiely to be identified as the authors of the editorial material, and of the authors for their individual chapters, has been asserted in accordance with sections 77 and 78 of the Copyright, Designs and Patents Act 1988.

All rights reserved. No part of this book may be reprinted or reproduced or utilised in any form or by any electronic, mechanical, or other means, now known or hereafter invented, including photocopying and recording, or in any information storage or retrieval system, without permission in writing from the publishers.

Trademark notice: Product or corporate names may be trademarks or registered trademarks, and are used only for identification and explanation without intent to infringe.

British Library Cataloguing-in-Publication Data
A catalogue record for this book is available from the British Library

Library of Congress Cataloging-in-Publication Data
Names: DuBois, Thomas David, 1969– editor. | Kiely, Jan, 1965– editor.
Title: Fieldwork in modern Chinese history : a research guide / edited by Thomas David DuBois and Jan Kiely.
Description: London; New York : Routledge/Taylor & Francis Group, 2020. |
Series: The Historical Anthropology of Chinese Society Series; 3. | Includes bibliographical references and index.
Identifiers: LCCN 2019031949 | ISBN 9780367263911 (hardback) | ISBN 9780429293078 (ebook)
Subjects: LCSH: China—History—Study and teaching. | History—China—Research. | History—Fieldwork.
Classification: LCC DS734.95.F54 2020 | DDC 951.0072/3—dc23
LC record available at https://lccn.loc.gov/2019031949

ISBN: 978-0-367-26391-1 (hbk)
ISBN: 978-0-429-29307-8 (ebk)

Typeset in Times New Roman
by codeMantra

Contents

List of contributors ix
Editors' preface: Fieldwork in Modern Chinese History xiii
THOMAS DAVID DUBOIS AND JAN KIELY
Acknowledgments xxiii

SECTION 1
History and fieldwork in historical perspective 1

1 They went to the people but did they hear them? Comments on field research in China in the 1920s and 1930s 3
 DAVID FAURE

2 A brief history of Japanese field research on China 22
 LINDA GROVE

3 The traditionalist phase in Taiwan anthropology: 1960–1980 35
 MYRON L. COHEN

SECTION 2
Work reflections 49

4 Fieldwork for Ming historians 51
 MICHAEL SZONYI

5 Conducting fieldwork as a local: perspectives from Hulunbuir 61
 GUAN YUXIA, WITH ZHANG WEI

6 Who are they, and who am I?: discovering gender and ethnicity in the Sino-Tibetan borderland 69
 XIAOFEI KANG

vi Contents

7 Ritual performance in changing local society 82
STEPHEN JONES

8 Beyond the border of disciplines and societies: from fieldwork among the Lahu to the history of *bazi* basins 96
JIANXIONG MA

SECTION 3
Walking the ground, talking to people 107

9 Basic questions for fieldwork on pre-1949 Chinese society 109
JOHN LAGERWEY

10 Festivals in the field—a social historical perspective 125
PAUL R. KATZ

11 Doing historical-anthropological fieldwork in Jiangnan: Gazetteers, newspapers, and real life 137
VINCENT GOOSSAERT

12 Incorporating historical GIS in fieldwork on Chinese culture and religion 144
KENNETH DEAN

13 Walks in Canton: doing historical anthropology in a Chinese city 159
MAY BO CHING AND ZHIWEI LIU

14 Contextualizing ethnic classification: the case of *hemu* (合亩) among the Li of Hainan 178
XI HE

15 Mud on your boots: researching the social and environmental history of conservation in Baishui county, Shaanxi during the 1950s 188
MICAH S. MUSCOLINO

16 Medicine, health, and disease: among the barefoot doctors of Hangzhou 204
XIAOPING FANG

	Contents	vii
17	Discovering the Cultural Revolution in oral history GUOQIANG DONG	215
18	Walking a production chain: an interdisciplinary approach to the history of things THOMAS DAVID DUBOIS	224

SECTION 4
Finding and working with grassroots documents 237

19	Field research using contracts (*qiyue*): legal archives of late Qing and early Republican-era Longquan, Zhejiang ZHENGZHEN DU	239
20	Account books (*zhangben*) in local history studies YONGHUA LIU	252
21	Land and property deeds and urban studies: a case study of deeds collected by Ms. Liu SUJUAN HUANG	264
22	Genealogies and revolution in the Jiangxi Soviet WEIXIN RAO	275
23	Using local public security archives from the 1950s—Poyang county, Jiangxi SHIGU LIU	282
24	Exploring a northern Jiangsu county Intangible Cultural Heritage archive JAN KIELY	289
	Index	301

Contributors

May Bo Ching 程美寶 is Professor of History at City University of Hong Kong. Her major research interest is the social and cultural history of modern China. Recently, she has been studying how the regional culture of South China took shape in a trans-regional context in terms of sound, color, and taste.

Myron L. Cohen 孔邁隆 is Professor of Anthropology at Columbia University. He has done extensive fieldwork in Taiwan and in villages in northern, eastern, and western mainland China. His present writing concerns the historical anthropology of a community in southern Taiwan. His publications include *Kinship, Contract, Community, and State: Anthropological Perspectives on China* (2005) and *House United, House Divided: The Chinese Family in Taiwan* (1976). Professor Cohen received his PhD in anthropology from Columbia University in 1967, after having joined the Columbia faculty in 1966.

Kenneth Dean 丁荷生 is Lee Chair and James McGill Professor Emeritus of McGill University, and Professor in the Department of Chinese Studies at the National University of Singapore. He is the author of several books on Daoism and Chinese popular religion, and directed *Bored in Heaven: A Film about Ritual Sensation*, an 80-minute documentary film on ritual celebrations around Chinese New Year in Putian, Fujian, China. His current research concerns transnational trust and temple networks linking Singapore Chinese temples to Southeast China and Southeast Asia. As part of this project, he is conducting a survey of 800 Chinese temples in Singapore.

Guoqiang Dong 董国强 is Professor of History at Fudan University, working primarily in the area of Chinese modern political and social history.

Zhengzhen Du 杜正贞 is Professor and supervisor of doctoral students in the Department of History at Zhejiang University. Since earning her PhD in History from the Chinese University of Hong Kong, she has specialized in late imperial and modern Chinese social and legal history, with a particular interest in grassroots social organizations, rural life, and folk beliefs. Her published monographs include *"Cunshe" and the Gentry in Ming and Qing Times: Institutional Transformation in the Rural Society of*

x *Contributors*

Shanxi Province's Zezhou Prefecture and *Custom, Contracts and Rights in Highland Society in Modern Times*.

Thomas David DuBois 杜博思 is Professor of Humanities at Beijing Normal University. He has written extensively on the histories of Chinese religion, law, charity, and rural society, including *Sacred Village: Social Change and Religious Life in Rural North China* (2005), *Religion and the Making of Modern East Asia* (2011), and *Empire and the Meaning of Religion in Northeast Asia: Manchuria 1900–1945* (2017). His current work examines the productive, ecological, commercial, and culinary faces of China's cattle industries.

Xiaoping Fang 方小平 is Assistant Professor of History at School of Humanities, Nanyang Technological University, Singapore. His current research interests focus on the history of medicine, health, and disease in twentieth-century China, specializing in the post-1949 period. He is the author of *Barefoot Doctors and Western Medicine in China* (2012 and 2015). He is currently working on a book manuscript entitled *Global Pandemic, Local Politics: Disease and Social Restructuring in Mao's China*.

David Faure 科大卫 is Wei Lun Research Professor of Chinese History and coordinator of the Historical Anthropology of Chinese Society project at the Chinese University of Hong Kong.

Vincent Goossaert 高万桑 (PhD, École Pratique des Hautes Études, Paris, 1997) was a research fellow at the French National Centre for Scientific Research (CNRS) (1998–2012) and is now Professor of Daoism and Chinese religions at EPHE-PSL (Université Paris Sciences et Lettres); he has served as dean of its graduate school (2014–2018). His research deals with the social history of Chinese religion in late imperial and modern times. He is co-editor of *T'oung Pao*, a leading journal in sinology established in 1890.

Linda Grove 顾琳 is Professor Emerita, Sophia University (Tokyo). She first conducted fieldwork in Gaoyang County, Hebei, in 1980, and has been a member of collaborative groups that conducted fieldwork in Songjiang (Shanghai) in the early 1980s and follow-up studies of several of the *kankō chōsa* villages in the 1990s and the early twenty-first century. Her major fields of research include rural industrialization, business practices, rural economic change, and women's history.

Yuxia Guan 关宇霞 is an associate professor of psychology at Hulunbuir University. She is the author of *Reindeer-Breeding Evenks' Psychological Trauma during a Century of Change*. Her current research project on psychological transformation among Three Minority Ethnic Groups in North China has been supported by the Humanities and Social Sciences project of the China Ministry of Education.

Xi He 贺喜 is Assistant Professor in the Department of History, The Chinese University of Hong. She studies the history of local society and the common people. In her research, she focuses on two questions. One is how the image of a traditional China derived from the Song dynasty; the other is how concepts, images, and rituals of the new state and new citizen emerged when the Qing empire was replaced by the Republic.

Sujuan Huang 黄素娟 received her PhD in history from Sun Yat-sen University, and was visiting scholar at Harvard-Yanjing Institute, 2016–2017. She is now a researcher with the History of Southern Chinese Commerce research center at the Guangdong University of Finance, and lecturer of sociology at the Department of Humanities and Communication. Her research areas are the history of merchant networks in Guangdong, Hong Kong, and Macao, and modern urban history, including the evolution of urban forms, urban land rights, and city-rural relations.

Stephen Jones 钟思第 has been documenting living traditions of folk ritual and soundscape in rural China since 1986. His books include *Plucking the Winds*, two volumes of *Ritual and Music of North China* (both with DVDs), and *In Search of the Folk Daoists of North China*. His main focus since 2011 has been the Li family household Daoists of Shanxi, resulting in the film *Li Manshan: Portrait of a Folk Daoist* and the accompanying book *Daoist Priests of the Li Family: Ritual Life in Village China* (Three Pines Press). His blog has a wide range of related material.

Xiaofei Kang 康笑菲 is Associate Professor of Chinese religions at the George Washington University. She is currently working on gender, religion, and the twentieth-century Chinese Communist revolution.

Paul R. Katz 康豹 is Distinguished Research Fellow at the Institute of Modern History, Academia Sinica, and Program Director of the Chiang Ching-kuo Foundation for International Scholarly Exchange. His research centers on modern Chinese religious life, with his most recent monograph (*Religion in China and Its Modern Fate*) being published in early 2014. At present, he is completing a book manuscript on the interaction between Han and non-Han religious traditions in Southwest China entitled *Religion, Ethnicity, and Gender in Western Hunan during the Modern Era*.

Jan Kiely 楊凱里 is Professor and Associate Director of the Centre for China Studies at the Chinese University of Hong Kong. He is the author of *The Compelling Ideal: Thought Reform and the Prison in China, 1901–1956* (2014), and co-editor of *Modern Chinese Religion II: 1850–2015* (2015) and *Recovering Buddhism in Modern China* (2016).

John Lagerwey 勞格文 received his PhD in Chinese Studies at Harvard in 1975. He is currently Research Professor of Chinese Studies in the Centre for China Studies, Chinese University of Hong Kong. He is chief editor of some 40 volumes of ethnographic research and of eight volumes on periods of paradigm shift in Chinese religious history. His most recent authored books are *China, a Religious State* (2010) and *Paradigm Shifts in Early and Modern Chinese Religion: A History* (2018).

xii *Contributors*

Shigu Liu 劉詩古 is Assistant Professor in the History Department of Xiamen University. His main research interests combine fieldwork and official archives to study the social economic history of the Ming and Qing Dynasties, and the history of Chinese revolution in the twentieth century. His newest book is *Resources, Property Rights and Order: the Fishery Tax System and Lake Society in the Poyang Lake Region during the Ming and Qing Periods.*

Yonghua Liu 刘永华 (PhD, McGill) is Professor of History at Fudan University. His interests includes history of Confucian rituals, popular literacy, and interpersonal networks in late imperial and modern China. He is the author of *Confucian Rituals and Chinese Villagers* (2013).

Zhiwei Liu 刘志伟 is Professor of History at Sun Yat-sen University, Guangzhou. His major research interest is the social and economic history of Ming and Qing China. For years he has been examining how regional economics and societies of the Pearl River Delta evolved between the sixteenth and twentieth centuries.

Jianxiong Ma 马健雄 is an associate professor in anthropology at the Hong Kong University of Science and Technology. His works include *The Lahu Minority in Southwest China* (2013) and research articles on the historical formation of the Yunnan and Burma frontier and ecological conditions of cultural diversity in Southwest China.

Micah S. Muscolino 穆盛博 is Professor and Paul G. Pickowicz Endowed Chair in Modern Chinese History at the University of California, San Diego. He is author of *Fishing Wars and Environmental Change in Late Imperial and Modern China* (2009) and *The Ecology of War in China: Henan Province, the Yellow River, and Beyond* (2015). His current research focuses on the history of water and soil conservation in Northwest China from the 1940s to the present.

Weixin Rao 饶伟新 is Associate Professor in the Department of History at Xiamen University. His research focuses on the social and cultural history of rural China, with a particular interest in grassroots historical documents, in the late imperial and Republican periods.

Michael Szonyi 宋怡明 is the Frank Wen-hsiung Wu Memorial Professor of Chinese History and Director of the Fairbank Center for Chinese Studies at Harvard University. His books include *The Art of Being Governed: Everyday Politics in Late Imperial China* (2018), *A Companion to Chinese History* (2017), and *Cold War Island: Quemoy on the Frontline* (2008)

Wei Zhang 张微 earned her PhD in Behavioral and Health Sciences at Kyushu University, Japan. She now teaches cross-cultural psychology at Hulunbuir University.

Editors' preface
Fieldwork in Modern Chinese History

Thomas David DuBois and Jan Kiely

This volume introduces a selection of the many ways and reasons that fieldwork can contribute to research on China's modern history. Incubated in multi-disciplinary research collaborations, it presents experiences and perspectives of 26 scholars in eight countries. It seeks above all to be *useful*—a seminar of techniques and lessons learned over decades of work in the field *and* in the archive—for students and scholars, as well as for researchers outside academia.

This volume originates in "China in the Twentieth Century, Historical Anthropology," a two-year collaborative research project (2015–2017) based at the Chinese University of Hong Kong. The project was grounded in the combination of local fieldwork and document analysis research—an approach well established at the university's Centre for Historical Anthropology of Chinese Society, which, under its director David Faure, has become a gathering place for like-minded researchers from Hong Kong, China, and around the world.[1]

Emphasizing discussion and collaboration, this project was always foremost a journey of exploration, epitomized by its series of field trips to places as different as urban Guangzhou, pastoral Hulunbuir, temples in highland western Hunan, and the terraced fields of central Shaanxi. The goal of these trips was simply to walk slowly and see what we could see, both about the place, and about the unique research work that was being carried out by our colleagues there. The project took a similar approach to building ties between scholars. Much of this book's content grew organically out of conversations over workshop lunches, long bus rides, or field visits. It was during our final conference that Paul R. Katz suggested the idea of this book. We are especially grateful, moreover, to two "outsider" voices, Hans van de Ven and Janet Chen, who as our final conference's keynote speakers put squarely the fundamental questions that drive each of the chapters: "What do you actually *do* in the field? What difference does it make?"

China historians going into the field

Although scholars of China have long found inspiration in the writings of anthropologists and ethnographers studying other parts of the world, we also recognize our own tradition within the China field of reflection on fieldwork methods. China-specialist anthropologists have written on the practical aspects of fieldwork (most recently, Heimer and Thøgersen 2006, Cornet and Blumenfield 2015). In *A Thrice Told Tale* (1992), Margery Wolf provides thoughtful reflection on ethnographic authority and practice in response to postmodern critiques. In *Fieldwork Connections* (2007), Stevan Harrell combines narratives with his local collaborators, Bamo Ayi and Ma Lunzy, which explore their relationships and cultural positioning through years of fieldwork. Anyone wishing to delve further into the ethnographic practices of some of the senior scholars involved with our project might consult the introduction to David Faure's *The Structure of Chinese Rural Society* (1986), Daniel Overmeyer's edited volume, *Ethnography in China Today* (2002), Helen Siu's *Tracing China* (2016), as well as the published dialogue about historical anthropology research in China between Zhiwei Liu and the cultural critic Sun Ge (2014).[2]

Beyond the two eponymous disciplines, the broad tent of "historical anthropology" also includes the work of scholars trained as folklorists, sociologists, and psychologists, as well as pan-disciplinary studies of literature, music, and ritual. Historical anthropology thrives on this catholicity of insights and practices. David Faure (Chapter 1) is best recognized as a historian, but his doctorate was in sociology. He cites the anthropologists of ritual Gilbert Lewis (1980) and Victor Turner (1969), the English historical anthropologist Alan MacFarlane (2013), and the French medieval historian Jacques Le Goff (1986) as intellectual influences. Many of Faure's early collaborators were mainland Chinese historians of his generation, notably Zhiwei Liu (with May Bo Ching, Chapter 13), Zheng Zhenman, and Zhao Shiyu, all of whom were heirs to the early Chinese folklorists' and sociologists' quest to "go to the people" that Faure discusses in his chapter. These fieldwork-based historians, moreover, early on found common cause with such historically minded anthropologists as Myron L. Cohen (Chapter 3), and the Taiwan-based ethnographers he discusses in his chapter, and also Helen Siu (1989), Ho Ts'ui-p'ing, and others who in the 1980s pioneered the return of fieldwork focus from Hong Kong and Taiwan to the mainland.[3] This sphere of mutual interest also included scholars of local religion. The Parisian wing of this scholarship associated with Max Kaltenmark and Kristofer Schipper brings contributions from John Lagerwey (Chapter 9), and Vincent Goossaert (Chapter 11). From the North American wing inspired by the likes of Daniel Overmeyer, David Jordan, and Susan Naquin, there are the chapters by Paul R. Katz (Chapter 10), and Kenneth Dean (Chapter 12). The shared interest in ritual, folklore, and the centrality of music to this made us keen to include a piece by Stephen Jones (Chapter 7) based on his pioneering research in North China.

As our collaborative research project bounced along mountain roads or huddled in temporary classroom meeting spaces, our discussions recognized the many commonalities we had with other trajectories of twentieth-century

China scholarship. For instance, amid the rapidly growing body of research on the Mao era (1949–1976), we are interested in the growing convergence between the tradition of international scholarship extending from the two pioneering fieldwork research studies of Wugong village in Hebei by Friedman, Pickowicz, and Selden (1993, 2005) to the recent *Maoism at the Grassroots* volume edited by Brown and Johnson (2015),[4] and the 2015 discussions between Chinese historians of historical anthropology (including May Bo Ching, Zhiwei Liu, and Weixin Rao in this volume) and Chinese scholars of the history of the Communist revolution.[5] Both groups use voices and unofficial or specially collected sources from the grassroots to integrate the transformations of the Communist Revolution into the larger sweep of Chinese history. Many of those scholars, and notably Dong Guoqiang, Chapter 17 in this volume, remind us of the importance of incorporating oral history, a long-standing interest in twentieth-century studies (e.g., Wang Zheng (1999), Joshua Howard (2004), Danke Li (2009)), into our work. We hasten as well to mention the notable works of the anthropologists Laurel Bossen, Ellen Judd, Gregory Ruff, Janice Stockard, and Robert Weller, the sociologist Guo Yuhua (2013), and the historians Gail Hershatter (2006), Huaiyin Li (2005, 2010), Jacob Eyferth (2009), and Wang Di (2018) whose fieldwork-based historical studies represent essential reading. Alongside those volumes, we also must not overlook the earlier generation of historians, including Roxanne Prazniak and Stephen Averill, who went out of the archive looking for the local cultures to the Chinese revolution. Janet Chen helpfully reminded us that several generations of urban history were written by scholars with deep experience of the cities about which they wrote.

Considering the breadth of interests, it is fair to ask: what, if anything, does this loose assemblage of scholars hold in common? We feel confident that the authors in this volume would agree broadly on two basic premises: first, a belief that ordinary people and distinct local cultures are worth understanding, both for their own sake, and as representing an important perspective on the sweeping trends of historical change; and, second, a research method that prizes deep familiarity with a place, its physical contours, remnants from the past, and most notably its people, who often preserve not only memories, but also textual scripts, material objects, and oral and performative traditions. Beyond this, it is difficult to generalize. To the first two premises, we may add as a third tendency a reticence to impose ideas or methodology. The eclectic tradition of existing and ongoing scholarship precludes any attempt to define a "school" of historical anthropology.

Structure and chapters

The book is arranged in four sections:

Fieldwork in historical perspective: The first chapters introduce three waves of fieldwork. David Faure begins with the movement by Chinese intellectuals of the 1930s to rediscover China, and the problems they faced—and created—when they went "to the people." Linda Grove introduces the massive archive—much of which remains untapped—of Japanese fieldwork by scholars of the Mantetsu and Tōa Dōbun Shoin. Myron L. Cohen presents the golden age of Anglophone scholarship in Taiwan and Hong Kong during the 1960s and 1970s. Each of these chapters presents its wave of fieldwork as a distinct intellectual and social moment, one that grew out of particular needs and ideas, which, in turn, left a distinct logic imprinted on the archive of its own findings.

Work reflections: In this section, five authors look back on the questions they brought with them to the field, and the different ones that emerged and stayed with them long after they had returned home. Michael Szonyi begins with a very practical question: as a historian of the Ming dynasty, what can one today hope to find that has not been moved, destroyed, or forgotten? Xiaofei Kang examines how her external persona as an educated Chinese woman shaped her fieldwork in western Sichuan, both in relation to what she was able to see, and how she was seen herself. Jianxiong Ma emphasizes the importance of interdisciplinarity, showing how moving beyond the questions of his discipline of anthropology afforded him a new perspective on the history of the basin societies of mountainous Yunnan. A Han Chinese raised in the ethnically diverse region of Hulunbuir, Yuxia Guan examines what it means to conduct fieldwork as a "local." Finally, Stephen Jones reflects on his decades of work with musicians and ritual specialists, not only in China, but also with those same musicians on tour in Europe.

Walking the ground, talking to people: The longest section introduces a series of distinct techniques and topics. The first four chapters in this section are written by scholars known for their field research on local religion, and revolve loosely around ritual. But the similarity stops there. John Lagerwey's chapter takes the form of a commentary on the questionnaires he uses for guiding fieldwork collaborators in the study of patterns of ritual practice, lineage, and economy in local society. Paul Katz juxtaposes historical portrayals of a Taiwanese plague festival against his own experience in the field, while Vincent Goossaert compares portrayals of ritual specialists in the first modern newspapers with those in oral histories. In the first chapter to discuss large-scale, team-based fieldwork, Kenneth Dean presents the use of GIS (geographic information system) in his extensive geographical survey of the dispersal of Putian temples in China and Southeast Asia.

The next five chapters relate experiences with specific topics of fieldwork. In a first chapter primarily on urban history, May Bo Ching and Zhiwei Liu take us on a delightful walk around Guangzhou and bring before us the history that is still visible even in a modern city. Xi He stays in the South, but returns to the countryside, combining documentary

Editors' preface xvii

evidence with fieldwork to show how ethnologists of the 1950s mischaracterized and misunderstood the *hemu* land system of the Hainan Li. Xiaoping Fang brings us to the history of rural medical practice in the Mao era, showing how he followed personal networks of "barefoot doctors" in his research in rural Zhejiang. Guoqiang Dong discusses the experience of conducting oral histories of the Cultural Revolution and combining these with written sources uncovered in the field. In a chapter on ecological campaigns, Micah S. Muscolino stresses the importance of seeing and walking the actual landscape, and talking to the people who lived its transformations in the study of micro-level environmental history of the early PRC. Thomas David DuBois, finally, shows how following the physical journey of an object from raw material to finished commodity can lead the researcher across the many meanings and relations of production, commerce, and consumption.

Finding and working with grassroots documents: The fourth section includes six chapters about the documents that may be uncovered through fieldwork—the archive of the people. Some of these documents are held in private collections, by individual households, or stored with more or less care by government offices. Five chapters discuss different types of document in detail, showing how they can be found, used, and read. Each type of document tells a different story. Three chapters examine civic legal documents from the early twentieth century: Zhengzhen Du compares land sale contracts held in the Longquan county archives with information from civil suit case files, genealogies, and her own fieldwork. Liu Yonghua shows how the account books kept by booksellers in Huizhou reveal not only commercial practices, but also reading habits. Huang Sujuan examines the land deeds held by one Guangzhou household, exploring what these documents reveal about the changing legal context of property ownership. Rao Weixin explores one of the most elemental documents found in localities and family genealogies, revealing how they can illuminate obscured sides to the social history of the Communist revolution. Liu Shigu returns to legal documents but for early PRC history, sharing his and his collaborators' journey deep inside a county-level public security archive. Finally, Jan Kiely introduces the official collection of Intangible Cultural Heritage materials that he encountered in a Jiangsu county archive, discussing why and how they were collected, and how they might be used.

Because each of these four sections has a distinct purpose, each is formatted somewhat differently: some chapters in the first and last sections include footnotes, whereas in the interest of a smooth and unencumbered text, most of those in the middle sections contain only suggestions for additional readings.

Lessons

First and foremost, this book encourages scholars to explore, to learn from the places, documents, and people in field locations. We are calling for historians to go out of the archives and into the localities discussed in our documents or where the documents were produced in the belief that this is the most effective way to understand what the written sources actually mean. A theme that runs through all of the chapters is that the purpose of fieldwork is not simply to answer questions that have been incubated elsewhere. By learning what is important to people, fieldwork can be the source of the questions themselves. Talking to people, visiting a site, or experiencing a ritual are all irreplaceable ways of personally and viscerally understanding the processes that others have described in texts. Because fieldwork is exploration, it is not always necessary to have a detailed plan. Sometimes it is better to *not* have a plan, but rather to simply approach the field with eyes and mind open, following wherever opportunity leads.

Two additional themes run through the chapters. The first is the importance of ethics and honesty. Certain very sensitive topics are likely to present political problems, either for the researcher or those at the research site, although the nature and degree of this sort of difficulty ebbs and flows. Conversely, one must accept as inevitable a certain degree of subjectivity in any fieldwork research. Both the historical pieces, and the chapters by Kiely, Dong, and He each emphasize the ways that political context shapes fieldwork, a lesson that helps us better appreciate the value of officially promoted projects such as Intangible Cultural Heritage (ICH), while remaining cognizant of their limitations. The second is the importance of self-reflection. As a methodology, fieldwork tends toward confirmation bias. If we arrive at a site expecting or even seeking out certain ideas, attitudes, or phenomena, there's a good chance we will eventually find exactly what we expected, including someone willing to express these ideas in a convenient, evocative quote. As the opening chapters make clear, the danger of such preconceived notions is that we might not even notice them, especially if we are allowed to present ourselves as "experts" of whatever stripe. The chapters by Szonyi, Kang, Guan, Ma, and Jones most fully elucidate this point.

Finally, we do not consider this volume an overview summary. This is not a final word on this research method for historians of China, but it is collaborative work in progress that should be developed, critiqued, discussed, and debated, taken in new directions and expanded into unexamined realms. This book is an open invitation to anyone interested in joining the journey.

References/Further readings

Averill, Stephen C., *Revolution in the Highlands: China's Jinggangshan Base Area.* Lanham, MD: Rowman & Littlefield Publishers, 2006.

Bamo, Ayi, Stevan Harrell, and Lunzy Ma, *Fieldwork Connections: The Fabric of Ethnographic Collaboration in China and America*. Seattle: University of Washington Press, 2007.
Bonnin, Michel, *The Lost Generation: The Rustification of China's Educated Youth*. Translated by Krystyna Horko. Hong Kong: The Chinese University Press, 2013.
Bossen, Laurel and Hill Gates, *Bound Feet, Young Hands: Tracking the Demise of Footbinding in Village China*. Stanford, CA: Stanford University Press, 2017.
Bossen, Laurel, *Chinese Women and Rural Development: Sixty Years of Change in Lu Village, Yunnan*. Lanham, MD: Rowman & Littlefield Publishers, 2002.
Brown, Jeremy, and Matthew D. Johnson, eds., *Maoism at the Grassroots: Everyday Life in China;s Era of High Socialism*. Cambridge, MA: Harvard University Press, 2015.
Brown, Jeremy, *City versus Countryside in Mao's China: Negotiating the Divide*. New York: Cambridge University Press, 2012.
Ching May-bo 程美宝, Diyu wenhua yu guojia rentong: wanqing yilai 'guangdong wenhua' guan de xingcheng 地域文化与国家认同: 晚清以来「广东文化」观的形成 [Local Culture and National Identity: The Formation of the 'Guangdong Culture" Perspective since the Late Qing]. Beijing: Shenghuo, Dushu, Xinzhi Sanlian shudian, 2006.
Cohen, Myron, "Being Chinese: The Peripheralization of Traditional Identity," *Daedalus* 120, 2 (1991): 113–134.
Cohen, Myron, "Cultural and Political Inventions in Modern China: The Case of the Chinese 'Peasant,'" *Daedalus* 122, 2 (1993): 151–170.
Cornet, Candice, and Tami Blumenfeld, eds., *Doing Fieldwork in China…with Kids!: The Dynamics of Accompanied Fieldwork in the People's Republic*. Copenhagen: NIAS Press, 2015.
Dean, Kenneth, and Zheng Zhenman, *Ritual Alliances of the Putian Plain*. Leiden: Brill, 2010.
Diamant, Neil J., *Revolutionizing the Family: Politics, Love and Divorce in Urban and Rural China, 1949–1968*. Berkeley: University of California Press, 2000.
Dong Guoqiang, and Andrew Walder, "Nanjing's failed 'January Revolution' of 1967: The Inner Politics of a Provincial Power Seizure," *The China Quarterly* 203 (2010): 675–692.
DuBois, Thomas D., *The Sacred Village: Social Change and Religious Life in Rural North China*. Honolulu: University of Hawai'i Press, 2005.
DuBois, Thomas D., *Empire and the Meaning of Religion in Northeast Asia: Manchuria, 1900–1945*. Cambridge: Cambridge University Press, 2017.
DuBois, Thomas D., "Many Roads from Pasture to Plate: A Commodity Chain Approach to China's Beef Trade, 1732–1931," *Journal of Global History* 14, 1 (2019): 22–43.
Eyferth, Jacob, *Eating Rice from Bamboo Roots: The Social History of a Community of Handicraft Papermakers in Rural Sichuan, 1920–2000*. Cambridge: Harvard University Press, 2009.
Fang Xiaoping, *Barefoot Doctors and Western Medicine in China*. Rochester: University of Rochester Press, 2012.
Faure, David, *The Structure of Chinese Rural Society: Lineage and Village in the Eastern New Territories, Hong Kong*. Hong Kong: Oxford University Press, 1986.
Faure, David, and Xi He, eds., *The Fisher folk of Late Imperial and Modern China: An Historical Anthropology of Boat-and-shed Living*. Abdingdon, Oxon: Routledge, 2016.

Faure, David, and Ho Ts'ui-p'ing, eds., *Chieftains into Ancestors: Imperial Expansion and Indigenous Society in Southwest China*. Vancouver: University of British Columbia Press, 2013.

Faure, David and Ching May-bo 科大卫, 程美宝, "Lishi renleixuezhe zouxiang tianye yao zuo shenme 历史人类学者走向田野要做什么"[What should historical anthropology scholars do when they go into the field], *Minsu yanjiu* 民俗研究 2 (2016): 24–27.

Friedman, Edward, Paul G. Pickowicz, Mark Selden, with Kay Ann Johnson, *Chinese Village, Socialist State*. New Haven, CT: Yale University Press, 1993.

Friedman, Edward, Paul G. Pickowicz, and Mark Selden, *Revolution, Resistance, Reform in Village China*. New Haven, CT: Yale University Press, 2005.

Goossaert, Vincent, *The Taoists of Peking, 1800–1949: A Social History of Urban Clerics*. Cambridge, MA: Harvard University Asia Center, 2007.

Grove, Linda, *A Chinese Economic Revolution: Rural Entrepreneurship in the Twentieth Century*. Lanham, MD: Rowman & Littlefield, 2006.

Guo Yuhua 郭于華, Shoukuren de jiangshu: jicun lishi yu yizhong wenming luoji 受苦人的 講述: 驥村歷史與一種文明的邏輯 [Narratives of the Sufferers: The History of Ji Village and a Cultural Logic]. Xianggang: Zhongwen daxue chubanshe, 2013.

Heimer, Maria, and Stig Thøgersen, eds., *Doing Fieldwork in China*. Copenhagen: NIAS Press, 2006.

Hershatter, Gail, *The Gender of Memory: Rural Women and China's Collective Past*. Berkeley: University of California Press, 2011.

Howard, Joshua, *Workers at War: Labor in China's Arsenals, 1937–1953*. Stanford, CA: Stanford University Press, 2004.

Jordan, David K., and Daniel Overmeyer, *The Flying Phoenix: Aspects of Chinese Sectarianism in Taiwan*. Princeton, NJ: Princeton University Press, 1986.

Judd, Ellen R., *Gender and Power in Rural North China*. Stanford, CA: Stanford University Press, 1994.

Kang, Xiaofei, and Donald S. Sutton, *Contesting the Yellow Dragon: Ethnicity, Religion, and the State in the Sino-Tibetan Borderland*. Leiden: Brill, 2016.

Katz, Paul R., 康豹, Taiwan de wangye xinyang 台灣的王爺信仰 [The Cult of the Royal Lords in Taiwan]. Taipei: Shanding wenhua chubanshe, 1997.

Kiely, Jan, and J. Brooks Jessup, eds., *Recovering Buddhism in Modern China*. New York: Columbia University Press, 2016.

Lagerwey, John, *Paradigm Shifts in Early and Modern Chinese Religion*. Leiden: Brill, 2019.

Lagerwey, John, Vincent Goossaert, and Jan Kiely, eds. *Modern Chinese Religion II, 1850–2015*. Leiden: Brill, 2015.

Le Goff, Jacques, *The Birth of Purgatory*. Translated by Arthur Goldhammer. Chicago: University of Chicago Press, 1984.

Lewis, Gilbert, *Day of Shining Red: An Essay on Understanding Ritual*. Cambridge: Cambridge University Press, 1980.

Li, Danke, *Echoes of Chongqing: Women in Wartime China*. Urbana: University of Illinois Press, 2009.

Li, Huaiyin, *Village China under Socialism and Reform*. Stanford, CA: Stanford University Press, 2010.

Li, Huaiyin, *Village Governance in North China, 1875–1935*. Stanford, CA: Stanford University Press, 2005.

Liu Shigu 刘诗古, "'Shixu' xia de 'zhixu': xin zhongguo chengli chuqi tugai zhong de sifa shijian – dui Poyang xian 'bufa dizhu an' de jiedu yu fenxi 失序"下的 "秩序":新 中国成立初期土改中的司法实践——对鄱阳县 "不法地主案"的解读与分析" [Order under Disorder: The Judicial Practice of Land Reform in the Early Years of the New China – Interpretation and Analysis of the 'non-lawful landlord cases' in Poyang County] Jindaishi yanjiu 《近代史研究》6 (2015): 91–105.

Liu Zhiwei and Sun Ge 刘志伟, 孙歌, Zai lishi zhong xunzhao zhongguo: guanyu quyu shi yanjiu renshilun de duihua 在历史中寻找中国: 关于区域史研究认识论的对话 [Seeking China in History: A Dialogue on the Epistemology of Local Area Historical Research]. Xianggang: Dajia liangyou shuju, 2014.

Macfarlane, Alan, *History and Anthropology*. Create Space Independent Publishing Platform, 2013.

Muscolino, Micah, *The Ecology of War in China: Henan Province, the Yellow River, and Beyond*. Cambridge: Cambridge University Press, 2015.

Naquin, Susan, *Peking, Temples and City Life, 1400–1900*. Berkeley: University of California Press, 2001.

Overmeyer, Daniel, ed., *Ethnography in China Today: A Critical Assessment of Methods and Results*. Taipei: Yuan-Liou Publishing Co., Ltd., 2002.

Perry, Elizabeth J. and Li Xun, *Proletarian Power: Shanghai in the Cultural Revolution*. Boulder, CO: Westview Press, 1997.

Prazniak, Roxann, *Of Camel Kings and Other Things: Rural Rebels against Modernity in Late Imperial China*. Lanham, MD: Roman & Littlefield, 1999.

Ruff, Gregory, *Cadres and Kin: Making a Socialist Village in West China, 1921–1991*. Stanford, CA: Stanford University Press, 1998.

Schoenhals, Michael, *Spying for the People: Mao's Secret Agents, 1949–1967*. New York: Cambridge University Press, 2013.

Schmalzer, Sigrid, *Red Revolution, Green Revolution: Scientific Farming in Socialist China*. Chicago, IL: University of Chicago Press, 2016.

Siu, Helen F., *Agents and Victims in South China: Accomplices in Rural Revolution*. New Haven, CT: Yale University Press, 1989.

Siu, Helen F., *Tracing China: A Forty-year Ethnographic Journey*. Hong Kong: Hong Kong University Press, 2016.

Smith, Aminda M., *Thought Reform and China's Dangerous Classes: Reeducation, Resistance, and the People*. Lanham, MD: Rowman & Littlefield, 2013.

Stockard, Janice E., *Daughters of the Canton Delta: Marriage Patterns and Economic Strategies in South China, 1860–1930*. Stanford, CA: Stanford University Press, 1989.

Szonyi, Michael, ed., *A Companion to Chinese History*. Hoboken, NJ: John Wiley & Sons, Inc., 2017.

Szonyi, Michael, *Cold War Island: Quemoy on the Frontline*. Cambridge: Cambridge University Press, 2008.

Szonyi, Michael, *The Art of Being Governed: Everyday Politics in Late Imperial China*. Princeton, NJ: Princeton University Press, 2018.

Thaxton, Ralph, *Catastrophe and Contention in Rural China: Mao's Great Leap Forward Famine and the Origins of Righteous Resistance in Dafo Village*. Cambridge: Cambridge University Press, 2008.

Turner, Victor W., *The Ritual Process: Structure and Anti-Structure*. Chicago, IL: Aldine Publishing Co., 1969.

Wang, Di, *Violence and Order on the Chengdu Plain: The Story of Secret Brotherhood in Rural China*. Stanford, CA: Stanford University Press, 2018.

Wang, Zheng, *Women in the Chinese Enlightenment: Oral and Textual Histories*. Berkeley: University of California Press, 1999.

Weller, Robert, *Unities and Diversities in Chinese Religion*. Seattle: University of Washington Press, 1987.

Wolf, Margery, *A Thrice-told Tale: Feminism, Postmodernism, and Ethnographic Responsibility*. Stanford, CA: Stanford University Press, 1992.

Wu, Yiching, *The Cultural Revolution at the Margins: Chinese Socialism in Crisis*. Cambridge, MA: Harvard University Press, 2014.

Zhao, Shiyu 赵世瑜, Xiao lishi yu da lishi: quyu shehuishi de linian, fangfa yu shixian 小历史与大历史：区域社会史的理念、方法与实践 [Small History and big History: Theory, Method and Perspective in Local-Area Social History]. Beijing: Shenghuo, Dushu, Xinzhi Sanlian shudian, 2006.

"Shehui jingji shi shiyexia de zhongguo geming 社会经济史视野下的中国革命," Kaifang shidai《开放时代》, 2 (2015): 11–80.

Notes

1 The project was funded by an internal competitive grant, the Vice-Chancellor's One-Off Discretionary Fund Grant, and led by David Faure with the assistance of Jan Kiely. A joint initiative of the Centre of Historical Anthropology of Chinese Society and the Centre of China Studies at the Chinese University of Hong Kong, the project assembled an 18-member research team and involved collaborations with the University of Oxford, Guangdong University of Finance and Economics, Hulunbuir University, Jishou University, and Shanxi Normal University, and held four on-site workshops with introductions to fieldwork, as well as research methods workshop and a major international conference. The Centre for Historical Anthropology of Chinese Society was funded by a multi-year "Area of Excellence" grant from the Hong Kong Research Grants Council.
2 Another Chinese guide to the use of fieldwork in historical research is Dong Jianbo, *Shixue tianye diaocha: fangfa yu shijian* [Historical fieldwork: method and practice]. Shanghai cishu chubanshe, 2013.
3 See May-Bo Ching, "Chinese History in China: The State of the Field (1980s–2010s)," in Michael Szonyi, A Companion to Chinese History, David Faure and He Xi's introduction to *The Fisher Folks of Late Imperial and Modern China*, and Zhao Shiyu, *Xiao lishi yu da lishi: quyu shehuishi de linian, fangfa yu shijian* [Philosophy, method and practice of area social history]. Sanlian chubanshe, 2006.
4 And including the works of Michel Bonnin, Neil Diamant, Elizabeth Perry and Li Xun, Sigrid Schmalzer, Michael Schoenhals, Aminda Smith, Ralph Thaxton, and Wu Yiching, among others.
5 Liu Yonghua, Ying Xing, Liu Chang, et al., "Shehui jingji shi shiye xiade Zhongguo geming" [The Chinese Revolution in the eyes of socioeconomic history] *Kaifang shidai* 2 (2015) summarizes the conference held at Sun Yat-sen University, January 12–14, 2015. The contributions of Rao Weixin and Liu Shigu in this volume are representative of this new kind of work that brings local, fieldwork-based history together with the history of the revolution.

Acknowledgments

This volume was originally made possible by a Vice-Chancellor's One-Off Discretionary Fund Grant from the Chinese University of Hong Kong (CUHK), which supported the China in the Twentieth Century, Historical Anthropology collaborative research project in 2015–2017.

Special thanks are also due to the Centre for Historical Anthropology of Chinese Society, funded by a multi-year "Area of Excellence" grant from the Hong Kong Research Grants Council, and the Centre for China Studies at CUHK for hosting and administering this project. Dennis Chan from the Centre for China Studies staff, as well as several of the Centre's research postgraduate students, particularly Jia Luyang and Yan Yiqiao, contributed substantially to the success of project events.

We are also grateful to our project partners at the University of Oxford, Guangdong University of Finance and Economics, Hulunbuir University, Jishou University, and Shanxi Normal University for their support and hosting of workshops. We are grateful to all research project members, including those who are not represented in this volume, as well as all participants in the project workshops and culminating project conference held on December 19–20, 2016 at CUHK for the many contributions to discussions that inspired this volume. In particular, we would like to thank Gregor Benton, Igor Chabrowski, Aurore Dumont, Feng Xiaocai, Anthony Garnaut, Huang Jianxing, Loretta Kim, Luo Kanglong, Wu Hexian, and Wu Ka-ming. As the keynote commentators at the conference, Janet Chen and Hans van de Ven provided invaluable critiques and suggestions that influenced the development of this volume and for which we are most grateful. Similarly, the wide-ranging discussions on the nature of the historical anthropology approach in Chinese history the following year (December 15–16, 2017) at the Historical Anthropology of Chinese Society: Conclusion and New Beginnings Conference at CUHK were similarly stimulating. We would like to express our gratitude particularly for the commentary of Chang Jianhua, Chen Chunsheng, Liu Tik-sang, Michio Suenari, Zheng Zhenman, Zhao Shiyu, Ho Ts'ui-ping, and James Wilkerson.

Finally, we thank Li Lingjie, who provided the first cut translation of most of the chapters submitted in Chinese, as well as helpful commentary on those in English as well.

xxiv *Acknowledgments*

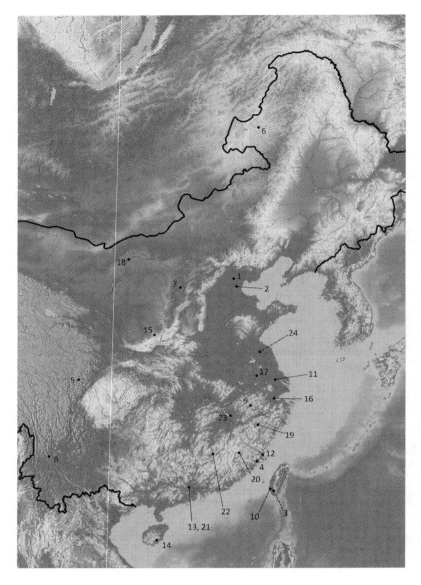

Image 1 Map of locations discussed in text.

Numbers refer to chapter numbers. Map compiled by DuBois from SRTM (Shuttle Radar Topography Mission) global elevation images available under Creative Commons CC0 license at maps-for-free.com

1 Miaofengshan (Faure)
2 Jinghai (Grove)

3   Meinong (Cohen)
4   Luozhou (Szonyi)
5   Songpan (Kang)
6   Hulunbuir (Guan)
7   Northern Shanxi (Jones)
8   Dali (Ma)
9   Huizhou (Lagerwey)
10 Tainan (Katz)
11 Jiangnan (Goossaert)
12 Putian (Dean)
13 Guangzhou (Liu and Ching)
14 Wuzhishan (He)
15 Baishui (Muscolino)
16 Hangzhou (Fang)
17 Nanjing (Dong)
18 Bayannur (DuBois)
19 Longquan (Du)
20 Sibao (Liu Yonghua)
21 Guangzhou (Huang)
22 Gannan (Rao)
23 Poyang (Liu Shigu)
24 Northern Jiangsu (Kiely)

Section 1
History and fieldwork in historical perspective

1 They went to the people but did they hear them? Comments on field research in China in the 1920s and 1930s

David Faure

Near Beijing is the hill known as Miaofengshan (妙峰山), where every year in the fourth lunar month, pilgrims trotted up rugged paths to pray at the Goddess of the Azure Mist Temple (碧霞元君庙) near its summit. Their annual trips were organized in Beijing city by "incense clubs" (*xiang hui* 香会). Involvement in the clubs being voluntary, their clientele very ordinary residents of Beijing, and the objective of the exercise tied closely to home and community, the annual pilgrimages to Miaofengshan, the pilgrims themselves and the clubs, would seem a fitting subject for any study of Beijing society.[1]

The study that made the custom of annual pilgrimage famous to China historians was conducted by Gu Jiegang (顾颉刚) (1893–1980) and his fellow Peking University students in 1925. Their reports were first serialized in the Beijing newspaper, *Capital Post* (*Jingbao* 京报), and then published as a monograph in 1928.[2] By the standards of present-day ethnography, the study was cursory. Gu and his team were at the temple for no more than three days. They made no stunning discoveries. They observed people burning incense and took note of the announcements issued by incense clubs and some of the many stele inscriptions found on the hill. The newspaper articles elicited some responses, which were included into the monograph. All in all, the reports were remarkable not for what they said but for adding everyday ritual practices onto the research agenda. Gu Jiegang knew that well. He said as much in the introduction he wrote to the account. That report, nevertheless, was the beginning of an effort to understand Chinese people on their own terms.

Minsu xue (民俗学): folklore studies

What Gu Jiegang and his team went on to report became the initiation of the discipline that came to be known as *minsu xue*, translated into English by participants in the *minsu xue* movement themselves as "folklore studies." Their interest had extended from a project to collect folksongs (*min'ge* 民歌), initiated by teachers at Peking University, Liu Bannong (刘半农), Shen Yinmo (沈尹默), and Zhou Zuoren (周作人) in 1918. Ambiguities were

4 David Faure

present from the beginning of the project. There were in the initiative the early rumblings of the recognition that Chinese literature should not consist of only what was acceptable to high society tastes sanitized by centuries of neo-Confucian strictures. The collectors of folksongs, as guardians of standards, drew the new line for acceptability at the boundaries of pornography (*yinhui* 淫秽). Moreover, under the rubric of what was soon to be constantly referred to as "going to the people," the initiative embodied an urge to document *minsu*, through folk literature, local aspirations, history, and custom. At the same time, the folksong collectors, as self-designated educators, were to guide such aspirations and customs toward new national goals so that the history of the local might eventually merge with that of the nation. The May Fourth Movement's "New Culture" project, from its start, was never only a fact-finding mission. Its proponents were self-styled reformers, rebels, and radicals who sought not only to learn about society but also to change it.[3]

As it evolved over the two years after the Miaofengshan study, "folklore studies" came to embrace not only the collection of folksongs but also reports on local customs (*fengsu* 风俗). The subject was also taken over from their teachers by the students: in 1925, Gu Jiegang was a 32-year-old starting out on his career and only hanging on in Peking University through short-term appointments. His companions on his Miaofengshan trip were even younger. Rong Zhaozu (容肇祖) (1897–1994) was 28, his brother Rong Geng (容庚) (1894–1983) was 31, as was Sun Fuyuan (孙伏园) (1894–1966), the recent Peking University graduate who had become an editor at the *Beijing Morning Post* (*chenbao* 晨报). What happened to the group was highly revealing to the history of folklore studies. Gu Jiegang contributed to the Peking University folksong collection from the time it was initiated and continued to patronize folklore studies for many years. He continued to study folksongs into the 1920s but built his reputation as the *enfant terrible* of the study of Chinese ancient history through his *Critiques of Ancient History* (*gushi bian* 古史辨), which went into publication from 1926. Rong Zhaozu, who graduated from Peking University in 1926 and taught at Sun Yat-sen University in Guangzhou from 1927, became more closely identified with the folklore movement than perhaps even Gu himself, but had built his reputation on textual studies. These were not of the folklore he collected, but of historical texts—some relating to folklore themes—which were well-grounded in bibliographic collections through the ages. Rong Geng subsequently became an ancient historian and philologist of the first order. Zhuang Yan (庄严) (–1980), the least known of the group, joined the Palace Museum as soon as he graduated from Peking University and devoted his entire life to that institution, first in Beijing and then in Taiwan.[4]

In 1925, the temple festival at Miaofengshan must have appeared a magical enactment of history to the young men who climbed to its top. They included not only Gu Jiegang's group, but also Li Jinghan (李景汉, 1895–1986), freshly returned from the University of California at Berkeley with a master's degree in sociology in 1924. Li published an account of his own visit to the Miaofengshan festival only months after Gu Jiegang did so. Li claimed that his associate, Sidney Gamble (1890–1968), who had published a social survey of Beijing in 1921 which mentioned Miaofengshan in a short paragraph on "temple market festivals," had visited the hill a year before just as the temple festival was coming to a close. Apparently Gamble found it so interesting that in 1925 he went there again with Li and two of his American friends. Li gave a fuller description of the worshippers than did Gu Jiegang. No doubt writing only from impression, he said 70–80 percent were peasants and 20–30 had come from cities; 70–80 percent were women; most had come from Beijing and its surroundings, but some had come from as far away as Tianjin, Baoding, Zhangjiakou, and even beyond the Great Wall. Only 10–20 percent had come with incense clubs; 20–30 came to give thanks to the goddess for having cured their parents and 50–60 to ask for blessings, relief from poverty, or for the birth of a son. He took less from the written records of the festival than did Gu and company, but he turned to their report to supplement his own account of the history of the temple and the incense clubs. Of the value of recording the festival, he had no doubt. He concluded his report advocating that other scholars should conduct studies into temple festivals on China's other famous mountains, Taishan, Wutai, Emei, Jiuhua, Luofu, and so on. As China was undergoing momentous changes, such studies were vital for preserving a record of disappearing traditions.[5]

Li Jinghan would seem to have been an unlikely folklore collector. He belonged to quite a different camp from the cultural historians who were gathering around Gu Jiegang. The sociologists were associated with the China Foundation for the Promotion of Education and Culture, an American effort drawing on funds that had derived from reparations demanded of the Qing dynasty government in the aftermath of the Boxer Rebellion. Only months before he joined Gamble on the Miaofengshan trip, he had conducted a survey on Beijing's rickshaw pullers, where his interests were entirely focused on their economic well-being. When, as a lecturer in sociology at Yanjing University, he took his class out to study the conditions of villages on the outskirts of Beijing, he was primarily interested, again, in the well-being of the villagers, their study being based on household survey and their report dealing primarily with population composition, occupations, incomes, and expenditures. The same interest he took with him when, in 1928, he became head of the social survey department of the China National Association of the Mass Education Movement which, with financial support from the YMCA, sought to reform villages in Ding county (定县) in Hebei province. His 800-page survey report provided a great deal of statistical data, but, sitting almost uncomfortably in between his chapters on living expenses and taxation were chapters on village entertainment, customs, religion, and festivals. He collected village songs and plays, which were published in 1933 by the Beijing Folklore Society and eventually translated into

English under Gamble's direction. The rhetoric was similar to that of the folklorists: knowledge of cultural life was important to any reform effort; entertainment could provide an entry into education; and survey of customs could identify those customs—such as foot binding of women—that needed to be reformed. Temples and temple festivals were so evidently the venues for playing out entertainment and customs that no further justification was needed for surveying them.[6]

Yet, the details that Li Jinghan included somewhat belie the instrumental view that he presented in his report. His report counted the number of temples and matched them to the populations of the 62 villages he surveyed, and he counted also the number of gods they housed, the number that housed earthen god statues, and the number that contained wall paintings. He was as interested in the financing of the temples as in the hagiographies of the gods and in the many practices related to them: women prayed to the Three Ladies for sons, and they did that by tying a red thread on their bodies, to which was attached a coin. The thread was wrapped round one of the little earthern babies that might be found on their altars so that it might be carried home and put under the bed. As to temple festivals, the biggest annual event was the four-day celebration at the temple of Hanzu (韩祖). The god had appeared as a mysterious old man to distribute buckwheat seeds to farmers of Ding and surrounding counties in some famine year of the past, and his festival drew a substantial clientele. This was an occasion for incense burning, offering new robes to the god, kowtowing to the god, not only at the temple, but every few steps along the way from the worshipper's home to it, and, then, of course, the hustle and bustle of business and entertainment, theater, and meals. Li Jinghan reported that at every annual festival more than 2,000 farm animals were sold at the fair associated with it. Obviously, observers such as Gu Jiegang, Rong Zhaozu, Sidney Gamble, and Li Jinghan were excited by what they saw at temple festivals. The songs, the lore, the theater, the ritual, and the commerce, all rolled together into one at temple fairs, and spoke to the researchers of outbursts of folk culture waiting to be studied.

The question of "methods" obsessed the students of the May Fourth generation. They were concerned with justifying their research in the interest of "scientific" understanding, a term that associates their work more with empiricism than with conjectures. And, they rather depended on their pursuit of "science" to distinguish their work from that charge from other May Fourth enthusiasts of tolerance for, if not encouragement of, superstition, a target straw man that May Fourth proponents had set up to stand as surrogate for China's backwardness. That obsession emerged in the many times the organizers of the 1918 Peking University folksong project reflected critically on their achievements. In 1922, the folklorists published their first magazine, *Songs* (*geyao* 歌谣). In 1923, they ventured into investigating customs (*fengsu diaocha* 风俗调查). Under the rubric of a customs investigation society (*fengsu diaocha hui*), they designed a questionnaire listing 54 items. Some of the questions were quite detailed. For example, under living conditions, they asked whether houses were made of timber, bamboo, brick, or earth, what furniture was found inside the houses, how the houses might be decorated outside, what conditions the sleeping area and toilets were found in, and where animals were kept. For funerals, they distinguished between the rich and the poor, and for sacrifice, if it was held in family temples, ancestral halls, at graves, or if it was made to the gods (rather than the ancestors). They distributed 3,000 copies of the questionnaire but received back only a handful (a total of 41 by 1924). Undeterred, they announced that they were determined to investigate into customs all over China and to "study them systematically" (*zuo xitong yanjiu* 作系统研究). Gu Jiegang writing in 1929 recalled that they were overwhelmed by the magnitude of the task.[7]

In the background, 1925 was a tumultuous year in Beijing. Sun Yat-sen died, the students were up in arms in the May 30th incident that followed, the warlord Zhang Zuolin took Beijing, and, even though Gu Jiegang's research continued, Peking University was defaulting on salaries. By 1926, he left Beijing for Xiamen where he spent an unhappy six months making an enemy of the powerful writer, Lu Xun, and moved on from Xiamen to the newly named Zhongshan University in Guangzhou. Rong Zhaozu followed much the same path, teaching at Xiamen upon graduation from Peking University in 1926 and moving to Zhongshan University in 1927. In Guangzhou, they were joined by Zhong Jingwen (钟敬文) (1903–2002), a young local folksong enthusiast who had contributed to *Songs*.[8] For a brief few years, Guangzhou became the center of the folklore movement and Zhongshan University published the Folklore series of books (*Guoli Zhongshan daxue minsu congshu* 国立中山大学民俗丛书). The question of "methods" remained a focus. Aside from the first three volumes, the first of which traced an evolutionary view on the mentality of primitive people, the other two reprinting essays written by Rong Zhaozu and Zhong Jingwen, the publications in Guangzhou showed collection but little analysis. Collection as an end in itself became a subject of contention, leading eventually to the university suspending support for the journal *Folklore* (*minsu* 民俗). Gu Jiegang in the journal's defense argued that collection must precede analysis and Rong Zhaozu held that while the analytic results of field work had yet to appear, Gu Jiegang had demonstrated that a folklorist view cast in ancient texts could yield interesting insights. More information needed to be collected in the field, and, as if one list of questions were deemed insufficient, Yang Chengzhi, in Guangzhou, translated the checklist from the work of an English folklorist, Charlotte Sophia Burne. That list, no more than the earlier list compiled in 1923, made no impact on published research.[9]

What to do with folk literature?

Up to 1929, "going to the people" had yielded the folklorists 20,000 folksongs and launched them onto the more comprehensive project of collecting folklore and customs. Despite their repeated efforts to "systematize" their work, most of the collection had been built up without recourse to the checklists they were drawing up. What does one do with a record of 20,000 folksongs? What does one learn from them about "the people"?

For most of the songs, the answer is: probably not very much, except in very general terms. Some of the volumes included in the Folklore series were purely descriptive: the *Love Songs of Taiwan* consists of 200 love songs collected in Taiwan, described in a single paragraph in the author's introduction as having been sung in a dialogue "by men to women, or men to men, or women to women, sometimes between two people, sometimes between a single person and a group, and sometimes by a solo singer." The *Folklore of Quanzhou* and the *Folklore of Guangzhou*, likewise, are exactly what the titles say they are. Those volumes were contributed by people outside the core group of folklorists around Gu Jiegang, some of whom apparently had had no previous connection with them let alone any awareness of their thoughts on "systematizing" the study of folksongs and folklore.

The interpretation of the folk literature undertaken by the core group of folklorists, that is to say, Gu Jiegang, Rong Zhaozu, and by the time they reached Guangzhou, also Zhong Jingwen, may be neatly summarized by Rong Zhaozu in his preface to his own volume in the Folklore series: "My original intention in writing these essays was to seek the truth of everything and every event, so that I might, in detail, write about their origins and development."[10]

Rong included in his volume, among other essays, his essay on the history of divination in China and his account of the evolution of the god known as the Erlang *shen*, fully illustrating his statement of purpose. Yet, of course, it was Gu Jiegang's study of the legend of Woman Meng Jiang (孟姜女) that exemplified best the method so described in action.

The story of Woman Meng Jiang is well known to most parts of China. As it was popularly known, her sorrow brought down the Great Wall of China, so that she might go beyond it to seek the body of her husband who had died in battle. With the knowledge of ancient texts that he was to exploit to the full in his *Critiques of Ancient History*, Gu Jiegang showed that there had historically been different versions of this story. The earliest version had it that Woman Meng Jiang cared about the proper rituals. Even in her grief for her husband, she demanded that respect be paid him in his home and not in the wild. The story was well known, for it was referred to in texts edited by disciples of Confucius, but the emphasis had changed. By the Warring States period, it was emphasized that she had wept on her husband's death, and, looking into other stories current at the time, Gu Jiegang found for the weeping connection to popular songs of the time which drew on the sound of weeping as a characteristic of their music. It was not until the Western Han dynasty that the signature narrative of bringing down a city wall came to be added to the tale, and even then, only by the Tang dynasty was it specified that the wall brought down was part of the Great Wall that had been built by the First Qin Emperor. How did that final addition to the story come about? Partly because of a conflation of two separate tales in the Tang, Gu said, and partly because by that time, the tale had become a popular theme that touched many families with husbands and wives separated by conscription into military service. Gu took the story into the Song dynasty, showing that the name Meng Jiang was given to the heroine of the tale only by then. Under Gu Jiegang's expert pen, illustrated with exhaustive citations and comparisons, what had been a simple folktale now bore layers of meaning imposed from the ages.[11]

Ironically, Gu Jiegang's achievement with the Woman Meng Jiang story does not provide a methodology for the students of folksongs, folklore, or even customs. The methodology that he employed on Woman Meng Jiang had little to do with folklore collections, but plenty to do with the very long established historical method of textual analysis. Maybe that was why, more than once, he distinguished between the collection of folklore at what he thought was the starting stage of the folklore movement and its analysis. The collection might be crude, but the latter should be systematic and scientific.

Moreover, his success in and advocacy for tracking the textual origins of folktales, far from being a revolutionary approach to the study of folktale, was precisely the objective aspired to by many a local historian throughout Chinese history.[12] The aspiration of seeking textual origins for folk practices, that is to say, stories, customs, and vocabularies, has been inherent in local histories that are now classed under *difangzhi* (地方志), often translated into English as "gazetteers." Most local histories, for instance, would give geographic information such as locations and terrain, places of interest, major events, and biographies of notable people, among which folklore would have been embedded. By the early years of the twentieth century, legal reform introduced the idea that if the written codes must be universally applied, they had to take into account local practices, especially in areas dealing with business (credit, contract), property (land ownership and transfer), and family relations (marriage, adoption, inheritance). Surveys into those subjects gave rise to a new sort of local history, referred to as the *xiangtu zhi* (乡土志 local history of the land), which was introduced into the school curriculum.[13] Therefore, while tracking origins might prove to be a means of historical understanding, it did not necessarily stand for neutrality in accepting "the people" on their own terms. Zhong Jingwen, who was to champion the cause of folklore studies from the 1920s until his death in 2002, might have perceived some of this aspect of Gu Jiegang's work in his various memoires, written in the 1980s and after. The folksong collection movement from Peking University, to Zhong Jingwen, was always described as only a preliminary stage in the folklore movement, and Gu Jiegang's celebrated Woman Meng Jiang, a "historical and geographic" approach. Zhao Shiyu, himself a Zhong Jingwen student, noted that change. According to Zhao, the departure was marked by "the search for typologies of folktales," as yet a subject not introduced through essays re-examining the whys and wherefores of folksong and folktale collection, but only in case studies.[14]

The turn to typologies was championed by the younger members of the folklorist movement, among whom should be counted Lou Zikuang (娄子匡 1907–2005), who became an enthusiastic participant from the time that Zhong Jingwen moved to Hangzhou in 1929. There might have been influence from British and Japanese folklorist practices behind Zhong and Lou, but the more direct influence seems to have been the prolific Zhao Jingshen (赵景深 1902–1985), who wrote a lengthy essay on the Cinderella "type" of folktale in the preface to the *Folktale of Guangzhou* volume in the Zhongshan University Folklore series.[15] Zhong Jingwen acknowledged that in his Guangzhou and Hangzhou days, he knew little of the theory of folklore, a subject he learnt to appreciate only in his later years. As he summarized it, the methodology consisted of comparing and contrasting different versions of a lore to establish its "original form," and to construct from that a history of its geographical spread.[16] Zhong himself, therefore, reconstructed as typologies the legends of songstresses, of the procreation of human beings after the great flood, and so on. By taking a universalist turn, Zhong Jingwen's methodology was moving away from Gu Jiegang's.

Nevertheless, much of folklore studies in China, in the 1930s or since, was much less ambitious than the universalist version of their theory might imply. Much of it took off from first proposition, that is, that folklore emerges from social groups. Zhong Jingwen's study of the tale of the songstress, Liu Miss 3 (Liu Sanjie 刘三姐), in 1982, well exemplifies what the proposition might mean. The Miss Liu legend is found widely in southwestern China where it was also common practice for local communities to stage singing contests (*gexu* 歌圩). While Miss Liu is credited by legend as having founded the singing contests, Zhong finds it more reasonable to assume the legendary character had been built on the roles of the songstresses who took part in them. That degree of clarity which characterizes Zhong Jingwen in 1982 was largely absent in his work in the 1920s and 1930s. Zhao Shiyu acknowledged that, in the final analysis, the folklorists did not conduct very much field work.[17] Indeed, the Miaofengshan study had sanctified field work and the slogan the folklorists created required their going to the people, but collecting, per se, required little field work, and putting specimens into typologies even less of it. In the 1920s and 1930s, as the folklorists effectively moved away, fieldwork was taken over by sociologists like Li Jinghan.

From community studies to class structure

Community studies in the 1920s and 1930s did not grow out of the folklorist tradition. There had long been a tradition to write about the Chinese village community, first by missionaries, and then by the economists. The missionaries often wrote with the view of converting Chinese people to Christianity, and, not surprising, they did not take kindly to villagers conducting sacrifices at the temples. The economists, on the other hand, were responding to rural poverty. They were concerned, therefore, with estimates of production and measures of the standard of living, and, in that context, cultural life entered into the formula primarily as an expense for religious practices and recreation. By the 1920s, a third constituency was entering the field in the form of the sociologists and anthropologists. One of the first sociologists to teach in China was Tao Menghe (陶孟和 1887–1960), who was trained at the London School of Economics and Political Science and taught in Peking University from 1914. He led the survey research department of the China Foundation for the Promotion of Education and Culture from its beginning in 1926. Li Jinghan moved from there to the Ding county project. Other universities founded sociology departments in the 1920s, and a prominent appointment among the sociologists was Wu Wenzao (吴文藻 1901–1985), who was trained in Columbia University and took up a teaching position at Yanjing University in 1929. By the 1930s, their students were conducting field surveys, some of which were community studies. One of Wu Wenzao's students was Fei Xiaotong (费孝通), who went from Yanjing to the London School of Economics and wrote his thesis on the village of Kaixiangong in Jiangsu province. His book, published in English in 1939, became a classic in the community studies literature.[18]

Morton Fried, commenting on the missionary accounts, criticized them not only for their lack of objectivity but also for their uncritical aggregation of information yielded from varied and unknown sources. He could have said the same about the economists and the sociologists and found support from Fei Xiaotong who famously made fun of the superficiality of the questionnaire techniques employed in J L Buck's monumental surveys.[19] As Fried pointed out, beyond the missionary interest, it was the growth of interest in anthropology—by which he meant research conducted by Wu Wenzao's students, including Fei Xiaotong—that prompted a spate of community studies in the 1930s and 1940s. However, Fried also lamented the community researchers' lack of interest in history, which is hard to understand given that community studies were almost always conducted to illuminate communal unity. Nevertheless, for Fried, history meant reference to the *difangzhi* local history, or, in the instance that found most favor with him, Chen Da's (陈达) study of emigrant communities in Fujian.[20] On this point, if one might adopt the position of the folklorists, there is scope for a refrain. Surely the history of any community far surpassed *difangzhi* and emigration, for would that not have been embodied in the "tradition" that had been passed down via folksongs, folklore and customs? It is only when the folklorist position is contrasted with the sociologist that the theoretical orientation of folklore tradition becomes obvious: the supposition that songs, lore, and customs contain a unique understanding that the people to be studied might identify with. The folklorists did not quite know what that understanding was, but they believed it was there.

Believing that the anthropologists were their allies, and, as championed by Zhong Jingwen, that folklore study as a discipline was also to include community study, the folklorists did not notice that the anthropologists, like themselves, might have gone to the people but made little effort to hear what the people had to say. With few exceptions, their community studies were conducted with the agenda of seeking practical applications for the rural economy and were not directed at understanding rural traditions.

As an example of community research that did not have the rural economy in its focus, it might be instructive to turn, first, to an account written by neither folklorist nor anthropologist, but by a conscientious and careful student, none other than Fu Sinian (傅斯年 1896–1950), whose stature was to dominate the May Fourth culture scene almost as much as Hu Shi (胡适). In 1920, Fu Sinian published an impressionistic essay on the villages of his home region, the northeastern corner of Shandong province. His general knowledge of the province informed him of the difference between this region and the rest of the province: big landlords were uncommon, and, so, the villages were small, the smaller ones being made up of 20 households and the larger ones 70–80 households. The villages took up their own defense but the households cooperated in little else. He described the daily lives of villagers, men and women, the daily and yearly rhythm, their household composition, means of production (farmland, spinning machines, looms), diet, clothing, and so on. Some of all that he had obviously seen with his own eyes. After the description of the material life came his description of village religion:

> It cannot be said the peasant's (*nongmin* 农民) religious spirit does not go deep, but the force of old religion is all but lost. His conception of gods and ghosts is governed by the psychology of fear and a superficial understanding. We see many dilapidated temples everywhere, and they stand witness to the weakness in the economy and decline of religious faith. When he is himself ill, when danger approaches, when his children are unwell, he goes to pray to the gods.[21]

This is not a description that demonstrates much understanding of village religion, but it illustrates the heart of the problem of writing about it. Fu Sinian had, indeed, seen the dilapidated temples, but he had not spoken to villagers for what they believed in. It might seem strange that the scholars who wanted "to go to the people" turned out to have been afraid or reluctant to talk to them about their religion. However, Fu Sinian was not alone.

The same lack of the villager's voice characterizes no less an accomplished ethnographer than Fei Xiaotong. Fei achieved instant fame when he wrote *Peasant Life in China*, published in 1939 with a preface by Bronislaw Malinowski.[22] In his introductory chapter, Fei tells his readers that he knew Kaixiangong village quite well, having visited it several times before his two-month sojourn there for research, having his sister (or cousin) working in the village, himself being a native of the county in which it was located and knowing the local dialect. He also said he spoke to the villagers and they were willing to speak to him. Readers of his autobiography, which he wrote many years later, would have come to a different view.[23] Fei entered Yanjing University in 1930 and was enrolled in classes given by Wu Wenzao in his first year of teaching. Fei came under Wu's influence as Wu groped toward "community studies." He heard Robert Park's lectures in 1933 and Radcliffe Brown's in 1935. Writing in his memoirs, he believed that Brown's social anthropology went deeper into an understanding of community than Park's sociology. He gave no indication if that was the reason he went to the London School of Economics for his doctoral research, for arrangement was made for him by Wu rather than by himself. As preparation for his doctoral training abroad, Wu also sent him to S M Shirokogoroff (1887–1939) at Qinghua University. Shirokogoroff was by 1933 already internationally known for his highly original research on Manchu shamanism, but he kept Fei as his assistant in physical anthropology. In this capacity, Fei spent a great deal of his time measuring the human body, of corpses, soldiers, and prisoners. His research trip to the Yao mountains of Guangxi in 1935 in which his newly wedded wife tragically died was likewise arranged by Shirokogoroff for him to measure the physique of the Yao.

Fei, therefore, had done no field work in Kaixiangong village up to the end of 1935. He went to Kaixiangong in 1936 after his accident in Guangxi to recover from his wounds, both physical and emotional, because his sister managed a silk improvement station in the village. In his two months in the village, he did indeed make observations of silkworm rearing and the silk trade, and he recorded that while on the boat journey to Britain, he managed to put those notes into order. Even after he arrived at LSE, it was his intention to write his thesis on the Yao people in Guangxi province. He recorded his first meeting with an LSE anthropologist in the person of Raymond Firth, who heard with no interest what he said about the Yao, but seized on the Kaixiangong research as a possibility when Fei mentioned it almost in passing. All this background is necessary for an understanding of the community ethnography that went into *Peasant Life in China*. It had come about almost as an accident. It was made up of some background information that could have been acquired from published sources or general observation, some detailed notes on the local economy, and, to make up for a thesis that would pass muster under the expertise of his eventual supervisor, none other than Malinowski himself, some very superficial comments on village religion. A short half chapter dealt with religion, but the rest of the book was a solid description of economic life.

Anyone who has read Malinowski would find it at least curious that Fei could have gotten away with so little discussion of the religious elements of economic life. His chapter on the calendar of work gives some clue in answer. The chapter cites Malinowski on the importance of reckoning time, backs that up with an outline of the 24 crucial seasonal events (*jieqi* 节气) in the lunar calendar, something that every student of China knows without conducting field work, and, as if to confirm his lack of field work, refers to a letter from his informant describing the two periods of the year when villagers had leisure.[24] It is as if Malinowski, hearing his chapter and the seasonal rhythm of work, had asked him when leisure fitted in, whereupon Fei wrote home to ask. He had not prepared it for the chapter. It was certainly not the result of field observation.

Community field work, therefore, did not always mean observation. More often, it meant interviews with local people who held official positions, usually about matters related to the economy and to administration. In that context, because it was well known that much business was conducted at temple fairs, quite a few studies listed when they were held and what was bought and sold. An exceptional detailed and poignant description was written by C.K. Yang (Yang Qingkun 杨庆堃 1911–1999), Fei Xiaotong's contemporary, in 1933. Having heard Robert Park, Yang went for doctoral training at the University of Michigan, and wrote the paper while a graduate student there, although it was published as a typescript only in 1944.[25] For another example, Qiao Qiming (乔启明 1897–1970) who studied in the Jinling University Department of Agricultural Economics under John Lossing Buck, also wrote an insightful essay on the village as a community at approximately the same time. He conducted a survey of all the villages within the neighborhood of a town near Nanjing, and through interviews with villagers, succeeded to mark on a map all earth-god shrines, temples, churches, villages, schools, general-purpose stores, teahouses, ancestral halls, public wells, brick kilns, cooperatives, and flour mills, and plotted on it the commercial, school, and temple-sacrifice demarcations. The paper is too brief for any analysis of what such territorial demarcations might have meant.[26] Nevertheless, the fact that it occurred to Qiao to mark them on the map indicates he was aware that territorial boundaries mattered in community studies. That seems like an obvious point to note, but it is an indication of how little local studies in the 1920s and 1930s appreciated the politics of village life that this was the only study that had made territory a focus.

Fei Xiaotong, C.K. Yang, and Qiao Qiming belonged to a new generation of scholars. They were students of the sociologists who had returned from Britain and the United States, Tao Menghe, Wu Wenzhao, Li Jinghan, and others, and they were trained in survey techniques which were very different from the home-grown variety that the folklorists had employed. The times were also changing. Whatever came to be said about the impact of international trade on the rural economy in China, from the last years of the Qing dynasty until the 1920s, farmers were riding the crest of rising prices and larger exports. By the end of the 1920s, the global Great Depression had brought down the silk industry, and, by the mid-1930s the United States Silver Purchase Act brought down the rice trade. In those difficult times, the term "rural bankruptcy" (*nongcun pochan* 农村破产) came to be popularized by the press. The downturn in the economy coincided with major political shifts, for the Nationalist Party (Guomindang), having successfully launched its Northern Expedition, was able to establish a government it dominated and to turn on the Chinese Communist Party. The 1930s became a decade of contradictions when the language of social class took root in social discussion. The Chinese Communist Party and its affiliates continued to advocate "land revolution" (*tudi geming* 土地革命), and the Guomindang and the Nanjing government implemented "rural rehabilitation" (*xiangcun jianshe* 乡村建设), which included the revival of rural industry—incorporated by Fei Xiaotong into his doctoral thesis—and moral rearmament—in the form of Liang Shuming's invocation of Confucianism in counterpoint with the Guomindang's New Life Movement. Indeed, village studies were conducted in the 1930s, but hardly any efforts were devoted to recording folklore or customs. The social program of the 1930s overwhelmed the folklorists. Local society was to be studied now not for what local people might want to think of their culture, but in terms of their class structure, which rested not on how they thought, but on how they made their livelihood.

As the class structure theory of society took hold, by accident more than design, community studies were driven to the southwest, and to peoples who had been designated non-Han. Out of the study of the minorities came China's most distinguished field workers of the 1930s: Ling Chunsheng (凌纯升), Rui Yifu (芮逸夫), and Yang Chengzhi (杨成志).[27] Lin Yuehua could have made a mark in Fujian. It was really a pity that he dramatized his research findings in the form of a novel, on which subject, Maurice Freedman, having tried to turn them into hard data, had this to say, "Of course, data taken from a work cast in the form of a novel must be inconclusive."[28]

The field now cleared of ethnographers, what did the sociologists make of villages in areas that were to be considered Han society, or sometimes, "China proper"? To answer this question, it is necessary to recognize that the field research explosion that exploded in quantity and magnitude in the 1920s and especially the 1930s shared two characteristics. First, much of it reported statistics. Second, almost all of it was carried out with a sense of mission to change society, whether it was raising literacy, alleviating poverty, promoting rural cooperatives, advancing the economy, exposing class exploitation, rural reconstruction, collecting tax, or, rather invidiously, preparing the field for the banks that were aiming to advance loans to farmers. There is perhaps no inherent reason why understanding local communities on their own terms could not be compatible with those traits. Yet, when those traits were put in place, field researchers ceased to write from their observations and reported their findings in the light, not of what they might observe around them, but as a shadow image of the distant world to which they wanted their surroundings to become.

The first social survey I know conducted in China was that reported in the *Journal of the North China Branch of the Royal Asiatic Society* in 1888 when foreigners in different parts of China gave their impressions on land productivity, prices, and ownership.[29] Beyond that, the best summary of the conduct of surveys is still Alfred Kaiming Chiu's doctoral thesis in 1933.[30] As anyone knows who has tried to arrive at statistical estimates for the Qing dynasty and the Republic, the drought of statistics up to the 1920s is followed by a tsunami. One only has to pick up any one of the 200 volumes of student reports produced by the Academy of Land Administration (*dizheng xueyuan* 地政学院) between 1932 and 1940 to be confronted with voluminous statistics collected through surveys by different branches of central and local governments, voluntary associations, universities, and the newspapers.[31] One should not let the statistics mislead. Few of them came from actual measurements taken by surveyors. Most were reported by respondents of one sort or another and anyone who wants to use those statistics would do well to ask how respondents were supposed to know how many acres were put under cultivation, what the population of the village or the county might be, not to say how many of those were landlords, or tenants, or half-landlords and half-tenants, or what even some of those terms might mean. The drive for the sham accuracy of statistics in those reports substituted pre-set classifications for the interest to observe. If there is any doubt about the condemnation I am invoking with this statement, I advise reading the diaries of the young people sent to conduct the surveys with the reports that they submitted. The surveyors in Changshu county in Jiangsu were swept off their feet when they confronted topless elderly village women as they remarked, "We couldn't imagine that the new life movement promoted in Germany had long been the practice here!" One sees surprises, questions, and doubts in the field diaries that are totally purged from the formal reports.[32]

Quite apart from the reliability of the statistics, the social program that bred the field research of the 1930s diverted interest from local society. The indictment sounds harsh, for was not the China National Association of the Mass Education Movement working in the villages, and, admirably, Li Jinghan living in a mud hut right in the model village of Zhaicheng (翟城) as he conducted his survey?[33] Charles Hayford, defending Li's survey, reminds us that we should read Li's own 828-page report of Ding county rather than Sidney Gamble's shorter account. Yet having done so, it is hard not to agree with Barrington Moore, also cited by Hayford, who complained that in the Gamble volume, "the social structure of this community is scarcely visible behind the mass of statistical data in this study."[34] Interestingly, chapters are included on religion, custom, entertainment, education, and even family (under "population"), but it is Chapter 3 "county government and other local organizations (*difang tuanti* 地方团体)" that is telling. Fifteen pages go into the county government, three into popular organizations under the county party office (peasant association, chamber of commerce, labor union, student association, women's association) and then five pages on former (*jiuyou*) local organizations, including the old agricultural association (*nonghui*), chamber of commerce, and so forth; and, only after those, comes a mention for village associations, including those for local defense.[35] I find that interesting, indeed, for what Li Jinghan produced in all his honesty was the Republican view of what society was becoming, so that what it had been might be tugged away safely out of harm's way, as nowadays we might do so by calling it all "intangible heritage." Interesting too, because Li Jinghan obviously knew there was a story to be told about how the Mass Education Movement might take root in Ding county and he did not divulge it. A social movement that put 400 schools into the county without upsetting some politics is almost incredible, and I have not yet seen any historical account that tells me what that politics consisted of.

The sociologists who wanted to reform Chinese society had little patience with what they found. They made their compromises with the powers that were in order to promote the programs for which they conducted their surveys. The description of village society they were prepared to divulge came close to the view that the government might have advocated. That approach brings us close to the Qing dynasty, a world in which the imperial realm ("society" had not yet made itself known) was defined in terms of provinces, prefectures, and counties, manned by officials who had passed the examination, skilled in the "statecraft" (*jingshi* 经世) of water control, famine relief, policing, tax collection, and legal adjudication, whose work was assisted by either the gentry (*shenshi*) who, aspiring to or having also passed the examination, saw eye-to-eye with the officialdom, or the clerks (*xuli*), power-wielding, and low-status people who nonetheless officialdom preferred to the gentry because it appointed them. That Qing dynasty world comes close to the orthodox version of Chinese society as taught in English in the 1950s, and, given some additional pages, we could document its heritage through the work of Fei Xiaotong, Wen Juntian (闻钧天), and then Xiao Gongquan (Hsiao Kung-chuan 萧公权).[36] Despite their starting point in community studies, in between their search for social classes and ready acceptance of the Republican model of rural governance, some time in the 1930s, the sociologists lost track of village society.

Hearing and listening

It is almost impossible to translate "hearing" and "listening" into Chinese to bring out the passive meaning of the one word and the active meaning of the other. It would be easy to charge the May Fourth generation who went to the people—to use Hung Chang-tai's term—with not hearing them. They probably did, as witness the surveyors' diaries, but their mission, as defined by the questions they were taught to ask, was not to listen. I have the experience of appearing in a Guangdong village in the 1980s in the company of a friend who wanted to know from someone we met how many "middle peasants" there had been in the village, and, when the villager could not answer the question, proceeded to explain to him what the "middle peasant" was. How on earth did the surveyors of the 1930s return with figures on the "middle peasant," a term that was ungrounded in village language, that was used without a common standard even by the surveyors themselves? Did they not hear the hesitation that responded to the question as it was posed?

18 *David Faure*

I worry at times if future generations might say the same of us. Given the last chance to record Ming and Qing society before the total destruction of its heritage, did my generation, guided by our hypotheses, only pick up what confirmed our preconceived beliefs? We have to trust that thanks to human incompetence, some researchers will slip through, as in the 1940s quite a few did, such as Li Shiyu who gave us one of the earlier studies of north China religious sects, and by the 1950s, Lu Yao, who spoke to the survivors from the Boxer Movement.[37] More importantly, we have to be able to learn to see the world from the vantage point, not of ourselves but of the people we are interested in. In order to do that, we have to learn to see how our models of their world differ from their models. Through my lifetime, students of Chinese society went through that learning exercise twice: once, when G. William Skinner, following from the nineteenth-century Western travelers in China (such as Arthur Smith in Shandong), brought us back to reality by reminding us that Chinese society was less structured in classes than in marketing systems,[38] and again, when Maurice Freedman discovered that south China lineages were really territorial communities built around the holding of property and not extensions of the family.[39] Those models have worked well in conversation with villagers because they have come closer to their models than previous efforts, but, of course, even then, they were not capturing imageries set in religion and folklore, as the Miaofengshan tradition of research had learnt.

The danger of every major discovery comes in its being accepted uncritically, so that we might think that having cited Skinner we are dispensed with the need to investigate variations in trading patterns and routes, or having read Freedman, we could assume that lineages might account for territorial organization in every part of China. The biblical adage "seek and you shall find" is a dangerous guiding principle for social research unless you add to that, "but please seek otherwise when you don't." Anthropologists are right in thinking they have to be critical of their own field methodology, and, as long as they do not turn self-examination into a substitute of the field work itself, historians who go into the field should do likewise. We can take our analyses to as far away from an unintended consequence as we might wish, but to speak and to listen to our villagers, we have to be able to communicate with them in their terms.

Notes

1 For a recent study, see Susan Naquin, *Peking, Temples and City Life, 1400–1900*, Berkeley: University of California Press, 2000, pp. 528–547.
2 Supplement (*fukan*) to *Jingbao*, May 13, 23, 29, June 6, July 17; Gu Jiegang ed. *Miaofengshan*, Guangzhou: Guoli Zhongshan daxue Yuyan lishixue yanjiusuo, 1928; reprinted in *Minguo congshu*, ser. 5, vol. 22, Shanghai: Shanghai shudian, 1996.
3 Contrasting versions of the movement may be found in Laurence A. Schneider, *Ku Chieh-kang and China's New History*, Berkeley: University of California

Comments on field research in China 19

Press, 1971, pp. 121–187 and Chang-tai Hung, *Going to the People, Chinese Intellectuals and Folk Literature, 1918–1937*, Cambridge, MA: Council on East Asian Studies, Harvard University, 1985.
4 Yang Kun, "Woguo minsuxue yundong shilüe" [Brief history of China's ethnology movement] in Yang Kun, *Minzu yanjiu wenji*, Beijing: Minzu chubanshe, 1991, pp. 210–237; Cheng Meibao, *Diyu wenhua yu guojia rentong, wan-Qing yilai "Guangdong wenhua" guan de xingcheng* [Regional culture and national identity: Forming views of "Cantonese culture" since the late Qing], Beijing: Xinhua 2006, pp. 213–260.
5 Li Jinghan, "Miaofengshan 'chaoding jinxiang' de diaocha," [A survey of the pilgrimage to Miaofengshan] *Shehuixue zazhi*, vol. 2: 5 and 6, 1925, pp. 1–42; Sidney Gamble, *Peking, A Social Survey*, New York: George H. Doran Co., 1921, pp. 228–229.
6 Charles W. Hayford, *To the People, James Yen and Village China*, New York: Columbia University Press, 1990, pp. 92–97; Sidney D. Gamble, *Chinese Village Plays from the Ting Hsien Region (Yang Ke Hsüan): A Collection of Forty-eight Chinese Rural Plays as Staged by Villagers from Ting Hsien in Northern China*, Amsterdam: Philo Press, 1970; Li Jinghan, *Dingxian shehui gaikuang diaocha* [Social survey of Dingxian], Beijing: Zhonghua pingmin jiaoyu cujin hui, 1933.
7 Rong Chaozu, "Beida geyao yanjiuhui ji fengsu diaochahui de jingguo," [History of the Beijing University folk song research and custom investigation society] *Minsu*, 1516, 1928, pp. 1–10, and no. 1718, pp. 14–31.
8 Zhao Shiyu, *Yanguang xiangxia de geming: Zhongguo xiandai minsuxue sixiang lun, 1918–1937* [Casting eyes downward: The intellectual revolution of modern Chinese folklore studies], Beijing: Beijing shifan daxue chubanshe, 1999, pp. 123–133.
9 Charlotte Sophia Burne (sic), *Minsu xue wenti ge* [Lattice of issues in folklore studies], transl. by Yang Chengzhi, Guangzhou: Guoli Zhongshan daxue Yuyan lishi yanjiusuo, 1928.
10 Rong Zhaozu, *Mixin yu chuanshuo, Zhongshan daxue minsu congshu* [Superstitions and tales, Sun Yat-Sen University collected folklore materials], vol. 2, Guangzhou: Guolin Zhongshan daxue yuyan lishi xue yanjiusuo, minsu xuehui, 1928–1929, rep. Taipei: Folklore Books Company Ltd., 1959, p. 1.
11 The three volumes Gu Jiegang produced on Woman Meng and related essays are included in Gu Jiegang, *Gu Jiegang quanji* [collected works of Gu Jiegang], Beijing: Zhonghua shuju, 2011, vol. 15.
12 To his credit, Gu Jiegang realized more than many China historians that the search for origin was not the objective of textual studies. See his comment at ibid. p. 89, where he eschewed commenting on the "reality" of Woman Meng in favor of learning from variations of the story through place and time the history of local variations, popular thought, and literati efforts.
13 Cheng Meibao, *Diyu wenhua yu guojia rentong*, pp. 96–108; Qiu Zhihong, "Qingmo Minchu de xiguan diaocha yu xiandai minshang faxue de jianli," [Investigation of customs and formation of formation of civil law in the late Qing and early Republic] in Huang Xingtao and Xia Mingfang, eds. *Qingmo Minguo shehui diaocha yu xiandai shehui kexue xingqi* [Late Qing and early Republican social investigations and the formation of modern social science], Xiamen: Fujian jiaoyu chubanshe, 2008, pp. 341–379.
14 Zhao Shiyu, *Yanguang xiangxia de geming*, pp. 188–189.
15 Liu Wanzhang, ed. *Guangzhou minjian gushi, Zhongshan daxue minsu congshu* [Guangzhou folktales, Sun Yat-Sen University collected folklore materials], vol. 6, Guangzhou: Guoli Zhongshan daxue yuyan lishi xue yanjiusuo, minsu xuehui, 1928–1929, rep. Taipei: Folklore Books Company Ltd., 1959, pp. 1–14.

16 Zhong Jingwen, *Zhong Jingwen minsuxue lunji* [Zhong Jingwen essays on folklore studies], Shanghai: Shanghai wenyi chubanshe, 1998, pp. 150–151.
17 Zhao Shiyu, *Yanguang xiangxia de geming*, pp. 221–234.
18 On Wu Wenzao, see the biographical essays, including a memoire by his wife, the writer Bing Xin 冰心, in Wu Wenzao, *Renleixue shehuixue yanjiu wenji* [Social science research issues in anthropology], Beijing: Minzu chubanshe, 1990. Tao Menghe co-authored (with YK Leong, a Malayan overseas Chinese) one of the earliest ethnographies on local Chinese society published in English as *Village and Town Life in China*, London: George Allen & Unwin, 1915.
19 Hsiao-tung Fei and Chih-i Chang, *Earthbound China: A Study of Rural Economy in Yunnan*, 1949, rep. 2010, London: Routledge, pp. 1–7; Fei Xiaotong, *Neidi de nongcun* [Inland village], Shanghai: Shenghuo shudian, 1946, repr. in Fei Xiaotong, *Fei Xiaotong wenji* [Fei Xiaotong essays], Beijing: Qunyan chubanshe, 1999, vol. 4, pp. 189–190.
20 Morton H. Fried, "Community studies in China," *Far Eastern Quarterly*, 14:1, 1954, pp. 11–36; Chen Ta, *Emigrant Communities in South China: a Study of Overseas Migration and Its Influence on Standards of Living and Social Change*, Shanghai: Kelly & Walsh, 1939.
21 Meng Zhen (Fu Sinian), "Shandong di yibufen de nongmin zhuangkuang dalue ji," [A rough sketch of the conditions of some peasants in Shandong], Xin qingnian, vol. 7 no. 2, 1920, p. 148.
22 Hsiao-tung Fei, *Peasant Life in China, A Field Study of Country Life in the Yangtze Valley*, London: Kegan Paul, Trench, Trubner & Co., Ltd., 1939.
23 Fei Xiaotong, *Shicheng, buke, zhixue* [Teachers, studies, scholarship], Beijing: Sanlian, 2001.
24 Hsiao-tung Fei, *Peasant Life in China*, p. 149.
25 Ching-kun Yang, *A North China Local Market Economy: A Summary of a Study of Periodic Markets in Chowping hsien, Shantung*, New York: International Secretariat, Institute of Pacific Relations, 1944.
26 Qiao Qiming, "Jiangning xian Chunhua zhen xiangcun shehui zhi yanjiu," [Social system in villages of Jiangning County, Chunhua Township] *Jinling daxue nongxueyuan congkan*, 23, 1934, pp. 1–45.
27 Li Yiyuan, "Ling Chunsheng xiansheng dui Zhongguo minsuxue zhi gongxian" [Contribution of Mr. Ling Chunsheng to Chinese folklore], *Zhongyang yanjiuyuan minsuxue yanjiusuo jikan*, 29, 1970, pp. 1–10; Li Yiyuan, "Zhongguo minsu, shehui yu wenhua—Rui Yifu jiaoshou de xueshu chengjiu yu gongxian" [Chinese customs, society and culture—the scholarly accomplishments and contributions of Professor Rui Yifu], *Shihuo yuekan*, 11:7, 1981, pp. 295–304; Shi Aidong, "Zhongshan daxue minsu xuehui yu zaoqi xinan minsu diaocha" [Sun Yan-Sen University folklore society and early investigations of customs in the Southeast], *Wenhua yichan* 3, 2008, pp. 46–57.
28 Maurice Freedman, *Lineage Organization in Southeastern China*, London: Athlone Press, 1958. p. 98.
29 George Jamieson, "Tenure of Land in China and the Condition of the Rural Population," *Journal of the North China Branch of the Royal Asiatic Society* 23, 1888–1889, pp. 59–118.
30 Alfred Kai-ming Chiu, "Recent statistical surveys of the Chinese rural economy, 1912–1932: A Study of the Sources of Chinese Agricultural Statistics, Their Methods of Collecting Data and Their Findings about Rural Economic Conditions," unpublished Ph.D. dissertation, Harvard University, 1933.
31 Xiao Zheng, ed. *Minguo ershi niandai Zhongguo dalu tudi wenti ziliao* [Materials on land problems on the Chinese mainland during the second decade of the Republic], Taipei: Chengwen, 1977.

32 Xingzhengyuan nongcun fuxing weiyuanhui, ed. *Jiangsu sheng nongcun diaocha* [Investigation of rural Jiangsu], Shanghai: Shangwu, 1934, p. 80; and the plates for visual images of what the researchers saw. The survey was designed by Chen Hansheng, who made his reputation in classifying the Chinese peasantry. On the Russian influence that guided his thoughts, see Yung-chen Chiang, *Social Engineering and the Social Sciences in China, 1919–1949*, Cambridge: Cambridge University Press, 2001.
33 Li Jinghan, "Zhu zai nongcun congshi shehui diaocha suode de yinxiang" [The impression of social investigation comes from living in the village], *Shehui xuejie*, 4, 1930, pp. 1–14.
34 Charles W. Hayford, *To the People*, p. 96.
35 Li Jinghan, *Dingxian shehui gaikuang diaocha*, pp. 77–119.
36 Fei Xiaotong, *China's Gentry: Essays in Rural-urban Relations*, transl. Margaret Park Redfield, Chicago: University of Chicago Press, 1953; Wen Juntian, *Zhongguo baojia zhidu* [China's baojia system], Beijing: Shangwu, 1935; Hsiao Kung-chuan, *Rural China: Imperial Control in the Nineteenth Century*, Seattle: University of Washington Press, 1960.
37 Li Shiyu, *Xiandai Huabei mimi zongjiao* [Secret religion in contemporary North China], Studia Serica, Monographs Ser. B No. 4, n.p., 1948; Lu Yao, *Shandong Yihetuan diaocha ziliao xuanbian* [Selected sources from the Shandong Yihetuan], Jinan: Qilu shushe, 1980; Lu Yao and Cheng Xiao, *Yihetuan yundongshi yanjiu* [Study of the Yihetuan movement], Jinan: Qilu shushe, 1988.
38 G. William Skinner, "Marketing and Social Structure in Rural China," *Journal of Asian Studies*, 24:1, 1964–1965, pp. 3–43, vol. 24: 2 pp. 195–228, and vol. 24:3, pp. 363–399; Arthur Smith, *Village Life in China: A Study in Sociology*, Edinburgh: Oliphant, Anderson and Ferrier, 1900.
39 Maurice Freedman, *Lineage Organization in Southeastern China*, and *Chinese Lineage and Society: Fukien and Kwantung*, London: Athlone Press, 1966.

2 A brief history of Japanese field research on China

Linda Grove

In 1980, having spent nine months at the Economic Research Institute at Nankai University as a visiting scholar, I returned to Tokyo and was invited to join a small research group that was studying rural change in pre-1949 China. The group met once a month to read and discuss materials from the Survey of Chinese Rural Customs (*Chūgoku nōson kankō chōsa* 中国農村慣行調査), a six-volume collection of the interview records of a wartime project on customary law in rural North China that is now recognized as one of the most important sources for understanding social life in rural China before 1949. Our multi-university group was led by Uchiyama Masao 内山雅生 and Mitani Takashi 三谷孝, and included Hamaguchi Nobuko 浜口允子, Kasahara Tokushi 笠原十九司, Nakao Katsumi 中生勝美, Suetsugu Reiko 末次玲子, and myself. The materials we were reading, usually referred to as the *kankō chōsa*, were the product of a major wartime research project conducted by the research bureau of the South Manchurian Railroad in collaboration with legal scholars from Tokyo University. The research team had selected six villages in Hebei and Shandong Provinces and conducted intensive research, interviewing a wide range of individuals in each of the villages, recording the interviews in question-and-answer format. The project was designed to study what the researchers called "customary law" (*kankō* 慣行), a broadly defined investigation that looked at practices related to family and family organization, lineage organization and functions, economic activities, landholding and customs related to selling, renting and mortgaging land, markets and market practices, religious activities, annual ceremonies, births and deaths, marriages and funerals, village leadership, village governance, village relations with township and county governments, and much more. After the war, participants in the research project edited the materials and published six large volumes in the original question-and-answer format. The format of the reports has preserved the voices—including dissonant views—of village leaders and ordinary peasants, and allows us now, decades after the materials were collected, to read and make our own judgments about family and lineage, property rights and inheritance, economic activities, village organizations, village religious life, and much more.

In the early 1980s when I joined the research group, use of the *kankō chōsa* materials was controversial. The research teams had carried out the study under the Japanese occupation and team members had often been accompanied by military guards when they visited the villages. Many scholars in Japan believed that the circumstances under which the materials had been collected had tainted the materials; there were sharp debates within the Japanese research community between those who used the reports as a way to understand village life and those who believed the materials were a product of Japan's aggression in China and thus should not be used. These debates took place during the Vietnam War, at a time when progressive scholars in Japan, as well as those in the United States and Europe, were giving a serious thought to the ways in which imperialist state policies had shaped academic discourse in the past, and how they continued to do so in the present. The *kankō chōsa* materials were seen by more left-leaning scholars as a prime example of "colonial research" designed to aid an imperialist state in its efforts to control a subordinate population.

While use of the materials in Japan—to say nothing of China—was once controversial, the value of the materials has now been widely recognized, and scholars at Central China Normal University (Huazhong Shifan Daxue 华中师范大学) have a major project to publish Mantetsu materials (of which the *kankō chōsa* are only a small part) in Chinese. The first volume of the translation series was published by the China Social Science Press (中国社会科学出版社) in 2016, followed by additional volumes in 2017 and 2018.[1] Project organizers at the university's Institute of China Rural Studies estimate that the translation series will eventually include 100 volumes of translated materials. I have written elsewhere about the use of these materials and the rich accumulation of follow-up studies by both Chinese and Japanese scholars.[2] The first major studies using the Mantetsu materials were the work of American and Japanese scholars, but in recent years Chinese scholars have also used the *kankō chōsa* materials as the base for follow-up studies. In 2014, I met the authors of one of the most comprehensive Chinese follow-up studies, which is on the village of Lengshuigou in the suburbs of the Shandong provincial capital of Jinan. Over the last several years, we have worked together to translate their work into English.[3] Many of the follow-up studies on the "*kankō chōsa* villages" have been undertaken in a spirit very similar to that reflected in other projects described in this volume: earlier surveys serve as historical resources on rural practices, which can then be compared to data and knowledge gained through contemporary fieldwork.

In this chapter, I present a brief history of Japanese fieldwork studies on various aspects of Chinese economy and society. While the *kankō chōsa* volumes are among the best-known results of Japanese survey and field research efforts in China, they follow in a long tradition of research on China that can be traced back to the mid-nineteenth century. In what follows I will briefly trace several lines of development, looking first at efforts to understand the Chinese economy and business practices, then at efforts to

24 *Linda Grove*

understand customary legal institutions, and finally at the *kankō chōsa* and other related research activities.

Economic and business practices

From Sakoku (seclusion)「鎖国」*to building an information society*

For more than two centuries of the Edo era (1603–1868), Japan was essentially closed to relations with the outside world. The Dutch and Chinese merchant communities, the only foreigners allowed to trade, were restricted to small enclaves in the port of Nagasaki on the southern island of Kyushu, and Japanese were not allowed to travel outside of the Japanese islands. What knowledge Japanese had of the outside world came through books— mostly imported from China—and through contact with Chinese visitors and "Dutch learning" through intermediaries in Nagasaki. Although contact was limited, there is no question that at least some Japanese officials were curious about the outside world. One of the most interesting signs of this curiosity was a book on customs in Qing China, edited by Nakagawa Tadateru, who was the ranking administrative official in Nagasaki from 1795 to 1797. He organized the official translators to question the Qing merchants who came to Nagasaki about customs in their home territories of Jiangnan and Fujian, producing a massive illustrated book *Record of Qing customs* (*Shinzoku kibun*) 清俗紀聞.[4] The book includes sections on annual ceremonies, life cycle rituals, daily life (cooking, cleaning, bathing), daily use items, implements used for cooking and cleaning, farming, religious ceremonies, and so forth.

Consular reports on economy and trade

After Japan was opened to international trade in 1858, there was an urgent need to gather and distribute information on the outside world not only to officials, but also to merchants, trading companies, and individuals who were interested in participating in international commerce. Since there was limited recent history of contact with foreign countries, those who wanted to get involved in trade had few ideas of what goods—beyond the silk and tea that foreign merchants desired—might be sold in foreign markets. The Meiji government set out to remedy this situation by setting up consular stations overseas, and directing the consular officers to report regularly on economic developments as well as political trends.[5] While almost all modern states' diplomatic services are charged with regular reporting on political and economic developments in the countries where they are located, one characteristic of the Japanese customs service was an effort to disseminate widely economic information to the general public. The consular reports, which were published under different names, began in 1881 and continued until 1943; they were published and openly distributed to members of the business community as well as the general public to aid their efforts in entering foreign markets.[6] On the basis of the data collected by consular officials, the "Japan-China Trade Institute" (*Nisshin bōeki kenkyūjō* 日清貿易研究所) a Japanese-Qing trade research organization in Shanghai in 1892 published the first comprehensive guide to Chinese economy and society, the Shinkoku tsūshō sōran 清国通商総覧 in three volumes with more than 2,000 pages.[7]

Tōa Dōbun Shoin and field research on the Chinese economy

As the Japanese government and Japanese businesses began to enter the Chinese market in the late nineteenth century, they realized they needed to recruit employees who knew the Chinese language and had knowledge of the Chinese business and political worlds. This demand led to the establishment of the *Tōa Dōbun Shoin* (East Asia Research Institute 東亜同文書院) in Shanghai. The school recruited students from all over Japan, with individual prefectures offering scholarships to successful candidates, who undertook a four-year curriculum that stressed language study (Chinese and English) as well as classes on politics, law, economics and business practices. According to Douglas Reynolds, more than 5,000 Japanese students attended classes, more than 3,500 graduated, and some 1,000 were in the school at the end of the war in 1945.[8] One feature of the school's training program was a graduation field trip. Senior students were divided into small groups of four to five members; each group decided on its own itinerary and undertook to provide a comprehensive survey of the cities and towns they visited, submitting a report on their return to Shanghai. Faculty and researchers at the school used the material gathered by the students to compile a series of volumes on Chinese provinces and on Chinese economic practices.[9] The research division of the school edited a bi-monthly journal, *China* (*Shina* 支那), which also drew on the research reports of students and faculty members.[10] I have in my collection a special issue from 1913 on the trade in China of miscellaneous goods, with detailed reports on markets for all kinds of consumer goods. These books and journals, along with dozens of specialized books on different industrial sectors, paid close attention to material culture and fashion. For example, guides to the textile trade include detailed descriptions of what kinds of cloth were sold, in which regional markets, and how local consumers used different products.

The leading Chinese business practices expert Negishi Tadashi 根岸佶 (1874–1971), who taught at the Tōa Dōbun Shoin in the early twentieth century before returning to Japan to teach at the Higher Commercial School (later Hitotsubashi University), continued to serve as research advisor for the Tōa Dōbun Shoin and used data from the student reports along with his own extensive research. He published an authoritative series of books on

26 *Linda Grove*

Chinese commercial practice, including a well-regarded work on Chinese guilds, and a massive study of Chinese business partnerships.[11] In recent years, scholars have rediscovered the materials compiled by the students and faculty of the Tōa Dōbun Shoin, and edited and printed the field reports as well as the trip diaries from the student field trips. These materials make for fascinating reading, not only for what they tell us about various regions of China, but also for what they have to say about the state of Sino-Japanese relations in different eras.[12]

Other economic and business studies

The description so far represents only a small part of the rich Japanese research on China's economy, business practices, and society. As the Japanese government and businesses became more involved in China, the demand for detailed studies of local economy and business practices increased, and various organizations began to publish articles and reports on specific industries and local markets. We can find quite useful reports in the pages of business journals (for example, the Japanese textile organization's journal), the newsletters of Japanese Chambers of Commerce in Japan as well as the Chambers of Commerce set up by Japanese business people in different Chinese cities, and privately published reports by business people in China.

One example comes from a businessman in North China, who published a series of reports on the cotton trade in North China based on his own detailed fieldtrips in Hebei and Shanxi in the late 1920s and early 1930s: "Riben Shiliaozhong de Zhongguo Jingji Huodong; Zhongguo Beifang de Quyu Jingji Wangluo" 日本史料中的中国经济活动: 中国北方的区域经济网络, in *Guojia Shiyexia de Difang* 国家视野下的地方 (上海人民出版社, 2014, 88–101). His field trip diaries include very interesting information on travel itineraries, the state of roads, railroads and lodging facilities, costs of travel, etc. The archives of a number of Japanese trading companies with activities in China, for example, the Mitsui Bunko (www.mitsui-bunko.or.jp/archives/englishguide.html), which holds the records of one of Japan's largest general trading firms Mitsui Bussan, also hold collections of important company-directed surveys. Yushodo Shoten put out in 2010 a digital reproduction of the newspapers published by Japanese Chambers of Commerce in East Asia between 1903 and 1945 (東アジア日本人商工会議所関係資料). The collection, on 20 DVDs, includes the newspapers published by the Japanese Chambers of Commerce in various cities in Korea, Manchuria, and Taiwan, as well as those published in Beijing, Tianjin, Chefoo, Jinan, Qingdao, Shanghai, Nanjing, Xuzhou, Hankou, Guangdong, Xiamen, and Hong Kong, and in several Southeast Asian cities. Another useful source is the digitalized newspaper clipping collection maintained by the Kobe University Library (www.lib.kobe-u.ac.jp/sinbun/e-index.html). The clipping files were created, beginning in 1911, by the Kobe Higher Commercial School, and cover the period from 1911 to the end of the war in 1945.

Legal institutions and customary law

A second major stream of Japanese research on prewar China began in the wake of the Sino-Japanese War of 1894–1895, when the Treaty of Shimonoseki ceded Taiwan to Japan as its first colony. In the late 1890s, the Japanese colonial government faced many challenges in trying to gain administrative control over the newly acquired territory. Gotō Shinpei 後藤新平, who was appointed as head of the Civil Affairs division of the colonial government, was convinced that one of the keys to successful colonial administration was to survey and register land. Customary practices in Taiwan related to land ownership rights were complicated and had to be understood if disputes over land ownership (and tax responsibilities) were to be resolved. Gotō and his colleagues organized the "special research group on Taiwan customs" (*Rinji Taiwan kyūkan chōsakai* 臨時台湾旧慣調査会), which included legal experts, to begin a study of customary law in Taiwan. This group examined earlier Qing legal regulations and practices, looked at contracts and documents, checked on customary practices in economic exchanges, interviewed indigenous (non-Han) groups about customs, and examined legal practices in the treaty port areas. A major aim of the project was to gain a thorough understanding of customary practices, also referred to as "private law 私法" with regard to property rights, family law (including on marriage, divorce, inheritance, adoptions), rights and practices related to movable property, and various legal aspects of commerce and industry including the organization of merchant firms, handling of debt and bankruptcy, exchange methods and so forth.[13]

In 1906, following the Russo-Japanese war, Gotō was appointed as the first director of the newly established South Manchurian Railway Company (hereafter Mantetsu). Under his direction, Mantetsu established a Research Bureau, and one of the first tasks assigned to the bureau was a survey of customary law in the Chinese Northeast ("Manchuria"). One of the core aims of the surveys was to gain a grasp of the land system in that region; investigators surveyed both Qing legal practices and local adaptations. Researchers were dispatched to villages in various parts of the region to interview village leaders about customary practices with regard to ownership rights, land sales, inheritance practices, and contracts.

As Japanese influence in China grew, the Mantetsu Research Bureau expanded its activities, setting up branch offices in various parts of China, with researchers carrying out a wide range of research projects. While many of the projects focused on economic issues, circulation of goods, production and sales of specific commodities, and commercial customs, research projects also included broader investigations of social life.

Mantetsu and village studies in China

The *kankō chōsa* studies on the six North China villages are the best known of the Mantetsu Research Bureau's studies on rural China—but they are far from being its only work on rural China. There were a number of studies of economic conditions in the Northeast, a comprehensive set of studies of agricultural practices in Eastern Hebei, and another set of village studies carried out during the war on villages in the Yangzi delta region. Philip Huang made extensive use of the East Hebei village studies in his *Peasant Economy and Social Change in North China* (1985). A collaborative research project involving four American scholars (Elizabeth Perry, Joseph Esherick, Philip Huang, and me) and scholars from the history department of Nanjing University in the early 1980s did field work in the small town of Huayangqiao 华阳桥 and four nearby villages in Songjiang 松江 county (Shanghai) that had been studied by the Mantetsu Research Bureau in the early 1940s. Huang's book *The Peasant Family and Rural Development in the Yangzi Delta, 1350–1988* came out of that project.[14]

The North China six-village *kankō chōsa* studies grew out of these earlier traditions of the study of customary law and economic relations, bringing together researchers from the Mantetsu with scholars at Tokyo University. The two groups jointly drafted a research agenda and recruited researchers to participate in the project. At the time, the Mantetsu research bureau had a large staff of talented researchers, many of whom held what might be described as "progressive" views. It was difficult for such individuals to find work in Japan in the 1930s, and as a result, some of them had taken up positions with the Research Bureau in China where ideological restrictions were considerably looser. Japanese scholarship in this period was influenced by Western academic analytical traditions that included Marxist notions of social relations and class, an influence that can be found in the way researchers formulated questions about land ownership, relations between landlords and tenants, and the influence of such relations on village politics. This interpretative language was shared across the political spectrum and use of such formulations can be found in descriptions of Chinese rural society not only in academic work but also in surveys undertaken by the Japanese military.

The *kankō chōsa* project had been designed to run for many years, and the North China village studies were envisioned as the first stage of a project that would eventually apply the same methods to studies of other regions of China. The studies were brought to a sudden end in September 1942 when the Kwantung Army launched a purge against what it believed were leftist scholars working for the Research Bureau.[15] After the war, scholars who had been involved with the project, including Niida Noboru, a Tokyo University professor and one of Japan's leading experts on Chinese law, took on the task of organizing and publishing the research records. Although the first volume of the series won a major prize, sales were not very encouraging. In the 1970s when I arrived in Japan to work on a dissertation on rural North China before and during the Anti-Japanese War, one could occasionally find a copy of the first volume of the *kankō chōsa* in a Tokyo used book store. Attitudes toward the value of the records began to change in the late

1970s, and in 1981, the Iwanami Publishing Company responded to the new demand and put out a reprint edition.

The kankō chōsa tradition and contemporary Japanese field work in China

By the late 1980s, Chinese scholars were willing to entertain the idea of conducting collaborative fieldwork with foreign scholars. Following long discussions, our research group reached an agreement with Prof. Wei Hongyun and his colleagues at Nankai University's history department to launch a project to restudy several of the *kankō chōsa* villages. With funding from the Japanese Society for the Promotion of Science and the Mitsubishi and Toyota foundations, over the next five years we paid multiple visits to the villages, and in 1999 and 2000 published two large volumes with the Japanese translations of the interview transcripts from those many visits.[16]

Our main concern in undertaking the project was to try to understand how the grand narratives of PRC history had played out at the "grassroots" level in each of the villages. The members of our group, with the exception of Nakao Katsumi, who is an anthropologist, were all historians, and we were primarily intent on recording the experiences of our informants, in their own words. (All interviews were recorded, and later transcribed by Chinese assistants, including several who were graduate students at Nankai at the time.) Each of the group members had an area of special interest, and we all took responsibility for collecting the life histories of informants. The first person who interviewed a villager would begin by discussing the person's life history: family, schooling (if any), marriage, children, work, and positions held in the village at different times. We conducted interviews in the mornings and afternoons and met every evening to exchange information on the day's interviews and to suggest follow-up interviews by someone with a more specialized interest in a particular topic. For example, my own special area of responsibility was to try to grasp the overall picture of economic development in a village from the late 1940s to the early 1990s; so, I spent a lot of time talking to team and village accountants. I was also responsible for work on non-agricultural activities, markets, and marketing and so talked to villagers who specialized in cash crops and non-agricultural activities, both during the Maoist era and during the reform period. I also visited and interviewed all of the villagers who had set up shops or small workshops, or those who worked in trade. This included, for example, in Pingyuan 平原 county in northwest Shandong a young couple who were running a putting-out operation in which village girls and women wove baskets for overseas markets, as well as interviews with men in a village in Jinghai 静海 county (Tianjin) who had set up a metal working factory that made auto parts under contract to a state firm. I also talked to village leaders and others who had been involved in collective factories in the pre-reform era. Another member of our group was responsible for trying to plot the political history of each village and concentrated on interviewing production team and brigade leaders from different eras, as well as on collecting accounts from many individuals about the various political movements in the villages starting with land reform and continuing through collectivization, the socialist education movement and the Cultural Revolution. Our anthropologist worked on family and lineage activities, life cycle and annual rituals, and the changing state of relations between villagers, while another member who was interested in education spent many hours talking to villagers about their school days and interviewing village school teachers. In addition to publishing the interview transcripts in Japanese, in 2000 we produced a semi-popular book for use in college-level classes, *Mura kara Chūgoku wo yomu* 村から中国を読む (*Reading China from the Village*). Our Nankai colleagues published, in 2010, four volumes that include the Chinese transcripts of all our interviews, as well as material that Prof. Zhang Si collected from his work on another Mantetsu village.[17]

Most of the members of our research team, both Chinese and Japanese, were historians, and we had hoped to combine the use of village written records with what we had learned from oral history interviews. We soon learned that few of our villages had good archives. For example, in my efforts to understand the broad outlines of village economic development, I sought copies of the annual statistical reports on agricultural and other forms of economic activity; but even such basic materials were lacking in some cases. None of the villages we studied had anything that looked like a "village archive." Where written records survived, it was due to the individual efforts of people who had been involved in creating them. For example, if the same individual had served as the village or team accountant for a number of years, the chances that s/he had kept copies of the records were higher; if, however, there had been frequent changes in village accountants, then often the village had not retained copies of the records they had submitted. We also discovered that village statistical records were considerably more problematic after the breakup of the commune and the turn to family-based farming and other economic activity.

We all dreamed of finding the kinds of records that Prof. Zhang Si found when he took Nankai students to one of the *kankō chōsa* villages that we had not been able to study, the village of Houjiaying 侯家营 in Changli County 昌黎, Hebei. Zhang uncovered village records, going back to the 1950s, that included economic records, village accounts and receipts, "class archives" from the time of the Socialist Education movement, and much more. Zhang and his students were able to use the records, together with their own fieldwork, to produce an interesting volume that includes an analysis of contacts with organizations and regions outside the village based on the receipts held by the village accountant, a record of books in the village reading room and movies that were shown, as well as numerous other reports on changes in village life.[18]

Although the *kankō chōsa* project was undertaken some eight decades ago, it continues to have an influence on contemporary Japanese scholarship. Many of the contemporary Japanese scholars conducting fieldwork in China are historians, and all have been influenced to some degree by the tradition of the *kankō chōsa* studies. Sato Yoshifumi, a social historian at Hitotsubashi University who works on Jiangnan, has suggested that one of the ways in which the *kankō chōsa* tradition influences contemporary work is the practice of transcribing interviews into texts.[19]

One of the advantages of this approach—of transcribing interviews and converting them into texts—is the accumulation of extensive interview files, some of which have been published, both by individual scholars and as group projects. We can imagine that scholars 20 or 50 years in the future may refer to this body of research, just as we look back today to the *kankō chōsa* records.

One of the factors that has contributed to this particular style of research is the way in which projects are funded. Much of the funding for research is provided by the JSPS (Japan Society for the Promotion of Science), an independent administrative unit closely affiliated with the Ministry of Education, that manages government funding in the social sciences, humanities, and natural sciences. JSPS encourages large-scale, multi-year research projects that include scholars from several universities. Fieldwork in China is most commonly undertaken by groups, rather than by individuals, and in order to allow for better coordination, group members work out pre-fieldwork common protocols and record and share data gathered among all of the members of the group. In some cases—as in our project on the *kankō chōsa* villages—transcripts have been published, but in many other cases members of a research group have published research articles in collective volumes but have not published the original data which the project gathered. These fieldwork records provide important records on rapidly changing Chinese society. However, if future scholars are to benefit from this work, we must find ways to build a public archive for the storage of fieldwork records. Without collective initiatives, the records of interviews and other data collected during fieldwork projects will be lost.[20]

Useful sources for access to Japanese research, including field research

This list is certainly not comprehensive but will provide at least a short introduction to some of the bibliographies and digital sites for finding Japanese research materials, primarily from the prewar and wartime periods.

1   For contemporary research, the best starting place is https://researchmap.jp/ which is a comprehensive listing of Japanese researchers, with a keyword search function. Most Japanese universities maintain their own databases of their research scholars, and upload data to this national

database, which is maintained by the National Institute of Informatics (NII). NII also maintains a database of all projects that have received funding from the Japan Society for the Promotion of Science (https://kaken.nii.ac.jp/), which can be searched by keyword as well as by the name of a scholar).

2 Japan Center for Asian Historical Records (JACAR) (www.jacar.go.jp/english/about/outline.html) is the website for searching historical archives. This project, launched in 1994, now has more than 30,000,000 images (as of April 2016) that can be viewed online, with new items added every year. Items come from the National Archives, Foreign Ministry Archives, and Military Archives. There are explanations in Japanese, English, Chinese, and Korean, although most of the documents are in Japanese.

3 National Diet Library Digital Collections (http://dl.ndl.go.jp/): the National Diet Library has digitalized almost all of its collection and has made them available for reading online books that are no longer under copyright. Their collection includes many of the items discussed in this short introduction.

4 Tōyō Bunkō Modern China Collection Digital Library www.tbcas.jp/ja/lib/lib1/ has digitalized many of its Japanese books and made them available for reading online. The Documentation Center for China Studies (DCCS) at Tōyō Bunkō is one of the six research bases of the intra-university center for China Area Studies, created under the National Institute for Humanities in 2007.

5 Mantetsu Research Bureau: the best catalog of Mantetsu Research, *Kyū Shokuminchi Kankei Kikan Kankōbutsu Sōgō Mokuroku—Minami Manshū Tetsudō Kabushiki Kaisha Hen* 旧植民地関係機関刊行物総合目録—南満州鉄道株式会社編, was produced by the Institute of Developing Economies in 1979. The National Diet Library has an online guide to finding resources on Manchuria and Mantetsu publications, which includes links to the holdings in various Chinese libraries (https://rnavi.ndl.go.jp/research_guide/entry/theme-asia-131.php#2-1).

6 Kōain publications: the Kōain 興亜院 was a research organization set up by the Japanese cabinet in 1938 to gather information on various parts of Asia. A research group at Tōyō Bunkō has put out a guide, including a 100-page bibliography, of research reports produced by various subordinate organizations. See *Kōain to Senji Chūgoku Chōsa* 興亜院と戦時中国調査 [Kōain and wartime research in China]. Iwanami shōten, 2002.

Notes

1 The general title for the series is *Mantie Nongcun Diaocha* (满铁农村调查).
2 Linda Grove, "Revisiting the *kankō chōsa* Villages: A Review of Chinese and Japanese Studies of North China Rural Society," *International Journal of Asian Studies* 11:1 (2014), 77–98.

3 Lin Juren and Xie Yuxi, *A Century of Change in a Chinese Village: The Crisis of the Countryside*, edited by Linda Grove. Lanham, MD: Rowman & Littlefield, 2018.
4 A Chinese translation was published by Zhonghua Shuju in 2006.
5 Tsunoyama Sakae 角山栄 has written extensively on government efforts to collect economic and trade information. See his *"Tsūsho kokka" Nihon no jōhō senryoku ryōji hōkoku wo yomu*「通商国家」日本の情報戦略: 領事報告を読む [Information Strategy of Japan as a "Trading Nation"—Reading the Consular Reports]. Tokyo: Nihon Hōsō, 1988.
6 For a short, general description in English, see Sakae Tsunoyama, "Japanese Consular Reports," *Business History* 23:3 (1981), 284–287; Tsunoyama also edited a volume that includes the Tables of Contents of consular reports from 1881 to 1913, *Ryōji hōkoku shiryō: shūryoku mokuroku* 領事報告資料:収録目録 [Consular reports: compilation and index] put out by Yushodo, to accompany a microfilm set of the reports.
7 This book can be read online at the National Diet Library (http://dl.ndl.go.jp/info:ndljp/pid/994021) or downloaded from a number of Chinese websites.
8 Douglas Reynolds, "Chinese Area Studies in Prewar China: Japan's Tōa Dōbun Shoin in Shanghai, 1900–1945," *Journal of Asian Studies* 45:5 (1986), 945–970.
9 The two series include: *Shina Keizai Zensho* 支那経済全書, a multi-volume series taking up important sectors in the Chinese economy, and *Shina Shōbetsu Zenshi* 支那省別全誌 with volumes providing detailed surveys of each province. Both series are available from the National Diet Library's digital library. A photo reprint version of the economic series was put out in China by the Beijing: Zhongguo xianzhi shuju 中国线装书局 in 2015.
10 The term "Shina" is a Japanese translation of the English word "China." Until 1911, Japanese commonly referred to China using the dynastic Qing name; following the fall of the Qing dynasty, "Shina" was often used to refer to the Republic of China. However, Chinese diplomats protested this use, and after the end of the war, it fell out of use both among scholars and among the general public, to be replaced by Zhongguo 中國, usually pronounced following the Japanese reading of the Chinese characters.
11 The latter 600-page volume, *Shōji ni kansuru Kankō Chōsa Hōkokusho—Gōko no Kenkyū* 商事に関する慣行調査報告書合股の研究 [Investigation of commercial practices], published by the Tōa Kenkyūjō in 1943, is still the authoritative work on Chinese business practices in the prewar period. It can be read online at the National Diet Library (http://dl.ndl.go.jp/info:ndljp/pid/1272898).
12 For an overview, see Fuji Yoshihisa 藤田佳久, *Tōa Dōbun Shoinsei ga Kirokushita Kindai Chūgoku no Chiikizō* 東亜同文書院生が記録した近代中国の地域像 [Images in different regions in modern China as recorded by students of the Tōa Dōbun Shoin] (Tokyo: Nakanishiya shuppan 2011). Fujita was involved in the editing and publishing of the original reports of student field trips. The overall title for the series is Tōa Dōbun Shoin Dai Chōsa Ryokō Kiroku 東亜同文書院・大調査旅行記録 [Index of Tōa Dōbun Shoin investigations], and at least five volumes have been published. The National Library of China Press has published a collection of the student reports, based on photo reproduction of the handwritten originals under the title Dongya Tongwenyuan Zhongguo Diaocha Shougao Congkan 东亚同文书院中国调查手稿丛刊 [Collected hand written materials of the Tōa Dōbun shown China investigations]. Part 1 was published by Beijing: Zhongguo shehui kexueyuan in 2016 and part 2 in 2017.
13 On the relationship between these early studies and the later development of Japanese anthropology, see Nakao Katsumi 中生勝美, *Kindai Nihon no Jinruigakushi—Teikoku to shokuminchi no kioku* 近代日本の人類学史——帝国と植民地の記憶. Tokyo: Fukyōsha, 2016. The first chapter deals with the Taiwan surveys.

14 All of the interviews were recorded. Our original plan had been to publish interview records, *kankō chōsa* style. While members of the research team have copies of the interview transcripts, these have not been published.
15 In September 1942, 24 of the researchers were arrested by the Kwangtung Army, beginning a purge of liberal and progressive researchers working in Manchuria and China; it eventually extended to include journalists and researchers in Japan proper. The Keio scholar Matsumura Takao has described the purge of researchers as a "frame up."
16 The Japanese transcripts were published by Tokyo: Kyuko Shoin in two volumes in 1999 and 2000, *Chūgoku Nōson Henkaku to Kazoku, Sonraku, Kokka* 中国農村変革と家族・村落・国家 [Transformation of the Chinese village: family, village and state].
17 Prof. Zhang Si was a graduate student at Nankai and assisted with the original research before earning a PhD at Tokyo University; other Nankai graduate students who assisted with the work include Qi Jianmin who earned PhD degrees from Nankai and Tokyo University and is now a professor at University of Nagasaki, Li Enmin who holds two doctorate degrees, from Nankai and Hitotsubashi University, and teaches at Obirin University in Japan, and Jiang Pei, now the Dean of the School of History at Nankai. The Chinese transcripts are in a four-volume set, edited by Wei Hongyun, Mitani Takashi, and Zhang Si, *Ershi shiji Huabei nongcun diaocha jilu* 二十世纪华北农村调查记录 [Record of the 20th century north China investigations] published in 2012 by Beijing: Shehui kexue wenxian chubanshe.
18 See Zhang Si 张思, Houjiaying—yige Huabei cunzhuang de xiandai licheng 侯家营——一个华北村庄的现代历程 [Houjiaying—modernization process of a north China village]. Tianjin: Tianjin guji chubanshe, 2010.
19 Sato Yoshifumi, "Rekishigakusha no fuierdowaku –kōnan chiiki shakaishi chōsa no bae" 佐藤仁史、"歴史学者の行うフィールドワーク——江南地域社会史調査の場合" [Historians' fieldwork-the case of social science investigations in Jiangnan] in Nishizawa Haruhiko and Kawai Hironao 西澤春彦、河合洋尚、*Fuierudowaku Chūgoku to iu genba, jinruigaku to iu jissen* フィールドワーク：中国という現場、人類学という実践 [Fieldwork, anthropological practice on the ground in China]. Tokyo: *Fukyōsha* (2017), 419–443.
20 The Center for Social Science Research on Japan at the University of Tokyo, Institute of Social Science, has created a depository for survey data on Japan that archives and shares the data collected by individual scholars and groups. However, so far there is no similar depository for fieldwork materials collected by Japanese scholars working on areas other than Japan.

3 The traditionalist phase in Taiwan anthropology
1960–1980

Myron L. Cohen

The heyday of anthropological research on the Han in Taiwan during the 1960s was geared to what I call a *traditionalist* orientation. Anthropological fieldwork, certainly including mine, during that time tended to view Taiwan within the framework of late imperial China, rather than with an interest in contemporary Taiwan society or in social change under Japanese colonial and then Nationalist (Guomindang, KMT) rule. Social change in Taiwan (and Hong Kong) was of little interest given what were thought to be the massive transformations taking place in Maoist China. In this chapter, I deal with traditionalism, non-traditionalism, and post-traditionalism in Taiwan fieldwork, with the latter phase conditioned by the opening of mainland China to fieldwork and the consequent massive shift in anthropological attention to the People's Republic. In a parallel development, traditionalism morphed into historical anthropology, which has attracted the attention of some anthropologists doing research on Taiwan, Hong Kong, and mainland China. It is obvious that fieldwork requires one to make choices regarding what to study, and where. Anthropological research on Taiwan during the 1960s and 1970s shows how such choices can be powerfully shaped by preexisting dominant discourses within the profession.

Traditionalism

For the generation of American anthropologists who later were to go to Taiwan, the source of their traditionalist orientation was the literature (and lectures) they were exposed to during their graduate work. As far as I was concerned, as a graduate student, a good deal of the theory taught at Columbia was preparation for Taiwan fieldwork only in the sense that it encouraged me to look for facts on the ground, and not spin webs in the air. The intellectual environment, in other words, was strongly objective, especially under the impact of Marvin Harris and his "cultural materialism." It meant that one went to the field site to count things, see things, and observe behavior. You focused more on behavior than on what people told you. Now, of course, in "post post-modern" times, the reverse is often true.

The American anthropology graduate students in those days generally did little background reading on Taiwan. One exception was George W. Barclay's *Colonial Development and Population in Taiwan*,[1] which was well known. It was a good book based on excellent Japanese census data. With no relevant special courses on offer, Taiwan was something you just had to try to figure out. For example, when Arthur Wolf did his fieldwork in Taiwan, he did not even know there were household registers, which the Japanese started in 1905. I was the one who told him about them, and he eventually made his whole career from these records. I learned of them from Burton Pasternak, only when we were both in Taiwan. Pasternak, for his part, was informed of their existence by local informants during his fieldwork in southern Taiwan. The point is that, for these American students, there was very little background information floating around. Most preparation involved the anthropology of the Chinese mainland, not Taiwan. The ethnographic problems I had been exposed to related to what was the China anthropology of those days, namely, the writings of Fei Xiaotong, Lin Yaohua, Francis L.K. Hsu, Sidney Gamble, Marion Levy, and Olga Lang, among others. In these works, the overwhelming emphasis was on "traditional" culture, although Lang and Levy were interested in both tradition and "modernization," especially with reference to social change in China's urban centers.[2]

As a graduate student, I was trained in that particular atmosphere. The Qing Dynasty, at the time, had been over for only about 50 years. The memory was not that distant, and, as of 1950, most people in China were still living according to Qing-period basic life patterns. Things had changed, life had become harder for many of them, but the patterns were still very much in evidence. G. William Skinner conducted his fieldwork near Chengdu in the late 1940s, where most people still lived in what was Qing dynasty culture. Skinner estimated that at that time only 10 percent of China's population was culturally impacted by modernization. Traditionalism was linked to the close fieldwork experiences of many people. Skinner, like my Columbia advisor Morton Fried, came out of what in many ways was still "Old China." Fried's fieldwork in Chuxian (滁縣), Anhui Province, ended when he fled his field site in the face of the approaching People's Liberation Army, but it had involved a focus on a merchant family organized along traditional lines.[3]

Skinner and Maurice Freedman were major figures in the American and British worlds of China anthropology. In an era of grand visions in anthropology, those of Skinner and Freedman were different, with both nested in Chinese studies. Like Fried, Skinner's traditionalism came out of his own fieldwork. Skinner had lived with a Hakka family outside of Chengdu on a farm, which is probably now a parking lot, or an apartment block. He was very interested in contemporary China, but his sentiments were more aligned with a focus on traditional China, and they remained so throughout his career. This is because he was interested in pre-industrial demographic and economic patterns. His marketing system approach is premised on a pre-industrial economy, with pre-industrial technology.[4]

In contrast, Maurice Freedman's first book, *Chinese Family and Marriage in Singapore* (1957), is certainly non-traditionalist.[5] In this book, Freedman deals with the collapse of tradition and the shape of modernity in an urban environment. Yet, when he shifted his focus to China, he reversed himself, and, with minor exceptions, would not leave the Qing period. He did return to his Singapore work at several points and, in contrast to his China focus, for Singapore he even wrote a paper called "The Rout of Custom."[6] When *Lineage Organization in Southeastern China* came out, it was as if he had never even written his first book. He dealt with lineage organization, with a focus on the Qing. He went from almost sociological urban fieldwork in a British colony straight into classic British social anthropology, albeit armchair anthropology, dealing with well-integrated lineages. It was really his second book on China, *Chinese Lineage and Society: Fukien and Kwangtung* (1966), that helped define China anthropology at that time.[7] Those doing fieldwork in Taiwan frequently noted the weakness of lineages there, a point made only in reaction to Freedman's book. Freedman did not provide a full picture of lineage organization because he did not treat them as large-scale business enterprises with offices and account books. He thought of them more in terms of kinship structures, which they were, but they were more than that. Freedman could have done fieldwork in the New Territories of Hong Kong on the lineages he wrote about, but his was purely a library project based on documentary sources. Later Freedman did do fieldwork in the New Territories, but this had to be cut short due to illness.

For those doing fieldwork, the functionalist vision of China was not simply a product of American and British social anthropological theory. Part of it came from Chinese culture itself. Yin and yang, in an inclusive cosmology, and the integrated character of traditional Chinese culture was what was so attractive. This vision did not ignore conflict, but placed it in the context of a working system.

At the same time that anthropological interest in China was growing, in the 1950s and 1960s, anthropologists could only do fieldwork in Taiwan or Hong Kong. Those going to do fieldwork there were already predisposed to look for tradition. As far as a focus on Hong Kong fieldwork was concerned, I discussed that possibility with my advisor, Morton Fried. His response was, "No, they're too Westernized!" His strongly felt traditionalism was formed through his fieldwork in Chuxian. The dominant traditionalist mode also produced an intellectual lack of interest in the People's Republic of China, the expression of which was sometimes pronounced. One very eminent anthropologist said, in those days, that the study of the PRC was "boring." For this generation, traditional China still had a strange glitter, a kind of other-authenticity. The PRC in comparison seemed to be mundane, with people giving orders to build wells, canals, and "backyard furnaces," as if the Great Leap Forward or the Cultural Revolution were mundane! In contrast, the PRC was exciting for a few American and British anthropologists who politically were very much to the left, saw "tradition" as backward and "feudal," and, under certain circumstances, were indeed permitted to do fieldwork in China, where professional anthropology otherwise had been closed down.

At that time, there was no "Taiwan anthropology" as such, but there were anthropologists doing fieldwork in Taiwan. For many in the older generation it was "China Studies" in Taiwan. The same applies to Hong Kong. Additional pressures helped to define the direction that anthropology took in those two parts of what had been the Qing dynasty, what Maurice Freedman tellingly referred to as "residual China." One was the emphasis of Contemporary China Studies on political economy, linked to what was almost an academic cleavage between the study of "traditional" and "modern" China. Modern China was the China of Mao Zedong, Land Reform, collectivization, Communist Party organization, and all that. Mao was modern China, in that perspective.

Among the first American anthropologists to go to Taiwan were Bernard and Rita Gallin, Arthur and Margery Wolf, and Norma Diamond, in the late 1950s. They were the 1950s generation, mine was of the mid-1960s, and also included Burton Pasternak, David Jordan, Donald DeGlopper, Stephan Feuchtwang, and others. The third, larger generation of fieldworkers was mainly made up of the students of earlier generations, and included Emily Martin Ahern, Joseph Bosco, Chung-min Chen, Lawrence Crissman, Hill Gates, Stevan Harrell, Lydia Kung, Steven Sangren, Gary Seaman, Thomas Shaw, and Alexander Yin. These generations of anthropologists made up the Taiwan component of what I call the "Hong Kong-Taiwan era" of Chinese studies. The Hong Kong-based anthropologists included Barbara Ward, Marjorie Topley, Hugh Baker, and Jack Potter, followed later by James and Rubie Watson. There was constant interaction between Taiwan and Hong Kong anthropologists during this period. Both groups were well represented in a series of conferences and conference volumes sponsored by the American Council of Learned Societies and the Social Science Research Council. In 1980, the first of several Sinological conferences in Taiwan was sponsored by the Academia Sinica, in Nangang, Taipei, and included anthropology panels with papers based upon fieldwork in Taiwan and Hong Kong. Such fieldwork came to comprise the basis of an anthropology united by a shared focus on a Chinese tradition, giving this research a place within the larger field of Chinese studies.

In preparation for my own fieldwork, I had written to the anthropologist Li Yih-Yuan (李亦園) and applied to be a visiting scholar at the Academia Sinica's Institute of Ethnology, of which he was director. The Institute housed some of the classic figures in China Anthropology: Rui Yi-Fu (芮逸夫), the great archaeologist Li Ji (李濟), and Ling Chun-Sheng (凌純聲), among others. It was a supportive atmosphere, and during my first year in Taiwan, when I lived in Taipei, I went once or twice a week to the institute to do research in the Academia Sinica libraries and go to talks. Like me, Burton Pasternak, a Columbia University PhD, was also a visiting scholar at the Institute of Ethnology. He also wound up doing fieldwork in south Taiwan, at the southern end of the Hakka belt, in Datie Village (打鐵村).

During this period, I asked friends at the Academia Sinica to suggest good possibilities for fieldwork on a "traditional" Hakka village. More than one replied "Meinong." One of my friends in the Institute of History introduced me to Mr. Lin Guangchun, who was from Meinong. So I went to Meinong, escorted on the first trip by Mr. Lin. There, I stayed with his family a couple of times. To choose a village, Mr. Lin and I went from one to another by car or motorcycle. I recorded visits to 11 villages, and finally found one that seemed just right for my work. It was Daqixia (大崎下), where I was to spend one and a half years. I also visited villages in the northern Taiwan Miaoli regions, but did not choose them because, in the anthropological vision of those days, a cohesive social system was highly desirable as an object of a "community study," and one seemed to be found in Meinong.

In arranging the fieldwork, my affiliation with the Institute of Ethnology was vital because the institute provided an official document or *gongwen* (公文), which was very powerful. Li Yih-Yuan, as Institute director, was able to issue this valuable certificate. This was during the Martial Law period in Taiwan, and an official document from a government institution like the Institute of Ethnology was very effective. So, when I first went to my field site in Meinong, I went straight to the Township Government (鎮公所) and showed the Township Head (鎮長) my *gongwen*. After I had introduced myself, I told him, "I'm looking for a village to do fieldwork." "Fine" he said. Then, about a few days or maybe a week later, I was at the home of my assistant one afternoon, and someone came up on a bicycle and told him, not me, "The police want to see you." I immediately gave him my *gongwen*. He went to the police, showed them the *gongwen*, and said, "I'm helping the government!" The police never bothered us again, and from then on, we were on very friendly terms with them.

Early in my first stay in Meinong, when I was looking for a field site, the entire Township was involved in the large-scale Rite of Cosmic Renewal, or *dajiao* (打醮). The massive *dajiao* mobilization was impressive. For part of a day, I joined a procession of about 10,000 people, or 20 percent of the population, that made its way, together with the gods, along all of the Township's major roads, with most of Meinong's other residents making roadside offerings as the procession passed. The key temple where the rites were being held, and to where the gods were being taken, was the Wugumiao (五穀廟), or Temple of the Five Grains. I stayed in that temple for a night. There I met my research assistant, Mr. Robert Chung 鍾福松 (sadly, he passed away on April 19, 2018). He knew the local people and was involved in negotiating my living arrangements. He himself was a local, so it was very easy for him to arrange things on my behalf. I was the first foreigner he had ever spoken with; he was fluent in English, which he had learned by listening to BBC broadcasts.

The village I finally chose as a field site seemed to me big enough to be complicated, and small enough to be doable, which was the way I thought about things at that time. People mentioned that there were large families, but that did not sink in until I encountered this incredible family situation. Once I got to the village, I was very happy with my choice, indeed I was very grateful. I sought out some of the more influential people in the village for it was very important to explain to them what I wanted to do, and get their permission. Having introduced myself to the local government and to the police, it then was crucial to gain acceptance in the village. One village resident was an elected Kaohsiung County assembly member, and I wound up taking my meals with his brother's family. The two brothers were among the people from whom I sought permission to work in the village.

Robert Chung, my field assistant, was of critical assistance. I felt satisfied that I was getting what I wanted. My big discovery involving gender issues was women's private money, which in Meinong is called *segoy*, the Hakka term, or *sifangqian* (私房錢) in Mandarin. One day I was outside when I chanced upon two middle-aged women behind the house where I had my sleeping quarters. One was giving a large stack of bills to the other. Later I asked my assistant "What was all that about?" He replied, "Oh, that's *sifangqian*." This opened up for me the whole world of women's private money and its link to joint family organization.

People were very friendly. They thought my doing research in the village was a bit peculiar, but there was no hostility. I think part of the reason was the way they had been prepared by my research assistant, who came from a nearby village and was well known. At least two families saw my presence as providing "a free English teacher." They had kids in school and English was a big thing for them. I did give English lessons. Not formally, but I did practice speaking with them. My daily routine, if there was nothing special, was to walk through the village so as to pass by every residential compound. I would walk, usually with my assistant, and greet whomever I met. People got used to me just walking around and being in contact with everybody. I would ask questions as they popped up. The routine would be interrupted by such major events as weddings, funerals, or meetings, which I would attend.

Generally, in those early experiences, I had no idea of what I would find and what I did find astonished me: in the village were thriving large joint families (大家庭)! I could not believe that here, in the 1960s, there actually were families of 30 or 40 people! These were not families in any vague sense. They had a common budget; they lived and ate together, and of course, each married couple had their own room. The various daughters-in-law took care of the kitchen in shifts under their mother-in-law. These families seemed straight out of the *Dream of the Red Chamber* (紅樓夢) or Ba Jin's *Family* (家). I simply did not anticipate this. Nothing in my reading had led me to expect to find them here. The theoretical stance of Morton Fried, Marion Levy, and many others, was that joint families were characteristic of the gentry, and not of the common people. The poor peasants had simpler families.

Of course, the construction of a gentry-commoner contrast pertained to late imperial China. In Meinong, however, I saw dirt farmers living in these large families, so my first thought was that the earlier view of the place of joint families in Chinese society had to be wrong. Joint families and the local focus on tobacco cultivation seemed to be mutually supportive. One of the richer farmers had five or six large tobacco-curing buildings, and his family numbered in the fifties. I wanted to see such families in operation, so I arranged to live with three families at once, which worked out quite well.

I rented rooms from each of these three families. All were big, joint families, presenting a fantastic opportunity to distinguish common structure from the unique. Every person had his or her own personality, obviously, but I asked: was this structure the combined product of each individual's particular characteristics? No, because the shared pattern of joint family organization was obvious. Involved in this were some basic structures of Chinese culture itself. It was not class, it was what allowed family features to be expressed, and what stopped them from expression. That is the way I thought of it, but only after I was there for a while.[8] These family arrangements were still going strong when I was there, but were beginning to dissipate at the edges. Ten or 15 years later, the joint families were gone.

In that period, I had my meals with one family. The place where I slept was in the compound of the second family. My office where I worked was with the third. I paid for three places. Where I ate, I paid the family head or one of his four married adult sons, all of whom lived together as one family. There were 35 family members in total. I rented my office from a relatively poor joint family. My office, with a dirt floor, was next to a water buffalo pen. In the compound with my sleeping quarters, I did not pay the family head, who was elderly and retired from active management of family affairs, but rather his son, who ran the family. I made monthly payments, and tried to pay everyone the same day, so I would not forget.

Among anthropologists, there was much discussion then, which continues to this day, about the advantages and disadvantages of multi-sited fieldwork. In my case, the advantages were greater because, if you want to do detailed work, you have to stay in one place or otherwise commit to multi-year fieldwork. Nevertheless, there was a "multi-sited" aspect to my fieldwork, and it was exciting to live with three families at once; in a family situation, you can talk in ways you cannot elsewhere, for example, about gender relationships. Having encountered such village families, it was difficult not to think of traditional China—the academic forces encouraging traditionalism were mightily boosted by what I found at my field site. Yet, in my case, I wrote against the prevalent literature on China, arguing that, as opposed to the idea of the joint family as an elite institution, it was one product of certain dynamics at play that infused the entire Chinese family system. I was interacting with the China literature. Still, my experience in Meinong was a powerful personal reinforcement to the mission that pervaded the field at the time.

When I first went to Meinong, many people could not speak "Taiwanese," which was the dominant Minnan language. They could speak Hakka, and either Japanese or Mandarin, depending on their age. In the village, kids would call me *a-mi-e* (阿美子), a familiar but not endearing Hakka term for "American." Those already in school could speak Mandarin and would use that language so their parents would not understand what they were saying. In families with schoolteachers, Mandarin might also be spoken in the household. Adult men could speak Japanese, but not all the women. At the time of Japan's surrender, many women in Meinong had not gone to school. The Japanese-era household registers show that, starting around 1944, people started switching to Japanese names, which made them eligible for special food rations. But as soon as Japan surrendered, they quickly went back to their original names in Chinese. They used to call Japanese names "four legs" (四腳, or *sigok*) because most consisted of four characters, while Chinese names commonly had three. "Four legs" suggested an animal.

My second major field trip to Meinong was a joint project with Burton Pasternak in 1971, supported by a National Science Foundation grant. Our idea was to study not just a village, but the entire township as a total social system. Skinner was very enthusiastic about the project, because he was all in favor of what he called a "local systems" approach. So were Maurice Freedman and Morton Fried. The guiding vision was that everything is integrated. It is not that there was no conflict, but that all the parts fit together, and the task was to find that integrated entity. In terms of fieldwork, our goal was to get as much information as possible about the entire township; almost 50 years later, I am still using that material. This includes such records for the entire township as the land and household registration records, going back to the years of Japanese rule, as well as our own surveys of temples, and more. Pasternak wrote a book using just the Japanese-period household records of Longdu Village (龍肚庄).[9] I wrote some articles using these materials, and I am still trying to come up with a *magnum opus* that will capture the dimensions of Meinong society during the Qing period.

In those days of my initial fieldwork, there were still old people who had been born during the Qing dynasty and clearly remembered the early Japanese colonial era. One woman was 11 when the Japanese occupied her village. She told me how she saw Japanese soldiers poking bayonets into haystacks to see if anyone was hiding. They had just seized the area in late 1895, after some nasty battles. Older people still had the late imperial Qing narrative in their heads. For example, they talked about a man with an imperial *jiansheng* (監生) degree. Then they would add, with some contempt, that "it was bought" (買的). Purchased degrees were common. Most if not all of Meinong's wealthier men, and there were not many of them, had purchased *jiansheng* degrees from the local Fengshan County Yamen (鳳山衙門). Everybody learned from their parent's discussions about life during the Qing period and the Japanese conquest. After all, it had been only 69 years since the dynasty had ceded the island to Japan.

The dominance of traditionalism in the anthropological studies of Taiwan continued into the later 1980s, largely because the results of earlier fieldwork were being continually published. Steven Sangren's first book, *History and Magical Power in a Chinese Community*, was based on fieldwork in Ta-ch'i Town (Daqi大溪) in northern Taiwan and presented a highly sophisticated view of Chinese religion. When I was reviewing the manuscript for Stanford University Press, I looked at my computer monitor, ancient by present-day standards, and noticed that on it was written "Made in Ta-Ch'i Taiwan!" Sangren does not tell us that Ta-Ch'i was sending computers all over the world, although he does note in the book's introduction that economic globalization is impacting this area. From then on, however, his focus is squarely on the popular religion deeply rooted in tradition. This is what I have in mind when I speak of "traditionalism." It was not Taiwan Studies; it was the "Hong Kong-Taiwan" era of China anthropology. When that era ended, with the opening of China, many anthropologists and their students moved right into "China Studies," showing how their interest had never been in Taiwan itself.

Traditionalism was reflected in the titles of anthropological monographs published in that period based on Taiwan research. Instead of any mention of "Taiwan," there was "Kinship in a Chinese Village," "Social Change in a Chinese Village," "Religion in a Chinese village," and so forth. In those days, the Taiwan Independence Movement was really anti-KMT, and anti-mainlander. It was a domestic movement largely irrelevant to China. With Taiwan villages identified as *Chinese* villages, support for the KMT position that "Taiwan is part of China, and we are China's legitimate rulers" might be implied. In that atmosphere, it was radical for some scholars, like Norma Diamond, to refer specifically in her book title to "Taiwan."[10] Although anthropologists in other fields would not have had any concern with the assertion that fieldwork in Taiwan had value because Taiwan was of anthropological interest in its own right, a common response from those in the field of China studies was that "no one is interested in Taiwan." Fieldwork in Taiwan was largely held to be contributing to Chinese studies, and not to the study of Taiwan. In China at the time, there was collectivization, the Great Leap Forward, and then the Cultural Revolution, but there was no way an anthropologist could study such massive movements if based in Taipei. Therefore, the focus was on traditional Chinese culture, as seen through Taiwan. Had I been studying a Taiwanese factory in the 1960s, and notwithstanding how this might link to broader anthropological concerns of that time, I might also try to push the point that I was doing fieldwork contributing to Chinese studies. To this, a common response was that "Taiwan is different." Even fully traditionalist subjects such as women's private money or family division contracts might fall victim to the "Taiwan is different" syndrome, but for the reason that these challenged dominant perceptions of Chinese "peasant" backwardness.

Nevertheless, during the Taiwan-Hong Kong era of China anthropology, there was substantial research, which did increase our understanding of late Imperial China. Conferences bringing together social historians working on the Qing with anthropologists doing fieldwork in Hong Kong and Taiwan made for a good intellectual fit. At that time, the community of Hong Kong and Taiwan anthropologists really enjoyed their fieldwork, and their enthusiasm fed into the traditionalist stance, with contemporary China largely missing from the discussion. Yet when China did open up in 1979–1980, anthropologists did not hesitate to go there, and their focus was on the contemporary.

Non-traditionalism

In the 1950s and 1960s, the overwhelming orientation of the Institute of Ethnology was on the non-Han, be these mainland China peoples, with the results of earlier pre-1949 fieldwork used for analysis and publication, or the Taiwan aborigines, who were now the fieldwork focus. It was a very sensitive issue as to whether anthropologists should study the Han Chinese, who were held to be more advanced and therefore more appropriate for study by sociologists, not anthropologists. That non-Han orientation was shared by anthropologists in China and in Taiwan.

There had been two anthropology factions in China. The northern faction, which included Fei Xiaotong, was more to the left politically than the southern, and most of its members stayed in China. Many in the southern faction came to Taiwan. While both groups largely focused on non-Han peoples, the northern faction showed increasing willingness to add the Han to their research agenda. The southern faction, represented, for instance, by Rui Yi-Fu and his study of the Miao, was characterized by an overwhelming focus on the non-Han.

The narrative of the Chiang Kai-Shek government in Taiwan was that "we represent the real China" and with the Communists destroying Chinese culture, Taiwan was now China's bastion. When elementary and high school students learned about history, it was the history of China. Taiwan was dealt with scarcely, if at all, and there was certainly no Institute of Taiwan Studies at Academia Sinica. The idea that the Taiwanese were Han Chinese was important in this political context. Whereas Chinese anthropologists studied the non-Han, the American anthropologists were coming to study the Han, because they were interested in Chinese culture. Li Yih-Yuan was instrumental in bringing Chinese anthropologists into fieldwork among the Taiwan Han. He originally went to Taiwan as a student, to study at National Taiwan University, not as a refugee. He was born in Fujian and came to Taiwan in 1948 when Chiang Kai-Shek was still in China, and when the KMT still controlled a large part of the mainland. Li himself had done fieldwork among overseas Chinese and in a Taiwanese village. Chen Qilu, the eminent Taiwanese anthropologist specializing in aboriginal art, was friends with Morton Fried and other foreign anthropologists. For his Columbia PhD in anthropology, Chen's brother-in-law, Tang Meijun, wrote an interesting dissertation on urban families in Taipei, and that too was framed as a study of *Chinese* family organization. Things did begin to change among the younger generation, however.

Still, anti-traditionalism was very strong among Chinese intellectuals in Taiwan who had lived through the May Fourth movement on the mainland. It was difficult for them to study "backward" Han customs such as ancestor worship and religious ceremonies. There were interesting parallels between what was going on at the same time in both Taiwan and the mainland with respect to attitudes toward "superstition" and "backwardness." Both places exuded the shared sense that, if Chinese intellectuals were to study the Han Chinese, the focus should be on social change and modernization. On Taiwan, this anti-traditionalism was absorbed into the Mainlander-Taiwanese distinction. Many mainlanders expressed the view that the Taiwanese were superstitious. For example, I listened to a Mandarin radio program in the 1960s which mocked shamans, who were important in Taiwanese popular religion." Why do they have to make such a racket and disturb neighbors?" the narrator asked. In those days, it was commonly asserted that *baibai* (拜拜), or Taiwanese religious activity, was very wasteful (浪費), and should be banned or controlled. Some anthropologists like Li Yih-yuan, who wrote articles such as "Let's Discuss *Baibai* Calmly," countered these attitudes.[11]

Post-traditionalism and the emergence of historical anthropology

During the height of the traditionalist phase of Taiwan anthropology, there were exceptions to this orientation. Robert H. Silin, for example, did fieldwork in Taiwan factories.[12] Another important exception was the organization in 1976 of a conference with an explicit focus on Taiwan as Taiwan, the edited proceedings of which were published in 1981.[13] That conference was enriched by the tension between those looking at China through Taiwan, and those looking at a Taiwan unto itself. However, it was not until anthropologists left Taiwan, when China opened up to anthropological fieldwork, that research on Taiwan became "Taiwan Studies."

In one respect, the abandonment of Taiwan by many anthropologists interested in China was a healthy development, because those who remained to do fieldwork in Taiwan did so out of an interest in Taiwan as such. Reinforcing this transition was the fact that life in Taiwan has changed dramatically. The Taiwan countryside now provides very few remnants of the Qing dynasty. However, local religion, for example, still has its historical roots and has evolved on its own terms.

Yet, with Taiwan fieldwork moving away from the goal of shedding light on late Imperial China, anthropological interest in late Imperial China has morphed into historical anthropology, both in Taiwan and in the mainland. To study Taiwan historically, when it was a prefecture of Fujian Province and, at the end, a province of imperial China in its own right, certainly contributes to an understanding of imperial China beyond Taiwan. For historical anthropology research, Taiwan is extraordinarily well endowed with documentary records that facilitate very close and detailed historical ethnographies shedding much light on life during late imperial times.

One of my own present research projects is the historical anthropology of Meinong, and this is intimately linked to China Studies. It is a study of a community in Imperial China during the Qing, and one of the main issues is the strength of the Chinese state's cultural presence, even in such a remote place. Meinong was in the backwaters of the empire, but it nevertheless was deeply involved with the Chinese state, socially and culturally. That changed when the Meinong area came under Japanese control. I am undertaking this project because of the many good local documents from Meinong, which allow for this kind of examination of state-society relations during the Qing period. What I find astonishing is how consciousness of the dynasty pervaded local culture. People constantly traveled back and forth between Meinong and the mainland, and during the Qing, much of Meinong's population consisted of mainland-born immigrants. I look at state-society interaction as an active, creative process in terms of local culture. As far as late imperial China is concerned, local culture was a product of state functioning and reproduction in combination with local historical development. The two reproductive processes were intimately connected, as surely was the case everywhere among the Han Chinese. Taiwan was a prefecture and then a province of the Qing empire, and, indeed, was treated as part of "China Proper," unlike the major non-Han imperial domains, such as Manchuria, Mongolia, Chinese Turkestan and Tibet.

What I am calling historical anthropology takes the anthropological imagination—formed and sustained through ethnographic fieldwork among living peoples—and applies it to past societies. Ethnographic research almost by definition focuses on the small scale; in anthropology such research takes the classical form of "participant observation," whereby long-term fieldwork through socially intimate interaction between the researcher and his or her objects of research hopefully provides knowledge and understanding unobtainable through other means. Given such circumstances of scholarship, to speak of "historical anthropology" as a research strategy might seem to be an oxymoron: reliance upon documents or other products of the past, even within a limited field setting providing physical and oral historical context, cannot capture the rich ethnographic detail required for the totalizing, "thick" cultural description and analysis that are the goals of ethnographic endeavor. This said, there remains the obvious fact that ethnography, being restricted to the present, leaves beyond its purview the cultural and social dimensions of much of the human experience. It is also true that by its very nature historical anthropology as a research technique is highly dependent upon the availability of documentary evidence. In ethnography, the people are there and the real issue (other than the competence of the researcher) is whether they are accessible. In historical anthropology, researching the past requires ample and detailed documentation within and with reference to the chosen field setting. The field site must be both accessible and worth getting to in respect of the data available there.

Historical anthropology is not in the first instance the product of archival research, for it requires long-term fieldwork at a particular site for which ample documentation is also available. Indeed, the anthropologist doing this fieldwork may have to obtain the documents from a wide variety of sources, often through borrowing, copying, and returning papers, the most important of which may be the various documents of their predecessors or ancestors still held onto by local families or institutions. It thus requires considerable fieldwork simply to create the archive, which will have its greatest value precisely through its links to the ethnographic findings also resulting from that fieldwork. For such historical anthropology, documentation should be informative regarding intimate social relations of the kind that anthropologists otherwise seek to identify and describe through ethnographic study. Historical anthropology of this kind cannot be done everywhere with the same degree of documentary support. Late imperial China was notable for the importance of written documents in everyday life, with the result that Chinese sites are potentially advantageous for historical anthropological research. In recent years, increasing numbers of such documents have become available for research, including land transfer contracts, family division agreements, temple records, family or association account books, and genealogies. Unfortunately, given China's tumultuous history during recent centuries, these materials have not always survived in quantities sufficient to provide the basis for a detailed exploration of social relations and cultural patterns within a community setting. Thus, in China communities vary in terms of the availability of documentary resources required for the practice of historical anthropology. In this respect, Taiwan may be better off than much of mainland China, for although the island has had its share of suffering, it at least escaped certain recent calamities of the twentieth century. Still, in spite of the losses associated with such events on the mainland, many documents did survive, thus confirming their importance and common use in late imperial China. It is no wonder that historical anthropology is now a major component of the anthropological profession in mainland China as well as in Hong Kong and Taiwan.

Notes

1 W. Barclay's *Colonial Development and Population in Taiwan.* Princeton: Princeton University Press, 1954.
2 Lang, Olga. *Chinese Family and Society.* New Haven: Yale University Press, 1946; Levy, Marion J., Jr. *The Family Revolution in Modern China.* Cambridge, MA: Harvard University Press, 1949.

3 See Fried, Morton H. *Fabric of Chinese Society: A Study of the Social Life of a Chinese County Seat.* New York: Praeger, 1953.
4 Skinner, G. William. "Marketing and Social Structure in Rural China, Parts I and II." *Journal of Asian Studies* 24 (1964–65): pp. 3–43, 195–228.
5 Maurice Freedman's *Chinese Family and Marriage in Singapore.* London: H.M. Stationery Office, 1957.
6 Maurice Freedman, *Chinese Family Law in Singapore: The Rout of Custom. In Family Law in Asia and Africa.* J.N.D. Anderson, ed. pp. 49–72. London: Allen and Unwin, 1968.
7 Maurice Freedman, *Chinese Lineage and Society: Fukien and Kwangtung.* London: Athelone Press, 1966. London: Athlone Press.
8 See my *House United, House Divided: The Chinese Family in Taiwan.* New York: Columbia University Press, 1976.
9 Pasternak, Burton. *Guests in the Dragon: Social Demography of a Chinese District, 1895–1946.* New York: Columbia University Press, 1983.
10 Diamond, Norma. *K'un Shen: A Taiwan Village.* New York, Holt, Rinehart and Winston, 1969.
11 *Pingxin Lun Baibai* 平心論拜拜。*Zhongguo Luntan* 中國論壇1(8) (1976): 20–21. (Reprinted in Belief and Culture 信仰與文化. Taipei: Chuliu Books 巨流圖書公司, 1978, pp. 117–124).
12 Robert H. Silin, *Leadership and Values: The Organization of Large-scale Taiwanese Enterprises.* Cambridge, MA: East Asian Research Center, Harvard University: Distributed by Harvard University Press, 1976.
13 Emily Martin Ahern and Hill Gates, eds., *The Anthropology of Taiwanese Society.* Stanford, CA: Stanford University Press, 1981.

Section 2
Work reflections

4 Fieldwork for Ming historians
Michael Szonyi

What can a scholar whose main period of interest is the fourteenth century to seventeenth century learn by hanging out in villages in the twenty-first century? Why don't you just work in a library like a normal Ming historian? These are reasonable questions to ask, and certainly the colleagues who referee my grant proposals ask me them all the time. In this essay, I'll suggest some answers, and try to explain why fieldwork in the Chinese countryside is a defining element of my historical practice.

I am fortunate to have had two excellent teachers who were pioneers in this type of work—David Faure and Zheng Zhenman, whose fieldwork skills are the stuff of legend. But much of what I know about fieldwork was learned through trial and error, simply by going to places that I was interested in. In the three decades that I've been doing fieldwork, I've spent time in the countryside with dozens of mentors, colleagues, and students. Sometimes this has been for my own research, sometimes for collaborative research, and sometimes I've tagged along as other people do research on topics that I know nothing about. I made and continue to make many blunders. I've pushed people too hard and too early in our interactions to share their genealogy, generating suspicion and tension. I've thoughtlessly brought into the open disagreements over some sensitive historical issue, leading to awkwardness that I'm sure persisted long after I was back on campus. And sometimes I've just wasted time, my own and that of other people.

All of these errors are permanently recorded in my own internal ledger of professional failings, but none—so far at least—have been fatal either figuratively or literally. The main lesson I've learned is that there is no single right way to do fieldwork, which means everything I say below should be taken with a grain of salt. This may seem self-evident, but being mindful of it might help the fieldworker to stay of good cheer when things seem to be going badly (I'm sure I'm not the only scholar of China who occasionally falls into what I call "black China moods"). It also helps scholars find their own way to a fieldwork approach that works for them. Some people are able to show up at a rural home without any introduction, ask to see private documents, and happily pull out their camera and start photographing. I can't do that. I don't feel comfortable demanding to see documents until I've had a chance to interact and form a relationship with people first. This might make me a little slower than others at collecting documents, but I think it makes me more effective as a historian in the long run. Watching educated, urban people talk over illiterate peasants as if they were not even in the room has taught me a lot about how I want to be a respectful fieldworker.

What I do in the field—the answer to the two questions above—can really be boiled down to two things (my comments here are limited to my research on premodern history; my fieldwork experience studying contemporary topics would be another story). First, I collect texts—genealogies, stone inscriptions, land deeds and contracts, ritual texts, and many other types besides. In this sense, the distinction between fieldwork and archival work is a false one. Fieldwork literally creates the archive I use. Every society privileges certain genres of texts over others. Because of the specific forms that this privileging has taken in China, vast quantities of historical documents remain in the hands of villagers, or on stone inscriptions erected in village temples, rather than in formal libraries and archives. In the case of genealogies, I estimate that in Fujian at least the total number extant is some two orders of magnitude greater than the number found in libraries.[1] Similarly, as Zheng Zhenman and Kenneth Dean have found, there are certainly thousands, perhaps tens of thousands of inscriptions in village temples in Fujian that had never previously been known to scholars. Findings from other parts of China suggest similar results. That being said, some of the types of material I gather in the field—folklore, oral history, and in particular observations of ritual performance—would strike traditional historians as unorthodox. Indeed, I continue to take delight in "discovering" new genres of texts that either I did not know existed or, more interestingly, did not realize were actually historical texts that might be useful.

Second, I use fieldwork to put the different parts of the archive in dialogue with one another, to illuminate the connections, tensions, contradictions, and discrepancies between the different parts for the purposes of exploring historical questions. A few examples can illustrate this point.

Sometimes the archive produced by fieldwork confirms or elaborates on a story in the official archive. For example, the early Ming *Veritable Records* (*Ming Shilu* 明實錄) as well as many local gazetteers record that in the 1380s, the emperor received disturbing reports that troops stationed close to their home villages on the southeast coast were creating problems for both military discipline and local order. In response, he ordered that troops be transferred to garrisons some distance away from their native place. That is as much as the official archive can tell us. The fieldwork-produced archive both confirms the official archive and provides far more detail. Members of the Ni 倪 lineage, who live on the site of the former Jinmen Battalion, told me that they had settled there when their ancestor was "transferred" there in the early Ming (though I was interviewing the family for my book *Cold War Island*, sheer force of habit meant that I still asked my interviewees about their ancestral origins). Sure enough, this story also appeared in their genealogy, explaining how their ancestral home was in Fuzhou, 300 kilometers to the north, where their early ancestor was conscripted, stationed, and later transferred from. This issue turned out to be of much greater, even central, importance to my next project, which led to *The Art of Being Governed*. By repeating the exercise up and down the coast, I was able to trace with some precision the circuits of movement created by the emperor's policy decision in the 1380s, with consequences for Ming soldiers and their descendants up to the present day. In general I wouldn't advise students to treat family legends of ancestral origin as historical facts. But in this case the consistency between the official archive, the fieldwork archive, and the folkloric record confirm that we should treat what ordinary people have to say, even about the history of their distant ancestors, with respect.

Sometimes, the juxtaposition of multiple archives can be productive by suggesting not consistency but the opposite. The Chen lineage of Luozhou 螺州, near Fuzhou—one of the subjects of my book *Practicing Kinship*—were, by the late Qing, one of the most prominent lineages of the region, which produced multiple examination graduates and high officials. I first learned of the family by reading multiple versions of their genealogy on microfilm in the library of the Church of the Latter Day Saints in London. Through a series of chance events and the kind introduction of a member of the lineage living in the United States, I was able to visit Luozhou and eventually lived there for several months, first in the ancestral hall and later in the home of a villager. Like most Fujian lineages, the Chen trace their ancestry back to Tang dynasty migrants from central China. They did not claim to have moved directly from central China to Fuzhou more than a thousand years ago. Rather, their genealogy reported that their distant ancestors had first settled in a neighboring county. Then, centuries later, the lineage's founding ancestor had moved to Luozhou in the early Ming, by marrying uxorilocally into a Luozhou family. The Luozhou Chen had retained a ritual tie to the original settlement in the neighboring county, the two groups visiting one another during the festival season in the first month of the Lunar New Year. When I was doing this research in the early 1990s, these visits had just been revived after the hiatus of the Mao years. I dutifully made plans to travel to that place of first settlement in search of further genealogical evidence and in the hope of cross-referencing the various genealogies.

In one of those offhand comments that I could have just ignored but that would prove to be hugely significant, a friend and lineage organizer told me not to waste my time exploring the specific genealogical links between the two groups. "The relationship between us and them," he told me,

> is false. We don't really belong to the same line. To tell the truth, our founding ancestor was Chen Youliang 陳友諒. Doesn't it say in the genealogy that our founding ancestor moved [here] in the time of [founding Ming emperor] Zhu Yuanzhang 朱元璋? After Chen Youliang was

defeated by Zhu Yuanzhang, he fled here to hide. If anyone had known that our ancestor was Chen Youliang, Zhu Yuanzhang would have had him killed. So he pretended to be from [the neighboring county]. It's not really true.

It turned out that many older men in the lineage would, if prompted, offer a similar account.

Once I started asking about Chen Youliang, I was often told another story: that when the ancestral hall was desecrated during the campaigns of the early 1960s, a genealogical record found in the back of an ancestral tablet referred to Chen Youliang as the lineage's founding ancestor. Who was Chen Youliang? Chen Youliang was one of Zhu Yuanzhang's leading rivals in the wars of the late Yuan; he was decisively defeated at the Battle of Lake Poyang in 1363, whereupon his surviving followers scattered. In the Fuzhou region, as in many parts of South China, Chen is said to be the progenitor of the Dan 蜑, a much discriminated-against status group who lived afloat on their boats and primarily made their living from fishing. The claim of a connection to Chen Youliang is thus a marker—emic, etic, or perhaps both—of Dan identity.

Materials in the official archive that had mystified me, such as a gazetteer biography of a lineage member who had successfully gained for the lineage an exemption on a fishing-boat tax, suddenly made more sense. But what these stories really told me was that despite their high status by the late Qing, at some point in the past the Chen had identified themselves or been identified as Dan. This suggested that the genealogical account was not—or was not only—a historical record but also a political claim. If the Chen were descended from migrants from central China who were already living in the region by the late Tang, they could *not* have been Dan boat people who settled there only in the early Ming.

The lineage had multiple stories, circulating in multiple registers, about their origins. Eventually this proved to be a major breakthrough in my dissertation, leading me to see that many of the genealogies I had collected in my fieldwork could be read as a claim about origins in a context where origins mattered to status. This was a very concrete illustration of the point made long ago by Maurice Freedman that genealogies are political documents.

While the kind of fieldwork that I do is very different from the ethnographic fieldwork of the anthropologist, this example does illustrate the benefits of building relationships in the community. One often reads in ethnography of how months of living in the community are what enable the ethnographer to "ask the right question." In this case, I never asked the right question. Rather, a close and cordial relationship that had developed with a villager made it possible for me to hear a chance remark that opened up a new intellectual possibility.

Historians juxtapose and reconcile conflicting sources all the time. There is nothing in either of the stories above that is especially fieldwork specific except that I would never have been able to collect these sources—neither the genealogies nor the oral accounts—without going into the field. So let me next provide an example where the sources are not the traditional ones of a historian and are themselves products of my fieldwork methods. *The Art of Being Governed* is a study of hereditary military households (*junhu* 軍戶) in the Ming dynasty, and their interaction with state institutions and state agents. Many such households did not actually serve as soldiers but as farmers in military colonies (*juntun* 軍屯), raising food for their colleagues in the garrisons. In the colonies, hereditary military households faced not only challenges of dealing with the military system but also with the existing residents of the surrounding area. Scholars have tried to trace this history, but the official archive allows only a very thin and unsatisfying description. For the fieldwork-oriented historian, the next step is obvious—go to the places where these people lived and see what you can find.

Gao Zhifeng, a graduate student at Xiamen University, first introduced me to Hutou 湖頭 township in Fujian, the site of his dissertation research. Hutou, a river basin in the highlands upriver from Quanzhou, was the site of a number of Ming military colonies serving the nearby coastal garrisons. Following the basic dictum of "in the village, look for the temple; in the temple, look for the stone inscriptions" (在村找庙, 在庙找碑), we visited a temple I call the Temple with Two Gods, and found there a number of stone inscriptions dating back to the Ming. Although there must have been hundreds of thousands or even millions of such small, village temples in China before 1949, this was a promising start. For this temple was a local institution that had clearly endured since the time when military households were stationed in the region. There is of course nothing unusual about a temple having two gods—many temples have two gods; some temples have even more than two gods. But the various inscriptions hinted at two very different explanations for why this particular temple had two gods. On the walls of this temple, as in most temples, were handwritten "red posters" (红版). These are the equivalent for Chinese temples of financial statements. They record temple income and expenditures, as well as details of leadership roles. They are pasted on the walls of the temple each year, and typically never removed, to ensure transparency. Because the annual temple festival is the largest expenditure of the year, the costs are shared among the participating villages, and the red poster records this. It can therefore serve as a guide to the social entities comprising the institution's network. The poster also indicates the order in which the festival procession visits the participating villages. A single red poster thus allows us to see the scope of participation in temple affairs. Comparing red posters for multiple years, we learned that while there was some variation in participation, a core of about a dozen villages had joined the festival since its revival a decade ago.

Our next step was to collect genealogies from lineages in those villages. It soon became evident that the lineages living in Hutou today could be divided into three groups: those who had been settled since before the Ming;

former military households who had settled there in the early Ming, and those that had settled there subsequently. Since it was the first two groups that were of greatest relevance, we focused on their genealogies. These two different groups of families remember the history of their temple very differently. Each claims that the temple was first founded in honor of a different god, with the other god being a later interloper. These competing perspectives are matched in the inscriptional record. The local folkloric record and the manuscripts of local Daoist priests also hint at the tension between these two versions of local history.

By placing these contradictory sources in relation to one another and to what I knew of the local history, I was able to develop an account that is both compelling and, I think, accurate. Local society must have been thrown into some turmoil by the arrival of the military colonists in the early Ming. This group used their special connections to the Ming state to insert a new god, one who represented their interests and their power, into the existing local temple, displacing the original chief deity and pushing him into a subordinate position. The different stories in the genealogies and inscriptions are a reflection of this power shift. Ultimately a compromise was worked out that enabled both groups to participate in the temple, to agree to disagree on the temple origins, and to join together for the annual procession festival and associated rituals. The compromise is visible today even though the institutions that generated the new social relations that lie behind the compromise are long gone.

The Temple with Two Gods has thus been both arena for and expression of a centuries-long negotiation between two groups—the original inhabitants and the soldier-households that were assigned there in the early Ming. The whole history of the encounter between the two groups can be told through the history of this temple, and indeed, barring the discovery of some new and authoritative account can *only* be told through the history of this temple. In general I would not argue for the superiority of fieldwork methods over other methods. But in this case, fieldwork practice not only created the archive that enabled this research, it also made possible a different kind of history that would simply not have been possible using more traditional methods.

To further develop the theme mentioned above, that fieldwork-based methods are not as dissimilar from more traditional approaches as they might seem, I suggest below a number of ways in which the work I do in villages resembles the work I do in the formal archive.

Both approaches entail an enormous amount of wasted time, of tracking down leads that end up going nowhere. Many genealogies and stone inscriptions are formulaic. Sometimes even trying to collect them proves impossible. Many elements of a ritual are dull, or worse. At the conclusion of the Hutou ritual, every family in the host village presents the gods with a ritually slaughtered pig. During one of my visits, I persuaded the Daoist priests to allow me to accompany them to a nearby village to observe this ritual. It turns out that pig butchery is more or less as I might have expected; it's not a very pleasant thing to watch, and there is not a lot it can teach us about Ming history.

First, I have tried in this chapter to refrain from giving too much avuncular advice, but middle-aged (and tenured) me wishes I could go back and tell younger (graduate student) me not to take these wrong-turns and delays so seriously. A few hours watching pigs be killed; the day I spent waiting outside an ancestral hall for the watchman to return with the key so I could look at a genealogy (he never came!) or the long journey into the mountains by bus and tractor to visit a temple, only to be told that "if you were really a scholar you would have come in a black car with officials from the county" did not spell the end of my career. And if nothing else they gave me good yarns to spin at the hotel bar after many a conference. But intellectually they are not so different from days spent in a library reading a text that turned out not to answer the questions I was interested in.

Second, with both types of sources—though perhaps more with non-traditional ones—it is all too easy to get trapped in a logic of verification. Were the Chen really originally Dan fisherfolk? Which god was really the first god? It took me many years to realize that for anyone but the local people themselves these are not interesting historical questions. The interesting questions involve understanding what kinds of arguments and claims are being made in these documents. As Li Ren-yuan has pointed out in his recent dissertation, the costs of producing a genealogy or a stone inscription were not trivial.[2] Why did people think this material was worth recording? How was a local community different after a text existed than it had been before? In other words, what were the conditions of production of these texts? One should ask the very same questions of any text, whether it is in a library or in a village.

Third, there is the importance of the serendipitous encounter—the chance remark and idle comment that almost certainly matters more than hours and hours of diligent recording. For all but the most ardent post-modernist, this role of chance offends our sense that our work is objective, even scientific. But I'm not sure it is all that different from our discoveries in the archive. How many times have I photocopied a document in the archives, forgotten about it, and then months or even years later read it again and realized that the real significance of the text for my research lay not in the passage that led me to make the copy in the first place, but on another part of the page? For that matter, how many times have I missed something crucial in the library or the archives because I was too tired, or bored, or distracted? (However, I am quite sure I have never missed anything in the library because I was too drunk on sweet-potato liquor. This particular hazard is definitely unique to fieldwork-based approaches.)

One way in which fieldwork really does differ from archival research—though not from oral history methods—is the much greater role that living people play in one's work. While most people in the Chinese countryside are unfailingly helpful and obliging, the fieldworker soon develops a catalog of people who cannot be avoided, but who do not make one's research any easier:

- local cadres who think the only purpose of your research is to demonstrate the distinctiveness of their area. Thankfully, when working on premodern topics one rarely encounters cadres who see one's research as potentially digging up some unfortunate event that could land them in trouble;
- scholars who know that the answer to your every question is already contained in their unpublished manuscript locked up in their desk;
- informants who want nothing more than to make the interviewer happy and will say whatever they think will accomplish that (a related sub-category is people who just want the interviewer to go away);
- informants who think "Chinese traditional culture" is the answer to any question. In a sense, these people do not understand that China has a history (a related sub-category in this case is people who assume "what we did when I was young" is more or less synonymous with "in the Ming dynasty").

Of course, none of these people are being deliberately unhelpful, and in many cases quite the opposite. But finding an appropriate way to respond and continue working with them is a challenge for every fieldworker. The even more vexing question is how the fieldworker can repay her debts to the countless people, many anonymous, who help in her research over the years. In this regard, the historical fieldworker faces similar dilemmas to the anthropologist.

I should admit that to some extent—though this is not something I would ever write in a grant proposal—my answers to the questions posed in the first paragraph are rationalizations for personal preference. I find it interesting and fulfilling to spend time in the Chinese countryside, for reasons that go well beyond the needs of my research. There are two quite different contexts in which I do so, and I enjoy both for different reasons. Some of my visits to the countryside are in ordinary time, and give me a chance to observe the quotidian, hum-drum rhythms of everyday life. I talk to people about the research topics that interest me, but also about their lives more broadly, as they go about their daily tasks. Other visits are scheduled around festival time, when every day is a spectacle of rituals, firecrackers and incense, and feasting. The people I talk with on these visits know very well why I have come to *qiao renao* (瞧热闹)—to watch and enjoy the excitement, literally "the heat and the noise."

Like most academic historians of China, I teach about modern and contemporary China and have a strong personal interest in what is going on in China today. An incidental benefit of my fieldwork is that it sometimes gives me insights into some aspect of life in China today that I would never have if I only spent time in the cities that house universities and libraries. The many unfinished, apparently abandoned, houses in some Fujian villages could be easily mistaken for a sign of a burst housing bubble. But repeated visits over the course of several years, and conversations with village residents working in factories elsewhere who return for the Lunar New Year festival, suggest a different explanation, one that has to do with the challenges migrant laborers face in access to credit. With no way to get a mortgage, they build their home in stages, adding floor one year, covering the bare concrete in tile another.

I'm Canadian, and over the years I have become used to the stock elements of the Chinese cultural repertoire that come up whenever Canada is mentioned—Bai Qiu-en (白求恩 Norman Bethune), Da Shan (大山 the *xiangsheng* 相聲 performer Mark Roswell), and so on. One day an old township cadre who was helping me gather the genealogies of military households gave me a different take. "Canada..." he said, "is unfriendly to China." Whatever could he mean? "You gave a work permit to Lai Changxing 賴昌星." Lai was the chief suspect in a massive corruption scandal who sought asylum in Canada. He was indeed granted permission to work while his asylum claim was evaluated (he was eventually returned to China), but the issue was a little more complicated than a deliberate snub by Canada against China. Who would have expected to learn a lesson about media control in contemporary China in this remote and isolated coastal community?

I don't think the last word on fieldwork methods for historical research has been written. Today new digital tools offer intriguing new possibilities for analysis of fieldwork-based research. For example, most of the stone inscriptions in temples and ancestral halls include donation records, long lists of names, and details of the size of their donations. Indeed, this is often the bulk of the inscription text. How can we use this information? As noted above, where the social affiliation of the donors is mentioned—lineage or lineage branch, village or neighborhood, or some other social organization like a guildhall—it can be used to reconstruct the social networks of the institution to which the donation is made. We can also look for the names of prominent people to get a sense of the kinds of activities of local elites—so-and-so donated to both the local temple and a nearby Buddhist monastery. But in general, I've never found much use for these records—the lists of names and amounts donated are just too long to keep track of. In places where we have both inscriptions and genealogies, though, it would not be difficult to cross-reference the two, and look for patterns. Where almost everyone in a lineage has contributed to a construction project, these patterns might well indicate the distribution of wealth across the lineage (though individual differences in commitment to the project might also be relevant). And—even more ambitious—where there are multiple inscriptions commemorating multiple reconstructions over the years, we could use these to show variation over time. So far as I know, no one has yet undertaken such research, but the possibilities are there.

The biggest pitfalls of using fieldwork-collected sources, of both the orthodox and the more unusual kind, are actually the same as those we face with all our sources—of treating them uncritically, of neglecting the conditions of their production. It is all too easy to treat a recently revived ritual simply as a remnant or survival of unchanging traditional or premodern practice, ignoring that the ritual is shaped by both history and contemporaneity (by contemporaneity I mean that the ritual is performed by people in the present, with their own needs and concerns, and faithfulness to tradition is but one of those concerns). Think of how and why community leaders today strive to present any ritual as an example of "intangible cultural heritage." It is almost certainly not because they hold this category itself in any particular esteem, but to forestall alternative understandings.[3]

As David Holm once remarked, China today is in the midst of a simultaneous cultural revival and cultural extinction episode. Temples are often barely reconstructed before they are bulldozed; lineages devote huge resources to compiling their genealogy even as their membership scatters from the village. This situation makes the task of historical fieldwork both urgent and significant; the fruits of this revival should be taken full advantage of before they disappear forever. The situation also calls on us to reflect seriously on the implications and importance of fieldwork-based research for our understanding of China present and China past, even the distant past of the Ming.

Notes

1 For how I arrive at this estimate, see *The Art of Being Governed*, 247n30.
2 Li Renyuan, "Making Texts in Villages: Textual Production in Rural China during the Ming-Qing Period." Ph.D. diss., Harvard University, 2014.
3 Kenneth Dean and Thomas Lamarre. "Ritual Matters." In *Impacts of Modernities*, edited by Thomas Lamarre and Kang Nae-hui, 257–284. Hong Kong: Hong Kong University Press, 2004, 257–284.

Further Reading

Dean, Kenneth, "Introduction", Special Issue on Stone Inscriptions, Local History, and Fieldwork, *Minsu quyi* 67, 3 (2010): 1–63.

Faure, David, *Emperor and Ancestor: State and Lineage in South China*. Stanford, CA: Stanford University Press, 2007.

Miles, Steven, *Upriver Journeys: Diaspora and Empire in Southern China, 1570–1850*. Cambridge: Harvard University Asia Center, 2017.

Siu, Helen and Liu Zhiwei, "Lineage, Market, Pirate, and Dan: Ethnicity in the Pearl River Delta of South China," in Pamela Crossley, Helen Siu and Donald Sutton, eds, *Empire at the Margins: Culture, Ethnicity and Frontier in Early Modern China*. Berkeley: University of California Press, 2006, 285–310.

Szonyi, Michael, *Practicing Kinship: Lineage and Descent in Late Imperial China*. Stanford: Stanford University Press, 2002.

Szonyi, Michael, *Cold War Island: Quemoy on the Front Line*. Cambridge: Cambridge University Press, 2008.

Szonyi, Michael, *The Art of Being Governed: Everyday Politics in Late Imperial China*. Princeton, NJ: Princeton University Press, 2018.

5 Conducting fieldwork as a local
Perspectives from Hulunbuir

Guan Yuxia, with Zhang Wei

Hulunbuir (Hulunbeier 呼伦贝尔) is a vast region of grassland and forest near the borders of Russia and Mongolia. Home to Mongol, Daur, Evenki, Oroqen, and other Chinese minority peoples, some may imagine that Hulunbuir is a place where people all ride horses and wear minority costumes, but in fact the mix of ethnicities and cultures is much more rich and complex than that.

I am a native of this place, born in Nanlu 南麓, on the eastern side of the Khingan (Xing'an 兴安) mountains. Known as Lingdong 岭东 (East of the Mountains), this region is dominated by agriculture, and is predominantly Han Chinese. Growing up, I had so little awareness of ethnic culture that I dated my husband for more than half a year before realizing that he was ethnic Mongol. After graduation and marriage, I moved with my husband to Beilu 北麓, in the pastoral area known as Lingxi 岭西 (West of the Mountains). It was in this part of Hulunbuir that I came to encounter different ethnicities, and to understand ethnic difference more clearly. Only after living in an area dominated by Mongolian ethnicity did I start to perceive these characteristics in my husband's appearance and personality. My point is that in a multiethnic region like Hulunbuir, even locals will have very different experiences of culture and lifestyle, even if they do not immediately recognize them as such.

There are many advantages to conducting research as a local: it is less expensive, and more convenient to travel, and easier to find introductions. As a local, you can find the best person to serve as a bridge to local communities, and you will be more easily accepted by the people you interview. I benefit especially from my marriage. As soon as I tell local people that my husband is ethnic Mongol, faces and words relax, and I can feel that I have been accepted as an insider. But this is just a way of entering the field. Throughout our relationship, I must continue to take active steps to deepen trust.

Having been accepted as an insider, I can gain access to deeper levels of information. Yet at the same time, we must always try to maintain aspects of an outsider's perspective, to ensure the sensitivity and objectivity of our research. And certainly, the question of how an outsider can use materials gained as an insider raises serious ethical concerns.

The advantages of conducting local research as a local

While it may be possible to conduct interviews remotely, or by inviting our subjects to meet us in a mutually convenient location, conducting our research on-site is less disruptive to our interview subjects, which, in turn, allows us to work at our own pace, and to delve more deeply in our questions. At the same time, speaking with people in their own communities can also make interview subjects more aware of maintaining a good appearance, and less willing to reveal negative information to outsiders.

I first traveled with colleagues to conduct interviews in the forested region of Genhe (根河) known as Aoluguya 敖鲁古雅 during Spring Festival. The woman who we knew as Elder Sister Wang brought us to a house, where a few families had gathered for a night of eating and drinking. It was just after two o'clock in the afternoon, and the people in the house were already quite drunk, and seemed to be on the verge of an argument. When we entered, a few people at first looked at us in shock, but seeing that we had been brought by Elder Sister Wang, they greeted us warmly. Elder Sister Wang had grown up in this area, and had not been back for a year, but remained very close to the people from her hometown. After she told the group that we had come to do interviews, voices in the room quieted, and a woman (we later learned her name was Xiaoping) quickly took us three outsiders to another room and closed the door. At that time, I presumed she was taking us into the other room because it was quiet, and so we wouldn't be disturbed by the noise of the drinking party. But I wondered: why did she do it so quickly? Later I noticed the concern on Xiaoping's face when she asked us where we were from, and whether we were there to conduct interviews (采访) or an investigation (调研)? But as soon as I told Xiaoping that we were from Hailar, her face immediately relaxed. She even did a little dance, and sang out, "They're not experts from Beijing! Nothing to fear! Nothing to fear!" At that moment, I honestly didn't know whether to laugh or cry. After a time, I came to realize that Xiaoping had rushed us out of the room because she had taken us for the sort of experts and reporters that had previously come to report on the problem of alcoholism, an experience that had left bad feelings in the community. Later, she showed us two albums full of precious old photographs, but before we could finish looking, the people at the table beckoned us to come over and have a drink with them. Once people knew that we were from Hailar, they all accepted us. As locals, and as Elder Sister Wang's friends, we were accepted with local hospitality, and were invited to come over and drink at the table. They even returned to arguing right in front of us, with no concern whatsoever. It would be unlikely for an outsider to witness such a scene.

Many outsiders will have the impression that everyone in this region is a heavy drinker. Actually, because people from Aoluguya have this reputation, they do not like to associate with outsiders. But, if you understand their history, you will understand them. Aoluguya people have been hunting in the forests of the Beili area since the seventeenth century. The average temperature is −5°C, and at times it is as low as −50°C. In this region, many people drink strong alcohol to steel themselves against the extreme cold. Men and women drink, and there are people who can drink heavily (three cups) and not appear intoxicated. In the 1950s, the government initiated a 30-year forest development resources plan, which resulted in the Aoluguya people losing their hunting grounds and being resettled into this district. Although they have more recently begun receiving resources through preferential government policies, and now have both comfortable housing and sufficient food and clothing, many were unable to adapt to this settled lifestyle. Alcohol became a way of dealing with the boredom and sense of dislocation. After 2012, cultural and ecotourism introduced ways for the Aoluguya to improve their economic situation. These new economic opportunities, plus the resurgence of traditional methods of raising deer and the new hope of ecological recovery gave the Aoluguya a way to reconnect to their past, and a new hope for their future. Alcoholism declined in relative terms, although alcohol remains an important part of everyday life, and is still customarily presented to guests. Fieldworkers with a good tolerance for alcohol, those who can put away a few drinks, will be accepted more quickly by their hosts. In order to avoid giving offense, we often make the excuse of having to drive or having an allergy in order to avoid excessive drinking. The hosts never force the issue, yet seeing their disappointed faces, and watching them drinking freely, one suddenly becomes aware of having been relegated to the status of outsider.

Of course, not every local researcher can easily be accepted; one also needs a good go-between to act as a bridge. This person needs to be trusted within the community, since the faith in the researcher is built on confidence in the introduction. At the same time, the go-between needs to trust us, needs to understand us and our research, and needs to believe that our research will benefit the community and bring no harm. Only then will she introduce you to the really important, central people. Elder Sister Wang was one of the few people from her community that was able to leave home and go to work in the city. She has done many good things for her community, and her father is a trusted leader. Because of this, Wang enjoys great trust among the people there, and some of the same age still refer to her respectfully as "elder sister." I was originally introduced to Elder Sister Wang by my husband and, through a four-hour conversation about our research, found her to be a very open-minded woman. For her part, she reckoned that I must be trustworthy, and agreed to personally accompany us to conduct fieldwork, because she felt that our work would benefit her community.

This experience with Elder Sister Wang reminds us of the ways that a good intermediary not only helps launch the fieldwork smoothly, but also can provide important information. Once before embarking on a fieldwork to Oroqen Autonomous Banner, I contacted the head of the local ethnicities study society. He told us that Huma County (呼玛县) in Heilongjiang was planning to hold a "river sacrifice" (祭江). We could not pass up such an important ritual. The Oroqen had only this one remaining shaman, who we were told was, in fact, the last practicing shaman in the entire area. Traditional Oroqen belief views shamans as emissaries between heaven and earth, and between humans and spirits. They communicate to the spirits our wishes to have a good life, to be healed of sickness, and to exorcize harmful forces and demons. We changed our research plan itinerary to attend the ritual, taking a small airplane to the Oroqen banner, and then traveling 500 kilometers by car to arrive at our destination.

The river sacrifice was scheduled to start at nine o'clock in the morning, but the preparations began three hours earlier. We went down to the riverbank with the organizers, who carried all sorts of sacrifices they had prepared the day before to place on the ritual platform. Offerings included fruit, raw and cooked fish, beef, sheep, and deer meat, which were given in order to pray for a good year of fishing on the river. After the offerings had all been arranged on large plates, the unmarried men helped the shaman put on her "Buddhist" robes and hat ("Buddhist" is frequently used as general term for religious) in a tent that had been erected beforehand. Once dressed, the shaman used dried moss gathered from nearby mountains to light a small fire, and began to pray, all while constantly adding small pieces of dried moss to the fire. Before the actual ritual, she prayed continuously for about 40 minutes. Although the ritual is in spring, and the thawed river was flowing, snow and ice lined the banks. Even in our down-filled coats, we were chilled to the bone, and it felt like the prayer would go on forever.

The old shaman was 83 *sui*, and not in robust health—the real organizer of the event was the shaman's niece, whom we called Elder Sister Fang 芳. She was responsible for the entire event, from the clothes the shaman wore during the actual ritual, to the prayer scarves (*fudai* 福带, like the Mongolian *hadag*, called *siwa* in Oroqen), and offerings that are given to the worshippers. Other people followed Fang's direction throughout the activity. Elder Sister Fang had very high prestige among the worshippers, having revived the spring river blessing ritual four years before. Elder Sister Fang was 60 *sui*, and, since retiring from her job, has been steadily working to record and systematize this region's ethnic culture. Reviving the shaman river blessing ritual was a way of continuing these traditions. Since the old shaman is her aunt (all of the ethnic groups in this area are more or less closely related), and has no children, Elder Sister Fang took on the duty of caring for her. With such help, her aunt is strong enough to endure a five hour ritual, though each time she goes through a period of being very ill and tired afterwards. Hearing all of this, I felt an immense rush of admiration for the old shaman and Elder Sister Fang.

At the same time, I felt extremely fortunate to have been able to observe and participate in this ceremony. Because we know, after the death of this old shaman, this activity will be completely gone, and those after us will never have the opportunity to experience it in person. This sense of respect for ethnic culture and gratitude to ethnic communities is a prerequisite for any fieldworker, and an essential attitude for any successful field work.

Shamanism is an important part of the beliefs of the northern nationalities. When dancing, drumming, and singing invite the spirits to possess her, the shaman's body becomes a bridge between spirits and humans, and her spirit "leaves its shell" to go and communicate with the spirits. During this time, the shaman can lose consciousness, become mute, enter a trance, or become extremely agitated. Scholars call this process "shaman possession" or "shamanistic dreaming."

Nonetheless, although the river blessing ceremony went on for a long time and completed the full ritual sequence, the shaman never entered a state of possession. The key element of shamanistic practice was already missing, and much of what once was at the core of shamanism is now gone. During the Cultural Revolution, shamanism was seen as superstition and its practitioners attacked. The public display of spirit possession was completely stopped, and new shamans have not revived it. Even after the ban on shamanism was rescinded, the revival has only been partial, at least in the realm of practice. Now those who get sick are more likely to visit modern medical specialists instead of going to a shaman. Few people are actually expecting to change the outcome of their illness. The river blessing in Huma County was thus organized in order to revive an ethnic cultural tradition, rather than to increase the fortune of the fishing industry. I wondered how the gathered spectators would have even reacted had the shaman actually gone into trance during the ceremony?

Deepening trust

After the intermediary has built the bridge to the local community, we face the important task of deepening trust and engaging the active interest of our interviewees. Mutual empathy and respect must come naturally, and are inseparable from our own status, motives, and beliefs. Many people are initially drawn to conduct fieldwork among ethnic communities out of curiosity or a search for the exotic. Even after these misconceptions are corrected, we remain unable to escape our own subjectivity. As much as I try to remain objective in my work, there is no question that my status as the only Han member of my husband's family shapes my view of the Mongols and of other northern nationalities. At a certain point, it is foolish, and even a bit dishonest, to hide what are very natural feelings of concern and affection for people that you have come to know well.

Developing good rapport with our interviewees often requires doing some homework in advance. We must first go through people (including our intermediaries) to collect as much information as possible on local society. Along with reading research reports, and ethnic gazetteers, we must also grasp geography, weather, and history as well as materials related to our specific research project: diaries, newspapers, cultural works, and legends. From our intermediary, we learn interviewees' names, work, and family situation. If we have done our homework, we can have in our minds a vivid and specific understanding before embarking on our fieldwork. Thus, when I am talking with an informant on a particular occasion, I will grasp that such and such person is the shaman's daughter, who was the old chief's daughter, and other such vital information. Moreover, the more information we have, the more able we are to pick up on implied meanings, and know what should not be asked about. For example, if we know that a woman is not married, you will know not to ask questions about how many children she has, or where her husband works. At the same time, it is important that our interactions with the interviewees should not be overly influenced by written materials or the opinions of your intermediary, but instead seek to be as objective and value-neutral as possible.

To conduct fieldwork in ethnic areas, you will also need to understand the community's taboos. To forest-dwelling minorities like Aoluguya and Oroqen, fire is both important and dangerous. There are many taboos about worship of fire spirits and the use of fire: we cannot throw things or splash water into a fire, or walk over the spot where a fire has burned, and must give the fire a sacrifice of cooked meat before using it. If we do not observe these taboos, or inadvertently break them, even if we are not directly criticized by the host, we will still make the host unhappy because such transgressions bring bad luck to the home. Sometimes politely refusing hospitality can give offense. The custom among these groups is to offer the spirits a large piece of cooked meat from the spine of a horse or deer. Afterwards, that meat is considered the most honored meal to offer guests. When eaten, it is cut with a knife into small pieces. The guest must use both hands to accept this meat and to place it in her mouth. If a guest hesitates or suggests by word or manner that the meat is unsanitary or too greasy, it will be very insulting to the host. If the host sees that the guest enjoys the meat, he may prepare some for the guest to take home. Refusing this gift will leave a bad impression. Take the gift, and if you feel it is necessary to repay the host, it is better to present an appropriate reciprocal gift later.

Apart from what we may learn from the content of conversation, communication during fieldwork is itself a means of increasing trust with your interviewees. We may try to maintain a value-neutral stance, but we still have feelings. When our interviewees tell us their stories, showing that we understand their emotions of happiness, pain, conflict, or anger makes them more willing to share these feelings. Even while remaining objective, it is important to use questions and physical gestures to listen in a way that displays empathy and attention. If we overlook this human connection, hearing the words but offering no response, or cutting short a conversation because it is not going in the direction we want, we will give the impression of being nothing more than tape recorders. Who would want to communicate with that?

Preparing an appropriate gift to present is also a way of deepening emotional ties between the interviewer and interviewee. When we go to conduct fieldwork, we are frequently disturbing people's lives or taking their time. Giving a gift is one way to express thanks, and the choice of gift is very important. If you are coming from outside the area, the choice is easy. Simply bring an item that is not available locally, which interviewees will consider interesting or to have commemorative value. If you are local, nothing you bring is likely to be so new to them, so bring something that they could use or would like. On one of our trips, our interviewee's 13-year-old daughter really admired a colleague's scarf and wouldn't put it down. So, my colleague gave the girl her scarf, which wasn't expensive and had no particular emotional value. Seeing how happy this simple gesture had made the girl, her father went to extra lengths to help us in our work. On another occasion, we went to visit a 70-year-old woman, and our go-between told us to bring a bottle of alcohol and some drinking snacks, since the woman liked to drink but was prevented from doing so by her family. That town only had two sad little shops, with little on the shelves. We could only buy a bottle of alcohol, some jars of fruit, and some sausage. Although the food was simple, we had a few drinks with the woman, and once she started talking, we learned that her daughters had all died young, and that she was now living a lonely life with her grandson's family. Although, of course, we knew not to let the woman drink too much, the drinking helped her with her pain.

In fact, some things are universal. Everyone needs to face the realities of sickness and death, and the daily trifles of eating and drinking. As researchers, we start from what we as humans share and go to the points of difference and individuality, so that our interviewees can understand our commonalities and are more willing to accept us. Sometimes this is as simple as a shared hobby. One of our colleagues is very skilled at making soap, and on one field trip, encountered a family that makes its own soap using sheep fat. This colleague shared a number of her soap-making methods with the family, and thereafter all of our interactions were very smooth. We talk to our interviewees about steaming bread, pickling vegetables, our preference of skin care products, all sorts of things. In the end, the aim of all investigation is understanding, and any true understanding must be mutual.

Ethical problems encountered in local investigations

In China, most fieldwork investigators are employees at universities or research institutes. Urban scholars live in the city and do their investigation in the countryside, and find most intermediaries among the rural intellectuals, who themselves have a certain social position. Because of this, our interviewees sometimes assume that we are connected to high officials, and refrain from asking us about the reason for our investigation. If our articles end up touching upon private or family secrets or gossip, unless it is something really scandalous, the interviewee is not likely to question or object, and many of our research subjects never even see our publications. These all raise serious ethical issues. We must respect our research partners, and be completely forthcoming about our research intentions, and about potential publications that could cause them problems. When the research is complete, we should allow them to review what we have written and give their informed consent. Changing names is a good way, but since many investigations are very detailed, the identities of euphemized individuals can sometimes be guessed.

Even if there is no power imbalance in the relationship, our interview subjects are often friends of friends, and may thus come to see us as friends, as well. For example, Elder Sister Wang and her aunt would discuss numerous issues about people in the area. Without worrying about my presence, they might say that this family's child had gotten drunk, injured someone in a fight and ended up in jail, or that woman beats her husband, and similar such statements. As a bystander, I benefit because their conversation touches upon matters that I want to know about but cannot ask directly. But these are all family secrets and gossip. At such times, I think: how could I possibly publish these things? From an ethical standpoint, I cannot. If my research really needs this sort of information, I should go to the people involved, wait for an appropriate moment to ask them directly, and get firsthand information from them. I will then know that the material is reliable and objective, and that I am not repeating information that might be incorrect or even dangerous.

The point is that there are many ways to be or become a "local." Regardless of where one is from, friendships, introductions, and local knowledge all give the researcher special access to a community. Being a local makes conducting research convenient, but its privileged access demands constant attention to our ethical responsibilities. We approach these topics with caution not simply because we live in the same city as our interviewees, or because we met them through friends or family, but because we care for and respect the people we work with. Looking back on my own research, I recognize that being an insider has helped my research, and how much I have gained personally from building these relationships. This gives me all the more reason to reflect on how I affect the communities where I work.

6 Who are they, and who am I?
Discovering gender and ethnicity in the Sino-Tibetan borderland

Xiaofei Kang

While staying in Beijing in the summer of 2017, I received a package from Songpan 松潘, a rural town in northwestern Sichuan where I had carried out intermittent fieldwork from 2003 to 2009. In the package I found several pairs of colorfully embroidered homemade slippers and a handwritten note: "Dear sister, these are more comfortable than what you would buy from the stores. Please take them back home to America." The slippers and the note were from Xiaohui, one of the daughters-in-law of the Zhang family with whom I stayed for several summers while in Songpan. Long after the fieldwork findings were published, every once in a while, I would still receive a package, an email, or a message on WeChat—a popular Chinese social media application—from the Zhang family, and we frequently exchange holiday greetings and updates on our children.

My ongoing connections with Songpan may sound familiar to other ethnographers. After all, our ability to reach to the inner core of local life depends largely on how well we have established local contacts. But it is rare to have the chance to reflect upon the personal encounters and subjective complications of ethnography. We are trained to be neutral observers, not to interfere with local lives, and we try to process ethnographic materials as objectively as possible.

I do value the established methods of objective ethnography and fact-seeking history, which combines ethnography with textual sources. However, this volume also provides a good opportunity for us to ask questions about the process. As much as we recognize the equal importance of ethnography and archives, shouldn't we also pay attention to the fundamental differences between these two kinds of sources? What distinguishes the way historians conduct fieldwork from how they process texts? However, subjectively textual sources were written and no matter how many different ways readers respond to them, the texts themselves remain the same. As such, except for those who study the materiality of the texts, historians' interactions with texts are very much unidirectional.

The same is not true for fieldwork. The people we encounter in the field think and talk back and forth with the ethnographer. Their interactions with the ethnographer are not only intentional representations, but also the product of particular contexts. Unless it is faithfully recorded and intentionally shared, the exchange with the ethnographer is also a one-time experience—it cannot be reproduced and verified by other scholars. Furthermore, the presence of an outsider inevitably creates new power relations in local family and community life. How a visiting scholar is perceived will have an immediate impact on what she observes. Besides, if an ethnographer has lived among the local people, eaten meals, and shared drinks around the same stove and under one roof, how could she remain totally detached from their everyday joys and sorrows, worries, and concerns? More often than not, these people have welcomed her not so much because they see themselves as the objects of her study, but because they can relate to her in terms of the multiple social roles in their own life: as a daughter, mother, urbanite, teacher, tourist, Han Chinese, overseas Chinese, or a "foreigner." Ethnographic findings are inevitably conditioned by the personal nature of field encounters as well as by the subjective constructions crafted between the ethnographer and the people she studies.

In this essay I draw on my own fieldwork experiences to address some of the issues I have raised above. For me, fieldwork is a journey of discovery. It contributes not only to understanding of larger academic themes of religion, state, and society over a long period of history, but also to the ethnographer's view of her own self as well as to that of the people she studies. The academic and the personal are inseparable. As a female ethnographer studying religion in an ethnically diverse region of southwest China, my journey of discovery hinged on understanding how gender and ethnicity played a critical role in forming connections in and beyond the field: how they defined the kind of information I collected, and in what ways they helped develop my own sense of multiple identities, as a Han Chinese woman, a female traveler, a foreign-trained female scholar, and perhaps many more.

The site and the ethnographic research

In late imperial times, Songpan was a garrison town. Located on the eastern edge of the Tibetan plateau, it lies about 400 kilometers north from Chengdu, the capital city of Sichuan province. It was viewed as a "lone city suspended in the land of 'barbarians'" and became the county seat during Republican times. Under the PRC, the town and its namesake county have been placed under the jurisdiction of the Aba Tibetan (and Qiang after 1987) Autonomous Prefecture 阿壩藏族(羌族)自治州. The indigenous peoples who have lived here are identified as Tibetans and Qiang in modern times. Since Ming times, Han and Hui Chinese have established settlements along the Min and Fu rivers, which cut through the mountain ranges to flow southwards to the Chengdu Plain.

My collaborator Donald Sutton and I started fieldwork here in 2003. What first drew our attention was Huanglong 黄龍 (Yellow Dragon), an old multi-ethnic pilgrimage center about 55 kilometers east of Songpan city.

In the 1980s, Huanglong, along with Jiuzhaigou 九寨溝 in the neighboring county, became a popular national tourist destination. In 1992, Huanglong was recognized as a UNESCO World Nature Heritage Reserve. The main tourist appeal of Huanglong is its picturesque scenery, with hundreds of colorful pools cascading down the 7.5 kilometers long and 1.5 kilometers wide slopes of the limestone valley. Huanglong temple (*Huanglong si* 黃龍寺) sits on a hill that overlooks the Huanglong valley. A god called Yellow Dragon the Perfected (*Huanglong zhenren* 黃龍真人) is worshiped here. Behind the valley stands the snow-capped 5,588-meter-high Tibetan holy mountain Shar dung ri (Ch. Xuebaoding 雪寶頂). On the 15th day of the sixth month of the lunar calendar, Han Chinese and Qiang come to celebrate the temple festival honoring Yellow Dragon the Perfected; Tibetans arrive at the same spot to finish their annual pilgrimage of circumambulating Shar dung ri.

Our research began with the examination of twentieth-century and contemporary struggles over religion, tourism, and ethnicity at Huanglong. Later we extended our scope of inquiries and placed Huanglong's transformation within the larger framework of the whole Songpan/Shar khog region, involving Han, Hui, Tibetan, and to a lesser degree, Qiang communities, and in light of the changing roles of the Chinese state through Ming, Qing, Republic, and into PRC times. The nature of such a project required us to combine archival research with extensive fieldwork. Given the political sensitivity of the ethnic area, we opted to bypass the official institutional channels and to build our own connections from grassroots. We did this by meeting pilgrims on the road and locating local interpreters of the Songpan dialect through personal friends in Beijing and Chengdu. We were lucky to find a dedicated college student, a Songpan native who was studying finance in Chengdu. We benefited greatly from his (and later his younger sister's) local knowledge and resources.

The primary goal of the collaborative project was to explore ethnicity, religion, and the Chinese state. Gender was not in the research plan, but as I will document below, it was constantly present in the fieldwork. The interconnections of gender and ethnicity shaped my ethnographic experiences and gradually revealed their importance in my academic inquiries.

Gender and ethnicity at work I: being foreign and coming from the outside

In the first two summers, Don and I often worked together. Walking the pilgrimage path and sojourning at Huanglong during the temple festival, our differences in gender were always perceived in relation to our age and race. On first encounters, the local people often took me, a younger Chinese woman, as the tour guide and interpreter of a senior Caucasian man. This caused many unpleasant experiences for both of us. For example, sometimes even if it was Don who asked a question, in clear Mandarin, some of them would answer me, assuming that I would provide the translation for him.

After a meal at a restaurant, the waiter/waitress would often hand the bill to me without even asking, expecting me to take care of it just as other tour guides did for their foreign customers. Going into the field without official patronage also posed serious challenges: all foreigners had to stay in three-star or higher hotels and register with their passports. If a foreigner stayed elsewhere overnight, the host had the responsibility to report him/her to the local police office, which would evict him/her immediately.

As we had visited the site multiple times and stayed for longer periods, the local people saw us as pilgrim-tourists or journalists: only the power of Yellow Dragon the Perfected could draw someone to the temple festival year after year, and only reporters would ask this many questions. Local officials and government employees seemed to hold similar views, and hence viewed us with suspicion. Our explanations that we were university professors fell on deaf ears; officials tended to associate our work with foreign media and the US government. Through the introduction of a Chinese professor who visited the US multiple times, we met a young Tibetan woman who had a bachelor degree from the Central University for Nationalities in Beijing and was then working in the Songpan county government. After I had developed a friendship with her, she once asked me privately, "So just tell me the truth, you really are here to collect information for the American government, right?"

In fact, one of our great discoveries in the field was that no one believed in academic research for its own sake. Everybody assumed that we were there with a hidden agenda—for better or worse. Our collaboration had to overcome and play with these local expectations, official suspicions, and the general perceptions of the hierarchical relationship of gender, age, and race. The arrival of tourism to the area had brought unprecedented opportunities as well as resource competition between local state agencies and local communities. The latter were just learning how to draw upon outside forces to counterbalance the overpowering state. Lay and religious leaders showed great enthusiasm for talking to Don, a "real foreigner," whom they believed would report on their culture and religion to the outside world and help promote their economic and cultural interests. They were particularly straightforward with Don about the intricate political situations, assuming that reaching out to foreign media would win them a sympathetic audience and give them increased leverage in their struggles with state agencies.

I cannot speak here for Don concerning his own rich experiences in the field. I can only document the personal experiences of a native-born Chinese and US-based female scholar. In the eyes of the officials and government staff, I was less suspicious than a "real" foreigner and certainly less politically capable/dangerous. As such, I was able to wander around and socialize more freely. Like any ordinary Chinese citizen, I could stay in lower-end hotels where only Chinese tourists were allowed. I was also able to venture into Tibetan, Qiang, Han, and Hui communities incognito, staying under the official radar. In these local encounters, the kind of information I could obtain depended on two factors: first, how locals perceived my various social roles, and second, how I subconsciously or deliberately positioned myself in these roles.

Historically the Hui and Han were both outsiders who established settlements within and around garrison towns and joined force to fight against indigenous "Fan (番)" rebellions, but religious differences and competition for local resources also created tensions and occasional bloody feuds between the two communities. Until tourist development began to change the residential settlements around 2005, the complex Hui-Han relationship was well reflected in the layout of the Songpan city: most of the Hui population lived in the northern part of the city, and the Han settled in the south. The two were separated by the Min river that cut through the city, and connected through a narrow bridge called Gu Song 古松— literally, Ancient Songpan.

In the eyes of many Hui Muslims and Tibetans, I remained a foreign journalist/scholar or interpreter. Don and I visited the two mosques in the northern part of the Songpan city multiple times. I also conducted several individual interviews with local Hui men, who knew well that I worked with a foreigner. In this context I found it much easier to talk to the men both inside and outside the mosque than to their wives and other Hui women—the latter always deferred conversations I initiated to their men, even when I deliberately asked "womanly" questions, such as about children, daily chores, and food. The male leaders of one mosque invited us to witness the communal meal that was supposedly for Hui only, and they encouraged me to take pictures during their prayers—all under the premise that I was an intermediary who would publicize Hui Muslim culture to the outside world. My own gender and ethnicity, as a Han Chinese woman, mattered little in these encounters.

For the Hui who were not aware of my foreign background, however, I appeared to be none other than a Han Chinese. Two middle-aged Hui women once kindly stopped me as I entered the Han Chinese-run City God Temple, reminding me that I had to be ritually clean (not menstruating) so that I would not offend the god inside and bring myself troubles from the unseen world. I also experienced the mistrust and even hostility that a Han woman would likely experience if she ventured into the Hui sacred ground as a stranger: one day when I attempted to enter the mosque without the presence of either Don or my familiar mosque members, two Hui teenagers yelled "go away, you dirty Han!" and hurled rocks at me. This gave me pause, and I pondered: should I pose as a Han Chinese woman and follow the local religious code? Or should I insist on my role as an American researcher? In either role, I felt as though I was stranded on that narrow bridge over the Min River, bearing the weighty history of "Ancient Songpan" that stretched back several hundred years.

The Tibetan monks saw me primarily through the struggle of their local Bon monastery to contend for its historical ownership of the Middle Temple in Huanglong. Tibetans had made Shar dung ri a holy mountain in the 1100s at the latest. While some Chinese sources claim that the Chinese had built the three Huanglong temples in the 1300s, what remains today, the Rear Temple on the top, Middle Temple 1,000 meters below, and the ruins of the Front temple at the foothill, can only be traced to the 1700s. Conversations with the Tibetan monks challenged the Chinese and English eyewitness accounts of the three Chinese temples from the late nineteenth and early twentieth centuries. The monks contended that Sertso (Golden Lakes), which was later named Huanglong in Chinese, had always been within the ritual territory of their own monastery. A lama from their monastery had built the Middle Temple as a Tibetan monastic school in 1904, and Tibetan acolytes continued to live here after 1941, when a Japanese bombing of Songpan city forced the Nationalist-run professional school to move into the temple. After being destroyed during Maoist times, the temple was renovated in 2003 by local Han Chinese and then contracted out by the Huanglong Management Bureau as a tourist enterprise.

The monks eagerly approached me in the hope that I could bring either media coverage or sponsorship from wealthy coastal areas that would hold back the combined power of local state and capital. One of the leading monks, in his late thirties, invited me to his living quarters in his monastery on the tourist highway to Huanglong, and to his private residence in Songpan town several times. The same monk and his abbot also knocked at my hotel door around 8 pm, after I just returned from a long day of fieldwork. They stayed for the next two hours talking about the unjust treatment the monastery had received from the county government regarding their claim to Huanglong temple. Neither the two monastics nor I were concerned with the gender implications of the timing and space of the visits. Yet even when we had developed an amicable relationship, I was still obliged to obey the gender rules of the Tibetan monastic community: no woman was allowed to enter the Bon monasteries. When I finally arrived at the doorstep of the above-mentioned monastery, I had to wait outside, watching with admiration as my monk friends and my Tibetan interpreter took my then nine-year-old son inside for a courtesy tour.

Gender worked both ways on other occasions. There were plenty of times that I consciously used the excuse of being a woman to dodge the local Han and Tibetan dinner etiquette of heavy drinking expected of an honored guest from faraway. When I trudged over bushes on the high mountains with the sole company of my interpreter—a young woman in her early twenties—and faced the potential danger of wild predators, I wished to summon a more militant spirit and masculine prowess within myself. Sometimes it was not animals, but unknown men in the unfamiliar terrain that tested my gender weakness or strength. One time I had to trace the background of a layman who came to preside over the Huanglong temple in the 1980s to a village about 50 kilometers south of Songpan town. Hitchhiking was a common local practice, but not a wise choice when all other passengers got off midway, leaving me alone with a foulmouthed, violent-tempered male driver. I grew

Who are they, and who am I? 75

increasingly alert when he began to throw questions my way about my age, profession, and purpose of visit. It took me a while to realize that the driver was busy figuring out how deep he could reach into my pocket: was I a tourist, an urbanite visiting local relatives, a reporter, or a cadre dispatched by the higher level government? Non-locals were routinely cheated in Songpan to pay higher prices for food, transportation, and other services. I was never so happy to be ripped off as when I arrived safely at the village.

Gender and ethnicity at work II: finding a family

My interactions with local Han Chinese women had a completely different dynamic, as my perceived role quickly shifted from an understanding of me as a foreign scholar/journalist to treating me as a Han Chinese tourist and, then, to embracing me as a close member of a local family. During the first two summers of fieldwork, Don and I were focused on the Huanglong temple festival. We made the acquaintance of many Han Chinese elderly women along the pilgrimage route and learned a great deal about local lore and Han Chinese ritual practices at the site. Unlike in the Hui mosques and Tibetan monasteries, I met no restrictions going in and out of the Han Chinese ritual spaces. The aforementioned local interpreters we hired were indispensable in conveying both my questions and my enthusiasm about Huanglong to these women. My digital camera also worked wonders—in 2003 it was still a novelty in this part of China, and many rural women considered it a special treat to have their own photos taken. They were even more impressed when they could see the pictures on the camera right away, to the extent that some of them even abandoned their scripture chanting sessions so that they could take a look at the photos. For most of them, my status as a scholar/journalist offered them an opportunity not so much to have their stories told, but to see a technological wonder that they could enjoy. Even the woman who indeed had a story to tell, the Li Popo 李婆婆 (Granny Li) whom we will meet below, did not shy away from marveling at her own images in every photo I took of her.

The photos eventually opened a new door for me. I printed the photos in Beijing and sent them back to Songpan. Soon I received a thank-you note from the granddaughter of Zhang Popo 張婆婆 (Granny Zhang)—whom I had met at Huanglong. When I returned to Songpan the next summer, I found Zhang Popo and the whole Zhang family, and was invited to stay in their house-compound. Zhang Popo's husband had died years before. She had three sons and two daughters, all married. The youngest son's family was elsewhere in Sichuan, and only came back to visit on major holidays. The two daughters married locally and lived in the same town: one ran a tea house, and the other was a middle-school teacher. Only Zhang Popo and the families of the eldest and the second son lived in the Zhang house-compound. Zhang Popo lived in the front section with the family of her second son; this family was comprised of a truck driver, his wife (Xiaohui, who sent me the slippers), and their then eight-year-old son. Passing through the family's vegetable plot, a pig pen, and the Zhang family's common bathroom, one got to the rear section where the eldest son's family had built a two-story house. The eldest son and his wife were both long-time contract workers for the county government. They resided in the dorm of the county government and came home only occasionally. They offered to let me stay in their room, while their teenage daughter lived in the other room. They rented the second story to a newlywed Tibetan couple, both of whom were elementary school teachers.

Once I became a resident in the Zhang-family house, I began to acquire a new social life in Songpan. The Zhangs welcomed me into their home not as tenants but as a new family relative. The very first thing we did in the Zhang-family dinner gathering was to compare our ages so that we could set up the family order: the eldest Zhang couple became my "big brother and sister (*dage* 大哥, *dajie* 大姐)"; I became "Elder Sister Kang (*Kangjie* 康姐)" for the younger couple, and "auntie (*ayi* 阿姨)" for all the Zhang-family children. A few days later, in another family gathering, the younger couple proposed that their son call me "*ganma* 乾媽"—the closest English equivalent being "godmother." I never took the initiative to make Zhang Popo my own "*ganma*" as the local custom probably expected me to, but she did increasingly treat me as a daughter. I followed her to her community temple work every day and to other temples on major festivals. Everywhere we went, she introduced me as "a relative from Beijing." When she made monetary donations on behalf of her whole family for divine blessings, she always asked the man in charge of the accounting book to jot down the name of each and every one of her children and grandchildren, and then added my name as well as the name of my husband and son. On our way back from a major temple festival, we took home several *mantou* 饅頭 and apples, which were our fair share from the offering table. Upon meeting a neighbor, she urged me to hide them, so that the two of us became the guardians of the Zhang family's fruits as well as the family's divine blessings.

Thanks to Zhang Popo, I entered into the religious world of the elderly Han Chinese women. Here I completely lost my role as a foreign scholar/journalist and became a "relative from Beijing." Even though I still struggled with the local dialect, I was able to mingle with the older women without an interpreter. Sometimes I would simply turn to a school-aged grandchild of any of the elder ladies when I needed to figure out some key terms. I also changed my working habits: I used to have a notebook in hand the first summer and tried to record everything my interviewee said on spot. Now I went about the local business following Zhang Popo, and only wrote a "diary" at the end of each day. It is also important to note that, once they had accepted me into their temple community, these women completely neglected my literacy and instead appreciated my labor. Nobody expected me to write their names down or record the donations or read the scriptures for them—for these jobs they routinely hired one or more literate men. But when I was the

Who are they, and who am I? 77

only one capable of moving a heavy pot of flour from one end of the temple kitchen to the other and when I spent the whole day making *mantou* and washing dishes in the smoky kitchen with these elder women, I won many praises and made friends instantly. In the religious world of these women, labor, rather than text and literacy, was the most important way to accumulate merit for themselves and their families. Now I belonged to the circle of local Han Chinese women and established an affiliation with a particular Han Chinese temple community run by these women.

These women's temple was indeed small, comprising of two rooms of roughly ten by ten meters and a slightly larger courtyard. From the outside, it looked just like any other low-lying farm house buried in the narrow alleys of Songpan's southern outskirts. Yet only after I had joined the circle did I find out that however small, this temple testified to the vicissitudes of Han Chinese religious life in the history of Songpan. A much larger and grandiose Temple of the Eastern Peak (*Dongyue miao* 東岳廟) had stood here in Qing times. It was destroyed in the devastating Tibetan uprising in 1911, rebuilt in 1916, and likely already desecrated well before the Maoist period. Had these women not rescued this small quarter from the commune's storage house in the 1980s and remade it into a Guanyin Hall, no traces of the historic Temple of the Eastern Peak would have ever been left.

Gender and ethnicity at work III: making friends

From 2005 to 2009, I stayed with the Zhang family during several summer visits and passed the time, day in and day out, with their kids, family, and friends, at no time drawing any official notice. I also built connections beyond the circle of elderly women in Zhang Popo's temple community. Over one family dinner conversation, for example, a niece of the Zhang family's eldest daughter-in-law dropped by. We ended up chatting for two hours about her new career as a local tour guide. Topics ranged from the required training and credentials to the great pressure tour guides faced because their only source of income was from commissions. And she knew all the tourist traps in Songpan region. "If they could not sell a piece of (fake) Tibetan jade for 50 yuan, they would just add two more zeros after 50, and it would be sold in one day!" The family setting of the conversation provided a different perspective on the inner working of the tourist industry, and it revealed a side of a tour guide's life that one rarely saw in official media, never heard from tourists, or ever experienced when we played tourists ourselves.

I also sojourned frequently with the locals to a tea house run by the women of the Zhang family. It was here that one of the Zhang's granddaughters introduced me to her classmate, the grandson of Li Popo, an elderly woman who took upon herself the grand task of renovating temples at Huanglong and in Songpan city. I had met Li Popo the year before at the Huanglong temple festival, and she knew me as a tourist and then as a journalist. Our relationship became much closer when her grandson took me to meet her again in their dark and damp hut by the Min River bank inside Songpan city. From then on, every time I visited her, she would hold my hands, offer me food, and recount to me stories about her own life and those of others—whether I asked or not. She also expected me to come back to Songpan every summer. One year she had kept a small bag of locally grown rare medicinal herbs that she had collected for me; another year she presented me with two booklets of hand-copied scriptures, saying: "I don't know how to read, but I know this is great stuff and will bring you blessings, so take them with you." Thanks to Li Popo's help, we were able to fill an important gap in Huanglong's textual history. She brought us to meet another elder woman who as a homeless young girl lived in the Rear Temple. She grew up there under the care of the then Daoist priest Yao Shanren 姚善人, who had presided over the Huanglong temple since the early 1920s, and whose tragic death during Maoist times has become a local legend, although one that is never mentioned in publications.

The Tibetan tenants of the Zhang house turned out to be some of the best friends I would make in Songpan; through them we gained a solid entry into the local Tibetan communities. The husband, Dorje, is from a Tibetan hamlet in Shar khog, the regional focus of our study. He is proud and passionate about his Bon religion and Tibetan culture. His wife, Wang Fang, is a Han who grew up in the Tibetan grassland, and therefore, is a "naturalized" Shar khog Tibetan. We had numerous conversations in the Zhang-family courtyard, over Tibetan karaoke in their living room, and at their gatherings with friends in Songpan's tea houses. Dorje introduced us to his close friend Tashi, who had a bachelor degree in Tibetan language and literature from the Northwestern University for Nationalities. The two of them served as our Tibetan interpreters in the field and translated difficult classical Tibetan texts for us. They took us to their home villages, where we met their families, friends, folklorists, as well as abbots, lamas, and monks in the local monasteries. They also brought us to many camping gatherings and on pilgrimage trips with their families and friends.

The insights we thus gained into the local Tibetan society greatly complemented what we learned from the Tibetan monastic communities I mentioned above. First, the visits to their home villages allowed us to make much better sense in both historical and geographic terms how these Tibetan hamlets have been organized around different monasteries, how during Ming, Qing, and Republican times they developed different relationships with the Chinese garrison towns, and in what ways the current tourist economy intensified the internal competitions and conflicts within these Tibetan monasteries and their communities.

Second, we already had observed that Tibetan elements were ubiquitous in the elder Han Chinese women's ritual settings and ritual activities. Certain Tibetan monasteries, such as the one I mentioned above, also served as mediators between the Han and Tibetan communities. Forming a sisterhood with Wang Fang and many of her female friends, and watching them traversing at ease across multiple linguistic, ethnic, and cultural boundaries, I came to realize at a personal level how deeply a common Songpan-regional identity, largely as a reaction to the ethnoreligious policies in force since the early PRC, has been entrenched in the everyday activities of local life cutting across ethnic and religious lines. It revealed how much the concept of "sinicization" along China's ethnic frontiers needs to be seriously questioned. Third, as Dorje's friend, I developed a different rapport with the Tibetan monks, abbots, and officials than I had with those I met on my own at the pilgrimage site. I was addressed in familial terms, Sister Kang, as I was by Zhang-family members; clearly I was no longer perceived as a foreigner nor as merely a Han Chinese woman. More often than not, my educational background and my American experiences made me an intellectual friend and resource in Dorje and Wang Fang's social circle. One of their friends, an unemployed Tibetan with a college degree, once asked me to write him a recommendation letter to support his application for a teaching job. A Hui colleague at Dorje's elementary school was curious about how math was taught in American grade schools. With Wang Fang and two of her Han and Tibetan girlfriends, I discussed interracial romances and marriages in the US, and the list of topics goes on.

In turn, I learned about local culture in the informal gatherings of this social circle: I heard about the internal conflicts among the different Tibetan Bon monasteries over the religious resources in the tourist economy; I witnessed the blunt discriminatory remarks by a Tibetan Gelugpa follower against the Bon religion—made right in front of Dorje and Tashi; and I discussed with a Tibetan county official his dual commitments, when with utmost sincerity he stated that "in my office I serve the Communist party, and at home I pray to the Dalai Lama." This county official was originally from a Tibetan hamlet neighboring Dorje's village, and the two have been friends since childhood. His hamlet was conveniently located along the tourist highway from Songpan to Huanglong. At one point in 2007, Dorje and I spent an afternoon in a tea house with this friend, who expected me to use my full intellectual power to help him brainstorm plans to lure more urban Chinese tourists to visit the mountain-top business stand his family had set up. The key was to offer "an authentic (i.e., 'exotic') Tibetan experience," ranging from decorating the site with colorful prayer banners, making offerings of barley tea and white *khatak* (Chinese: *hada* 哈達), dressing the guides in Tibetan costumes, and taking tourists on a two-hour horse-riding experience. To my amazement, I found myself participating in the local entrepreneurial production of commodifying Tibetanness—the very subject of my own scholarly critique.

Afterthoughts

When we step out of the archives, we must acknowledge that to a large extent, ethnographic materials are simultaneously shaped by who we are and what we encounter in the field. In ethnically diverse Songpan, my personal background, in terms of gender, ethnicity, as well as age and education, affected the ways in which I engaged with the local people from different backgrounds and having different agendas. This does not mean that we should value one form of engagement more than the other. We remain outsiders for some and become friends and family members for others—all for good reasons. Indeed, any of the perceived and realized social roles can open up meaningful windows into the rich textures of local life.

Whether my largely anecdotal and highly personal accounts of fieldwork could be used as a methodological guide will be for readers to decide, but I do like to use these on-the-ground experiences to draw attention to three important aspects of doing ethnography in the study of Chinese history. First, more collaboration is needed in fieldwork. As I have indicated earlier in this essay, personal differences among ethnographers in terms of their gender, ethnicity, age, and other backgrounds elicit different local reactions and place pre-existing local politics into sharper focus. Having more collaborators in the field will provide more comprehensive perspectives, much in the same way that we would collect as many different kinds of written sources as possible on a subject matter of research.

Second, ethnographic work is important in its own right, but also makes archival research more imperative. The two mutually complement each other and allow historians to make better sense of particular places. My ethnographic experiences with the Tibetan monks and in and out of the Hui mosques can only be fully understood in light of the region's long history of ethnic tension and the local reactions to current official ethnic policies—all of which have been well documented in written sources. My temple work with elderly Han women, in contrast, reveals the critical role of elder women in Chinese religious lives; their contribution has been rarely recorded in historical writings.

Third, and most important, we cannot underestimate the personal impact of ethnography beyond its original research purposes. Few of my personal stories from Songpan made it into the book Don and I wrote, but these personal experiences raised my awareness of gender and identity and opened it to such new dimensions: as a Han Chinese woman interacting with pride, prejudice, friendship, and care from Hui, Tibetan, and Han community members, or as an overseas Chinese woman scholar working in between a male Caucasian colleague and rural inhabitants of different ethnic backgrounds in China. My conversations with Dorje and Wang Fang about bilingual and bicultural education does not stop with the publication of the book: I raised my son to be fluent in both English and Mandarin, and they strive hard to teach their kids Tibetan while the only language Songpan's elementary school uses is Mandarin. The motherly love of Zhang Popo and Li Popo stays with me even after they passed away one after the other in late 2009 and early 2010. In reflecting on their lives, I cannot help but make comparisons between theirs and the life of my own mother. They are of more or less the same age, and all three lived through poverty and hardship before and during Maoist times. But my mother's urban and educated background sets her apart—especially with respect to experiences with religion and with Maoist revolutionary heritage. The comparisons spark my intellectual curiosity about the issues of women, gender, and religion during the twentieth-century Chinese revolution. This has evolved into the subject of my current project.

And, the female bonding from Songpan continues to this day, as I brought Xiaohui's embroidered slippers back home to America. They were custom made for me, and they are indeed, very comfortable.

Note: I have used pseudonyms for all the people I encountered in my fieldwork.

References and Further Readings

Fu Chongju 傅崇矩 and Zhang Dian 張典, *Songpan xianzhi* 松潘縣志. 1924.

Kang, Xiaofei, "Two Temples, Three Religions, and a Tourist Attraction: Contesting the Sacred Space on China's Ethnic Frontier." *Modern China* 35.3 (2009): 227–255.

———, "Rural Women, Old Age, and Temple Work: A Case from Northwestern Sichuan." *China Perspectives* 4 (2009): 42–52.

Kang, Xiaofei and Donald S. Sutton, *Contesting the Yellow Dragon: Ethnicity, Religion, and the State in the Sino-Tibetan Borderland.* Leiden: Brill, 2016.

Songpan xianzhi bianzuan weiyuanhui 松潘縣志編纂委員會, *Songpan xianzhi* 松潘縣志. Beijing: Minzu chubanshe, 1999.

Sutton, Donald S. and Xiaofei Kang, "Recasting Religion and Ethnicity: Tourism and Socialism in Northern Sichuan, 1992–2005." In Thomas DuBois, ed., *Casting Faiths: The Construction of Religion in East and Southeast Asia.* New York: Palgrave Macmillan, 2009: 190–214.

Zhili Songpan tingzhi 直隸松潘廳志. 1812. Comp. Wen Chenggong 溫承恭.

7 Ritual performance in changing local society

Stephen Jones

Further to my various books, my blog is full of reflections on fieldwork.[1] My work is based on the lives of ritual performers and patrons in changing modern society. Studying ritual as I do involves engagement with *performance*. So given that texts are expressed through *sound*, I consider soundscape intrinsic to ritual studies, informing the study of changing ritual practice. Other major themes in this chapter are rapport and the life stories of all kinds of participants in local ritual culture.

My ethnography of the Gaoluo village ritual association in Hebei (from 1989 to 2003) may be seen as a blueprint for my later in-depth study with the Li family Daoists in Shanxi (going back to 1991). The subject of the former was an amateur village-wide ritual group, whereas the latter are an extended occupational family of household Daoist ritual specialists; but the principles of "thick description," documenting change over a lifetime, and through participant observation, remain similar.

I tend to float between different levels—from regional to local surveys, then perhaps to a single village, or even one family. Both the wider outlines (*pucha* 普查) of general surveys, and settling into a long-term base (*dundian* 蹲点) are necessary. Thus, my study of Gaoluo drew upon our general survey of over a hundred villages in the vicinity; and my work with the Li family Daoists was based on long-term explorations in Yanggao county and elsewhere in north Shanxi. Since 2005, taking the Li family on tour in Europe has not only enabled me to continue my studies with them, but has also allowed me to observe our relationship in another context.

Background

Amidst the substantial methodological literature, I am inspired by the "thick description" of Clifford Geertz, and by Bruce Jackson's brilliant *Fieldwork*. Bruno Nettl's *The Study of Ethnomusicology: Thirty-one Issues and Concepts* is essential reading for performance. Ethnographies from nearer home can be stimulating, such as (for Western art music) Christopher Small's *Musicking*.

Almost anything can be fieldwork, such as talking to your mum, or your kids, or going clubbing—although we're unlikely to undertake all three at the same time. But I refer here to spending time with Chinese people in the countryside, which requires a rather different set of skills from hanging out with rock musicians in Beijing, for instance.

Fieldwork by Chinese scholars has a long history, but has thrived since the 1980s. Plenty of Chinese ethnographers are doing great work, not least my long-term colleagues Xue Yibing and Zhang Zhentao. They are much better equipped than me for such work.

In those early days after the 1980s' reforms, Chinese musical fieldwork was rather mechanical: the main object was to collect material in the form of musical pieces, conceived of as rather fixed and detached from changing social context. Foreign scholars like Antoinet Schimmelpenninck were at the forefront of broadening the subject; her inclusion of the performers in the frame has borne fruit in Chinese and foreign work.

Local cultural workers were previously valuable sources, but more recently the influence of the Intangible Cultural Heritage project has had a damaging effect on serious scholarship. So when you arrive in a county-town in China in search of leads to ritual activity in the area, far more promising than becoming ensnared at the Bureau of Culture is to visit the funeral shops. Some shops are actually run by household Daoists; but whoever runs them, they all have close contacts with both ritual specialists and shawm bands, as well as geomancers, cooks, grave-diggers, and so on. They can soon tell you where to find the best bands, and when funerals are coming up. All this makes platitudinous banquets with local cultural officials pleasantly superfluous.

Rapport

A lot has been written about personal interaction in fieldwork, though less for China. We all have different personalities; some of us may seem more outgoing than others. It is an unfair accident of birth and upbringing. Musicians will be more forthcoming with people they feel comfortable with. Of course, fieldwork manuals talk about good *guanxi*, but it's more. We respect people that we talk to, but we also aspire to some sort of equality, hoping to be neither obsequious nor superior. On the agenda here are sociability, informality, enthusiasm, empathy, and humor—all without naivety or romanticism! We do naturally adapt our behavior to different situations—I'm much more sociable in China than in my native England. Fieldwork may be an unending amount of work, but it's endless inspiration too: and one works better when inspired.

I do bear in mind Nigel Barley's warning (*The innocent anthropologist*, 56):

> Much nonsense has been written, by people who should know better, about the anthropologist being "accepted." It is sometimes suggested that an alien people will somehow come to view the visitor of distinct race and culture as in every way similar to the locals. This is, alas,

unlikely. The best one can probably hope for is to be viewed as a harmless idiot who brings certain advantages to this village.

By the way, I'm not a harmless idiot, I often feel like a harm*ful* idiot: I hope it's a coincidence that everywhere I go, the local traditions go down the drain…

Our ways of repaying all this hospitality are variable, depending on our means and inclinations. One may send photos and videos to one's hosts, and organize tours. Chinese colleagues have gone so far as to install running water for them or find urban jobs for their relatives.

Obviously, a brief interview with a stranger is likely to yield less interesting or reliable results than long-term acquaintance. But I do take on board the notion of stranger value. On the one hand (Jackson, *Fieldwork*, 69–70, after Goldstein),

> The collector who comes from afar and will disappear again will be able to collect materials and information which might not be divulged to one who has a long-term residence in the same area.

On the other hand, there's the local insider's assumption that "You will never understand this music" (Nettl, *Ethnomusicology*, ch. 11). "Stranger value" wouldn't apply if a middle-aged English academic were to descend on a bunch of Newcastle punks; they would quite rightly tell me to get lost—although possibly not in those precise words. Chinese villagers are more hospitable.

And then, who is an insider? What of urban Chinese? How might an urban-educated male Fujianese get along with female spirit mediums in rural Shanxi?

Chinese fieldworkers

Over my three decades of doing fieldwork in China, the nature of the equipment we use, and fieldworkers themselves, has changed just as much as our objects of study and the rest of the population—of course just like anywhere else, and over earlier periods of ethnographic history.

Wonderful fieldwork in the 1950s, led by scholars such as Yang Yinliu, was undertaken with very limited resources. Through the 1990s, when my trusty fieldwork companion Xue Yibing and I went on long fieldtrips together, I used to show up at Beijing train station with a heavy bag full of audio and video tapes, dozens of films for my camera, a bulky array of batteries and chargers, and even a few spare clothes—besides my heavy equipment bag with a camera, a camcorder, a tape recorder, leads, and so on. And even that was very modest compared with the lists advised by some earnest ethnomusicologists, giving an inventory that would be the envy of a major military invasion force.

Meanwhile, Xue Yibing just brought a slim shoulder-bag containing only his little notebook, a biro, and a toothbrush. Out of all our combined equipment, it was his notebook that would turn out to be most precious.

Sometimes—not always—we managed to hire a clapped-out old minivan. To find ritual activity, we just had to "go down" to the villages and hope. Not only were there no smartphones, very few villages even had a landline. As soon as we "went down," we were cut off from all contact with the outside world.

Fast-forward to the last few years when young Chinese fieldworkers take an array of high-class audio and video equipment, laptops, and smartphones, with which few foreign scholars of their age can now compete. Smartphones give fieldworkers instant access to all kinds of information—one could virtually do everything, including taking photos and recordings, with just a phone. Chinese fieldworkers often drive impressive, robust off-road vehicles, with GPS to help them navigate and find villages. The road network is vastly improved; local tracks may still be very basic, but motorways have expanded a lot. And among these young music fieldworkers, women are now in a clear majority. Chinese students also now have some grounding in international ethnomusicology. Fieldworkers change, just like their objects of study.

Recently on Twitter, an urban Chinese labor activist responded to my post on village ritual with a succinct and intriguing reaction: "I don't like local Chinese rural customs!" "Well, tough!," I wanted to respond. But actually it highlights an important issue: the alienation of educated urbanites from rural life. Rural customs are what rural dwellers *do*; it's hard to belittle the former without rejecting the latter. This feeling that Chinese tradition is "backward" dates back well before the twentieth century, despite the efforts of Chinese folklorists since the 1920s.

Today those older urbanites who endured banishment to impoverished villages under Maoism have good reason to feel ambivalent about rural culture. My splendid Beijing fieldworker friends have some painful memories—starving in Shandong around 1960, witnessing colleagues being crushed to death in dangerous mines in Gansu in the Cultural Revolution. For our local assistants, the countryside may have even more direct associations: I sometimes found myself taking them back to the very villages where they had taken part in "tempering through manual labour" during the Four Cleanups campaigns of the early 1960s. From bitter personal experience, these people have no reason to idealize rural life. Thankfully, the bright new generation of Chinese fieldworkers have been spared such sufferings—though this also makes it harder for them to empathize with the life stories of our village hosts.

So as our fieldwork in Hebei and Shanxi took off in the 1990s, my friends must have felt as if they were being dragged back into "going down to the countryside to join in the brigade." But it wasn't me who was dragging them—I was *following* them—and they too were following in the footsteps of previous generations of intrepid Chinese fieldworkers. We were all aware of the phrase attributed to Confucius, no less: "When the rites are lost, seek them throughout the countryside" (*li shi qiu zhuye* 礼失求诸野).

Occasional forays were all very well, but I began to feel the need for longer stays. For me—safely armed with my passport and return air-ticket—sleeping on the *kang* brick-bed of my wonderful host Cai An in Gaoluo, fetching water from the well, slurping noodles with *doufu* and cabbage from chipped bowls at funerals, and even visiting the latrine by the pigsty, still had a certain exotic *frisson*.

While my Chinese friends shared my excitement at discovering such a wealth of material on ritual life in society, their other consolation was that this new rural exile was (semi-) voluntary—and that there was a clear time-limit on it. In those days, their living conditions in the dilapidated Music Research Institute in Beijing were far less comfortable than they were later to become, with the huge improvement in living standards and their own growing reputation. But apart from the demands on their time in Beijing, they might find more extended stays somewhat beyond the call of duty. Still, these fieldworkers entered the fray with spirit, and the fruits of their labors are outstanding.

Younger city folk may not have had to endure rural life like their elders. But steeped in pop music and video games, when they are dragged back to the poor countryside to attend the funeral of a grandparent, they too may find village customs irrevocably tainted by poverty and backwardness. Moreover, apart from those duped by the media into regarding folk culture as a theme park, younger city folk—not least those bravely seeking social justice—have been further alienated by rosy state cultural propaganda.

But ethnographers don't have to be misguided mouthpieces for official patriotism. Our job is not to *praise* rural life, but to truthfully *document* it, without romanticizing it as some ideal "living fossil" of an illusory golden age. Along with any grandeur that pundits may impute to ritual in rural China, there also belong power struggles, violence, the plight of women and blind outcast shawm players, and all kinds of tribulations under imperial, Maoist, and other modern regimes. And when studying folk culture, it is worth noting the alienation of younger urban dwellers from it. Indeed, just as I'm not naturally a great admirer of English Morris dancing, getting to know a little about it reveals how it fits into the changing social culture of rural England. However, rapidly the Chinese rural population has been diminishing since the 1980s, documenting rural life remains just as important as studying urbanites—of all kinds and classes, including the workers' struggle and their expressive culture.

That said, descriptive ethnography doesn't necessarily imply standing aside entirely from judgment. Now, as it happens I do admire many aspects of village ritual, but that's not the point. More adventurous fieldworkers (like De Martino in post-war south Italy) may seek to spell out some respects in which ritual is life-enhancing, offering consolation and cohesion;

or, conversely, ways in which it serves to entrench delusion and conflict, or fortify irrational power. Or—quite likely—they may entertain both hypotheses at once. Both need to be tested, not assumed. So to that underwhelmed Chinese activist on Twitter, I might say, as the great Tsinghua University-based anthropologist Guo Yuhua can tell you,[2] far from obstructing the quest for social justice, ethnography can be a contribution to it. Apart from urban workers, if anyone has been downtrodden, it is the peasantry.

The official version may seek to reify and sanitize culture, yet factory workers, household Daoists, women, village cadres, spirit mediums, army recruits, sectarians, vagrants, and entrepreneurs are all part of the social spectrum, and their lives deserve to be documented.[3] But we have to be with them. I note some handy Maoist clichés that have relevance for fieldwork:

- *chiku* 吃苦 "eating bitterness."
- *santong* 三同 "the three togethers" (eating, living, and laboring together).
- *dundian* 蹲点 ("squat"; more generously defined in my dictionary as *"stay at a selected grass-roots unit to help improve its work and gain first-hand experience for guiding overall work"*).
- *gen qunzhong dacheng yipian* 跟群众打成一片 "becoming at one with the masses." I'm always struck by the irony of hanging out with Chinese peasants whose whole life-experience and world-view are totally different from my own.
- *buna qunzhong yizhenyixian* 不拿群众一针一线 "not taking a single needle or thread from the masses."

My point here is to get over the empty formalism of such slogans and see through to the sincere humanity that once inspired them.

I was wont to keep my head shaved even before I began doing fieldwork in China. But since the older generation of peasants in north China tend to do so (mainly for the sake of hygiene), I emulate them while I'm there. Early in the course of my long-term work with the ritual association of Gaoluo, one demonstration of our developing relationship was my decision to have my hair cut in the village. I later wrote (*Plucking the winds*, pp. 205–6):

> I admired the closely cropped heads of many of the musicians, and tend to do without much hair in the summer myself. He Junqi (then 54), a regular visitor to He Qing's house, son of the sweet elderly flautist He Yi, used to cut the musicians' hair for them, so I asked him if he'd like to do mine. Everyone stood round having a good laugh, while He Junqi gave me the most meticulous haircut and shave of my life, scouring my scalp with local "White Cat" washing-powder.

I think we all use teamwork to some extent, finding good regional and local scholars to work with—and perhaps supporting their own work. I have always relied heavily on my Beijing colleagues to make notes, at least until circumstance and greater familiarity lend me the confidence to spend time with villagers on my own.

A small fieldwork team may be good up to a point. It depends partly on one's means, but the group perhaps shouldn't be too large. I like the informality and flexibility of working alone, but it is a bit much to take photos and videos and make notes and distribute cigarettes all at once. I'm still very attached to the detailed notes of my Chinese colleagues. For me, fieldwork is a constant discovery of how inaccurate and superficial my previous notes were.

As to time-frame, repeated visits over a long period are valuable, such as Friedman, Pickowicz, and Selden's work in Raoyang, or my own on Gaoluo and with the Li family in Yanggao.

Ethnography and Daoism

The personal accounts of biography and thick descriptions of ethnography have flourished for all kinds of Chinese people—factory workers, villagers, vagrants, cadres, and so on. We have some fine studies of local figures in modern rural China, including ritual organizers and musicians. Beneath the broad umbrella of Chinese ethnography, religion in reform-era China has become a lively topic, with studies of all kinds of religious practitioners and groups.

Field reports on local Daoist ritual groups have multiplied since the 1980s, and constantly amaze me in their detail. Still, many of the authors were trained quickly in a fine if rigid template. The template is impeccable as far as it goes, but unless used judiciously it may result merely in long inventories that discourage nuance.

In total contrast with ritual itself, both ritual manuals and scholarly publications are silent and inanimate. One can't record everything on audio or video (and even if we could, using media without text would leave unclear how many of the Chinese characters should be written). I used to use video mainly to film ritual—only later did I begin to record informal situations. Documenting ritual in video is no easy task, but to do so on paper alone is still more of a challenge. While many scholars use video, very few edited films have been published. My 2015 film on the Li family Daoists complements my 2016 book, and both are updated on my blog.[4]

The main agenda of most projects on local Daoist ritual is the collecting of manuscripts, not human context or social change. To take a book out of the library you don't have to get to know the librarian, one might say. This agenda yields fine results within its own archeological terms; but what it *isn't* is ethnography. Concerned largely with salvage, such studies tend to convey a rather timeless image; only the very occasional sentence suggests that any social (or indeed ritual) changes may have occurred since the nineteenth century.

So, just as for any social group, and practitioners of any religious affiliation, the current lives of Daoists (of all types) deserve study. Since even ethnographers of modern religion may hesitate to enter a field that demands such highly specialized training, one might suppose that the first to tackle the subject would be the scholars of Daoism. But with their sinological expertise in such arcane arts being so very hard-earned, the weight of scholarship on early Daoist texts tends to dominate their energy at the expense of modern social history. To a mindset that seeks the ancient, the complex, and the mystical, it may seem irrelevant to document twentieth-century change. Thus, the vast body of reports on local Daoist traditions, devoid largely of context, may appear as an autonomous zone fated to remain adrift from wider fields of inquiry. As Vincent Goossaert observes, "I believe there cannot be a history of Daoism without the Daoists—all of them." While a few scholars have taken up the story of modern local temple Daoists, studies of household Daoists from this perspective are still sadly lacking. Context, whether ancient or modern, is in short supply in Daoist ritual studies. All the laborious spadework of documenting texts is admirable and necessary, but it is only one aspect of the task confronting us. Indeed, the ethnographer and even the historian might go further. Context doesn't have to be subsidiary to written or even oral text; one might consider it as the main topic, the text merely one of its subsidiary manifestations.

Ethnographic fieldwork spans time, embracing not just contemporary observation but also oral history going back at least several decades, and indeed the collection of historical artifacts. Yet despite all the voluminous field reports on household Daoist groups, details on their changing social lives and ritual practices since 1949 are sparse. Such field studies are hardly of a type that anthropologists would recognize as ethnography. The whole enterprise was made possible by observing ritual and collecting material in the field, but it still tends to focus on salvage; even the oral history there usually refers to recollections of the period *before* 1949. Salvage may indeed be a valuable aspect of fieldwork. But a focus on recreating former glories tends to downplay modern change. Chinese musicology also still remains prone to the "living fossils" craze that was rife in the 1980s, with fieldwork often seeking to glorify the majesty of early Chinese culture.

Globally, some of the most thoughtful reflections on the tension between preservation and the documenting of social change, and about fieldwork on the past, are now found in music studies. It has long been the norm to discover "endangered" traditions, so we should get used to it. A ritual observed and described, or even a ritual manual, cannot exist outside of context. Of course, all this is a universal issue. Histories of Christianity in medieval England will naturally differ from an ethnography of parish activities there in the 1980s, even if many of their ancient texts may be similar. It is reasonable to visit an English village church today with a view to collecting material to reconstruct the medieval liturgical scene there; an account of *current* religious life there would probably come from a different type of scholar. Bach scholars can do fine work on Leipzig church life in the 1730s without studying Bach as performed in churches and concert halls since the 1950s.

In the 1940s, Grootaers' project documenting "cultic buildings" around the peripheries of Yanggao was ambitious enough without further describing ritual life at the time.

One may document all kinds of detail. Even within the traditional musicology of Western art music, the watermarks on Bach manuscripts, the layout of his house, and his tribulations with patrons and fellow-musicians are all illuminating aspects of Bach scholarship. Ethnomusicologists have long widened their focus from the "great composers" to everyday musical life in a broad range of societies, even incorporating the modern social history of Western art music into the picture.

Meanwhile, scholars of Daoist ritual have remained keener to document the nitty-gritty of Song-dynasty texts than to describe the details of current performance practice within a society in change. But having gone all that way and gotten our feet dirty, it may seem eccentric to engage only in salvage, while not documenting the situation under our noses—especially when we know so little about it, and since it can provide by far the most detailed material. I might not argue with a division of labor, but at present most research speaks almost entirely to previous eras without the benefit of modern observation.

Unpacking "Daoist music," and participant observation

As I explained above, my subject is Daoist ritual, not "Daoist music." The texts of Daoist ritual are never read silently; they are performed aloud, and never in ordinary speech mode. So if we wish to understand Daoist ritual, it is not enough just to write about the ancient origins of the texts on the page; we have no choice but to address performance and sound—they are intrinsic. One might even suggest that the texts studied by scholars of Daoist ritual hardly have any real existence outside their sound. We may read ritual manuals, analyze doctrine therein, and so on, but these texts exist to be performed. The main medium through which they are performed is sound, and the sounds by which they are communicated are largely "musical." That's why we need films, too.

The content and structure of ritual manuals rarely yield clear clues as to how to perform them: whether sung slowly, recited, chanted fast, solo or tutti, and so on. On a practical level, when we consult a silent manual surely it is worth knowing that it takes less time to whip through a long prose passage of several pages than to sing a slow melismatic hymn of only five couplets.

Oral aspects of transmission are important. The melodies of the Li family's vocal liturgy were never notated until local scholars, and Li Qing, did so in the 1980s. Even their texts, contained in ritual manuals, were rarely consulted. By contrast, the percussion patterns and the melodies for *shengguan* melodic instrumental ensemble have long been notated. But as with the vocal texts, this was merely as an aid to memory, and again some Daoists would learn both mainly orally. One point of such study is to reveal the technical complexities of what Daoists have to do, apart from any doctrinal elements. This also reveals subtle changes in ritual performance practice over a lifetime.

Participant observation

The emphasis on performance leads us to another tenet of ethnography: participant observation. It is a routine expectation in ethnomusicology, but still virtually unknown either in Chinese musicology or in studies of Chinese ritual.

I've made laughable attempts to learn the wild music of shawm bands in Shanxi and Shaanbei, and the more stately music of the Gaoluo ritual association; and I've become an occasional deputy with the Li family Daoists (when they're desperate!). For Daoist ritual, the early leads of Kristofer Schipper and Michael Saso have hardly been followed—and only partly because scholarly visits, however frequent, are mostly brief.

Without necessarily demanding a thorough training, there are significant benefits to taking part in ritual performance and acquiring as much basic practical familiarity as one can. Doing so shows a willingness to engage and also helps us think up useful questions. However, inept my own attempts, they have been a great help in documenting ritual detail—performance, not just texts—as in my accounts of the Presenting Offerings and Invitation ritual segments (*Daoist priests*, 208–9, 264, 298–307). Thus, to learn the basics of singing the hymns, noting repeated phrases not shown in the manuals, the syncopated cadences on percussion, and the way that interludes for the large cymbals dovetail with the verses gives us insights into how Daoist ritual actually works, and what is involved in learning to be a Daoist.[5]

The 1949 barrier

Though historians always study change, some sinologists consider modern change to be terminally radical and destructive. But in the case of Daoist ritual, for instance, such a rationale seems paltry when all take pride in the enrichment of the database by observing recent material. Only current ethnography will yield thick description.

The supposed decline of Daoism has been lamented regularly throughout history. Regular upheavals have occurred. We may regard them as brief interruptions with no long-term assaults on ideology; but now that we witness the enduring energy of religious activity today, the Maoist era too may look like another temporary crisis. Daoists continue to adapt to society and negotiate new challenges as they always have done.

Even historians mainly concerned with recreating the pre-1949 ritual scene rely heavily on recent material—the whole impetus behind the new discoveries is visiting Daoists and observing their rituals. But such reports provide little context, tending to refrain from describing social or ritual change since the 1940s—which happens to be the most detailed material available to us, right before our eyes and ears.

If we are all "blind people groping at the elephant," there is indeed an elephant in the room: self-censorship. For many years, both in China and abroad, anthropologists (not to mention modern historians and the media) have been documenting the Maoist and reform eras with a certain candor, pushing back old boundaries. There are some fine Chinese projects on the oral history of Maoism, such as those of Guo Yuhua and Wu Wenguang. But this has been slow to filter down to the other humanities and to local society.

Religious practice since 1949—whether savagely repressed or tacitly maintained—still appears to be a sensitive issue. Ironically, modern history is not entirely about political campaigns; general social and economic trends also need discussion, but they too are casualties of this taboo mentality. But such idealization of both present and past feeds into the rose-tinted patriotic subtext of recent cultural heritage projects. It is not only religion that is sensitive. When discussing with Chinese colleagues about the lack of detail on modern history in reports on local folk culture, one often hears the riposte "Everyone knows what happened since 1949—there's no need to discuss it." Such a conspiracy of silence is both erroneous and dangerous, repressing memory.

Thus, I seek not a normative reconstruction of some timeless ancient wisdom, but a descriptive account of ritual life within changing modern society. We should neither dismiss the present by seeking "living fossils" nor romanticize it by ignoring change. Fieldwork reveals the limitations of what historical sources can teach us, prompting questions that might otherwise never arise. We should not be reluctant to describe the subtle changes wrought since around 2000 by migration, mobiles and motor-bikes; or fees, the pool of disciples, degrees of expertise within a band, flexibility in choice of ritual segments and texts, the changing discrimination of patrons, and so on. While hoping to recreate as much of the past as possible, we should avoid privileging it. I try to show what it is, and was, like to be a village Daoist—now, under Maoism, and before the revolution.

One example of the fruits of fieldwork is the 1942 temple stele that we found bearing the names of Li Manshan's forebears. Supposing that someone like Grootaers had found the temple (which is rather remote from any village) at the time, they would be most unlikely either to notice those five names near the foot of the stele or to identify them as a group of household Daoists. Even supposing they did somehow learn all this, the information would mean little without being able to trace the position of the lineage at the time and how they practice today—knowing about Li Qing, his son Li Manshan, and the latter's son Li Bin, learning their life stories, their ritual practices, and so on. We can hardly expect historical sources from earlier centuries to provide such rich information.

In Daoism, fieldwork allows us to overturn naïve assumptions about Quanzhen and Zhengyi branches, which can no longer be seen as a simple temple–folk dichotomy.[6]

Questionnaires, language, and diaries

Various templates have been published, from the 1964 *Minjian yinyue caifang shouce* 间音乐采访手册 (for music) to more recent lists for Daoist ritual. One will have one's own working list, which should be updated daily. Always consider the answers! They should give rise to further questions not on our original list; one must always be flexible, following the flow of the conversation, and *listening*. One hopes to prompt people to talk at length—so avoid questions that invite simple Yes/No replies! As I commented (*Daoist priests of the Li family*, pp. 33–4):

> We have to learn to latch onto troublesome terms like "in the past" (*guoqu*) or "originally" (*yuanxian*). I'm getting better at leaping in and asking, "You mean in the 1980s? Or before the Cultural Revolution?" or even more precisely, "Before the 1964 Four Cleanups, or before Li Qing went to Datong in 1958? Or before Liberation? Under the Japanese?" Even the seemingly mechanical task of eliciting dates requires imagination. Though not necessarily clear on dates, they may recall how old they were the last time they performed such and such a ritual, or we may ask questions like "Was Li Peisen still alive?" or "Before your first son was born?"
>
> One day, admiring the trendy outfit that Li Manshan's second daughter Li Min has bought for her young son, I observe, "Funny, in the past one never had to worry about fashion for kids' clothing, either in China or England!" She has an astute come-back: "How do you mean, 'in the past'?!" Me: "Ha—that's what I'm always asking your dad!" Hoist on my own petard.

Consider how to translate questions conceived from the comfort of one's home into a language suitable to the local context.[7] One aspect of respecting our local hosts, and "abiding by local customs" (*ruxiang suisu* 入乡随俗), is that fieldworkers should be careful not to inflict their educated vocabulary on locals. You wouldn't use academic language in talking to old-time musicians in Kentucky—even if they may understand it, or even adopt it temporarily for our benefit. Vocabulary reflects world-view, so we should try and latch onto it.

Some terms are just a matter of basic fluency: one never "plays" (*yanzou* 演奏) instruments, for example, but (according to their means of sound production) one blows (*chui* 吹), beats (*da* 打), bows (*la* 拉), or plucks (*tan* 弹) them. In Yanggao, the often-used term *kabulei* ("fantastic") would be *kebulai* in standard Chinese, but *bucuo* is the standard urban version. I like *duohuir* ("When?"), more classically economical than the cumbersome standard *shenme shihou*. Tradition ("*chuantong*" 传统) is *lao guiju* 老规矩.

Of course it would be silly to try and go native; we can only retain our personality. But little efforts to adapt to our mentors' world-view pay dividends. Often we will seek a more idiomatic way of expressing our own scholarly vocabulary. In my blog post I give some random examples from my fieldwork experience in ritual and musical life, mainly in north China. Few terms can be applied casually across the board: precisely because they are local, one can't even expect to use a Shaanbei term for spirit medium in north Shanxi—still less in Guangxi or Fujian.

Thus, folk ritual groups are not tuan 团, but *ban* 班, *she* 社, *hui* 会, *tang* 堂, *tan* 坛; their "performance" is not *yanchu* 演出 or *biaoyan* 表演 but *yingmenshi* 应门事 (responding to household ritual), *songjing* 送经 (escorting the scriptures), or *chuhui* 出会 (going out as an association). Ritual specialists (in our weird language, *yishi zhixingren* 仪式执行人!) may be *fashi* 法师, *shigong* 师公, *zhangjiaode* 掌教的; a folk Daoist (rarely "*daoshi* 道士") may be *laodao* 老道, *yinyang* 阴阳, *erzhai* 二宅, and so on; spirit mediums are not *shenpo* 神婆/*shenhan* 神汉 but *daxian* 大仙, *xiangtou* 香头, *matong* 马童, *shen guan* 神官, *dingshende* 顶神的, and so on.

For ritual manuals, I never hear *keyiben* 科仪本 in the north, only *jingshu* 经书, *jingben* 经本, *jingjuan* 经卷, or just *shu* 书. Percussion is not *dajiyue* 打击乐 but *faqi* 法器, *jiahuo* 家伙, *xiangqi* 响器, and so on.

An instructive method is to ask our hosts to compile a diary of their activities (*Daoist priests*, 18–21). On my blog, my diary of our 2017 French tour makes a nice contrast with Li Bin's hectic ritual schedule back home since their return.[8]

Talking of emic/etic enquiry, here's a vignette from the Li band's 2012 tour of Italy (Daoist priests, p. 336):

> Third Tiger is as curious as ever, always asking weird "etic" questions like "Why are Italian number-plates smaller at the front than at the back?" Bemused, I later ask several Italian friends, who have never noticed either. It strikes me that this is probably just the kind of abstruse question that we fieldworkers ask all the time, and I'm sure my enquiries in Yanggao sound just as fatuous. I must cite Nigel Barley (*The innocent anthropologist*, p. 82):

> They missed out the essential piece of information that made things comprehensible. No one told me that the village was where the Master of the Earth, the man who controlled the fertility of all plants, lived, and that consequently various parts of the ceremony would be different from elsewhere. This was fair enough; some things are too obvious to mention. If we were explaining to a Dowayo how to drive a car, we should tell him all sorts of things about gears and road signs before mentioning that one tried not to hit other cars.

In sum, while engaging fully with ritual texts and performance, my work with the Li family suggests a less compartmentalized, more humane context-based model for Chinese ritual studies; an interest in people's lives and life stories, thick description, and even modest participant observation will all bear fruit.

Notes

1. https://stephenjones.blog/category/fieldwork/. This article is also based on Appendix 1 of my book *Daoist priests of the Li family*, where you can find further references.
2. https://stephenjones.blog/2018/06/19/guo-yuhua/
3. https://stephenjones.blog/2018/08/26/yanggao-personalities/
4. See, for example, the whole series of field reports from March 2018: links here https://stephenjones.blog/2018/04/16/home-with-master-daoist/
5. https://stephenjones.blog/participant-observation/
6. https://stephenjones.blog/zhengyi-and-quanzhen/
7. https://stephenjones.blog/2017/03/17/vocabularies-educated-and-local/
8. https://stephenjones.blog/2017/05/27/the-li-band-in-france-notes/, https://stephenjones.blog/2017/08/21/daoist-diary/

Further Reading

Barley, Nigel. *The innocent anthropologist: notes from a mud hut*. London: Penguin, 1983.
Friedman, Edward, Paul Pickowicz, and Mark Selden. *Chinese village, socialist state*. New Haven: Yale University Press, 1991.
———. *Revolution, resistance, and reform in village China*. New Haven: Yale University Press, 2005.
Guo Yuhua 郭于华. *Shoukurende jiangshu: Jicun lishi yu yizhong wenming de luoji* 受苦人的讲述：与一种文明的逻辑 [Narratives of the sufferers: the history of Jicun and the logic of civilization]. Hong Kong: Chinese University Press, 2013.
Jackson, Bruce. *Fieldwork*. Urbana: University of Illinois Press, 1987.
Jones, Stephen. *Plucking the winds: lives of village musicians in old and new China*. Leiden: CHIME Foundation. With CD. 2004.
———. *Ritual and music of north China: shawm bands in Shanxi*. Aldershot: Ashgate. With DVD, 2007.
———. *Ritual and music of north China, volume 2: Shaanbei*. Aldershot: Ashgate. With DVD, 2009.
———. *In search of the folk Daoists of north China*. Aldershot: Ashgate, 2010.
———. *Li Manshan: portrait of a folk Daoist*. 82-minute film. Edited by Michele Banal, 2015. https://stephenjones.blog/the-film/
———. *Daoist priests of the Li family: ritual life in village China*, St. Petersburg, FL: Three Pines Press, 2016.
Nettl, Bruno. *The study of ethnomusicology: thirty-three discussions*. Urbana: University of Illinois Press, 2015.
Small, Christopher. *Musicking: the meanings of performance and listening*. Hanover: University Press of New England, 1998.

8 Beyond the border of disciplines and societies
From fieldwork among the Lahu to the history of *bazi* basins

Jianxiong Ma

China's southwestern Yunnan province is known for its rugged highland terrain, challenging transportation routes, rich local cultures, ethnic minorities, and frontier setting. The region's natives are well familiar with their province's complex ethnic relationships, diverse languages, and religious beliefs. Having grown up in Dali 大理 in the west of the province, my interests were shaped by this multicultural environment. The summer after I graduated from Yunnan University, I had a chance to visit the Chinese reaches of the Salween River valley with one of my teachers, Professor Xiao Ying 肖迎, to study the history of local Lisu 傈僳 communities. This experience conducting on-site investigation convinced me to pursue an academic career in anthropology. In 1994, I entered the ethnography program at Yunnan Nationalities University, under the supervision of Professor Huang Huikun 黄惠锟, a historian of the Dai 傣, who had been the secretary of the director of the provincial Nationality Affairs Office, and later became the vice president of our university. He approved and supported my fieldwork plan, and offered helpful advice on doing field work among the Lahu 拉祜. The following year, I started my fieldwork at Ban village 班村 among the Lahu in Lancang 澜沧 Lahu Autonomous County on the Yunnan-Myanmar border. This village has since been my fieldwork site for more than 20 years. I return to Ban village regularly every year to visit friends, and study changes in the everyday lives of my Lahu informants. Through long-term fieldwork, I have gradually learned how to observe, describe and study local life from an anthropological perspective.

I also came to realize that in a huge, diverse, and historically rich society like China, macrocontexts must be considered in combination with the specific mechanisms of cultural and social change in individual communities. As an anthropologist, I pursue questions that relate to the unity and the diversity of human societies, and seek to understand the process behind the dynamic meanings of social relations and social agency. As a historian, I show how these questions and meanings change over time. But ultimately, my research concerns emerge less from disciplines than from my personal experience of conducting fieldwork, and from my interest in historical change along the frontier between China and Southeast Asia.

Fieldwork in a Lahu village and the history of frontier society

In order to conduct anthropological field work, I lived in Ban village with an informant family, learned Lahu language with the villagers, and participated in the daily activities of my friends. I shared such tasks as cutting firewood, herding cattle, and working in the fields, all the while keeping notes. Social activities, such as building grass houses, as well as weddings, funerals, and healing rituals, were all important opportunities to learn with my informants. I recorded names of heads of families, their genealogies, kinship ties, religious beliefs and rituals, festivals, as well as the location of farms, irrigation ditches, markets, notable localities, and places of migration. Only a small portion of this information was actually used in my dissertation. I continued to conduct fieldwork during my doctoral studies at the Hong Kong University of Science and Technology, spending another nine months at Ban village in 2004–2005 and noting the many changes over the years. I still return at least once a year to stay for few days or weeks, and value my good friendships with my friends in the village.

Along with this long-term anthropological fieldwork, I sought out historical sources at the townships of Lancang County and recorded oral histories of the social changes that people have experienced. As historical participants, these informants shared memories that became very helpful to my understanding of local society and the social-political changes that have occurred since the 1940s. However, such accounts must be closely cross-checked against many others if we are to reconstruct an accurate version of local historical events. In some cases, I recorded my informants' oral histories numerous times in different living contexts, then scoured local archives at township, county, city, and provincial levels. I was fortunate to find large amounts of archival material that related well to what I had learned from my informants. These included data about households and family members, farm land records, implementation of government policies, and reports sent by local cadres to higher leaders.

I consider local archives to be of two types: (1) original archives from official bureaus, including meeting records, investigation records, government papers, and official statistical data and (2) collections of local publications, including contemporary gazetteers, collections of cultural materials (*wenshi ziliao* 文史资料), publications by local Literary and Art Circles (*wenlian* 文联), yearbooks, government annual reports, and publications by the local Party History Office (*dangshi ban* 党史办). In the process of collecting these materials, one can also form personal connections and friendships with local scholars, cadres, and historians. Such local intellectuals are key informants, facilitators, and guides, who can explain their thoughts and choices made in the way they construct their narratives of local history. Moreover, they are quite often important social agents in local affairs. Our research frequently starts from these local connections with native historians, and over the long term, becomes an ongoing exchange and dialogue with them.

Since I was both a student and a local, the staff at the official archives were especially willing to help me to locate the material I needed. While not everyone will be in such an advantageous position, it is still worth investing the time to build personal connections and friendships. With the villagers as well, if I visited them frequently, they viewed me as trustworthy and helpful. Through these experiences, I gained greater appreciation of the complexity of social relations, and how this understanding could be deepened by participation in the local community. In the process, I recognized that as an anthropologist, I also had to understand and explain the relationship between historical facts and historical interpretation, since a local historical narrative takes shape gradually as the people there come to understand and interpret the same past that is documented in records, publications, stories, or rituals. With this in mind, I aim to place what we learned from historical documents into the context of actual individual lives, experiences that unfolded amid the course of social-political change. In this way, I could learn how to grasp the dynamic and diverse possibilities of social change and cultural values behind people's interpretations of history.

Understanding local history

In 1948, a group of Chinese Communist Party members, who had been part of the overseas party branch in Bangkok, returned to Yunnan and established a Chinese Communist Party (CCP)-led guerrilla group among the ethnic minorities, and a People's Government at Menglian 孟连 County. I sought to understand how this local CCP government became established at the frontier, and how its policies on minority affairs related to Land Reform and to the policies of the Yunnan provincial Committee of Frontier and Minority Affairs after 1953. After I worked out a basic outline of historical events, the next step was to seek interviews to record life histories of important officials and villagers who had experienced these events. I later checked these stories against archival records of meetings, battles, social movements, and the formation of local autonomous county governments. Finally, I assembled all of these historical accounts, documents, and memories into a larger narrative about land policy and construction of local political authority.

My next task was to understand how these policies affected cultural and social ties in terms of collective labor and kinship ties. One cannot separate local society from broader historical transformations related to labor cooperation, land property succession. The process of policy-making was intimately tied to the everyday views and social change among ethnic minorities on the frontier. Because Land Reform was not carried out in this frontier region, ownership of land remained with individual families, meaning that people in Ban village people were uniquely able to transform kinship groups into production teams (生产队). When in the 1980s, the People's Communes were abolished and the Household Responsibility system reform was launched in the Lahu area, private land ownership was returned to individual families very quickly, earlier than in the rest of the province, demonstrating the resilience of social cooperation based on ties of marriage, kinship, and residence. This finding is important because it shows that the Communist Revolution and the establishment of a new government did not, despite the hiatus of the 1958–1980 period, fundamentally alter Lahu social ties related to farming land property rights.

Ritual in local context

Since the mid-1990s, minority communities on the southwest frontier have, despite the protections of the ethnic autonomous region system, remained under the shadow of financial policies that made county governments dependent on financial subsidies and special poverty relief resources distributed by the central and provincial governments. Local political elites, especially the powerful cadres that came from influential Han Chinese families, gradually came to control the channels and opportunities for gaining these resources. The politics of poverty relief and infrastructure building projects thereby became the basic mechanism to link local communities with the state. Yet this policy enlarged and reinforced the gap between the "backward" Lahu and the "advanced" Han with respect to resource competition and political inclusion/exclusion. After 2006, civil service recruitment was changed, so that new local cadres had to be selected from among college graduates. This meant ordinary villagers stood little chance of being promoted to be local-level cadres. Meanwhile, the education system and poverty relief projects increasingly created a new sort of inequality between Han and minorities in daily life. Poverty relief policies created pressure for minorities to be "modern like the Han" and to emigrate from the region, and this pressure became the source of painful identity struggles. Since the 1990s, the most significant outward migration in these areas has been that of minority women moving to marry Han husbands in such inner provinces as Henan, Shandong, Jiangsu, and Zhejiang. In the last ten years, growing numbers of male youths have joined the flood of migrant workers to find jobs in the cities. Significant numbers have committed suicide in their home villages, a phenomenon that has been interpreted by some as an extreme form of "escape" from both their place and identity as "frontier ethnic minorities."

In Ban village, the healing ritual (known in Lahu language as the ritual of "calling the souls") is a key to understanding the way people live and think about these changes. The villagers believe that each person has a pair of souls; when someone gets sick, it is because one of their souls has left the body and returned to the world of the dead to remain with the ancestral generation. In order to call the soul back, the patient's family should hold a healing ritual practiced by two male ritual specialists, who organize a group of ritual participants and sacrifices of chickens, pigs, or even oxen, to exchange them for the escaped soul of the unwell person. The healing ritual thus acts as a channel to provide resources for the world of the dead, where no productive possibilities exist. In the process, ritual specialists and relatives imagine a long procession of souls, traveling on the way toward the world of the dead. People come and go to this world to present gifts, to negotiate with the ancestors, and confer with the patient's soul to encourage it to return. If the person is seriously ill and dies, it means the pair of souls was not willing to return, and that the deceased had resettled himself or herself in the world of the dead. The ritual process is complex: sometimes the reason the soul leaves the body in the first place is because it has been bitten and occupied by a spirit. In such cases, the first task of the ritual specialists is to judge which kind of spirit this was. Second, in the main procedure of the ritual, participants walk in procession to the temple of god E Sha 厄沙, the great creator of the world, to ask permission and for the weapons—water and sand—needed to drive the biting spirit back to where it came from. The ritual to drive the spirit away is followed by a final procession of ritual journeying to the world of the dead to call the escaped soul back.

As important as the study of ritual has been in anthropology, I have found in my experience of analyzing Lahu healing rituals that existing theories of ritual process cannot help us fully explain why people want to imagine this journey to ask E Sha for weapons to drive spirits away before proceeding to the world of the dead. In effect, there are two separate parts to the healing ritual, one to drive away the biting spirit and another to retrieve the escaped soul, and both need to be understood in their specific local setting.

For the first part, the landmarks of the journey from the village to the temple of *E Sha* are described in detail. The march starts from Ban village and proceeds to the temple following a particular set route: first to Nanzha 南栅 village, then to Nanben 南本, on to Baka 坝卡, then Mengmian 勐缅, and Mengzhu 勐主, and Mengban 勐班. Having received the permission and weapons, they return to the village along the same route. For some years, I could not understand the meaning of the names of the landmarks on the road in the first half of the healing ritual. The ritual specialists told me that we were following the road taken by their ancestors, and must visit all of these places in order to gain the power to drive away the biting spirits. But if this ritual is held during the New Year festival, one crucial element will be added on the way back; after receiving the permission and weapons, the team also needs to search for the seeds to bring home fortune for the whole year. During the New Year festival, each family has to search for these seeds of fortune for the new annual cycle. These seeds, for example, the seed of good harvest, seed of rearing cattle, seed of money, can be found at different places along the road from the village to E Sha's temple.

After several years of studying historical documents, I came to realize that this procession represents a memory of wars and migrations over the last 200 years. Each of the sites visited had specific historical significance: Mengmian was the name of land where the ancestors of these villagers had inhabited, Nanzha was the location of the central temple, Mengzhu was the place of salt wells, and Mengban was a ferry point on the Mekong River. Ritual thus becomes a text for historical memory practiced in daily life; but its meaning is quite different from the history we read in official documents. Field data and historical archives are equally important for understanding the dynamics of local history and cultural meaning on the frontier. This perspective has led me to follow a specific method of reading historical archives and studying texts in the context of daily life based on my fieldwork experience. It has helped me to establish an analytical framework for studying local societies and communal relations from a macroscopic view of historical and geographic processes of state power and frontier reconstruction between China and Southeast Asia since the fourteenth century. This fundamentally involves the dual approaches that combine fieldwork and diverse types of historical texts recording multiple variations of memory and meaning.

Bazi basin society

Over recent years, I have sought to enlarge my study to encompass frontier society in general and the highland society of Southeast Asia so as to produce a synthetic analysis that links political geography, transportation routes, state institutions, Ming and Qing imperial cosmology, and frontier construction as seen from the viewpoint of local communities. My intention is to revise theoretical explanations of the dynamics of China's political unity and regional diversity. This begins with attention to the land. In Southwest China about 6 percent of terrain is flatlands or basins surrounded by mountains, known locally as *bazi*. Local communities located in *bazi* established networks of mule caravans that traversed the mountains and deep valleys along narrow paths on the ragged mountain ranges and river systems that linked the transportation systems of the Yangtze and the Irrawaddy Rivers. Together, these routes circulated trade materials of China's inner provinces with Burma, India, and the Tibetan Plateau. These geographic conditions, as well as cooperation between humans and animals that formed the mule caravan trade, actively shaped the construction of frontier society in Southwest China. To understand why the diversity of identities and cultures in this complex region did not affect political unity, I compare mountain and basin communities, their connections, economic independence, and political integration with state institutions. Unlike the northern and northwestern divide between pastoralists and agriculturalists, diverse cultures and ethnic identities along the Yunnan and highland Southeast Asia frontier were constructed in the complex environment of overlapping historical legacies and state politics, escalating altitudes, mountain topography, the influence of monsoons from the Indian and Pacific oceans, and numerous of forms of agriculture and animal husbandry.

Before the first system of modern roads was built in the 1930s, mule caravans were the central means of transport. I have researched the relationship between muleteers and their animals with respect to long-distance travel and daily exercise, the rearing and training of mules, veterinary practices, the trade in mules, and its cooperation with caravan business-based communities. The cooperation of men and mules not only made possible transportation in a large geographic space, but also wove communities in highlands and lowlands together through the integration of agriculture and animal husbandry. Human-animal cooperation was at the core of this system for centuries and exerted considerable social influence in this frontier area. Mule caravans and human labor linked important ports in Yunnan and Guizhou to different cities and towns into circulation of material and information. At ports like Xufu 叙府 (today's Yibin 宜宾) and Luzhou 泸州 in Sichuan, Zhenyuan 镇远 in Guizhou, Baise 百色 in Guangxi, Maohao 蛮耗 in Yunnan, and Bhamo 八莫 in Burma, navigable rivers met a land-based transportation system. Mule caravan transportation in the mountains integrated with the navigation systems around the Yangtze River, Dongting 洞庭 Lake, the Red River, and the Irrawaddy River, and from there to a global market. Exploring these transportation systems is one way our research on the frontier societies of the *bazi* basins and mountain communities has sought to surpass the categorization of ethnic minorities within state documents. Combining research methods from anthropology and history, we examine the creation and meaning of local communities, social and religious networks, and the social mobility of materials, information, and knowledge.

This project also aims to construct a model of historical geography of local society within the spatial ties of *bazi* basins. The *bazi* basins are scattered in the mountainous terrain like small islands or desert oases. Over time, they developed into cities or commercial towns supported by fertile farming lands for wet rice and by complex irrigation systems. Transportation routes oriented different parts of the province to different markets in China's inland provinces, Southeast Asia, and the Tibetan Plateau. In Yunnan, both Dali and Kunming have historically been political centers: Dali under the ancient kingdoms of Nanzhao 南诏 and Kunming under the Mongol Empire. Lijiang 丽江 became the northwest gate to Tibet; Tengchong 腾冲 was the west gate to Burma; Zhaotong 昭通 the northern gate to Sichuan and the Yangtze River ports of Xufu and Luzhou; Qujing 曲靖 the eastern gate to Guizhou; and Jianshui 建水 the gate to Vietnam.

In Guizhou, the Miaoling 苗岭 Mountain range is the province's "roof ridge," separating the province into northern and southern parts. Rivers from the northern slope of the range flow into the Yangtze River, whereas the southern slope rivers run southeast into the West River. Situated at the two ends of the Miaoling Mountain range, Qujing became the gate to the west, and Zhengyuan to the east, linking through the Dongting Lake navigation system to the rivers of western Hunan. This geography shaped the historical construction of Guizhou province. Because Guizhou performed a significant role in the transportation position between Yunnan and Hunan, the Ming and Qing states invested significant political resources in managing the east-west transportation routes from Qujing to Zhengyuan. But on the whole, the state ignored the local communities on the two slopes of the Miaoling Mountain range. Valleys and mountain communities along the tributaries of big rivers thus became stable geographic spaces for local chieftaincies of what is called the Xidong 溪峒 polities. In Guangxi, Baise became the historical gateway for goods transitioning from mule caravans coming from Yunnan to the West River-linked cities and tributary river ports that formed the transport network between Yunnan, Guizhou, the South China shipping system, and Pearl River delta. The West River water transportation thus bound together Nanning 南宁, Liuzhou 柳州, Wuzhou 梧州, Zhaoqing 肇庆, and Guangzhou into a multi-layer regional system of commodities, identities, and cultures. Figure 8.1 charts these key routes and connections.

In the Ming and the Qing dynasties, chieftains maintained local jurisdiction over the regions where official prefectures and counties had not been established. The political institution of chieftaincy therefore became the basis for stable local politics and identities that were guaranteed and sheltered under these geographic and environmental conditions. Seen from the perspective of local community, Ming and Qing state ideology and political institutions largely relied on the participation of local communal

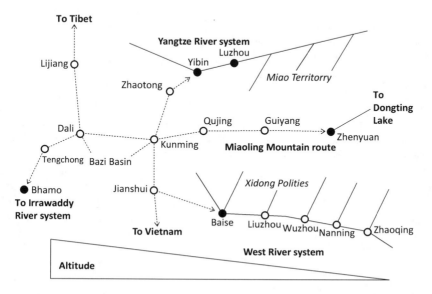

Figure 8.1 Communication routes in Southwest China. Dashed lines denote land routes and solid lines denote riverine systems. Filled circles indicate sites of transfer between land and water transport.

representatives. For example, cooperation with official institutions to maintain transportation systems was fundamental to communal affairs both in the basin and on the mountainsides. This task was assigned to the communities by county officials, but was run, in effect, as a kind of mule caravan business paid for by funds that were managed by village gentry in the names of communal temples. Yet, at the same time, this transportation system also embedded local communities in state political and economic institutions. Official travelers, tribute missions, long-distance traders, military forces and their caravans all had to work with villagers and their animals to maintain the routes, traveling services and the circulation of materials and information. Equally essential is to recognize how these forces shaped relationships and meanings within and between local communities. Particularly notable is the history of how common property management shifted from oversight by a few large Buddhist monasteries in the *bazi* basins, to a model that was village-based and organized around temples that were connected to irrigation systems. By seeking the perspective of local communities, our study asks questions about diversities and unities of ethnicity, ritual, cultural discourses and political processes within local environments, and from the vantage point of macrogeography.

Conclusion: blurred boundaries of fieldwork and historical documents

My experience of anthropological participant observation in studying rituals in Ban village has driven me to enlarge my vision from micro-scale questions about religious belief, ritual, and kinship ties to agriculture, to macro-scale questions about global connections, ethnicity and state frontiers, social conflicts and mining history, as well as the environmental condition and shared agency of human and animal relations. Questions from the small and large scale connect to each other because they are all derived from the dynamics of communication in a historical context. Within Yunnan, these questions could be expanded to explore different research topics around the mining industry, the jurisdictional systems of the Qing state, political integration of chieftains, the Qing-Burma wars, the change of state institutions in frontier society, and state practices such as colonization in Burma, border demarcation, and the ordering of farm land property rights among the Lahu. By synthetically combining the sources, arguments, and analytical tools of history and anthropology, as well as the concerns of geography and the natural environment, we find not just new answers, but also new points of view.

Acknowledgements

This research was supported by the Research Grants Council's (RGC's) General Research Fund Project (No. 16655916).

Further reading

Giersch, C. Patterson, *Asian Borderlands: The Transformation of Qing China's Yunnan Frontier*, Cambridge, MA: Harvard University Press. 2006.

Ma Jianxiong, "'Waize chaogong churu, neize wenwu wanglai' Mingqing yilai Zhaozhou bazi de shehui chongjian" ['When the Tributaries and Officials are Passing by': Social Re-construction from the Ming to the Qing of the Zhaozhou *bazi* Society], in Zhao Min and Tik-Sang Liu eds., *Yungui gaoyuan de bazi shehui: lishi renleixue de shiyexia de xinan bianjiang* [*The bazi Society of the Yun-Gui Plateau: Southwest Frontier in the Perspective of Historical Anthropology*], Kunming: Yunnan University Press, 2015, pp. 1–28.

Ma Jianxiong, "Richang shenghuozhongde 'lishi shijian:' Yunnan xinanbu Lahuzu shehui youguan 'xingfu' 'quanli' yu 'shengming' de yishi yu quanshi" ['Historical practice' in Daily Life: The Rituals and Interpretations about 'Fortunate', 'Power' and 'Life' in the Lahu in Southwest Yunnan], in Suinari Michio, Liu Zhiwei and Ma Guoqing eds, *Renleixue yu "lishi:" diyijie dong Ya renleixue luntan baogaoji* [*Anthropology and 'History': Papers from the First East Asia Anthropology Forum*], Beijing: Social Sciences Academic Press, 2014, pp. 111–116.

Ma, Jianxiong, "Ethnic Marginalization in China: The Case of the Lahu (Chapter 16)," in Zang Xiaowei ed., Handbook on Minorities in China, Cheltenham: Edward Elgar, pp. 364–382.

Ma, Jianxiong *Lahu Minority in Southwest China: A Response to Ethnic Marginalization on the Frontier*, London: Routledge, 2013.

Min Zhao and Tik-Sang Liu eds, *Yungui gaoyuande bazi shehui: lishi renleixie de shiye xia de xinan bianjiang* [The bazi Society of the Yun-Gui Plateau: Southwest Frontier in the Perspective of Historical Anthropology], Kunming: Yunnan University Press, 2015.

Section 3

Walking the ground, talking to people

9 Basic questions for fieldwork on pre-1949 Chinese society

John Lagerwey

In the 25 years I have been involved with collective fieldwork projects in China, my collaborators and I have always avoided using questionnaires, for the simple reason that they tend to impede the natural free-flow of questioning. Of course, we go into the field with specific questions in mind, and we do seek to find answers to them. But often the person we are interviewing will have no interest in or knowledge of these questions while at the same time being a rich source for something else altogether. So, one of our cardinal rules has always been to ask about what interests the interviewee. Also, the "art of the interview" takes into account that questions asked may draw blank looks and, therefore, require finding different paths to eliciting answers to those questions. The key to good interviewing is thorough knowledge of the subject so that the right questions keep bubbling up spontaneously, without consulting a crib. For example, if you are asking about local Daoists but do not already know a lot about local Daoism in the region, it will be very hard to get the answers you are looking for. Sometimes, that may even involve knowing that, locally, Daoists aren't called "Daoists"!

When we have, over the years, used questionnaires, it was to help our non-academic collaborators gain a better sense of the kind of information we were after. The fieldwork methods guide for research collaborators that I present below was devised with Wang Zhenzhong of Fudan University, my partner in the production of the *Huizhou Traditional Society Series* (*Huizhou chuantong shehui congshu* 徽州传统社会丛书). Lineage, the economy, and customs were the foci of our work.

However, before discussing methods, I would like to comment on my own reasons for doing the kind of fieldwork I do, because these reasons are always, if they are to be fruitful, deeply personal. That also means the reasons and objectives change with time and experience, so the guide I will be commenting on is the product of my own personal evolution with respect to what I hoped to learn from fieldwork. When I began doing fieldwork in the fall of 1980 in Taiwan, I had one goal: to observe and understand Daoist ritual in all its extraordinary detail. I started with the now celebrated Chen Rongsheng 陳榮盛 of Tainan whom I had met in Paris in 1977. In 1980, he took me on a trip to Taidong in southeastern Taiwan, and for three exalted days I did nothing but scribble in a large notebook, noting every gesture, movement, and burst of oboes or drums. These notes became the basis of my first book of ethnography. To my notes I added my knowledge of Daoist ritual history, which I had been studying feverishly ever since 1977, as well as the notes taken in two university courses Master Chen gave while in Paris. Back in Paris, I compared my notes with photocopies of the ritual texts Chen used. In the fall of 1981, after further observation of rituals in Tainan, I struck up an acquaintance with Zhu Kuncan 朱坤燦 in Taipei and began to follow him around. In the following years, I recorded with video cameras and traditional recording equipment the Daoist rituals of both southern and northern Taiwan, including the northern Fachang 法場 or exorcism. These recordings enabled me to watch and listen to the rituals repeatedly while looking at the texts, and do so often along with Zhu Kuncan. In the spring of 1987, I took as my master Zhu Kuncan's teacher, a Hakka from Zhongli, and I was all set to write a second book, this time on the rituals of Northern Taiwan.

But that was not to happen because in May 1987 I took information about the two main Daoist families of North Taiwan—the Lins and the Lius—to China, and discovered that the Lins lived inland some 50 kilometers from the coast in Zhao'an County (the southeastern-most county in Fujian), in Hakka territory: I had "discovered" infra-Han ethnicity and began to read up on it. Soon I had learned the "golden legend" of the Hakka, that they had migrated from North China in successive waves starting in the fourth century CE, and I began to dream that they had perhaps brought with them and preserved an early form of Heavenly Master Daoism.

Thinking I was on the verge of a major discovery, I carefully plotted a journey through "Hakkaland," starting with what I had learned was their "capital," Meixian, in northeastern Guangdong. Starting in the fall of 1989, this journey would take me to counties in Guangdong, Fujian, and Zhejiang provinces. As I discovered at my first stop, in Meixian, that the local Hakka had Daoist traditions quite unlike those of Zhao'an, the dream of a ground-breaking discovery was exploded right then and there. But while I thus learned that the questions that motivate us may prove utterly foolish, I also learned that shattered imaginings are even more instructive than proven hypotheses. It took time, but I eventually formulated it this way: "A good day in the field is when you start the day with your head full of neatly sorted facts and by evening are confronted by total chaos." That is, our questions and hypotheses may misguide us; the demonstrable facts on the ground do not. The greatest joys of fieldwork are the daily discoveries that undermine our theories.

But let us not exaggerate: we also gradually get better at what we are doing, more knowledgeable, and better at formulating hypotheses that prove a little closer to the facts. Meixian had no archaic Heavenly Master traditions, but it did have the traditions of the incense and flower monks (香花和尚) and of exorcists from the Lüshan tradition called *shangong* (○公[1]).

Moving on to Dabu, and then, into Fujian, to Yongding, Wuping, Changting, Ninghua, Jianning, and Taining counties—the Fujian Hakka universe from which the Meixian Hakka had emerged, I became as enamored of the differences encountered in each place as I had been previously of my dream of a unitary Hakka tradition. What do we do in the face of such variety? We press on. I visited 42 counties that year. Since this initial "hit and run" fieldwork, my fascination with this variety has never ceased, and it has shaped a larger conceptual perspective. Local customs are like jazz, infinite variations on a theme; China is like a giant puzzle of which each village is an integral piece; we will therefore never be able to answer the most basic question of all, "What is China?" My notion of a "great or big China" is, in this sense, even vaster than the state assertion of the "da guo" (大國, i.e., the political conception): it lies in the extraordinary diversity and richness of its local cultures.

Making progress took many years, fortuitous meetings and collaborations with other scholars. Pursuing more systematic fieldwork followed upon teaching in the Anthropology Department of the Chinese University of Hong Kong in the spring of 1990, and meeting Zhou Lifang, vice-president of the Fujian Folklore Society, who introduced me at lunch in Fuzhou to his son-in-law, Yang Yanjie 楊彥杰—my long-term partner in this project thereafter. Reading David Faure's work on a monolineage village in the Hong Kong New Territories built around its ancestor hall was eye-opening: when it came time to do the Daoist ritual of rituals, the Jiao 醮 offering, this village performed it in honor of the local earth god. This division meant that where the casual visitor sees one physical village, there are in fact two spiritual villages: one organized as a blood-based lineage, the other a divinely protected territory. Suddenly, I understood all of my fieldwork and studies of the history of Daoist ritual in a new light: there were two Chinas, one Confucian and the other Daoist. That view—almost a hypothesis!—inspired my first Chiang Ching-kuo project with Yang Yanjie and my other collaborators in Guangdong and Jiangxi. Yang Yanjie and I soon found that the two stories—that of religion and that of the lineage—were so intertwined that it would be sheer folly to try and separate them. Thus was born what would become another guiding principle to describe our work: *zhengti yanjiu* 整體研究, "study of the whole (social body)." Eventually this led us to add a third component: the economy.

Of course, a truly comprehensive study of any given village would require looking at more than these three areas, and years of work alongside specialists of geomancy, architecture, economic history, and the anthropology of family structure, to name but a few. Still, given the centrality of worship of the gods and ancestors in Chinese rural society, we believe our approach has contributed to developing a new way of appreciating China "from the bottom up."

Central to this method has been our close collaboration with small teams of local people and our own students to do fieldwork in the villages. The goal was always for them to write comprehensive essays on the villages or towns they studied. That is, we were not doing quantitative sociological research but qualitative exploration of local memory on selected topics. Over time, we came up with the following guide for collaborators that, through trial and error, has proved to yield the best results. Setting it out and discussing it illustrates not just an important specific aspect of our method but also what we came to focus on and why.[2]

"徽州传统社会丛书" 基本方法及内容
Basic Methods and Contents of the *Huizhou Traditional Society Series*

一、基本方法：以客观描述为主，主要用调查而来的口碑和地方文献，避免主观思考。解放后可一笔而过。

I. Basic method: focus principally on objective description, relying above all on local texts and oral information acquired through fieldwork. Avoid subjective speculation. Post-1949 can be touched on but nothing more.

Comment: Our principal collaborators were inevitably local "literati," with the common historians' prejudice in favor of written documentation. Such documents have obvious value but ignore the fine-grained accounts we sought of local festivals and social organization. On other topics, such as lineage origins and segmentation, oral and written witnesses may vary widely. Is an oral account not always subjective? Yes, but here "objective description" refers precisely to that subjective account as an integral part of local society, because such oral accounts represent the living memory of things and therefore have an "unvarnished" authenticity that written documents often lack. At the same time, to avoid becoming the prisoner of one person's subjectivity, key questions must be put many times to a range of individuals.

To give but two examples, when trying to reconstruct who sold what on an "old street" 老街, as old market streets are referred to, one person's memory will rarely be sufficient. The same is true when trying to reconstruct the organization of a local festival, or the order of the elements in a god-welcoming parade. Such complex subjects concerning an already distant past require the pooling of memories on the part of as many elderly men as accept to participate.

二、文章内容：绪论部分论述地理位置、人口、历史、经济、姓氏，以及当地对风水的基本认识。

II. Contents of essays: In the Introduction, give an account of geographical location, population, history, economy, surnames, and basic knowledge of local geomancy.

三、宗族：如是乡镇一级，应包括乡镇的所有宗族。主要内容：列表显示各族的基本人口，宗族基本分房情况，宗族住在多少村庄？宗族基本特色。

III. Lineage: If the focus is a township, all lineages in the township must be included. Key content: use a table to show each lineage's population, basic segmentation, and number of villages inhabited. Basic characteristics of the lineages.

Comment: What is sought here is a basic introduction to the main lineages from an historical point of view: putative time of arrival of the founding ancestor; basic facts concerning lineage segmentation, ancestor halls, and Qingming grave-sweeping; the current population of each segment.

(1) 来源: 哪里来? 什么时候来? 始祖传说故事。

1) Origins: Where do [the lineages] come from? When did they come? Tales of the founding ancestor.

Comment: What we are really after here are the mythical origins of the lineage because, in our experience, historical origins are often unknown, that is, clearly invented (sometimes it seems every lineage is descended from a high official!). This is, moreover, one point on which oral and written accounts will frequently differ. Written versions are typically found in the prefaces to local genealogies, meaning these must be read attentively in order to see the ever-evolving accounts of origins.

(2) 族谱: 用表来说明族谱历来的编纂情况, 编辑者是谁? 属第几代? 每一种谱包含多少房? 都应加以说明。编纂过程, 是否设立谱局? 谱局的组成, 如何分谱? 如何保管族谱?——上述几点, 也就是论述从编纂族谱到成谱后的所有运作过程。并将主要的谱序放在附录。

2) Genealogies: Use a table to explain the editorial history of the genealogies. Who edited each edition? What generation did he belong to? How many segments does each edition include? Each of these elements must be explained clearly. In the process of editing, do they set up a special genealogy office? How is it organized? How are genealogies distributed? How are they preserved? All the above points look at the entire process, from the editing of a genealogy to its conservation. All prefaces should be collected in an appendix.

Comment: These questions barely hint at the complex issues involved in the creation and use of clan genealogies. Genealogies usually begin as *xianghuo bu* 香火部, a family record associated with a single household and containing the information needed to know when sacrifices should be performed for individual deceased members of the household. A first genealogy will come later, usually produced by a single well-to-do segment with literate members. If the lineage continues to prosper, it may gradually come to incorporate all persons of the same surname in a given village or set of villages. Alternatively, a local group may simply be a part of a much larger group whose primary ancestor hall may even be in a different province. Prefaces are a key way for assessing how local a given genealogy is, or is not. Local help in reading a genealogy can be of the utmost importance for understanding the document, its origins, scope, and use.

The number and regularity with which local genealogies were edited is crucial to assessing much of the information included and a volume's overall credibility. Long gaps of a century or more between editions, or even between early ancestors with dates of birth and death, are obviously significant in this regard.

As to the overall editorial process, the taboos observed while editing and the manner of celebrating completion are the most revealing. For example, to avoid their pollution, women may be banned from the genealogy office; some places perform a Jiao (醮, Daoist offering) to give thanks for successful completion of the genealogy, but also to pacify all the ancestors who have been disturbed by the manipulation of their names; distribution may involve *qiangpu* 搶譜, pushing and shoving to be the first to "grab" a copy and rush home with it. A great variety of modes of conservation were practiced, the most common being to keep the central copy under lock and key, with access by non-lineage members being decided by committee; in other places, the responsibility of conservation was rotated, usually among segments. If a number of segments had each a full copy—or only their segment's section—these would have to be brought regularly to the common ancestor hall for verification. The reasons for all this care and concern were simple: the genealogy contained lineage secrets, including about property—houses, tombs, shops, land, and temples—and past court cases involving this property, but also about lineage structure and generational names and dates. Like all knowledge, access meant power and rights, which the lineage naturally wished to control.

Good genealogies are an extraordinary resource, notably for studying the demographic evolution and marital alliances of the lineage and the history of collective property accumulation. Such sources enable us to trace who the daughters married, how many sons died at birth or in childhood, and who migrated where and when. They may also contain the biographies of eminent clan members, including women, as well as accounts of local geomancy, the founding or restoration of ancestor halls and, occasionally, temples, and the "eight scenic sites" 八景 and a sketch-map of the village. However, they need to be read with a great deal of caution, especially for the earlier periods. This requires making a close examination of the prefaces and maintaining keen awareness of the following typical features: early generations have dates of birth and death recorded, but these then disappear for a number—as many as ten—of "single-son transmission" 單傳;[3] then, often with the first generation to produce an identifiable imperial official, usually a low-ranking one, death dates reappear, and in a somewhat later generation, birth dates are again recorded. These characteristic conventions of these compilations tend to reveal that everything noted before the first official appears is what I call "lineage myth-history." This is often made all the more apparent by the fact that the first generations, those with birth and death dates, are all celebrated with glorious biographies. And, at least, they are reported to have transited through such standard places as Shibi 石碧 in Ninghua 寧化 for the Hakka of Fujian and Meixian, Zhujixiang 珠璣巷 for people now living in Guangdong, Huangdun 黃墩 for citizens of Huizhou 徽州, or Dahuaishu 大槐樹 for many lineages in North China. In the south, including Huizhou, these are conventional ways of saying a lineage comes from North China and is therefore "authentically Chinese," not a "southern barbarian." To my knowledge, no study has been made of when these conventions first appeared in the genealogies of the various areas, but my impression in Hakka areas is that it is quite late, and therefore most probably designed to refute the "southern barbarian" accusation.

(3) 祠堂：用表将所有祠堂列出。哪一年建的？哪一年修的？谁建或修的？第几代人？与祠堂相关的风水故事，建筑特色，祠堂用法（如祭祖等）。祠堂等级，从家内的神龛到宗祠的相互关系。神主从家里什么时候移到祠堂，主要祭文抄入附录。

3) Ancestor Halls: Use a table to list all ancestor halls. In what year were they founded? Restored? By whom, and of what generation? Geomantic stories, architectural particularities, and use (as for worship of the ancestors) should all be covered. Starting at the base with family altars up to the pinnacle of the clan hall, what are the intermediate levels of the hierarchy of halls? When are ancestor tablets moved from home to hall? Copy the principal sacrifice prayers in an appendix.

Comment: The range of halls in some of the large southern lineages is truly staggering, with dozens of halls in some villages in Jiangxi and Fujian. Some of these halls also house extended families, while others are free-standing. Understanding what the deceptively simple term "lineage" means can in these cases require house-to-house and hall-to-hall investigation, which is as time-consuming as it is revealing. Deciphering accounts of hall geomancy is as difficult as it is important, because often intra-lineage rivalries are expressed by these tales. Dates of hall founding and restoration more commonly found in genealogies than in steles, which, in any case, rarely survive multiple centuries are essential for understanding the gradual construction of the local lineage over long periods of time. Ancestor halls often served as sites for funeral rites, not just the worship of the ancestors. In some villages, where the halls had been destroyed, people continued to perform these rites on the spot where the hall once stood. Where there was a hierarchy of halls, such rites took place in the segment—or even the sub-segment—hall.

All of this explains why the treatment of ancestor tablets also varies widely, ranging from the Jiangxi halls where only the "meritorious," who had purchased their place—or earned it by passing the exams—had tablets placed in serrated racks, to the collective tablets of Hakka Fujian. The latter seem to have been one response to an unmanageable accumulation of tablets. In Huizhou, by contrast, we heard often of tablets having to be cleared out of the hall after five generations and then buried in a geomantically significant "tomb." In some localities, tablets are placed in a hall as soon as the cycle of funeral rites is completed, but in other places this practice may be delayed for quite some time, even a generation or more, and then require a rite of transfer. All of this costs money, both to have one's child registered for inclusion in the next genealogy and to have one's tablet placed in a hall. For example, in one village in Liancheng County, Fujian, because the village/lineage hall was built on a *yin* 寅 "tiger" site, the genealogy could be taken out of its locked chest in a separate building behind the hall only once a year, during the first month, at a *yin* hour (3–5 a.m.). Only at that time could children be given a lineage name and have that name recorded on red slips of paper inserted in the genealogy, ready for inclusion in the next edition. This was also the only time we as outsiders were allowed to consult the lineage copy of the genealogy (which fortunately proved to be identical to one we had been able to borrow and photocopy from a lineage member).

(4) 坟墓: 主要坟墓, 风水, 仪式, 故事。

4) Tombs: The main tombs, their geomancy, associated rituals and tales.

Comment: Qingming 清明 Festival may last several weeks in some places (as we found regularly in Hakka Fujian), so that all 20–30 generations of tombs can be swept. It is, however, the relatively small number of tombs of which stories are told, always of geomantic import, that are most interesting. For instance, we were told that, generally, the Hakka prefer the tombs of their women to those of their men, because the latter are propitious for success in life while the former benefit the production of sons. Male offspring are, in the end, more important to lineage strength than the exam success of one individual or segment. We also heard stories of tombs whose geomancy favored non-lineage over lineage members—again the tombs of women (grandmothers). In one Yongding village, we were told that a local small lineage was forced to eliminate all second floors on their houses because the nearby large lineage had its principal graves on a low hill across the road, which meant this minor group were looking down on their larger, more powerful neighbors. Another role played by tombs in the geomantic conflicts between lineages was the phenomenon of eager occupation of "geomantically treasured sites" 風水寶地 by the creation of fake—empty—graves. This was also a way to fend off grave robbers, who would not know which of the five graves was the real one.

Other matters requiring attention are second burials, carried out normally in the eighth lunar month in Hakka Fujian. Often, these are put off until a geomantically "treasured site" has been found and purchased. In other villages, the casket is placed in what are locally called "ancestor halls" 祠堂 until the right site has been found. The village with the *yin* hall had dozens of these halls, all of them with geomantic "maps" in the genealogy. Even when there are no maps or birth dates, but only death dates, the precise orientation and positioning of each tomb is carefully recorded in the genealogy. This offers insight into the importance of "location" in local ritual life.

(5) 与其他宗族的关系: 通婚, 禁婚, 合作。包括大小姓关系, 佃仆 (伴亻当, 小姓, 祝活) 的情况。

5) Relations with other lineages: intermarriage, marriage interdiction, cooperation. (This includes relations with "little lineages" and tenants).

Comment: The reference to "little lineages" was meant to include a particularity of Huizhou society where hereditary gaps between the wealthy and the poor lineages involved serfdom. The poor provided not just agricultural and domestic labor but also ritual work for the rich. This explains why we even found "Daoist" villages, in effect, satellite lineages charged with handling all ritual (and musical) duties for the "big lineage" 大姓. Although it was not formulated in such stark hierarchical terms in Fujian and Jiangxi, we did find similar hereditary Daoist families or even villages, always belonging to small, poor lineages. In Huizhou, other hereditary families might be in charge of bridge maintenance and would therefore live in Bridge Village 橋頭村.

But it is not always the "big guy" who wins out: in Hakka Fujian we repeatedly heard tales of "contract laborers" 長工 who, having earned the trust of their employers, obtained the right to build a "straw hut" 茅棚 on his land. According to the stories, this was always on a site the laborer had learned, sometimes from a geomancer who had been treated contemptuously by the employer, was a "treasured site." In one case, it was because the ducks he guarded for the employer always went to that site to lay their eggs! Eventually, the laborer's lineage would completely replace that of the employer's.

It is rare to encounter stories about intermarriage between "big" and "little" lineages: this can be observed by simply tallying marriages with different surnames over the generations (and then asking where these other surnames lived). All the stories on this theme are about marriage interdiction. They are extremely common oral tales—and are often belied by information in the genealogy, making them all the more interesting because they contradict the written factual statements.

(6) 简略提一下宗族的主要人物（解放前）。

6) Mention briefly the principal personages of the lineage (before 1949).

Comment: Our chief focus being ethnography, not history, we have always avoided copying genealogies...

四、经济：

（1）农业：包括简单的灌溉系统介绍。土改之前的土地所有权，如有具体资料，请列表显示各类公产田，如族田、祭田、学田等（按时代列表）。如果可能，将此结果与分房问题相对照。如果本地有特产，要描述他的出产过程和买卖形式。

IV. Economy

1) Agriculture: This includes a brief introduction to the irrigation system. If there is concrete material for land ownership before Land Reform, make a chronological table that shows the various kinds of collective lands, such as lineage, sacrificial, and scholarship land. If possible, link this table to the various lineage segments. If there is some local special product, describe how it was produced, bought, and sold.

Comment: Information on types of land may be found in the richest genealogies. These report not only where these plots were to be found, but also which ancestor gave them to the lineage trust. Next we have to determine how they were managed, something that is rarely recorded in the written sources and therefore to be learned only from living or transmitted memory. Among the many special agricultural and natural bio-resource products described in the Hakka and Huizhou series are tea, persimmons, cane sugar, fish fry, tea oil, and even rice. These stories are always fascinating, both in terms of everyday technologies and skills and the manner in which such products were marketed. Not to be neglected are the special markets for plow oxen, usually associated with a temple festival called the "oxen assembly" 牛會. In the forested areas of Huizhou and Hakka Fujian and Jiangxi, lumber was a big business that has left a trove of fascinating stories about planting, harvesting, and transport. These relate, for instance, the experience of dragging great logs down to the nearest stream, then riding them bronco-style during spring floods on the local streams, downriver to port towns where they could be lashed into small and then ever larger rafts that could be floated all the way down the Yangzi River.

非农业经济：怎么组织？谁组织？有没有会？股分会？产品卖到哪里？如何运出？本村有多少人参与运货活动？有无佃仆参加这些经济活动？货的价钱、脚费？与此非经济活动相关的神明崇拜，以及相关仪式，忌讳等。以本地为中心的对外交通情况，当地是否有信客？如何活动？

2) Non-agricultural economy: How was it organized and by whom? Were there associations and, if so, with shares? Where were the products sold? How were they transported? How many people in the village were involved in such transport? Did serfs participate in this economic activity? How much did the product cost? What about transport? What god worship, rituals, and taboos were associated with this economic activity? With regard to a given place and its transport system, were there local letter-bearers? How did that work?

Comment: The last question particularly concerns Huizhou and the coastal areas of Fujian, where long-distance and especially overseas trade were flourishing in the late imperial period. As for associations, these were of every kind, and not just commercial, including associations for bridge and dam maintenance, crop-watching, market control, porters, and boatmen, and also for temples and even their gods. These associations were frequently composed of share-holders, whose stake/or share in some cases were hereditary and in others were transferable through sale. Some temples and their gods were directly associated with commerce, as in the "guilds" 會館 (usually organized by locality, not type of trade), but also the Mazu temples located in river ports or the Wutong temples in the market towns. Along the rivers where there were dangerous passages of rapids, there would often be a temple on a hill, facing upstream to "control the dragon" 鎮龍. The boatmen would go to pray there before continuing, sometimes portaging boat and cargo around the rapids. There were also taboos aplenty—and also secret language—in the practice of the various trades, everything from river transport to tree-forestry. Lineages and villages specialized in many handicraft products, from pewter-ware to ceramics, shoes of straw and recycled cloth, bamboo ware, and so forth. Paper production was fundamental to the Fujian Hakka economy; paper was thus, together with rice and salt, the most commonly portered good. In general, learning in detail about portering and boat transport is among the most fascinating paths to gain insight into the networks of local society. These networks are inseparable from those of rotating markets whose fixed alternating dates (within a ten-day period) made it possible for small-scale businessmen managing their own transport to go from one day to the next to a different market. This, in turn, opens up the possibility of comparing market and marriage networks.

五、民俗

V. Customs

（1）用示意图表示本地（如村落）所有烧香的地方，对各类神明（如土地神、树神等）要有完整的交代，一年什么时候拜，与这些神明相关的传说、活动，如何组织？相关的庙宇什么时候建？如有祭文，请将祭文全文列于附录。

这一部分，应特别关注与求雨、求子、寄子、朝山进香有关的神明。

1) Sketch a map that shows all places (if it is a village) for burning incense. Each god, including the earth god, tree gods, and others, must be presented thoroughly. When are they worshiped in the course of the year? What stories are told of them? What activities involve them, and how are they organized? When were the relevant temples built? If there are writs for sacrifice, place them in an appendix.

In this section, special attention must be paid to the gods addressed with prayers for rain or children, children adopted out to the gods, and pilgrimages to their sites of worship.

Comment: This is the core inquiry for understanding local society as it expresses itself in its religious practices. Equal attention needs to be paid to individual practices like praying for children or adopting them out to the gods and to collective ones like praying for rain or going on pilgrimage. Yet, it is in the collective acts of worship that local social organization becomes clear, including relations between lineages or villages that share a common temple and its god. Critically important is to determine the criteria for selecting leaders, the way they are chosen (i.e., through negotiation, wealth, rotation, or divination), how responsibility for the multiple activities associated with worship is apportioned, the specific details of rituals performed in their honor, whether by Buddhists, Daoists, Confucian masters of rites 禮生, spirit mediums, or the villagers themselves.

Local gods accumulate tales, some of them found far and wide, others thoroughly local. Typical stories tell of the god selecting a locality by being carried in, set down for a rest, and then being too heavy to pick up to go further, or by being flushed downstream during a flood; it might speak of a log that, no matter how often it was pushed away from the river bank, insistently floated back to the same place, often going upstream to get there. Also frequent are tales of young maidens who, along the god's parade route, wished to be married to someone as handsome and that very night die and become the god's wife. Contests between gods over the location of their temple and, more generally, miracle tales of all kinds—principally of healing and protection—are also common.

But it is the rituals—and associated taboos—that are the most important for understanding the unique character of each place. Starting at the lowest level, the adoption out of a child may be to a higher goddess like Guanyin, but it is more typically to a camphor tree or a rock associated with the local earth god, probably situated at the village water exit 水口. Children are taught to respect these humble earth gods who protect villages from their downstream position at the water exit: if a child comes home with a bellyache, the first question to be asked is whether he urinated near the earth god altar 壇. Pilgrimages to distant places, sometimes to pray for rain, but usually simply a regular practice involving local associations or even a whole village, are one of the most important forms of local ritual practice. They may require the accompaniment of a Daoist priest or *fashi* 法師, but many do not. A typical form is the organization of pilgrimages to nearby sacred mountains and their temples. These may be mountains only known locally, or famous mountains like Mount Jiuhua 九華山, which attract pilgrims from a vast area. One particular form of pilgrimage widely practiced in the southeast is "going to fetch incense fire" 取火/割火, normally from the "ancestral temple" 祖廟 of the god worshiped in the village temple. This will usually coincide with the village's most important annual festival, for the "birthday" of their god.

(2) 歲时节日: 主要节庆, 相关的筹备活动, 节庆中使用的食品、供品、节庆的组织、费用, 以及相关故事。过渡仪式: 怀孕, 出生, 小孩治病, 寄子, 婚姻, 死亡。如果死亡有请道士、和尚做超度, 可以展开写。

2) Festival days: the chief festivals, how they are prepared, including food, offerings, organization, cost, and tales of the gods. Rites of passage: pregnancy, birth, healing of small children, their adoption out to gods, marriage, death. If Daoists or Buddhist monks are invited to perform death rituals, these can be described at length.

Comment: In China as elsewhere, festivals define a society, that is, its sense of self and other, how it sees and organizes itself. Among them are "pan-Chinese" festivals like Duanwu 端午, but these are always celebrated in unique ways locally. In parts of Huizhou, for example, it is the time to "jump Zhongkui" 跳鍾馗.[4] Where dragon boat races were done, usually at the level of the market town, this invariably involved competitions between lineages or villages, each with its own color boat. As a sign of the ancient link between these races and sending off epidemic gods 瘟神, the boats were often stored in temples dedicated to these gods. The races are often associated as well with stories of boats overturning and all rowers drowning.

Major rituals like Jiao 醮 will normally require Buddhist or Daoist priests, but there are also festival rituals done entirely by lay persons. The dragon lantern parades of Gutian 古田 in Liancheng County, Fujian, for example, involve competitions between lineages: one has the longest, a second the tallest, and a third the most beautiful dragon. The Hua and Jiang lineages, who have the longest dragon, alternate taking charge of the ritual, with the lineage in charge in a given year going to pay homage with the dragon to the other lineage at its lineage hall. The long planks of the dragon are assembled on a slope leading out of the village and through the fields at the foot of barren hills. Each of some 100–200 planks—each 2.5 meters in length, with

5 lanterns on it—has its place assigned to it ahead of time with a number. At the top, the massive papier-mâché head—for whom a special sacrifice has been performed by the family which has won the privilege of producing it—is set down on the far side of a small rivulet coming down from the hills. When the planks forming the dragon's body have all been linked together, they must be linked last of all to the head, which is designated not by a number but as "Heaven," just as the papier-mâché tail emplacement is marked as "Earth." This means that the numbered planks in-between represent "human beings": society. The linking of the body to the head, one on either side of the rivulet, repairs (reverses?) the geomantic severing of the dragon artery that enters the village at that point. As for the tail, it is never joined to the body, lest the dragon become too real and fly off!

Such rituals are the quintessence of "popular religion," entirely organized by and for the people without the help of any religious specialists. As such, they are the best illustration of what is rightfully called "local autonomy."

More than anything, special festival foods leave indelible impressions in young minds and thereby contribute powerfully to the creation and transmission of local custom: thorough description is indispensable. Offerings, likewise, are often unique to festivals and extraordinary expressions of local creativity. Among them are what I call "food sculpture," with whole navies of ducks, large cucumbers peeled to resemble dragons, and complex objects made of glutinous rice. Festivals are also inseparable from the craft of papier-mâché objects: giant decorative lanterns 華燈 for New Year's festivals, giant Guanyins 觀音大士 to control the "orphan souls" 孤魂 invited to Universal Salvation 普渡 rituals, and marshals 元帥 to line the path to Heaven for memorial presentations 進表 in Daoist Jiao.

To these we may add the houses 靈屋 and other paraphernalia sent by burning to the deceased during salvation rituals 超渡, perhaps the most important form of rite of passage. Such rites are essentially lay rites and customs that may or may not involve religious specialists. That is why, even though there may be considerable overlap from place to place, we always seek out comprehensive, detailed accounts of marrying and burying. Always, it is the "small differences" of practices often described as "largely the same, with small differences" 大同小異 that reveal local particularity.

It is by means of all these rites and customs, through their organization and repeated practice, that local society is constructed.

(3)　另外，如果是乡镇，请将老街上的店铺、寺庙、祠堂列表，画出示意图，并加以说明：谁开的？做什么样的买卖？有多少资本？买卖如何运作？

3) In addition, if the focus is a township seat, draw up tables of the shops, temples, and ancestor halls on the "old street," and sketch a map of them, together with an explanation: whose shops were these? What kind of business did they engage in? How much capital did they have? How was business carried on?

Comment: Much to our surprise, and even in our most recent experience (Suichang in SW Zhejiang, in 2017), one only need find the right elder gentlemen in order to get a full account of who owned what shops and did what kind of business, who was a local or an outsider, and where goods came from and were sold to. Typically, small eateries were run by locals, while shops requiring the import of goods from elsewhere were run by outsiders. These "old (market) streets" are particularly interesting because they are always multi-lineage or even simply multi-surname, and therefore, by the way market town festivals are organized, show the central role played by religious practices in transcending lineage, as do the many multi-village rural festivals built around a common temple and its god.

Concluding note

As our reliance on oral accounts and the often flawed or censored memories that provide them may seem to be a guarantee of subjective inaccuracy, I will add here a few words of explanation

First, while we obviously did not shun the use of local written sources of all kinds—genealogies, account books, contracts, and steles—we relied in the first place on oral accounts because they alone give access to the living memory of local social organization and sense of identity as seen in festivals and other ritual and economic activities or in tales told of local gods, ancestors, tombs, and inter- and intra-lineage conflict. That is, most of the information we were interested in is simply not to be found in written documents. Donor steles in a local temple may provide precious dated information about which individuals and lineages supported the temple at various times over the centuries, but they will not say anything about the conflicts and competition for control and status that local people can recount. An account book that gives details of expenses for a festival or a marriage offers a vividly concrete sense of the component parts of such events, but it cannot match a full oral recounting of preparations for and enactment of the event, including, for example, unwritten rules of precedence or procession order. Oral tales of the gods give unique insights into how the people imagined them, intimately and with a great deal of humor: when these stories are told, they invariably provoke laughter. Put simply, oral culture is common culture, which brings us far closer to core concerns and interests than written culture. Finally, there is one particular social group of special relevance to the oral approach: religious specialists. No one knows as well as they do the local tales, taboos, unwritten rules of social interaction, and ritual calendars and practices of the living culture. Not only do they have their own manuscript traditions, but they also accumulate unmatchable experience, often over generations, of local social dynamics and of the relationship between the visible and invisible worlds.

"徽州传统社会丛书" 基本方法及内容

一、基本方法：以客观描述为主，主要用调查而来的口碑和地方文献，避免主观思考。解放后可一笔而过。

二、文章内容：绪论部分论述地理位置、人口、历史、经济、姓氏，以及当地对风水的基本认识。

1、宗族：如是乡镇一级，应包括乡镇的所有宗族。主要内容：列表显示各族的基本人口，宗族基本分房情况，宗族住在多少村庄？宗族基本特色。

   来源：哪里来？什么时候来？始祖传说故事。
   族谱：用表来说明族谱历来的编纂情况，编辑者是谁？属第几代？每一种谱包含多少房？都应加以说明。编纂过程，是否设立谱局？谱局的组成，如何分谱？如何保管族谱？——上述几点，也就是论述从编纂族谱到成谱后的所有运作过程。并将主要的谱序放在附录。
   祠堂：用表将所有祠堂列出。哪一年建的？哪一年修的？谁建或修的？第几代人？与祠堂相关的风水故事，建筑特色，祠堂用法（如祭祖等）。祠堂等级，从家内的神龛到宗祠的相互关系。神主从家里什么时候移到祠堂，主要祭文抄入附录。
   坟墓：主要坟墓，风水，仪式，故事。
   与其他宗族的关系：通婚，禁婚，合作。包括大小姓关系，佃仆（伴亻当，小姓，祝活）的情况。
   简略提一下宗族的主要人物（解放前）。

2、经济：

   农业：包括简单的灌溉系统介绍。土改之前的土地所有权，如有具体资料，请列表显示各类公产田，如族田、祭田、学田等（按时代列表）。如果可能，将此结果与分房问题相对照。如果本地有特产，要描述他的出产过程和买卖形式。
   非农业经济：怎么组织？谁组织？有没有会？股分会？产品卖到哪里？如何运出？本村有多少人参与运货活动？有无佃仆参加这些经济活动？货的价钱、脚费？与此非经济活动相关的神明崇拜，以及相关仪式，忌讳等。
   以本地为中心的对外交通情况，当地是否有信客？如何活动？

3、民俗：

   (1) 用示意图表示本地（如村落）所有烧香的地方，对各类神明（如土地神、树神等）要有完整的交代，一年什么时候拜，与这些神明相关的传说、活动，如何组织？相关的庙宇什么时候建？如有祭文，请将祭文全文列于附录。
      这一部分，应特别关注与求雨、求子、寄子、朝山进香有关的神明。
   (2) 岁时节日：主要节庆，相关的筹备活动，节庆中使用的食品、供品，节庆的组织、费用，以及相关故事。过渡仪式：怀孕，出生，小孩治病，寄子，婚姻，死亡。如果死亡有请道士、和尚做超度，可以展开写。
      另外，如果是乡镇，请将老街上的店铺、寺庙、祠堂列表，画出示意图，并加以说明： 谁开的？做什么样的买卖？有多少资本？买卖如何运作？

Notes

1 The character used to write *shan* is an invented one that looks like a Daoist talisman and is found in no dictionary. Such Daoists are called *shangong* in Hakka parts of southwestern Fujian and northeastern Guangdong. As they are never called *daoshi*, until I learned what they were called, I could not find them.
2 Lest there be any misunderstanding, this was NOT a questionnaire to be taken along and consulted when interviewing. It was something for our collaborators

to consult privately, to give them an idea of the type of question to which we would like them to find answers. It did not aim at some kind of statistical survey, but was just to help the fieldworkers check on themselves: on what they had already learned and what they still needed to learn in order to write the kinds of essays we were looking for. Once a local author had produced an essay, we would often go back with them into the field to ask further questions in order to illustrate to the author where he needed to dig deeper. Often essays went through three to four versions before they were ready for publication.

3 Typically, the founder, said to have been a high official, will be said to have several sons, but all but one will be said to have "moved elsewhere" and will therefore have no descendants' names in the genealogy. Following generations may have the same phenomenon, or else simply record only a single son, and this may then continue for as much as a dozen generations before more complete—and plausible—information begins to appear. The same is true for the marriages of daughters or the out-migration of clearly identified individuals: these are usually phenomena that are recorded only well into lineage history, from the mid-Qing, for example.

4 Zhongkui is the exorcist par excellence; "jumping," no doubt because the activity does in fact involve hopping, is the standard vernacular verb for playing a ritual role. Mediums, for example, are often referred to as *tiaotong*, "leaping lads."

10 Festivals in the field—a social historical perspective

Paul R. Katz

This chapter examines the ways in which fieldwork can help social historians uncover relationships and tensions in Han Chinese or non-Han communities that archival materials and other documents tend to overlook. It shows that the social meanings attributed to festivals are regularly contested, while also pointing out that not all participants in these ritual events are as concerned with the politics of temple management or the details of liturgical practice as local elites who organize them or the ritual specialists who preside over them. On a broader level, this chapter stresses the value of ethnographic data for complimenting historical accounts of Chinese religious life while providing us with new perspectives on this topic.

The data presented below derive from field research I undertook in the southern Taiwan fishing port of Donggang 東港 (Pingdong 屏東 County) during the summer and autumn of 1988 while collecting data for my doctoral thesis on plague god cults and festivals. While the focus of my dissertation was on late imperial Zhejiang 浙江, fieldwork in Donggang proved vital for enhancing my understanding of how such beliefs and practices actually played out on the ground. Fieldwork may not be essential for all forms of social historical research, but it certainly is for studying festivals. This is because one must experience such events firsthand in order to fathom not only how various rites are performed, but also the dazzling diversity of views that people bring to such events. Such data cannot be learned by relying solely on historical writings, which are often frustratingly sketchy or even biased. As I will show below, even the most detailed Qing-dynasty gazetteer accounts of plague expulsion festivals provide only a bare-boned summary of these events, often spiced up with criticisms of their cost, with almost no data on the *people* who took part (the "anthro" of "anthropology" or "ethno" of "ethnography") and their motivations for doing so. Fieldwork alerts us to the presence of many different stakeholders in a festival, each of whom may possess very different needs and agendas.

The act of doing fieldwork can help historians more fully appreciate the fact that localities are archives in their own right containing a wealth of data related to a community's social history. However, as in archival research, a substantial time commitment is required. Graduate students and junior scholars should take advantage of their relative independence to do as much long-term ethnographic research as possible (I lived in Donggang for a six-month period, three months before and after the date of the festival in late October). One's early years as a scholar present a unique opportunity for in-depth and close-up observation, something that becomes much more difficult over time, especially if one is later tenure-track and/or starting a family.

First, some background: I graduated from Yale in 1984 with a degree in Chinese history and a profound interest in religious life, having been inspired by Jonathan Spence's lectures on White Lotus sectarian religion, the Taiping Civil War, and the Boxer Uprising, as well as Kang-i Sun Chang's excursions into the realm of late imperial Chinese fiction and its portrayals of that era's beliefs and practices. Then, while studying advanced Chinese in Taiwan, I got to know my "classmate" David Jordan, who took me with him to witness the huge plague festival (*wenjiao* 瘟醮) that was staged in Xigang 西港 Township (today's Tainan City) during the summer of 1985. The religious and social dynamism I experienced during that event convinced me to study its historical development in Zhejiang and other parts of South China, even as I recognized that I needed to do more systematic field research on such festivals in Taiwan over a sustained period of time (something relatively difficult to arrange in the PRC at the time). This was followed by three years of doctoral training at Princeton under the tutelage of Stephen Teiser (who guided me to better understand the state of the field and ritual theory) and Raoul Birnbaum (who was inspirational in helping me comprehend religion as a living system with powerful affective features), with kind assistance from Susan Naquin at the University of Pennsylvania (who provided rigorous instruction in the methods for doing social and religious history from below). While one may never be truly "ready" for one's first experiences in the field, this training established a foundation for studying the next round of plague festivals that would take place in Donggang and other parts of southern Taiwan in 1988, with my research being supported by a Luce Foundation fellowship to study at the Taiwan History Field Research Office at Academia Sinica (台灣史田野研究室; the predecessor of today's Taiwan History Institute).

I arrived in Taiwan in the spring of 1988, my project having been designed to pursue the following goals. First, I wanted to assess the diverse representations of Taiwanese plague gods (generally referred to as "Royal Lords" or *wangye* 王爺) by the men and women who take part in a festival, including temple committee members, Daoist priests (*daoshi* 道士), members of performance troupes, and local worshippers. These questions had been shaped by the 1985 edited volume entitled *Popular Culture in Late Imperial China* (especially James Watson's chapter on the "standardization" of local cults), David Faure's *The Structure of Rural Chinese Society* (1986) and Robert Weller's *Unities and Diversities in Chinese Religions*, which had just been published the previous year. In addition, the historian in me wished to trace how Taiwan's plague festivals had changed over time, including the number of villages participating and their locations, the size of the procession and its route, and especially the roles of temple committee members, Daoist priests, and other local elites in determining how a festival should be staged.

In order to achieve these goals, I knew that it would be necessary to adhere to rigorous research methods. It is absolutely essential to prepare fully before starting any fieldwork, including both documentary research and language training. Previous scholars had already done in-depth studies of the Xigang plague festival, most notably Liu Chih-wan 劉枝萬, who combined immersion in documentary data with his own ethnographic investigations. In order to avoid repeating his work, I chose another festival that was also well known but considerably less studied, namely, one held in the town of Donggang every three years and referred to as "Inviting the [Royal] Lords" or *yingwang* 迎王. At the time, relatively few historical materials were available for the study of Taiwanese communities. There were some writings by local elites (mainly current or former officials, school teachers), but these pale in both quantity and quality to the work of today's local experts (*wenshi gongzuozhe* 文史工作者). Only a few Western missionaries and travelers had recorded their experiences in Donggang, with little data on religious life. Still, based on library research and some exploratory trips to Donggang prior to commencing fieldwork, I was able to gain a preliminary understanding of the town's social and religious development.

In studying the history of Taiwan's plague festivals, the main texts that scholars rely on are local gazetteers, which provide basic descriptions of such practices that can help us understand their essential characteristics yet lack details on local interests and tensions that only fieldwork can provide. Take, for example, two gazetteers on today's Tainan City, the *Taiwan xianzhi* 臺灣縣志 (1720) and *Xuxiu Taiwan xianzhi* 續修臺灣縣志 (1807). The former work notes that plague festivals were staged every three years, with Daoist priests presiding over sacrifices to a plague boat, plus statues of three "plague kings" (*wenwang* 瘟王), with one member of the local elite (referred to as "someone with knowledge of such matters" or *xiaoshizhe* 曉事者) presenting offerings to the gods while kneeling. The plague boat was then either floated out to sea or burned. This description is followed by scathing remarks on the high costs of such rituals, as well as an account of Dutch sailors falling like flies after a battle with one plague boat, which the author dismisses as apocryphal. The second text contains detailed information on where Tainan's plague god temples were located as well as a brief description of plague god statues. It then stresses the role of local elites (*toujia* 頭家) in fund-raising activities, while decrying the festivals as "defrauding people of their wealth" (*liancai* 歛財). This work also describes Daoist priests presiding over plague festivals as well as their boat expulsion rites, before concluding with more critical comments on the expenses involved. The only mention of actual worshippers occurs in the latter text, which refers to "ignorant people completing to file indictments and petitions" (*yumin zhengtou gaodie* 愚民爭投告牒, most likely judicial rituals for underworld indictments). In short, while gazetteer accounts are invaluable for giving us a sense of *how* plague festivals could be staged in the past, they provide precious little information on *who* was involved and *why*.

Apart from reading historical documents, the other form of preparation involved three months of intensive training in Taiwanese, later supplemented with additional classes while in the field. This hardly made me fluent, but even spending a few months learning a language enables one to become much closer to informants by being able to do such basic things as expressing polite greetings, asking directions, and posing initial questions during an interview (with more complex issues requiring the help of a research assistant). Lack of training in Miao 苗 languages during my most recent research project on religious life in western Hunan (Xiangxi 湘西) has been a source of deep regret since I started that effort in 2010. Scholars intending to do fieldwork should never underestimate the fact that one cannot do local history without being able to fully communicate with the "locals."

Planning for fieldwork in Donggang also meant deciding where to start. I chose the temple responsible for organizing the plague festival every three years, namely, the Donglong Gong 東隆宮 (founded in the eighteenth century). My reason for doing so was straightforward: temples like the Donglong Gong sit at the heart of local networks of power, veritable nodes of social life where one can meet all the diverse individuals and interest groups who choose to participate in a festival, particularly the elites who sponsor them and the specialists in charge of their rituals. I often remind my students that the booklets (*jianjie* 簡介) prepared by large local temples are a veritable "Yellow Pages" for prominent local figures, most of whom support such sites and their ritual activities so as to accumulate the symbolic capital of having their names (and photos) included in such booklets (not to mention carved on inscriptions commemorating temple construction projects, with donor names listed alongside the amount donated in order of the size of each contribution). Once one has gotten a sense of the various networks circulating around a leading temple, one can then work to broaden one's fieldwork to encompass cooperating/competing temples and their various elites, as well as Daoist priests, performance troupes, local worshippers, and so forth.

In working to locate and interview informants, I strove to adhere to the same methodological strictures of social history: just as the historian doing archival research would be expected to locate the broadest possible source base (gazetteers, stele inscriptions, *biji* 筆記, newspaper articles, etc.), so too the historian doing fieldwork needs to seek out the widest range of informants, which in my case included the individuals and interest groups mentioned above. Since I was researching both social roles and historical change, my questions tended to center on issues such as who participated in the festival, how and why they chose to do so and for how long a period of time, where they lived and worked, etc. In interviewing informants, it soon became clear that it was best to adhere to oral history techniques by asking more open questions than focused ones, thereby allowing people to tell their own stories as opposed to addressing my scholarly agendas.

Working with informants involved considerable challenges, particularly the issue of whether or not to become initiated as a Daoist while studying the specialists who presided over the Donggang festival Lin. On the one hand, initiation would allow me to become familiar with the details of Daoist liturgical traditions, especially talismans, spells, mudras, etc. Only with such esoteric knowledge, can one hope to grasp the intricacies of the rituals being performed. On the other hand, obtaining such knowledge is often accompanied by the act of taking a vow not to divulge key details so as to present their being copied by rival specialists without having to invest the time and expense involved in studying under a master. In addition, the closer one becomes to any informant, the greater the risk one runs of having one's own views molded by their agendas. These considerations left me feeling rather uncomfortable with the ethics of becoming a ritual specialist (my then future wife was not too happy at the prospect either), yet at the same time, I could hardly hope to understand Daoist rites without establishing close personal relationships with Daoist masters. In the end, the Daoists and I reached a compromise whereby I accompanied the troupe during many of their rituals, while only publishing data on facets of their traditions that they were willing to share with the scholarly community through the articles I was writing (and showed them in advance).

As the date of the festival grew near, as well as during the actual event, the goals espoused by different participants and the tensions between them became increasingly evident, and it became possible to postulate their links to processes of historical change. Take, for example, the two groups mentioned above: local elites who manage temples plus their festivals, and ritual specialists who perform at these events. The Donglong Gong's *temple committee members* were mostly older elite males, who viewed the Royal Lords as high-ranking officials conducting tours of inspection. One informant described this as much like the visits of late-imperial provincial governors (*xunfu* 巡撫). These gods required regular worship in the temple during *siwang* 祀王 and *yanwang* 宴王 ceremonies. The committee members made every effort to control all aspects of the festival, and in particular, the procession and all rites performed both inside and outside the Donglong Gong. The *Daoist master* hired to lead his troupe in staging plague expulsion rituals considered the Royal Lords to be minor spirits invoked when dealing with contagious diseases. These spirits paled in stature next to Daoist deities. Moreover, he expressed considerable frustration at not being granted a greater role in the festival. In contrast to present-day Daoists from nearby Tainan as well as those mentioned in Qing-dynasty gazetteers, who could oversee a plague festival from beginning to end, this festival's Daoist troupe was merely asked to perform rites on the event's final day (most notably the "pacification of plagues" or *hewen* 和瘟), and then at a temporary altar set up just outside the Donglong Gong. They were not allowed to set foot inside the temple, a situation the troupe's leader referred to as being at "a place where heroes could not exert their prowess" (*yingxiong wu yongwu zhi di* 英雄無用武之地).

Many other agendas could be observed as well. *Leaders of smaller temples* that took part in the festival and sponsored troupes (*zhentou* 陣頭) to perform in the procession could embrace rather different views from those espoused by members of the Donglong Gong temple committee. Their main concerns were with the details of the procession route and the order of their troupe(s) in the procession. In addition, they felt it essential that the quality of their troupes' performances exceeds those of troupes sponsored by their neighbors, one oft-quoted expression in Taiwanese being *su-lang m-su-thin* 輸郎毋輸陣, meaning "one can lose out to individuals but not performance troupes." To them, the identities of the deities invited or the relative status of Daoists vis-à-vis temple committee members were of little or no concern. Similar views colored by local rivalries were expressed by *neighborhood heads* (referred to as *zongli* 總理, and their leader as *dazongli* 大總理). They also stressed that it had once been their duty to organize the festival, but that this task had been given to (or usurped by) the Donglong Gong temple committee. Similar tensions have marked the growth of other major festivals in Taiwan as they began to attract ever-larger donations in the thriving economy of the 1970s and 1980s. As for the *performance troupes*, these consisted of younger men (some with links to local gangs) who joined troupes (八家將, 宋江陣, 五靈聖將, 十三太保, 五毒大帝, etc.) in large part to demonstrate their skills in martial arts as well as possession techniques. Temple committee members often considered such troupes uncontrollable and even dangerous, especially when rivalries with other troupes escalated into brawls requiring mediation by local elders.

Finally, *male and female worshippers* from Donggang (as well as natives who had moved to other parts of Taiwan or even abroad but returned home every three years for the festival) generally had little interest in the tensions described. Instead, they made offerings to the Royal Lords to ensure peace and tranquility (*ping'an* 平安) for themselves and their families, while busying themselves in hosting banquets for friends and neighbors during the procession (*liushuixi* 流水席). Those who felt burdened by a sense of wrong-doing could go to the Donglong Gong to be symbolically punished in rites meant to imitate the tortures of the late imperial yamen, or dress up as criminals (*fanren* 犯人) by wearing small paper cangues during the procession. For such individuals, Donggang's plague festival could be both a rite of passage and a rite of affliction.

In contrast to gazetteer and other historical accounts, which describe festivals and criticize their cost while neglecting the people who took part, fieldwork along the lines described above allows us to see the different roles and views of the individuals and groups involved, thereby allowing us to attain a much more dynamic and complex picture of their historical development than one could hope to learn from archival sources. In other words, while reading texts like gazetteers can help us appreciate historical continuities in how plague festivals could be staged (including the prominent roles of local elites and Daoist priests), by doing fieldwork we can more fully comprehend the tensions involved in staging these rites, as well as get a better sense of a broader range of interest groups than those described in gazetteer accounts.

At the same time, there were some aspects that I overlooked. Early on in my fieldwork, I learned that the Donglong Gong used to have its own spirit-mediums (*jitong* 乩童, or *tang-ki* 童乩 in Taiwanese), but that they had left (or been forced out) during the 1970s and 1980s as the temple worked to "brand" itself to meet more "orthodox" criteria espoused by the state. These mediums then set up their own small shrines, some of which were quite active, but I did not do interviews with them. Since spirit-mediums often played key roles in the early growth stages of Royal Lords cults, this was a considerable oversight. The other group that I utterly neglected was local women. I have tried to make up for this in subsequent fieldwork, but have found that interviewing goes much more smoothly if done by a female research assistant.

To sum up, although the research procedures described above might seem more ethnographic than historical, the data collected as a result can help fill in gaps in our knowledge of religious life that historical sources either tend to neglect or else treat in a perfunctory manner. Be that as it may, field data can be useless unless it is recorded using the same methodological rigor that one brings to an archive; hence the need for detailed field notes. While one does not necessarily need to imitate precisely the anthropologist's diligence in compiling field notes, including on-the-spot jottings, a diary, a journal, and longer notes that can serve as the basis for scholarly articles, detailed and systematic records of what one has witnessed are essential, since one often forgets the finer points of fieldwork after returning to the ivory tower and needs to start writing up a thesis or prepare to publish or perish. Beginning in Donggang, and continuing up to my current work in western Hunan, I have found it helpful to prepare a standard form ahead of interviews, which can be used for filling in basic information and keeping track of questions, especially since discussions often wander from one's intended path (see below). This is because remembering when and where an interview was conducted, as well as detailed information on each informant's personal and professional background, can prove essential for trying to measure the significance of what was said during the interview. In addition, preparing tables listing what one considers to be essential data collected during interviews and field observations can be most helpful for summarizing what one has learned at a given point in time, as well as for considering how to present these data to people who have never visited one's field site, and assessing what needs to be asked to compensate for gaps in the data. I would also note that while the digital age provides endless temptations for making elaborate audio and video recordings of interviews and events, one should prioritize good notes, since without them such recordings can lose their meaning over time. Field notes not only provide a framework for one's research, they constitute much of its flesh and blood.

The data and discussions presented above suggest that systematic ethnography can go a long way in helping us to better understand Chinese religious life, while also allowing us to gain a more nuanced understanding of the agendas and tensions that diverse individuals and groups bring to ritual events like festivals. Achieving this goal requires flexibility in terms of adjusting hypotheses in light of the data collected, which in the case of my fieldwork in Donggang involved rethinking the roles played by Daoist priests when confronted by powerful temple committee members, as well as the tensions between local temples and the performance troupes they sponsored. This is critically important, because, as David Faure's chapter in this volume has shown, the modern history of Chinese ethnography has been in large part marked by tracing the origins of local beliefs and practices using methodologies that often did not rely on extensive fieldwork. Other projects were guided by a mission of achieving social reform that could taint the agendas of those who undertook them. As a result, while many ethnographers did "hear" (*ting* 聽) informants in the field, they often failed to listen and learn from (*tingqu* 聽取) what these informants had to say.

If one accepts the above principles, then one won't be surprised by discrepancies in informant accounts, because one is already on the lookout for diverse systems and sets of memories at work. One also won't be miffed if oral accounts differ from written texts. In fact, one should start questioning one's methodology should no such differences occur. One of the most instructive examples of this point may be found in Huang Meiying 黃美英's ethnographic studies on Taiwan's Mazu 媽祖 cults and pilgrimage networks. While most work on this topic has focused on how local elites rewrote temple histories and rearranged procession routes in order to enhance the "incense power" (*xianghuo quanwei* 香火權威) of the sacred sites they patronized and the rituals they staged, Huang's long-term observations of pilgrims (especially women worshippers) revealed that such disputes held little meaning for them. Many were largely unaware of and utterly uninterested in such issues, focusing instead on individual and family concerns. Moreover, even if they followed temple leaders in joining new pilgrimage routes, pilgrims would often make detours to the sites they had used to worship at out of force of habit (most commonly expressed as "being used to it" or *xiguanle* 習慣了). In short, ethnographic data on aspects of Chinese religious life such as plague festivals and Mazu cults should make us aware of the need to make every effort to avoid bringing preconceptions about how things work to the field; let the field data reshape one's hypotheses, and not vice versa.

It is my hope that this brief discussion might show, in essence, that doing fieldwork is not all that different from doing research at an archive. Both endeavors require preparation before starting, methodological rigor in posing questions and making records, and sensitivity to the nuances of the data being collected. However, while historical data can be highly complex in its own right, many guides and introductions to archival sources tend to present a rather systematic and finite set of structures, conventions, and languages that must be understood for doing research on such texts. In contrast, this chapter has revealed that doing fieldwork can result in a vision of local society as a physical and living "archive" exponentially more vibrant and less systematized than a collection of written texts, something often overlooked by the many conventional historians who tend to presume the opposite. If one can accept the fact that ethnographic investigations resemble historical research in possessing the potential to challenge us to look beyond conventional wisdom on a given topic, then we will be better equipped to grasp fieldwork's value in undertaking social historical research. In that sense, then, going into the field is really an act of leaving one archive and entering another.

Appendix A.10
Basic information form for ritual specialists

Editors' note: Unlike the list of questions that John Lagerwey discusses in his chapter, this form is intended to be filled in by the researcher as a way of keeping track of informants and their experiences, as well as the circumstances of when and where interviews took place. The form records basic information about the individuals being interviewed (in this case ritual specialists), including education, family, career choices (most specialists hold other jobs), apprenticeship, training, etc. There are also data on followers, any materials collected, and a list of further contacts.

神职人员基本资料表 坛名 _____ 纪录日期: _____

姓名:	性别:	职业:	访问日期:
职称:	出生年:	生肖:	年龄:
族群别:	村里别:	识字程度:	教育程度:
婚姻状况:	子女数:	祖传或私授:	

经历(村长、民代或其它宫堂要职):
联络电话:
个人及配偶居住地、族群别 居住地: □本地 □外地(本居地: _____ 何时迁来: _____) 配偶族群别: □同 □异(□苗族 □土家族 □汉族 □其它_____) 配偶村里别: □本庄 □非本庄(村别: _____)
成为神职人员背景及原因 成为神职人员年纪: _____ 原因: □父母引入 □长辈、亲友引介 □其它原因_____ 父是否为神职人员: □是 □否 父是否担任过庙中要职: □是 □否(_____) 母是否为神职人员: □是 □否 母是否担任过庙中要职: □是 □否(_____)

神职人员的训练过程(选任方式):_____
_____
个人宗教背景及仪式活动
◎是否同时拥有苗老师、土老师、客老师身分：□是 □否(先:_____后:_____)
◎是否同时拥有仙娘身分：□是 □否
◎是否同时参加地方庙坛活动：□是 □否(_____)
◎祖师爷是谁:_____
◎是否会向祖师爷请示自己家中的事务：□是(一年约有几次_____) □否
◎家中哪些事情会请示祖师爷：(□身体健康 □择吉日 □其它疑难_____)
◎一年约请示祖师爷几次：_____
◎有无得到祖师爷启示或帮助的亲身经历_____

◎除了科仪本以外，平时会看其它经书、宝卷：□是(例如：_____) □否

其它补充事项：

◎替信徒做法事纪录表：

顺序	性别	年龄	地点	外地人	日期	仪式性质	解决何种问题
1							
2							
3							

◎访问备忘录:____年___月__日____:____时间_____(地点)
一、访问过程概述：
_____
_____
_____

二、访问内容概述：
_____
_____三、待办事项：
_____备注：
_____

◎收集资料简表：

资料名称	出版单位	出版年代	采集地点	备注
1.				
2.				
3.				

◎本次拜访对象表：

受访者	身份	电话	地点(地址)	备注
1.				
2.				
3.				

◎下次待访名单：

受访者	身份	电话	地点(地址)	备注
1.				
2.				
3.				

Further Readings

Faure, David. *The Structure of Chinese Rural Society: Lineage and Village in the Eastern New Territories*. Hong Kong and New York: Oxford University Press, 1986.

Huang Mei-ying 黃美英. *Taiwan Mazu de xianghuo yu yishi* 台灣媽祖的香火與儀式 [Mazu Pilgrimage and Ritual in Taiwan]. Taipei: Zili wanbao chubanbu, 1994.

Johnson, David G., Andrew J. Nathan and Evelyn S. Rawski, eds., *Popular Culture in Late Imperial China*. Berkeley: University of California Press, 1985.

Kang Bao 康豹 (Paul R. Katz). *Taiwan de wangye xinyang* 台灣的王爺信仰 [The Cult of the Royal Lords in Taiwan]. Taipei: Shangding wenhua chubanshe, 1997.

Liu, Chih-wan 劉枝萬. *Taiwan minjian xinyang lunji* 台灣民間信仰論集 [Essays in Taiwan Popular Belief] Taipei: Lianjing chubanshe, 1983.

Weller, Robert P. *Unities and Diversities in Chinese Religion*. Seattle: University of Washington Press, 1987.

11 Doing historical-anthropological fieldwork in Jiangnan
Gazetteers, newspapers, and real life

Vincent Goossaert

The following rambling thoughts spring from an ongoing (in truth, incipient) project about the religious structures of Jiangnan 江南 society and their role in the evolution of that region from early modern to modern to contemporary times. This project shares a lot with those discussed in the other chapters of the present volume, but one characteristic of Jiangnan needs to be spelled out: the overabundance of written, published historical material. Because Jiangnan was rich and densely inhabited by a highly literate populace, even villages have their own pre-1949 level gazetteers (which are so much more interesting to read than administrative-level gazetteers); not to mention local literati's memoirs, diaries, collectanea, and so forth. Epigraphy, however, is in contrast to other regions, less systematically collected and published, and has in many cases been thoroughly destroyed. The overabundance of sources is thus both a blessing and a curse. The former because it allows for more fine-grained examination of historical evolution than is possible in many places; the latter because it seems to question the very need for fieldwork.

Jiangnan after 1860 was also special because of the city of Shanghai, with its unique concentration of capital and technology. A huge proportion of the printed material for modern China (1890–1940) was produced there, often with regional audiences in mind. The output of religious books in Shanghai was staggering, but so was that of popular novels, material for the performing arts, and the press, that discussed religion, local society, and performing arts at great length. I have developed a particular interest in the newspapers, notably *Shenbao* 申報, which was established in the international concession in 1872, and is widely available, including in a digital, searchable form. Until about 1900, *Shenbao* ran enormous numbers of reports on local society and religious life. It continued to do so after that date, but less frequently.

Such abundance of pre-1900 descriptions of religious life should invite a skepticism that remains at an implicit, if not subconscious level for many scholars: how "ethnographic" are the early modern "quasi-ethnographic records" of local social life, and in particular, of religious life? This is a tricky question. It is easy to dismiss press records as biased by all sorts of prejudices and agendas—as press records often are. These writings never pretend to adhere to critical distance and axiological neutrality; most of the time (albeit not always) they take stands, criticize, and argue for reforms. And yet, if one is to understand in some detail how a procession took place in Shanghai, or any other Jiangnan city in the late Qing or Republican period, one would be very hard put indeed to find a more precise description (How many people? What kind of performing troupes, and in what order? What itinerary? How long did it last? What was the role of women?). The question of the "ethnographic" value of stories in *biji* 筆記 anecdotes has been discussed at some length—even though the extreme abundance and richness of *biji* stories about religious life in modern Jiangnan has hardly begun to be tapped—but similar reflection is required about press reports. Both sorts of record have an advantage over descriptions in local gazetteers (even the township and village-level gazetteers) in that they discuss individual cases and deviations from the norm, whereas gazetteers tend to provide an ideal-typical description. For instance, when studying the great *saihui* 賽會 processions in late Qing Jiangnan, I could in some cases, thanks to the *Shenbao*, follow the modifications and negotiations around the order and composition of the procession, year after year, rather than be content with one description. This is ethnographic quality: things that are always different from the norm.

Because of the availability of such sources, a substantial amount of research has been conducted in Jiangnan (as elsewhere) that poses anthropological questions to historical material. But for all its contributions and inherent interest, this research is not the same as the historical anthropology practiced by many of the contributors to this volume. The distinction seems to me to hinge on avoiding four major and basic oversights:

1 *Not doing fieldwork at all.* This is actually the main drawback of much of the best work on the topic, notably many studies by Chinese scholars who, unlike me, understand local dialects. The kinds of sources noted above make it easy enough to come up with lifelike, rich descriptions of festivals, sacrifices, and family rituals in Jiangnan, all without leaving one's office. Yet in doing so, one can easily misread the sources, fail to see the systemic logic that holds all the different elements of local socio-religious life together, and neglect certain elements little mentioned in the sources (such as the roles of women, spirit-mediums, vernacular performers of *baojuan* 寶卷, and so-called "sectarian" movements). And one will miss a good part of the meaning of the rituals due to being unfamiliar with the liturgy (published descriptions of festivals hardly ever discuss the liturgy used by religious specialists). Yet another example is the specificity of certain social classes, such as the fishing people, *yumin* 漁民, who in Jiangnan as elsewhere in China, had and still have distinctive social organizations and rituals, that written sources tend to avoid discussing in detail—gazetteers in particular tend to abhor discussion of social, class, and ethnic difference.

2. *To believe uncritically in oral history.* This is the opposite pitfall to the previous one. We all know that people constantly reinvent their own life histories and memories as they go—indeed, we do so ourselves. A well-meaning fascination with "salvage anthropology" might lead us to invest extraordinary value in the oral memories of an old person who may be the last surviving witness to practices that are now long gone. And yet, a description not corroborated by textual sources is very difficult to use.

3. *Putting aside the transformations of modernity as being someone else's job.* I am in full sympathy with attempts to retrieve what is left of "traditional" society in the field, but it seems very difficult to understand what we see and hear in the field if we are not aware of all that took place in between the late imperial period and the present, including radical transformation of the administrative system, local power relations, economy, and ecology, as well as political movements that forced temples, cults, rituals, and communities to reinvent themselves, in appearance as well as in substance, in order to remain acceptable to some degree.

One such transformation is the changing position of spirit-mediums within the local socio-religious landscape. Currently, female *xiangtou* 香頭 (lit. "incense head," meaning a religious leader and organizer of festivals and pilgrimages—the *xiangtou* are often, but not necessarily mediums) plays a leading role in rebuilding temples, organizing pilgrimages, connecting ordinary people with religious specialists, and so forth. It is easy to suppose that such spirit-mediums represent an old and largely unchanged tradition, one that was long undetected by the state. Nothing could be less true. Mediums used to be regulated and embedded in local systems allocating ritual labor and roles; organizing large-scale rituals was the preserve of gentry men. The abolition of such local regulations by the state, accompanied by the destruction of clerical institutions and the demise of the gentry class that formerly organized religious events at all levels, has actually empowered female spirit-mediums. Clerics whom I have interviewed in Jiangnan claim that female mediums have much more power than before, and in a reversal of the former hierarchy, that they tend to lord this power over clerics. Clerics have their own reasons to make such claims, but historical documents tend to suggest there is some truth to them. This then must be understood as a direct result of the political changes of the twentieth century. Because there are so few written documents that were produced by or around spirit-mediums, these sources represent the most challenging aspect for a historical anthropology of local society; and yet it is an aspect that absolutely cannot be neglected.

Another aspect of the impact of historical change is the mobility of persons. One needs to get a sense of how to locate the people who once lived in the place of research interest. For instance, it has often become almost useless to interview the monks in the local temples in Jiangnan because the vast majority have been assigned or hired in that place recently, but were born several hundred kilometers away, and have no knowledge and little interest in local society and culture. Still, one cannot make assured claims that this or that thing mentioned never existed. The one person who knows some particular matter may be an old Daoist or Buddhist at-home priest who lived in the village for most of his life but now stays with his children somewhere else (monks will deny that there are married *heshang* 和尚, but there actually are, and they are very important and interesting informants).

Indeed, identifying a person who knows about the local territory is a concern for locals before it is one for the historical anthropologist. As in much of China, but on a particularly spectacular scale in industrialized Jiangnan, territories and their communities have been transformed over the last generation. Around Suzhou, villages initially rebuilt their territorial temples during the 1980s. These were razed together with the villages to give way to the industrial parks in the 1990s; subsequently, the villagers built shrines clustered around the sole surviving (higher-order) local temple. This temple was, in turn, torn down in the late 2000s, and in its place, the industrial park built a brand new, officially recognized Daoist temple with rows of statues of the village gods. Since that time, the villagers, who had been relocated and often dispersed, will travel to that temple in the middle of the factories to honor their village god, and to report to the god the death of family members (*baomiao* 報廟). Knowing who is one's village territorial god, and where to find him, has become a real, and sometimes tricky question for former villagers. Temple clerics often do not know, whereas spirit-mediums or *baojuan* performers frequently are better informed.

4 *Going to the field and asking questions before reading the written record about the place.* Informants in Jiangnan like elsewhere tend to give you as much information as you seem able to understand, not more—especially on sensitive topics like religion (aka "superstition"). If you ask large questions with standard *putonghua* vocabulary, you tend to be given general answers, worth little. If you want to see documents, it makes a difference to know what they are called locally. Bring copies of your own local documents and hint that you can make sense of them. If you want information about a ritual, you should know its specific local vocabulary. Lots of things never get mentioned in conversations if you don't say the particular words first. When you do, people often smile and say "oh, so you know" and, then, start speaking in more detail. Of course, the local scholars you work with know these things, but it may not come to their minds that you may be interested in them. Bringing along sources such as late Qing or Republican press reports or accounts from village gazetteers or *biji* stories about the local people's temples and festivals, highlighting the rare or bizarre terms and asking about

them (or, even better, showing that you have already more or less figured it out) can take you much further than just saying: "tell me about the festivals in your district."

As the above suggests, I strongly believe in the value of doing historical work on the available written evidence *and* going to the field. Of course, that kind of statement in no way prepares one for facing some hard facts about the discrepancies one encounters when using the two approaches in conjunction with each other.

What is there in the written sources that is not apparent in the field?

One of the things I learned from reading the sources on Jiangnan local society and religion was that it was highly regulated from below, not by the state. For instance, one could not hire a priest willy-nilly; it was necessary to abide by long-term, contractual and mutually binding relations built between families and their providers: Buddhists, Daoists, Confucian priests (*lisheng* 禮生), pariahs (*jianmin* 賤民, performing for weddings and funerals), musicians, diviners, carriers of sedans and coffins, firecracker specialists, and even spirit-mediums. These specialists would sue each other in court if one took a job in someone else's turf. That sort of regulation no longer exists. Some Western scholars appear incredulous when faced with these facts that run counter to their view that Chinese society is and has always been enthusiastically entrepreneurial, valuing competition, and that Chinese religion is one expression of this cultural love for unfettered competition. What is to be done when "impressions" from the field trump evidence from the documented record? To resolve this, one must ask the clerics. Most of those who I have interviewed recognize the technical terms formerly used for these contractual relationships (*mentu* 門圖/徒 or *menjuan* 門眷); some younger ones do not, but admit that this was the former principle underlying interactions between clerics and families. Indeed, some families have kept old *menjuan* contracts. To fully bring this tradition to light, however, one must understand how the regulation was dismantled—and that evidence is in newspapers and archives (local archives in the area are very difficult to access, with the important exception of the Shanghai Municipal Archives, which has very little pre-1912 material).

Another aspect of early modern religious life in Jiangnan that is very much present in the historical sources but is not readily apparent in the field is spirit-writing (*fuji* 扶乩, *fuluan* 扶鸞, *feiluan* 飛鸞, *jiangbi* 降筆). A good number of village and district gazetteers from before 1949 state unequivocally that each village had its spirit-writing group joined by all those of some literacy (men, and increasingly from the turn of the twentieth century, women as well). The press is also replete with reports on the practice. Because of the connection with the "sectarian" traditions such as Yiguandao, spirit-writing was severely repressed after 1949 and remained banned, hence its invisibility; but it has not disappeared. A large, very active pre-1949 network of spirit-writing temples based at Jin'gaishan 金蓋山 (Huzhou, northern Zhejiang) that I have studied linked temples that had after 1949 very different trajectories. Some were categorized by "outsider" Chinese Communist Party (CCP) cadres as "counter-revolutionary sects." These groups have not been revived to this day. Others in adjoining districts were luckier to be merely labeled as "superstitious," and thus, in several cases, have been allowed to reform, even though their specific cult practices and rituals clearly betray their spirit-writing origins. The Jin'gaishan network has partly been reconstituted, but with new forms of affiliation. It is thus necessary to know the history of the spirit-writing practice to understand these temples and the network, but one has to be careful when discussing it in the field.

What is there in the field that isn't in the textual sources?

As mentioned above, one of the many problems one runs into when doing purely textual historical anthropology is that some aspects of ritual and festive life go unreported even in the most "ethnographic" of written sources—and not necessarily because of a critical bias. For instance, Rostislav Berezkin (a specialist on *baojuan* traditions) and I have examined the pilgrimage to the Three Mao Brothers 三茅真君 at Maoshan 茅山, one of the most important pilgrimage destinations in modern and contemporary Jiangnan—on a par with the better known Buddhist (Guanyin) pilgrimages to Hangzhou and Putuoshan. When reviewing the evidence, we found that, whereas the *baojuan* and their performers are hardly discussed in historical records (including the press, which by contrast provides much information on the Three Mao Brothers spirit-mediums), field work evidence clearly reveals that they are at the core of the cult and the pilgrimage. Any village group doing the pilgrimage brings its own *baojuan* performer. As a result, the many versions of the *Sanmao baojuan* 三茅寶卷 that tell the story of the Three Mao Brothers are the most abundant source on the deities, their history, and the values they uphold. We also collected Daoist texts (as well as *baojuan*!) on the Three Mao Brothers from Daoists at Maoshan, but these texts are surprisingly few and late when compared to the *baojuan*.

The same holds for many if not most local cults. One very interesting case is that of the Wutong 五通 (Five Powers) and their cult center at Shangfangshan 上方山 near downtown Suzhou. These five brothers (together with their mother) who possess female spirit-mediums have a bad reputation in the historical sources, and the anecdotal literature, in particular, has led historians to describe them as demonic beings whom everyone—Daoists, Buddhists, state officials—attempts to suppress, subdue, and/or transform. Yet, fieldwork shows that the cult is thriving, and that the gods are not generally considered malevolent or even dangerous. The main written sources about them, again the *baojuan* Rostislav has collected from both the performers themselves and various collections in libraries, are the best source to study how local people see the Wutong and negotiate their moral value and their connection to them.

All the examples mentioned here show that when working on religion in Jiangnan, it is possible and rewarding to do either historical work with sources such as local gazetteers and newspapers, or ethnography, but that joining both is much more illuminating even if challenging. One of the challenges is that bridging the differences between what can be read in libraries and what can be seen in the field requires some understanding of the modern transformations of local society and religion over the last three generations (including the much understudied 1940s and 1950s). Yet another challenge is the question of scale. Ethnography by nature focuses on small-scale communities (a single village or sacred site) with welcome detail, but not always a clear sense of how that one community is specific or distinctive; research based on historical records easily compares different places that share common cults, rituals, practices, and social organization—but may also slip into over-generalization. To what extent Jiangnan is a coherent cultural entity that warrants a macro-level study (and where to trace its borders) is an open and often unaddressed question: this is indeed a general problem in the study of Chinese culture where geographical markers ("south," "north") are often purely rhetorical. Historical anthropology is likely the best way to identify the most relevant level of analysis between the village and the vast region home to hundreds of millions.

Further Reading

Dean, Kenneth and Zheng Zhenman, *Ritual Alliances of the Putian Plain*. Leiden; Boston: Brill, 2010, 2 vols.

DuBois, Thomas David, *Sacred Village: Social Change and Religious Life in Rural North China*. Honolulu: University of Hawaii Press, 2005.

Goossaert, Vincent, "The local politics of festivals: Hangzhou, 1850–1950," *Daoism Religion, History & Society*, 5, 2013, pp. 57–80.

———, "Wanqing ji Minguo shiqi Jiangnan diqu de yingshen saihui 晚清及民國時期江南地區的迎神賽會" [Festivals in Jiangnan during the Late Qing and Republican period], in *Gaibianle Zhongguo zongjiao de wushinian* 改變了中國宗教的50年, Paul R. Katz and Vincent Goossaert, eds. Taipei: Institute of Modern History, Academia Sinica, 2015, pp. 75–99.

———, "The Jin'gaishan network," in *Modern Urban Daoism*, Vincent Goossaert and Liu Xun, eds. London: Routledge, forthcoming.

———, "Irrepressible Female Piety. Late Imperial Bans on Women Visiting Temples," *Nan Nü. Men, Women and Gender in China*, 10 (2), 2008, pp. 212–241.

——— and Rostislav Berezkin. "The Three Mao Lords in modern Jiangnan. Cult and Pilgrimage between Daoism and *baojuan* recitation," *Bulletin de l'EFEO*, 99 (2012–2013), pp. 295–326.

Inlis, Alister David, *Hong Mai's Record of the Listener and Its Song Dynasty Context*. Albany: State University of New York Press, 2006.

Kang, Xiaofei and Donald S. Sutton. *Contesting the Yellow Dragon. Ethnicity, Religion, and the State in the Sino-Tibetan Borderland*. Leiden: Brill, 2016.

Katz, Paul R. *When Valleys Turned Blood Red: The Ta-pa-ni incident in Colonial Taiwan*. Honolulu: University of Hawai'i Press, 2005.

12 Incorporating historical GIS in fieldwork on Chinese culture and religion

Kenneth Dean

When I first began fieldwork on Chinese religion in Tainan, Taiwan, in 1984, I lived in one of the only apartment buildings then standing in Tainan city, situated at the end of Chung-shan Road. From my window, I could see much of the city. Almost every night, I could see fireworks shooting up from one temple or another as the birthdays of the gods were celebrated. I gradually developed a sense of the spatial distribution of the temples around the city, and the calendar of their festivals. I was fortunate to have had an introduction to the Daoist Master Chen Rongsheng 陈荣盛道长 from Professor Kristofer Schipper. Master Chen invited me to attend the rituals he performed in temples around the city throughout the year, which gave me another perspective on the hierarchy of urban temples. Research on the epigraphy of the temples of Tainan revealed that this hierarchy culminated in late imperial times in the City God temple, where the state cult intersected with Daoist rites, and from where the sedan chair of the City God was followed in a procession around the entire city by all the major temples of Tainan.

Spatial analysis provides different insights at different scales. The layout of each temple, and the actions of ritual specialists as well as worshippers inside that temple and in the courtyard and stage outside it are spaces of transformation that are essential to the analysis of ritual processes. Different flows of people, including ritual specialists, spirit mediums, villagers, and visitors, the movement of offerings, the burning of incense, spirit money, and the cooking of food, and the distinct uses of spaces according to the timing of events within an overall ritual event—all of these place-making activities can be analyzed from a spatial perspective that is as attentive to movement as to fixed sites, and to friction and sudden acceleration as well as to historical temporalities and long-term changes (Dean and Lamarre 2003, 2007; see also Lefebvre 1991).

One of my PhD advisors, G.W. Skinner, emphasized the importance of spatial analysis for many years. He successfully developed a historical GIS (geographical information system) approach (Skinner 1964–1966, 1985, 1994) as part of his analysis of nine macro-regions of China, combining an analysis of central place theory and marketing zones with an analysis of the geographical boundaries between regions (mountain ranges, drainage systems, hinterlands, passes, and roadways). He applied GIS methodology to a wide range of issues in Chinese studies, transforming the field by demonstrating that the presumed one-dimensional political geography of imperial China masked a range of diverse regional economic systems with their own cycles of rise and decline (Skinner 1985). However, his effort to extend his comparative GIS analysis to cultural and religious aspects of Chinese geography was never completed (see his 1994 geographic analysis of the Lingnan region, based on a set of over 100 variables—even in this study, cultural elements are not central to the analysis -see also the critique from a theory of geography perspective in Cartier 2004). This led some of his students, such as P. Steven Sangren (1987), to propose a cultural geographic analysis that went beyond the limits of market town central place theory, especially in relation to religious phenomena such as pilgrimages in Taiwan. Indeed, some religious sites thrive on their relative distance from city and market centers.

I was fortunate to continue my research after a year in Tainan at Xiamen University in Fujian in 1985–1987, just as the great founding temples of the main deity cults of that province were being restored and their rituals and processions re-invented (Dean 1993). During my fieldwork in Fujian, I began a 30-year research collaboration with Prof. Zheng Zhenman 郑振满 of Xiamen University. As a native of the Putian/Xianyou 莆田仙游 region, he helped me when I first began to study the spread of the Three in One sectarian syncretic religious movement founded by Lin Zhao'en 林兆恩 (1517–1598) in this area (Dean 1998). Later we worked together to locate, photograph, transcribe, edit, and publish local stone inscriptions on the history of religion from the greater Minnan 闽南 region (Dean and Zheng 1995, 2003, forthcoming). From 2001 to 2008, we collaborated on a village-by-village survey of ritual activities in a geographically defined region, the man-made alluvial irrigated plain to the west of Putian city (Dean and Zheng 2010). In the course of all this research, I moved from research on four major cult centers and their extended networks, to the distribution of 1,000 temples dedicated to Lin Zhao'en in the two counties of Putian and Xianyou, to a study of ritual activities in over 2,500 temples in 724 villages on the irrigated, alluvial Putian plain. In all these projects, questions of physical, religious, and cultural geography were central.

The gathering of stone inscriptions related to the history of religion in Fujian required us to ride for miles around the countryside on motorcycles. We went up and down deserted mountain roads searching for remote monasteries and the upstream weirs of irrigation systems. We rode into narrow, crowded village streets, searching for the temples inevitably to be found with an open courtyard at the center or at the edges of the village. We had plenty of accidents and mishaps along the way, losing skin, and blood as well as four out of six motorbikes. This was a great way to get a sense of the lay of the land, and I highly recommend it to anyone considering fieldwork in rural areas. It is hard to describe the joys of discovering, photographing, reading, and transcribing an ancient stone inscription after a day of searching; and one also quickly gains an understanding of the importance of the placement of steles. These are objects of public memory and local history.

One soon develops a sense of the contents of the inscriptions—stories of the powers of the god, the collective response and contributions of the villagers, and the cross-section of the village provided by the list of donations, sometimes arranged by quantity, sometimes by rank, or lineage, or territorial sub-division, or members in a ritual alliance. We saw hundreds of new inscriptions being carved and set up by reconstructed temples, describing the "kalpic disaster" of the Cultural Revolution and the "new spring wind" of the revival of religious traditions. Many included donations from Overseas Chinese from Southeast Asia and Taiwan compatriots, indicating a centuries-long transnational network, which we later followed to Singapore, Malaysia, Borneo, and Indonesia. All these inscriptions, like all other local historical documents, should be read "in situ." Only by interpreting them in relation to their geographical and socio-historical setting can these documents enable one to comprehend their roles within local society, and their processes of production, limited circulation, and preservation of memory and meaning.

The contrast between the Xinghua 兴化 region, made up of the two counties of Putian and Xianyou, and the rest of the greater Minnan region (traditionally divided into Quanzhou and Zhangzhou prefectures) made clear the significance of local geographically defined cultural regions. Putian and Xianyou counties have three million inhabitants who share a local dialect (topolect), cuisine, architecture, opera, pantheon of the gods, ritual traditions, customary practices, and, to some degree, a local cultural self-understanding. Xinghua and Minnan topolects are mutually unintelligible, and people on either side of these linguistic boundaries live in markedly different cultural universes.

In the course of our survey, we found one temple in a remote part of the Putian plain, set amidst salt-fields and brick kilns, which had been built in 1964, already a year into the Socialist Education Campaign. We found many temples that had been rebuilt, repaired, and reopened in 1979, some 15 years later. Villagers we met described meeting in secret during the Cultural Revolution, hiding statues of the gods and steles, and performing some rites in private. Others still bitterly lamented the destruction of ancient temples and statues. Daoist masters described periods of imprisonment and the impounding and often the destruction of their personal collections of liturgical manuscripts, altar hangings, and paintings. They described the slow and still ongoing process of rebuilding their ritual traditions, often by sharing fragmentary texts and performing simplified versions of rites. Over the next three decades, we would see a strong revival of Daoist ritual traditions, Buddhist, Three in One, and spirit medium rituals in the area. Seeing the intermixture of these different ritual traditions in the present day, sometimes within the same overall ritual event, led me to develop a new theory of the syncretic ritual field, a historically evolving mix of multiple liturgical frameworks, as it operated within Xinghua local culture (Dean 1998; Dean and Zheng 2010, ch. 10).

Attending and participating in local ritual events is a crucial way to gain deeper understanding of families, kinship systems, villages, ritual alliances, and geographic and cultural regions as a whole. There are rituals symbolically marking and actually generating each of these levels. During the first few years of our fieldwork together, Zheng Zhenman and I argued endlessly about the power and significance of rituals in generating (actual, experimental, and imagined) community, and, as we observed the spread and increasing scale and intensity of ritual events in the region, we gained deeper insights into the power and significance of local ritual traditions. Zheng Zhenman had a Marxist socio-economic perspective, with a deep knowledge of the Chinese imperial states' institutional history in terms of changing policies on taxation, registration of households, and local governance. He was also very familiar with the history of local land rights, and he developed a sophisticated model of continuously transforming family-lineage structures (Zheng 2001). Over the course of our fieldwork, he came to the realization that the ritual unification efforts of the founder of the Ming dynasty, known as the *sheji* (altar of the soil and grain) system, had left significant traces on the local ritual structure of the Putian area, and thus, on regional social and geographic history, but that this system had quickly mutated from the neo-classical order imposed by Zhu Yuanzhang and had become a new mixed form of *she-miao*—altars of the earth established *inside of* local god temples (Dean and Zheng, 2010, Part 2). These then became essential building blocks in the evolution of a system of local ritual alliances in the area. Many of these unique historical cultural features cannot be found in other, later developing regions (such as Taiwan, which was colonized primarily during the Qing period).

From 2001 to 2008, every summer we conducted a village by village survey of the religious sites and ritual activities of 1,500 villages, including those on the 424 square kilometer largely man-made (over a thousand years) irrigated alluvial plain west of Putian, and those located in several townships along the upper reaches of the Lai river. We eventually published findings on the Putian plain only, made up of 724 villages distributed over this plain and currently organized into 154 multi-village ritual alliances. We developed a historical GIS for this region, comprising multiple layers of maps based on databases of geo-referenced sites with temporal information added (e.g., including historically changing shorelines, irrigation systems, cities, towns and villages, temples, ancestral halls, Buddhist monasteries, and various shrines—all linked to founding dates where possible).

Our historical GIS system allowed us to reconstruct the process of the filling in of the bay, which reached to the gates of Putian in the Tang dynasty, and the settling of the reclaimed irrigated land with villages from the Tang, to the Song, Ming and into the early Qing, when the bay reached its current boundaries. Settlement filling into available spaces continued in satellite villages in the late Ming, Qing, and early Republican periods. Nowadays, the main tendency is the spread of the urban zone and township centers into and

148 Kenneth Dean

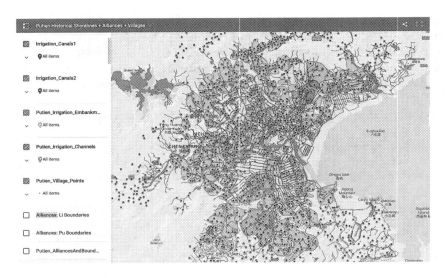

Figure 12.1 GIS Map of the Putian plain, showing village points, ritual alliances, and irrigation systems (screenshot from shgis.nus.edu.sg, 10.11.2018). The left hand menu allows the viewer to highlight different village networks.

over the surrounding villages. We were able to reconstruct the process of construction of multiple highly elaborate and interconnected irrigation systems, with sluice gates spaced at regular intervals, designed to prevent seawater from entering newly created rice fields at high tide while also allowing fresh water from the Mulan and the Qiulu rivers to be guided into the fields when needed, and sluiced out twice daily back into the receding tides of the sea.

We set about constructing this kind of historical GIS database in order to provide a more comprehensive approach to local religious and cultural history in a trans-local perspective and to demonstrate the role of ecological factors in local history, and to examine the impact of rapid urban development. We attempted a comprehensive survey of the population, lineages, temples, gods, and ritual activities of all 724 villages in the Putian alluvial plain. We then combined our survey results with geo-referenced points drawn from local historical sources (district gazetteers, irrigation system gazetteers, local literati writings, and gathered stone inscriptions). We entered data into our Putian historical GIS system to produce maps of the distribution of multiple cultural features. This provided a spatial dimension to cultural features by showing the distribution of lineages, literati, and temples of the local gods across the Putian area. We next developed an analysis of resulting patterns of distribution of cultural features over time. Our GIS system enabled us to map the entire Putian plain into 154 ritual alliances, consisting of alliances of three or four villages to larger alliances of 36 surrounding villages. The local term for these alliances is *qijing* 七境 (seven-fold ritual alliance).

We made several discoveries due to patterns that arose while comparing data within the GIS system. We found that there were a number of specific areas of high Confucian activity (high success rate in exams, presence of *paifang* 牌坊 commemorative arches, long-established major lineages). We also identified areas with little or no sign of Confucian activity, which by contrast were sub-regions characterized by a high degree of (sometimes collective) spirit medium training and ritual activity. This suggested a much more variegated cultural landscape—different cultural zones side by side in a close space—in late imperial China than is usually assumed.

We found strong evidence of a locally inflected pantheon with its own written sources and ritual forms. While we expected Mazu (Tianhou 妈祖/天后) to be the most common deity in the area, she is, in fact, in seventh place, with the God of Theater, Tian Gong Yuanshuai 田公元帅, in second place after the Earth God (who is much more complex in the Putian region due to the lingering influence of the Ming *sheji-gushe* 社稷古社 system). Commander Tian is the subject of many local myths, legends, ritual plays, and rites of deliverance that developed locally in the Putian region. We found evidence of the historical mixing of ritual traditions that greatly complicated our understanding of ritual events in Chinese popular religion and led to the elaboration of new theoretical perspectives on the "syncretic ritual field" (Dean 1998; Dean and Lamarre 2003, 2007).

I discovered the two earliest recorded ritual alliances (first mentioned in a Hongzhi 弘治 period prefectural gazetteer and dated around 1501) had formed as a result of disputes over water flow within the southern plains irrigation system (Dean and Zheng 2010). This then provided another hypothesis for the formation of the ritual alliances: these may have evolved to overcome the limitations of lineage land-holdings situated along smaller segments of the irrigation system that were not able to manage the escalating demands for water-usage, unpredictable tidal flows, and the need for water retention within canals, all in an increasingly complex system. Broader coalitions of lineages and villages, based in higher-order temples which functioned as management centers for larger irrigation systems, formed at this time into ritual alliances. But at the same time, much of the cohesion and strength of these alliances arose from the fact that many were formed out of the branch temples of founding *sheji* temples dating back to the early Ming. These hypotheses can be cross-checked and tested against data gathered in the historical GIS for Putian that we developed (Dean and Zheng 2010).

How can one build one's own historical GIS for the region under study?

To create a historical GIS of a particular region one must first have a clear sense of the geographical boundaries and features of the region, and some idea of its cultural historical uniqueness. Next, it is necessary to gather and digitize current maps of the region and, if possible, digitize historical maps of the region, and study records on the evolution of its geography. We were fortunate to be able to draw on historical boundary data published in the 2004 *Fujiansheng lishi dituji* 福建省历史地理图集 *(Collected maps on the Historical Geography of Fujian)*. One must select the most detailed base maps possible. For our project, we digitized and vectorized People's Liberation Army (PLA) topographical maps from 1960 at a scale of 1:20,000. We paid special attention to the tracing of irrigation systems, the shapes of housing clusters in the villages, and the location of villages, using a digitizing tool to inscribe lines and shapes (polygons) from traced maps onto a digitizing tablet. We added additional information and points from the *Gazetteer of Putian Placenames* and other local maps. We also included additional points based on our own on-the-ground survey. For each village or residential cluster, we sought to locate the lowest level independent ritual units. We digitized township boundaries from contemporary maps. Historical boundaries (based on the *Collected Historical Maps of Fujian*, 2004) were added to another layer of the map. Ritual alliance boundaries (based on information given in each village) were added as yet another layer. The maps were rubber-sheeted to fit satellite imagery purchased from Quickbird and LANDSAT. This provided additional verification for the locations of villages. Survey data were entered into a database (MySQL) and linked to the Attribute Tables in ArcGIS. A website is under construction that provides online maps to site visitors who can then view historical layers and ritual alliances, as well as the distribution of gods, lineages, and other features. Each point on the map is also an archive of information, photos, and texts from the temples of that village (shgis.nus.edu.sg under Linked Projects: Putian).

Much of the technology for this kind of research has advanced considerably since the time of our Putian survey. The extraordinary online resources of the Chinese Historical GIS (CHGIS) and Chinese Biographical Database (CBDB) based at Harvard University make it very convenient for anyone to download base maps for their particular regions of interest. Nowadays, one can access most GIS software tools using freeware such as QGIS. Most smart phones have built in GPS location finders, which can be set to automatically tag images and to create maps using GIS software. Google Maps enables one to build a simple GIS system made up of ten layers, and to add points and draw new layers using the KML software. Tutorials on this kind of software are available on *YouTube*, and most universities have GIS labs that can provide technical support for such projects. I look forward to multiple historical GIS projects in Chinese studies in the coming years. It does, however, require a lot of time and energy to conduct surveys using detailed questionnaires in specific sites in order to build up a database for GIS analysis.

Unfortunately, very little is known about the actual distribution of Chinese ritual traditions across China. The imperial, Republican, and contemporary regional gazetteers provide only fragmentary information on the numbers of temples, monasteries, ancestral halls, and sectarian halls in specific regions. By some estimates, including my own for the Putian area, available information amounts to less than 5–10 percent of what was there. More recent government issued statistics may push this number up to 10–30 percent, but this is still not very comprehensive. There is a great need for more comprehensive geographically based surveys of ritual activity in different areas of China. With the growth of Internet postings, it may be possible in some areas to reach something closer to 50–70 percent accuracy. Thus, for example, recent work on the spread of temples and monasteries in Xiamen city by Daniel Murray drew on such sources, as well as his own fieldwork, to map the locations of over 120 temples in the city, many of which were newly opened (Murray 2018). Researchers working on the historical geography of Beijing have documented the sites of over 1,000 temples there, of which only a handful remain. William Grootaers (1995) conducted surveys in northern China in the 1930s that found an average of 3–4 temples per village—similar to our findings in Putian in the 1990s. Much more survey work needs to be done to build up a more complete account of the distribution and nature of Chinese popular religious sites. Projects such as ours in Putian provide important "ground-truthing" correctives to dubious official statistics.

The situation in Taiwan is radically different, thanks to the work of the GIS center at the Academia Sinica. There, under the leadership of Dr. Fan Li-chun, a GIS map of over 15,000 temples across Taiwan has been developed. This dataset is geo-referenced by location and has information on the date of construction of temples, and it includes data on the deities worshipped and some of the rituals conducted on an annual basis. Photographs and other archival materials are included in the dataset. This is an extremely rich source for historical GIS work on Taiwanese history, and its links with Fujian, Chaozhou, and Hakka regions. More recently, even more fine-grained datasets of Taiwanese Buddhist institutions have been developed by research teams at Fagushan University.

What are the intellectual stakes in using this technology in fieldwork?

One of the key intellectual stakes of this research concerns theories of the relative centrality of irrigation to administration in Chinese culture. According to Karl Wittfogel, *Oriental Despotism* (1957), Chinese state authority was largely based on its ability to mobilize the population for the construction of vast water control systems (i.e., the Grand Canal). In contrast, J. Stephen Lansing, in *Priests and Progammers* (2007) argued that irrigation systems in Bali were self-organizing systems. The generation of large-scale crop rotation and decreased pest damage was achieved through the interaction of local village based irrigation temples scattered around the entire island of Bali. Our research in Putian revealed that the Song state under Wang Anshi 王安石 (1021–1086) did call for the construction of large-scale irrigation systems, but that it farmed the construction of these systems out to local entrepreneurs, who had to win the backing of local landlords and lineages. We demonstrated, based on a reading of local irrigation system gazetteers, stone inscriptions, and legal case documents, that the Mulan irrigation system grew too complex for lineage control by the mid-Ming, leading to the rise of a self-organizing system of regional ritual alliances (made up of multiple villages and lineages) into a system-wide hierarchy of irrigation management based in higher-order temples. The power of the state could still occasionally be accessed when breaking points in the system were reached. The state intervened on such occasions to set the distribution of water at key intersections in the system, but the long-term management and development of the irrigation remained in the hands of the local temples, ritual alliances, and higher-order temples. Thus, the Putian case is midway between the "Oriental Despotism" model described by Wittfogel, and the village-centered island-wide self-organizing system from below described by Lansing. The larger story, however, concerns the increasing degree of autonomy of the Chinese villages in controlling their own environmental resources from the mid-Ming onwards. Without the development of a historical GIS for the Putian plains, it would have been difficult to detect the underlying patterns or to test various hypotheses regarding historical developments in the region.

A second key intellectual issue is a comparative one—can the study of geographically determined regions reveal the development of local cultural institutions that led to cultural unification with the rest of China? For example, could we trace the rise and spread of a range of cultural institutions: temples to officially canonized local gods, standardized lineage halls, locally based philanthropic institutions, etc., which developed in one region, and then spread to other parts of China, contributing along the way to a growing set of elements defining Chinese culture? Alternatively, can local features suggest alternatives to centralization effects, particularly when the regions under study are located on the coast, with long historical ties to Southeast Asia as well as the imperial center?

One of the most significant insights gained from the comparative study of different historical regions is the rapid rise and spread of new religious and cultural phenomena. Some remain concentrated within a specific region, while others spread rapidly across regions and dialect areas. How we interpret such phenomena is a key question in Chinese Studies. David Faure (2007) introduced the term "ritual revolution" to describe the widespread adaptation of a specific model of the lineage form in the Pearl River delta in the sixteenth century. He argued this was a key mechanism for the recognition on the part of local people of their cultural identification with the state, and for achieving recognition from the state for the legality of household registration and land claims and hereditary rights. Together with Liu Zhiwei, he argued that different mechanisms had been adopted by the Chinese state at different times and places (Ke Dawei and Liu Zhiwei 2000, 2008).

Thus, they argued that Putian was absorbed into a unified state-defined culture in the Song, through the canonization of large numbers of local gods. The southwestern regions of China were absorbed in the late Ming by means of the gradual recognition and transformation of the *tusi* 土司 (native chiefdom) system by means of *guiliu* 归流 (return flow into the Chinese literati official order). In Hakka regions in the southeast, cultural unification involved first master-disciple transmission of written documents (i.e., local Daoist traditions) in the Ming, followed by a widespread conversion to Confucian lineage form in the early Qing.

However, the history of Putian did not come to a stop with its supposed integration into Chinese cultural unity by means of the canonization of local gods in the Song. More and more gods kept being produced in the Putian plains, to the point where we located over 1,200 gods in our surveys, half of whom were only known in a single village. Additional ritual "revolutions" continued to profoundly transform local society in Putian. This included the very early rise of the lineage form in Song and its spread throughout society by the mid-Ming (1100–1500). With the rise of new multi-village, multi-lineage ritual alliances with Daoist rites at higher-order temples entrusted with the maintenance of the irrigation systems in the alluvial coastal plain of Putian (1500–1750), lineages became absorbed into local ritual alliances and ritual activities. Lineages continuously underwent fundamental transformations through a development and decline cycle, as shown by Zheng (2001) from communal to hierarchical (with elites managing lineage trusts) to contractual (where shares in lineage investments could be purchased by non-lineage members). They also, along with temples and monasteries, were behind the formation of transnational networks reaching into Southeast Asia. These became circuits for the continual circular flow of people, ideas, ritual specialists and ritual artifacts. These circulations allow us to trace both ritual and institutional changes in Southeast Asia and back in Fujian.

Regarding these concerns, there is no question that comparative historical research would be greatly improved through the collective use of common GIS platforms—this would enable hypotheses to be tested across broader regions. However, to reach this stage of comparative analysis, historians will have to learn how to turn their data into databases compatible with GIS requirements, using standard geo-referencing as well as temporal coding. If this can be achieved, larger comparative paradigms can be tested against the emergent patterns and correlations within the data. Until that point, historical research will continue to rely on its own inevitably limited sources, much like traditional anthropology which often builds its models on the basis of research in a single village rather than on a survey of all the villages in a determined geographical setting. By broadening the evidential basis to all sites in a region, the entire combinatorial range of cultural features can be explored. Clearly this could lead to analysis based on breadth of coverage at the expense of depth of individual analysis—but this shortcoming can be mitigated by adding in data from frequent participant observation of ritual-events held within the region under study.

A historical GIS for Chinese temple networks across Southeast Asia

After concluding the Putian survey around 2008, Zheng Zhenman and I began exploring the overseas temple network that spread from Putian with the emigration of large numbers of male migrants in the late nineteenth century to Southeast Asia. We again used GIS technology to map the distribution of various temple and church networks that spread from Putian and Xianyou to various sites in Southeast Asia. We located 20 Xinghua temples in Singapore alone, along with four different native-place associations. Across Southeast Asia, we located dozens more Xinghua temples, ancestral halls, and *huiguan* 会馆. We explored the range of networks, their points of overlap, and the resources, people, ritual knowledge, and forms of spirit possession that flowed back and forth between the points in these networks at different times at different rates over the past 120 years. This is an ongoing project, which hopefully will be published soon.

In 2008, I began a project to map all the Chinese temples and native-place institutions in Singapore (Dean and Hue, 2017; Hue 2012). I did not anticipate at that time that the total figure would grow to include over 800 free standing temples, over 1,000 private spirit medium altars in Housing Development Block public housing units, 250 native-place associations and ancestral halls, 450 Christian churches, 100 mosques, 23 Indian temples, and countless unofficial religious and ritual sites (Dean 2015). This GIS mapping project has expanded since I moved to Singapore in 2015 (for preliminary results see the website: shgis.nus.edu.sg). Together with the Engineering and Computer Science Department, we developed an iPhone app which we hope to bring soon to the App Store. This Chinese Temple App asks users to take a series of photographs, starting with exterior shots, then the courtyard, then the main hall, then the god statues, then the principal cultural artifacts, then the posted written documents, and so forth, followed by a series of questions gathering basic data on the temple. All these data are automatically uploaded to our servers. Ultimately, we hope the public (and members of temples and associations) will use the App to send in corrections, new data, and video of ritual events. This is an example of Volunteer GIS. The aim is to develop a continuously expanding cultural database for the ritual activities of the Chinese (and other ethnic) communities of Singapore. The goals of this project are as follows: for Singapore, to study the distribution of Chinese temples by dialect group and link these to their home communities in Southeast and South China. For Southeast Asia, to map the networks of Chinese temples across the region historically, starting with the 1,500 plus dated inscriptions gathered and published by Franke (1985–1998); to map the distribution of cults created in Southeast Asia such as the Nine

Figure 12.2 Map of Singapore showing Chinese temples, *huiguan*, other religious buildings, and HDB boundaries (screenshot from shgis.nus.edu.sg, 10.11.2018). Each point links to a pop-up window containing relevant information.

Emperor Gods across Southeast Asia; and to examine changes to the network over time, including ritual changes originating in Southeast Asia and spreading back to China, or the repositioning of temples within division of incense networks whereby different nodes (say those in Singapore) become more central due to economic strength or ritual fervor. This project seeks to provide a new view of the multi-layered networks of transnational Chinese culture in interaction with regional cultures, from the ground up, rather than as imposed from above.

Transnational temple networks

A range of different networks link Singaporean temples, *huiguan*, lineage halls, and dialect communities to mother temples and ancestral sites across Southeast China. These networks can take the form of division of incense within popular god cults consecrated by dialect-specific, regional Daoist ritual traditions, master-disciple ties within Buddhist monastic networks, sectarian formations of many varieties, spirit-medium-led temples, business ties within native-place *huiguan* (usually based within temples), and ancestral ties to ancestral halls (sometimes with invented ancestors and kinship links based on common surnames). Many Singaporean temples, monasteries, nunneries, sectarian movements, *huiguan*, and ancestral halls have established strong local and regional (Southeast Asian) networks. These networks have yet to be mapped out and analyzed. Many of these temples have revived their ties to China in recent years through assisting in the reconstruction of halls and surrounding infrastructure, which was sorely needed after the destruction of the Cultural Revolution. Research on these networks is at a preliminary stage—many fundamental questions remain unanswered. In particular, the role of spirit mediums in maintaining temple followings and creating transnational networks remains to be explored.

So far, our research has successfully integrated multiple historical maps of Singapore (developed by the NUS Geography Department) as layers on a digital GIS base map. We have begun work building a biographical database of Singapore elites (linked to the GIS map), based on the CHGIS (Chinese Historical GIS) and CBDB (Chinese Biographical Database) models, developed at Harvard University. We are attempting to move beyond elite biographies by building up databases of genealogies, burial records, and demographic analysis of the dialect groups. We will develop social network analysis of connections and associational membership among the elite (currently, we have collected data on 1,500 Singaporeans and another 3,000 Southeast Asian Chinese). We hope to be able to incorporate data on Southeast Asian business history and networks, building on the collections in the Chinese Library of NUS: digital editions of Singaporean and Southeast Asian Chinese newspapers, rare books collection of several hundred temple and regional association commemorative volumes, Southeast Asian reference materials, links to oral histories in the Singapore National Archives, government records, digital image archives, and video footage.

What are the intellectual stakes in applying historical GIS to the study of Singapore and Southeast Asian Chinese transnational temple networks? Rem Koolhaus (1995), in his infamous essay "Songlines," described Singapore as a state-imposed *tabula rasa*, erasing history, imposing homogenous spaces, domesticating nature, fetishizing colonial heritage, and turning the place into one massive shopping mall. Singaporean cultural geographers have developed a much more complex account, emphasizing the power of the historical imagination to absorb and critique both nostalgia for the kampong and state constructed national heritage. Daniel Goh (2015) describes the constantly transforming forms and meanings of cultural hybridity, alternative modernity, and the continued power of ritual traditions "more powerful than culture or modernity" that create life "as-it-is," not an "as-if" alternate ritual world. In "Parallel Universes" (Dean 2015) I examined the evidence for the survival of cultural diversity in the proliferation of temples and associations but question the degree of interaction across cultural communities. Our Singapore Historical GIS (shgis.nus.edu.sg) provides maps and analytic resources to engage with these alternative perspectives on Singaporean culture, history, and current place-making activities.

As for the transnational networks linking Singapore and Southeast Asia to China, the historical GIS can reveal the historical depth and continuity of these networks, and the flows of people that made them significant. We can also show the scale of the reverse flow of people, money, and ritual knowledge after the end of the Cultural Revolution, to aid in the reconstruction of temples and ancestral halls and the re-invention of ritual traditions in Southeast and South China. This is in my view a movement of world-historical significance, because it has enabled these regions of China to have an alternative and richer sense of cultural past and future (historical memory and cultural aspirations) compared to more homogenized urban sites elsewhere in China.

These projects are ongoing, and hopefully reveal the potential for historical GIS in urban settings as well as in broader regional studies. I welcome students and scholars who would like to participate in building even more robust historical GIS models for the comparative study of Chinese ritual traditions in China and the broader Sinosphere.

References

Dean, Kenneth, "Parallel Universe: The Chinese Temples of Singapore." In Peter van der Veer, ed., *Handbook of Religion and the Asian City: Aspiration and Urbanization in the Twenty-First Century.* Berkeley: University of California Press, 2015: 273–298.

———, *Lord of the Three in One: The Spread of a Cult in Southeast China.* Princeton: Princeton University Press, 1998.

———, *Taoist Ritual and Popular Cults of Southeast China.* Princeton: Princeton University Press, 1993.

———, "Ritual Matters." In T. Lamarre and Kang Nae-he, eds., *Impacts of Modernities*, Hong Kong: University of Hong Kong Press, 2003: 257–284.

———, and Zheng Zhenman, *Epigraphical Materials on the History of Religion in Fujian: Xinghua Region* (1995); *Quanzhou Region*, 3 vols., (2004) *Zhangzhou Region*, 3 vols., forthcoming: Fuzhou: Fujian People's Press.

———, and Hue Guan Thye, *Chinese Epigraphic Materials in Singapore, 1819–1911*, Singapore: NUS Press, 2017.

———, and Thomas Lamarre, "Micro-sociology of the Ritual Event" (co-authored with Thomas Lamarre). In Anna Hickey-Moody and Peta Mahlins eds., *Deleuzian Encounters: Studies in Contemporary Social Issues*, London: Palgrave Macmillan, 2007: 181–197.

———, *Ritual Alliances of the Putian Plains: Vol. 1: Historical Introduction to the Return of the Gods: Vol. 2: A Survey of Village Temples and Ritual Activities*, Leiden: Brill, 2010.

Franke, Wolfgang and Chen Tie Fan, eds., *Chinese Epigraphic Materials in Malaysia*, 2 vols. Kuala Lumpur: University of Malaysia Press, 1980–1985.

———, *Chinese Epigraphic Materials in Indonesia*, collected, annotated, and edited by Wolfgang Franke, with the Collaboration of Claudine Salmon and Anthony Siu, and with the Assistance of Hu Luyun and Teo Lee Kheng, Singapore: Nanyang Xuehui, 3 vols in 4, 1988–97.

Franke, Wolfgang, editor, with editorial assistance from Liu Lifang, and assistance from Hu Junyin and Zhang Liqing, *Taiguo Hua wen ming ke hui bian (Chinese epigraphic Materials in Thailand).* Taibei: Xinwenfeng chuban gongsi, 1998.

Fujiansheng fangzhi difang weiyuanhui, ed., *Fujiansheng lishi dituji (Collected Maps on the Historical Geography of Fujian)*. Fuzhou: Fujiansheng ditu chubanshe 2004.

Goh, Daniel P.S., "In Place of Ritual: Global City, Sacred Space, and the Guanyin Temple in Singapore." In Peter van der Veer, ed., *Handbook of Religion and the Asian City: Aspiration and Urbanization in the Twenty-First Century*. Berkeley: University of California Press, 2015: 21–36.

Grootaers, W.A., Shiyu Li, and Fushi Wang, *The Sanctuaries in a North-China City: A Complete Survey of the Cultic Buildings in the City of Hsüan-hua (Chahar)*. Bruxelles: Institut belge des hautes études chinoises, 1995.

Hue, Guan Thye, "The Evolution of the Singapore United Temple: The Transformation of Chinese Temples in the Chinese Southern Diapora." *Chinese Southern Diaspora Studies*, Vol. 5, 2012: 157–174.

Ke, D. (David Faure) and Liu, Zhiwei, "Standardisation" or "Becoming Orthodox"? Examining Greater Chinese Cultural Unity from the Perspective of Popular Beliefs and Ritual Practices'" (in Chinese). *Lishi renleixue xuekan (History and Anthropology)*, Vol. 6, 2008: 1–21.

———, "Lineage and the Identification with the State of Local Society: The Ideological Foundations of the Development of the Lineage in Ming and Qing South China (in Chinese)'." *Lishi yanjiu (Historical Research)*, 3, 2000: 3–14.

Koolhaas, Rem, "Singapore Songlines." In Rem Koolhaas and Bruce Mau, ed. S, M, X, XL: OMA, Monacelli Press, 1995.

Lansing, J. Stephen, *Priest and Programmers: Technologies of Power in the Engineered Landscape of Bali*. Princeton: Princeton University Press, 2007.

Lefebvre, Henri, *The Production of Space*, trans. D. Nicholson-Smith, Oxford: Blackwell, 1991.

Murray, Daniel M., "The City God Returns: The Organised and Contagious Networks of the Xiamen City God Temple." *The Asia Pacific Journal of Anthropology*, 19. 4 (2018): 281–297.

Sangren, P. Steven, *History and Magical Power in a Chinese Community* Stanford: Stanford University Press, 1987.

Skinner, G.W., "Creolized Chinese Societies in Southeast Asia." In A. Reid, ed. *Sojourners and Settlers; histories of Southeast Asia and the Chinese*. Australia: Allen and Unwin, 1996: 51–93.

———, "Differential development in Lingnan." In *The Economic Transformation of South China: Reform and Development in the Post-Mao Era*, edited by Thomas P. Lyons and Victor Nee. Ithaca: Cornell East Asia Program, 1994: 17–54.

———, "Presidential address: The structure of Chinese history." *Journal of Asian Studies* 44. 2 (1985): 271–292.

———, "Marketing and social structure in rural China," Parts I, II, and III. *Journal of Asian Studies* 24, 1 (Nov. 1964): 3–44; 24, 2 (Feb. 1965): 195–228; 24, 3 (May 1965): 363–399.

Wittfogel, Karl, *Oriental Despotism: A Comparative study of total power*. New Haven: Yale University Press, 1957.

Zheng, Zhenman, *Family lineage organization and social change in Ming and Qing Fujian*. Translated by Michael Szonyi. Honolulu: University of Hawaii Press, 2001.

13 Walks in Canton
Doing historical anthropology in a Chinese city

May Bo Ching and Zhiwei Liu

Walking is probably one of the best exercises for practicing historical anthropology, regardless of how this discipline or approach is defined. To understand a community, be it urban or rural, we need to give it a walk, not just one but many. The aim of such walks is to establish a link between mind and feet, past and the present. As historians our craft lies in documentation, yet interpretation of documents calls for imagination inspired by everyday experiences. By walking we acquire a better sense of motion and direction to bring alive the texts and documents we read. Walking *away* from archives for a while will help us discover more out of archives. Ultimately, we still have to sit down to write, but the fluidity of our writing will no doubt be enhanced with the chemistry brought about by walking.

Students of Chinese historical anthropology are used to walking in villages. Some of them have become very skillful at visiting temples, observing rituals, interviewing local people, and taking photos of stone inscriptions and genealogies. Walking in cities may require some other techniques. One may also find temples, stone inscriptions, family records, and approachable people in cities, but because the city's population is in many cases made largely of migrants, and because most cities have undergone rapid development and redevelopment in the past one or two centuries, a walk in any Chinese city requires us to make extra effort to reconnect the imperial past with the present. As an experiment, we propose to start our walking exercise with Canton. Throughout this chapter, we prefer to call the city "Canton" as this term has been around for centuries longer than the *Pinyin* transliteration of "Guangzhou" 廣州. Like all other Chinese cities, Canton is typical as well as atypical. But being "representative" is not our concern. What we want to do with such a walk is to equip ourselves with some tools so that we can perceive the "Canton" of the past from the "Guangzhou" of the present. We trust that such tools are applicable to most other Chinese historical cities, although not many cities possess historical depth and cultural variety akin to Canton.

160 *May Bo Ching and Zhiwei Liu*

To start the walk, you may want to bring with you your smart-phone equipped with an interactive map for navigation. With such a map, you won't be surprised to find that you can locate historical place names that might be too obscure to be marked on a modern printed map. At the same time, to become familiar with historical place names, you should read as many old maps as possible, and you may want to select a few and bring them with you along your walk. Assuming you have already read some related literature, we don't think you need to bring with you any textual materials. If you need, you can still check and read *en route* a considerable amount of primary source materials available online with your smart-phone. But we don't think you should bother to do so. On the contrary, to trace your physical as well as your mental road map, we want you to go back to basics—bring a pen and a little notebook to jot notes and draw sketches. This will help you fabricate your own mental landscape which will then orient your writing at the end of the day. For this exercise, we have specially prepared a map with sites approximately located for your easy reference (Figure 13.1).

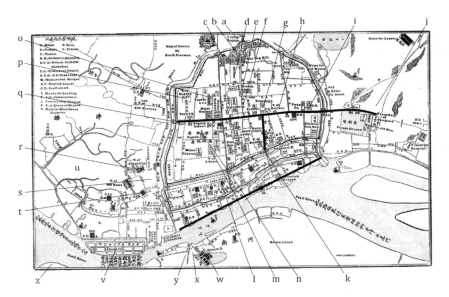

Figure 13.1 A map specially designed for the walk. Letters indicate the sites and the route described in the article. Modified on the basis of a map drawn probably by a Chinese around the 1880s, which was, in turn, a modification of an earlier one titled "Map of the City and entire suburbs of Canton" by Rev. D. Vrooman, 1860 (reprinted in Guangzhou shi Guihua Ju, Guangzhou shi Chengshi Jianshe Dang'anguan (eds.), *Tushuo Chengshi Wenmai: Guangzhou Gujin Dituji*, Guangzhou: Guangdongsheng Ditu chubanshe, 2010).

Capture the shape of the city and locate the starting point

We have to decide where to start our trail, as the selection of starting point indicates how you may want to narrate a history of your own. It is well known that the meaning of the Chinese word "*cheng*" 城 is multifold. In general, it refers to the city and its suburbs (*chengxiang* 城廂). In terms of physical construction, it includes the city wall and the moat (*chengqiang* 城牆 and *chenghao* 城濠). A Chinese imperial city in an administrative sense is therefore a walled enclosure within which various *yamens* (衙門 government offices) were set up. In Canton, the 1912 collapse of the imperial order was subsequently followed by the gradual removal of the city wall. The land on which the city walls previously stood and the extant streets and roads within the walled enclosure became the most convenient and reasonable sites for constructing modern motor roads. Hence, the "shape" of a modern city is often determined by the shape of its pre-twentieth-century walled counterpart.

Modern Guangzhou follows the contours of the bell-shaped walled city of Canton, which was built in 1380 by the Ming regime and modified in the early Qing period. Because almost all city walls in Canton had been torn down by the 1930s, and the first new motor roads were built upon the land left by the removal of the walls, walking along these roads today is therefore more or less like pacing the old city walls of the Ming and the Qing. People's Road 人民路 today stands on the land on which the western wall was erected, and Yuexiu Road 越秀路 is its counterpart in the east. Just above Yuexiu Road is the Donghaochong Viaduct 東濠涌高架. It is interesting to note that "Donghao chong," the current name of this elevated concrete and steel structure, literally means "East Moat." The East and the West Moats, together with the South Moat located along today's Dade 大德, Danan 大南, and Wenming 文明 Roads (all named after the inner gates on the southern wall during the Ming), functioned as a defensive barrier surrounding three sides of the city. On the northern edge, the city walls extended along Yuexiu Hill 越秀山, thus giving the city of Canton its unique bell shape, with the Five-Story Tower (*Wuceng Lou* 五層樓), also erected in 1380, sitting at the top of the dome. In 1563, a "new city" (*xincheng* 新城) was built to the south of the original city (then called the "old city," *laocheng* 老城) by extending the east and the west walls southwards and by building a new south wall on land formed from silted-up riverbed. Walking along Yide 一德, Taikang 泰康, and Wanfu 萬福 Roads today is comparable to walking along the new south wall between the sixteenth and the early twentieth century. In 1647, the Qing regime extended the west and east city walls further southward, reaching to the banks of the Pearl River and forming the "winged city," as the two extended walls resembled a pair of wings.

Encountering a Chinese city that has been evolving for two millennia (well before the Ming construction, the earliest walls were built in the Qin dynasty) forces us to think like the state. Standing in the Five-Story Tower places us atop of the walled city. Such a posture helps us think like the state in a physical sense. We therefore choose Five-Story Tower as our starting point for this walk (a). In temporal terms, it also means that we start our narratives of the history of Canton from the Ming, although we will soon see from the vast amount of archaeological finds that the city has a history going back more than 2,000 years.

From Exit A of the Yuexiu Park 越秀公園 Subway Station you will be led to the nearest park entrance through which you can walk uphill and arrive at the Five-Story Tower. Walking in the Park is not only good for our health, but also allows us to feel the elevation and observe how the northern part of the city wall was situated along the hill. Along the path you will see partial remains of the wall, which present to us at least three layers of history: the red sandstones at the bottom were laid in the Ming, on which layers of blue bricks were placed during the Qing, and more recently, a third layer was added as part of a restoration. Students of history should be able to distinguish various layers of history by identifying different materials available or applied in different periods.

The Five-Story Tower houses the Museum of Guangzhou, which displays the history of the city and the nearby area with interesting objects.[1] However, for the purpose of this walk, you should not spend too much time viewing the exhibits and instead go up to the top floor of the tower to take in the panoramic view of the city. Thirty years ago, you could see as far as the Pearl River from there. But today you will be disappointed, as modern skyscrapers block most of the views. It is time to use your imagination, and the official name of the tower, Zhenhai Lou 鎮海樓, Tower for Pacifying the Sea, might help. The naming of the tower indicated the expansion of the Ming Empire by suppressing opposition in the south. Leaning against the railings at the top floor (although you can't really do it due to safety concerns), you feel like the Ming Emperor overlooking the South Sea, reminding us that the Pearl River here is NOT a river, but is part of the sea subject to tidal influences. When local residents cross the river by ferry, they would call it "crossing the sea" (*guohai* 過海). Such local usages are crucial for us to appreciate the geographical feature of the city and the wider Pearl River Delta.

Leaving the Five-Story Tower, do not forget to turn around to salute the pair of stone lions who have been guarding the tower entrance for more than 600 years. They are worth a look as they represent the Ming style of stone lions, which appear more primitive than their elaborate Qing counterparts. Seldom do you see such stone lions in cities nowadays. Do have a look before their red sandstone becomes fully eroded.

Filled with a number of Republican monuments (b), the other parts of Yuexiu Park are also worth seeing: these include the 37-meter-high stone monument to Dr. Sun Yat-sen (completed 1930), the Library for Commemorating Commander Deng Zhongyuan 鄧仲元 (completed 1930), the Pavilion for Commemorating the 1922 Seamen Strike (completed 1933), and the Tombstone of Dr. Wu Tingfang 伍廷芳, the first Chinese legislator of Hong

Kong, and that of his son, the Nationalist diplomat Wu Chaoshu 伍朝樞. All these indicate the efforts made by the Nationalist Government to establish historic landmarks for a modern state. Yuexiu Park itself was one of the Republican municipal projects to create public spaces for modern citizens in the 1920s.

Attracted by sites of modern Chinese nationalism, one may easily overlook the remnants of old practices. Somewhere around the corner of the path leading to the Monument to Dr. Sun Yat-sen, it is not uncommon to find incense sticks placed by people from time to time, despite warnings issued by park security. The incense is probably not for worshipping the founder of the Republic but is a reminder of the former Guanyin Temple 觀音廟 on the hill. The temple no longer exists, but the stone arch inscribed with the two characters "Fo Shan" 佛山 (Buddha Hill) does, and people remember well that the hill is named "Guanyin Shan" 觀音山 (b). Evidently, there are people who try to maintain their own understanding, if not personal memories, of the place, in spite of the revolutionary efforts of place-making.

The uses of spaces as defined in imperial times, in fact, extend to the Nationalist and Communist epochs. Let us not linger at Yuexiu Park, but go and walk downhill along the "hundred-step ladder" and reach Yingyuan Road 應元路. It is named after the Daoist Sanyuan Palace (三元宮, Palace of the Three Primordials) (c), which is believed to have been built in the fourth century and was the site where Bao Gu 鮑姑, the wife of the Eastern Jin Daoist scholar Ge Hong 葛洪, practiced Daoist cultivation and alchemy. You will soon find that many temples and monasteries of this city are connected with early legends. We are not interested in judging whether these stories are true or not. It is enough that their survival implies the city has a history long enough to incorporate myths emerging since early times.

Along the axis, vertical and horizontal

Walk across Yingyuan Road, and you will be attracted by the spectacular Sun Yat-sen Memorial Hall (d) constructed in 1929 to commemorate the founder of the Republic (again!). You may be enthralled by its architectural splendor. Your intuition is not misguided, as it has been the center of state ceremonies since its founding. But to acquire a sense of space and direction, let us pass by and continue. Traversing Middle Dongfeng Road 東風中路, from north to south, you will pass, one after another, the buildings of the People's Congress of Guangzhou City, the Guangzhou Municipal Government (e), and then People's Park (f). These constructions witnessed numerous changes in the twentieth century, and yet their physical arrangement continues that of the imperial era. If you still remember that Five-Story Tower is located at the top of the dome, all the above-mentioned public constructions are developed along the north-south axis which divides the dome into two roughly equal halves, manifesting the symmetrical balance signified in most imperial Chinese cities.

The continuity is an outcome of practical concerns rather than "reactionary" choices. The consequence is that modern government offices were built along the imperial city's axis on which the old *yamen* were previously erected, turning the meaning of the Chinese word *"gong"* (公) from "official" (in this sense *guan* 官) to "public" (*gonggong* 公共). During the Qing period, the land where the Sun Yat-sen Memorial Hall is now located was the parade ground for the Qing army; to the south was the Guangdong Governor's Office. It would be easier for the Republican Government to put public buildings on land without much on it or that had been occupied by the former regime. The People's Republic Government inherited the legacies of the Republic and thus of the Ming and Qing dynasties. Today's Guangzhou Municipal Government was housed in the building of its Republican counterpart, which was built between 1929 and 1933. The People's Congress of Guangzhou City Building was built after 1949 as an auxiliary. To further appreciate the modern ideal of Republicanism, it is worth spending some time wandering in People's Park. Built in 1918, it was previously named the Central Park (*Zhongyang Gongyuan* 中央公園) and represented one of the earliest modern Chinese government attempts to construct public spaces and establish codes of civility. In fact, this was where Red Guard activists gathered during the short-lived Guangzhou Uprising in December 1927. After 1949, it was renamed "People's Park" (*Renmin Gongyuan* 人民公園) by the PRC government, and it is still meant to be a "public space" as defined by the state.

Leaving the South Gate of People's Park, you will find yourself on Zhongshan Fifth Road 中山五路. Turn east and walk to Zhongshan Fourth Road and you may look out over the Museum of the Palace of the Southern Yue Kingdom (g). Located next to the boisterous City God Temple, this museum deserves a bolder title. It houses the archaeological sites of the palaces built by two autonomous kingdoms in south China, the Southern Yue (204–111 BC) and the Southern Han (917–971), and, in addition, the relics and remains of multiple layers of cultural deposits left from the Qin dynasty to the modern era. Until the sites were excavated in the mid-1990s, no one realized that the palace and garden of the Southern Yue Kingdom was located across the north-south and east-west axis of the walled city, and that a millennium later the palace of Southern Han Kingdom was built upon the exact same site. Here are also found the remains of the buildings of the local administrations of the Tang, Ming, and Qing empires. Seldom do we find in China another old city of which the axis and center of imperial authority remains unchanged across 2,000 years. The site demonstrates how time is compressed within space, and how certain logics of historical continuity appear to have been in operation even when discontinuity was the norm. Visit the museum; go down to the site, and explore the depth of history buried beneath the modern commercial area.

You might not want to miss the City God Temple (h) (one of many in Canton, this one belonged to Guangzhou Prefecture), which is located just a few steps away. After all, the God was the spiritual symbol of an imperial city, and the earliest building of this City God Temple was said to be erected in accordance to the order issued by the Ming emperor in 1370. Built in that same year was the Panyu Confucian Temple (*Panyu Xuegong* 番禺學宮) (i), which is located to the east of the City God Temple. It retains the standard architectural layout of a late imperial Confucian Temple. Its presence reminds us of the fact that the walled city of the provincial capital was also where the Panyu and Nanhai County governments were located. Most people in Guangzhou today would find the name "Panyu Xuegong" unfamiliar, as they know it by the name "Nongjiangsuo" 農講所—the Peasant Movement Institute. Founded in 1924, the Institute was headed by Mao Zedong from May to September 1926. It is therefore a sacred site of Communist history, a fact that protected the Confucian Temple from damage during the political turmoil of the 1960s.

To gain a feeling for history, try to imagine that you are standing on the Street of Benevolence and Love (*Huiai Jie* 惠愛街) in Canton, rather than Zhongshan Road in Guangzhou. In the Qing dynasty, the Street of Benevolence and Love was the major avenue connecting the West Gate and East Gate, dividing the bell-shaped walled enclosure roughly into two halves, upper and lower. If you are already too tired to keep walking, we suggest that you take the tram running along Zhongshan Road. There are so many sites to see in the eastern part of the city; so, we should allow our historical imagination to be facilitated by the modern means of a tram traveling eastward from Zhongshan Fourth to Zhongshan First Road. Let's put back the Ming-Qing city map in your mind for a moment: once you pass Zhongshan Third Road, you are leaving the eastern city wall. You now should have a sense of the width of the enclosure and realize how small the old city was.

Mind you, the east- and then northward journey is one of death (j). Until the Qing period, lands in the eastern and northern suburbs were considered land of "fortune" (*fudi* 福地) good for burial. The impression extended well into the first half of the twentieth century. Here, you may want to pick up another geographical term commonly known to local people—"*gang*" 崗 (mount). Wherever there is a "*gang*," you may assume that there are or were burial places. Today many of these remaining "*gang*" are markers of Republican history. At the intersection of Zhongshan Third Road and Lingyuan West Road (陵園西路, lit. the West of the Graveyard), you will first find the "Red Flower Mount Tombs for the Four Martyrs" (*Honghuagang silieshi mu* 紅花崗四烈士墓, built 1923). From the northern part of Lingyuan West Road, you turn right and reach the Xianlie Road (先烈路, lit. Martyrs Road) and will see the "Yellow Flower Mount for the Seventy-Two Martyrs" (built 1912–1936). Further westward is the "Mausoleum of the 19th Route Army" (built 1933). Whereas the former two graveyards were built to commemorate the revolutionaries who sacrificed for the 1911 Revolution, the latter was for memorializing the soldiers of the Nationalist armies who died in the 1932 defense of Shanghai against the Japanese. If you visit the Red Flower

Mount Tombs, we can't resist urging you to have a look at the building of the late Qing Guangdong Provincial Assembly. Now housing the Guangdong Museum of Modern History, its neoclassical architectural style mirrors the short-lived experiment with parliamentary politics at the end of Qing dynasty.

Into the 1980s, the eastern suburb, in comparison with its western counterpart, was more spacious for urban development, and gradually a "new city axis" evolved further eastward in the 2000s along with which brand-new commercial, cultural, and recreational facilities arose. Nonetheless, for the purpose of our walk, let's head back to the old city to start our journey to the west.

Beijing Road, South End, Long Bund

You are now back on Zhongshan Fifth Road. Walk eastward and stop at the intersection of Beijing Road and Zhongshan Road. Head north and you will see a grand Western-style building standing at the end. Built between 1915 and 1919, it housed the Department of Finance of the Republican Guangdong Provincial Government. It continues to fulfill the same function for the provincial government nowadays. The same location was the site of the Office of the Provincial Administration Commission (*Buzhengsi* 布政司) under the Qing. Between the Department of Finance and the "Tianzi" (天字 lit., "the character 'sky'") Pier located at the southernmost tip along the river bank is Beijing Road, which was called "Shuangmendi" (雙門底, lit., "under the double gate") in the imperial times. Previously, leading down to the Great South Gate, the Shuangmendi thoroughfare formed another major north-south axis of the city.

Walking along Beijing Road, you will be able to envision what the roads were like over the past 1,000 years—from Southern Han (of the Five Dynasty and Ten Kingdoms), Song, Yuan, Ming, through the Qing—with the archaeological finds on display along the middle section of the road. Looking through the protective glass, you will be amazed by how roads of different dynasties, built with pebbles or bricks, were laid one on top of the other; and you can see that the ground surface of Beijing Road today is significantly elevated. Strolling along the historical roads, you should not miss the many bookstores along the eastern side of the road. Their presence reminds us that these were the sites where bookstores, woodblock presses and printers were located in the Qing and the Republican periods. It is not uncommon to find the place name "Shuangmendi" on the addresses of some well-known printers in Qing Canton. It took its name from the double gateway placed in a section of the wall dating from the Song. During the Ming, a tower was erected over the gateway. Inside the tower, a clepsydra made in the Yuan period was installed, implying that the imperial government tried to put into operation a uniform time for the city. Today, you can still see the remains of the towers at the southern part of Beijing Road.

At the intersection of Beijing Road and Xihu Road 西湖路, turn west and walk along Xihu Road to pay a quick visit to the archaeological site of a water gate (k). Now housed in a modern shopping mall, the water gate was constructed in the Western Han for flood control purposes. Thus, it must have been located next to the river bank, and its presence reminds you how wide the Pearl River used to be. The whole structure was made of wood. It is extraordinary to see such a large quantity of wood which has survived for more than 2,000 years! In the neighborhood of Xihu Road you will find a few remaining Qing architectural structures named either "ancestral hall" (*jiaci* 家祠) or "academy" (*shuyuan* 書院). These were built under different surnames by people from different parts of the province for their boys to study for the civil service examinations held in the provincial capital. These "ancestral halls" were once so numerous that they crowded one against the other and formed an unmistakable landscape of the city. Most of them were unfortunately torn down in the course of rapid urban development in the late 1990s, although the most conspicuous example, the Chen Family Temple 陳家祠 located on Zhongshan Seventh Road, is still in good shape and is definitely worth a visit.

The presence of the state in the past here can easily be felt on these streets. Walking along Beijing Road from the very north to the very south, you can tell how long and straight the road is. As students of history, we realize that, whereas roads are something taken for granted nowadays, road construction in the past was highly selective and was often an indicator of the presence of state authority. You may now understand why at the end of the road there was a pier and that it was named "Tianzi" 天字. "*Tian*" is the first character that appears in the *Thousand Character Classics* in which the first line read: "*Tian di xuan huang, Yu zhou hong huang*" 天地玄黃 宇宙洪荒 (The sky was black and earth yellow; space and time vast, limitless). This line was so well known that for numeration, the first character "*tian*" came to stand for number one. Walking southward, you are approaching thus the "Number One" Pier which was reserved for welcoming high officials coming from other parts of the empire to Guangdong to assume their duties. Getting off a ferry, stepping on the Tianzi Pier, and then walking along the Beijing Road from the south to the north, you might imagine yourself as such an official—albeit without a sedan chair!

We should bear in mind that the modern Chinese compound word for city—*chengshi* 城市—is a combination of walled enclosure (*cheng*) and markets (*shi*). Unlike some other provincial capitals of imperial China, the role of Canton in the Qing period was multifaceted: it was the center of provincial and county administrations, a port city supported by an outer port at Macau and an anchorage at Whampoa, and a distribution hub facilitated by a complex river network, with a commercial metropolis that emerged in the "South End" during the Ming and later in the "West End" in the Qing period. This is why we still find a number of huge wholesale markets along Danan Road 大南路, Dade Road 大德路, and Daxin Road 大新路—all being the streets running along the South End of the old city. The "new" city wall built in 1563 was meant to restrict the expansion of commercial activities, and yet its consequence was that more markets prospered along the bank of the Pearl River, as many buyers would have come to the city by river transport. Today you can still feel the flamboyance of the wholesale markets in this district, selling clothes, shoes, stationery, accessories, paper and plastic decorative items, dried seafood and sundries to customers from other parts of the country and from different parts of the world. People are so busy moving large bunches of goods with their trolleys. You'd better watch out!

Many of the place names in the South End and the West End bear the Chinese word "*lan*" 欄, which should not be mistaken as meaning railing, barrier, or barrister as explained in standard Chinese dictionaries. It is a Cantonese expression referring to wholesale markets. The term is now phasing out in Guangzhou today but still survives sporadically in Hong Kong, notably the *"guolan"* 果欄 (wholesaling market for fruit) in Yaumatei in Kowloon. The southward expansion of the market area reached its extreme

Figure 13.2 Map of "Canton with Suburbs and Honam," 1907, showing that the West End had become densely populated and urbanized by the 1900s. This is also one of the few early twentieth-century maps that show in detail the more developed parts of Honam Island (Surveyed by Mr. F. Schnock, Engineer, 1907, reprinted in *Tushuo Chengshi Wenmai: Guangzhou Gujin Dituji*).

at the turn of the twentieth century when a large-scale reclamation project was launched by Guangdong-Guangxi Governor-General Zhang Zhidong 張之洞, resulting in the construction of Changdi 長堤 (Long Bund) stretching along the western part of the South End. Today Changdi is quite quiet and you may enjoy a leisurely walk there. The tranquility is a result of its decline. Once an unsurpassed location for trendy department stores, fashionable hotels, large banks, theaters, teahouses, and cafes, receiving visitors and traders traveling from everywhere to Canton by ferry, Changdi lost its relevance due to the decline of water transport. To picture its ephemeral prosperity, you may raise your head to have a gaze at the Aiqun Building 愛群 and New Asia 新亞 Hotel which are still extant. You should be able to sense the pursuit of modernity by these early twentieth-century architects.

From Changdi at South End it is very easy for us to walk to the West End. But for the time being let's hold on and head back to the north to spend some more time in the western part of the walled city. We want to remind you of a few religious sites which you must not overlook.

Sacred sites in the secular world

From around the midst of Changdi you should now head north and walk toward Yide Road 一德路, where you will see the Sacred Heart Cathedral (l) that no one can miss. Constructed between 1863 and 1888 by Société des Missions Etrangères de Paris, the cathedral's architecture is undoubtedly worth careful appreciation. If we look at a pre-1860s map of the walled city, the location of the cathedral is also worth noticing. Its site was originally the residence of Guangdong-Guangxi Governor-General, which was destroyed during the Second Opium War, and was then obtained by the mission after signing an agreement with the Qing government. Despite its foreign origin, the locals gave the church a literally descriptive name: the "Stone House" (*shishi* 石室). The naming could not be more accurate, as the cathedral is entirely built of granite. Walking northward for about ten minutes, you will find the Temple of the Five Immortals 五仙觀 (m) on Huifu West Road 惠福西路. Founded in 1377, the temple carries significant meaning to the people of Canton. Legend has it that the Five Immortals came to the city riding on five rams which held sheaves of rice in their mouths. They left the sheaves of rice for the local people who had been suffering from famine. The rams turned into stone and the city became a prosperous place. They also gave the city the name "City of Rams" (*Yangcheng* 羊城).

Another ten minutes walk heading northward from the Temple of the Five Immortals will lead you to Guangta Road 光塔路, named after the 50-meter-high "Smooth Pagoda" (n) standing there. Standing further northward almost parallel to Smooth Pagoda is the 58-meter high "Flowery Pagoda" (Huata 花塔) (o). Before the French cathedral with its soaring steeple was put up, the Smooth Pagoda and the Flowery Pagoda must have appeared quite stunning in the city's skyline when few houses in Canton were more than two stories high.[2] Smooth Pagoda is a tall minaret which has smoothly tapering, circular walls first built in about 850 next to a mosque that was founded even earlier. It is said that the mosque is one of the oldest in the world and has been serving as a religious and cultural center for Muslims in China since the Tang dynasty. Today, the minaret remains to be the place where the muezzin leads Muslims in the call to prayer. The Flowery Pagoda is auxiliary to the Monastery of Six Banyan Trees (Liurong Si 六榕寺, founded 537 and rebuilt 989) of which the name was related to a visit in about 1100 by the celebrated poet Su Dongpo 蘇東坡, who was remembered for being moved to record the presence of six banyan trees in the courtyard.

Don't hesitate to stop by the mosque—visitors are welcome—and remember to observe the rules as you should do in every other place of worship. Part of the attraction is the setting. Sometimes you do not only *see* a site, but you also *smell* it. Entering Guangta Road, you will smell the lamb and beef sold and cooked specifically for the Huis and Muslims coming from different parts of the world. This is where the *"fanfang"* (蕃坊 foreign quarters) for the Arab and Persian in the Tang dynasty were once located. Several streets nearby still bear such old names as "Tianshuixiang" (甜水巷 Sweet Water Lane) and Manaoxiang (瑪瑙巷 Agate Lane) which reflect their original functions. Probably not coincidentally, almost a thousand years later in the Qing dynasty, these "foreign quarters" became "banner territory" (*qijie* 旗界), the district demarcated for bannermen stationed in Canton. You will still find such street names as "Jiangjun West" (將軍西路) and "Jiangjun East" (將軍東路) in this neighborhood, as this was where the Manchu Tartar General's residence was located (n).

Nor should you miss the Guangxiao Monastery (光孝寺) (p), one of the oldest extant Buddhist monasteries in China. Founded and named "Guangxiao" in 1151, the monastery stands on a site where an older counterpart was founded as early as 401. It was also famous for the arrival of many famous monks from afar, notably Huineng 惠能, the Sixth Patriarch of Chan Buddhism. Despite numerous refurbishments, the present architecture retains the style prevalent in the Southern Song. The iron *stupa* there cast in 967, with now only its lowest three layers remaining, is the best testimony of the Buddhist influence spread by the Southern Han Kings in South China—if you still remember we have already visited the site of his palace.

Wandering in this western section of the old city, you will find how close these historic religious sites are to each other. From the Sacred Heart Cathedral, walk about 700 meters northward to arrive at the Temple of the Five Immortals, 300 meters more to go to the Mosque at further north, and some 530 meters to Six Banyan Monastery. Between Six Banyan and Guangxiao located in the west is the shortest distance of around 330 meters. In other words, at average walking speed, one may pay a quick visit to all these sites of major religions of the world covering 1,600 years of history within half an hour! But now let's leave Guangxiao Monastery, pass the West Gate, and enter the more secular world of the West End.

West End, West End!

The history of the West End (*Xiguan* 西關) should be understood against the broader background of the "China trade" that started with the arrival of the Portuguese in Guangdong in the sixteenth century. The West End was originally a marshy area which had been vividly named "Bantang" (半塘/泮塘, lit., half of the place covered by ponds). Because foreigners were not allowed to enter the walled city, the West End became the only district where they could find lodging. The buildings resided in by foreign merchants were referred to as "factories," a common eighteenth-century word for a godown, trading station or warehouse. With Canton being designated the sole port for foreign trade in 1757, the development of the West End further accelerated between the 1700s and 1800s. The streets located at the rear of the factories, in particular the "Old China" and "New China" Streets, were international marketplaces, selling porcelain, silk, tea, and various arts and crafts to Western customers. Looking at the export paintings produced in this period, you will be struck by the images of the factories along the bund and the variety of commodities and the quality of art and craftworks sold in the shops nearby. But you will not find a trace of them in today's West End except a street named "Thirteen Hong Road" (Shisan Hang Lu 十三行路) at the rear of present-day Cultural Park (*Wenhua Gongyuan* 文化公園). There is no high-quality porcelain, silk, and tea in the West End today. It goes without saying that industries in China have transformed so drastically in the last century that traditional arts and crafts are no longer commonplace. With the political turmoil in the 1960s, reckless redevelopment in the 1990s and 2000s, merchants fled, natives moved out, and the West End today has become a place for buying cheap industrial products. Only the food sold there might give you a taste of the past.

But you can still appreciate the history of the West End by walking it. The street plan and certain sites still allow us to visualize bits and pieces of the past. Moreover, to understand more about this part of Canton, the best reference is probably *Walks in the City of Canton* by John Henry Gray (1875). Chapters four and five describe vividly the goods and trades available on different streets in the West End after the two Opium wars. Glance at the list of goods and services Gray recorded: cotton, hardware, poultry, egg, betel nut, rope, dye, flour, tobacco, tea, silk, porcelain, bird's nest, sandalwood, jade stone, horn lanterns, coconut shells, ivory, furniture, lacquer ware, musical instruments, looking glasses, fortune telling, and last but not least, a cat and dog restaurant. Have a cup of coffee somewhere and flip through the book (you can even find a pdf copy online) before you continue your journey.

Let's proceed now to a place named West Gate ("Ximen Kou" 西門口, now also a subway station) (q). Walking westward via the "West Gate" means that you are leaving the west wall and are entering the upper section of the Western Suburb. Walk southward along Renmin Road 人民路

until you arrive at Changshou East Road 長壽西路 along which you should walk further westward. Around that area you will see a huge jade and stone market. Filled with jade stones of various grades, genuine and fake, this market reminds us of Gray's description of the jade stone articles and glass bracelets once for sale on Changxing Street (長興街 no longer extant today) and the places nearby in the late nineteenth century. Gray mentions that the glass bracelets were bought in large quantities by the "Parsee and Mohammedan" merchants residing at Canton, who would then forward the goods to Bombay and Calcutta to be sold to Indian women. In the western section of Changshou East Road you will see Kangwang Road 康王路. Cross it, then you will find a small Qing-style building located next to the more well-known Hualin Monastery 華林寺 (r). Named "Jinlun Huiguan" 錦綸會館, the building was a silk weavers guild which witnessed the bloom of silk manufacturing in seventeenth- and eighteenth-century Canton. And, take a quick look at a small stone tablet nearby, which bears the characters "Xilai Chudi" (西來初地, the first touching of land on journeying from the west), at the junction of Shangjiu Road 上九路 and Yuqi Street 玉器街. Standing there for centuries, the tablet was erected to mark the arrival of the Indian monk Bodhidharma—also believed to be the founder of Hualin Monastery in Canton—by sea in 520. We don't know how true the story is, nor do we know when the tablet was put up, but like the water gate at Xihu Road, the tablet hints that 1,500 years ago it was located next to the river bank upon which Bodhidharma had landed.

Along the Shangjiu Road 上九路 (which has been named "Shangxia Jiu Pedestrian Mall" 上下九步行街 since the 1990s), keep walking westward. You will find on both sides of the road rows of *qilou* (騎樓 verandah buildings), which were constructed in the 1920s–1930s (s). Built with pavement-wide first floor canopies in a continuous corridor to protect pedestrians from sun and rain, these building are so "long" that people usually divided the house into two sections, running their shops in the front, and living in the rear. If you visit other south China cities such as Hong Kong, Macau, and Amoy (Xiamen), or some Chinese communities in Southeast Asia, you can find these similar verandah buildings. It is true that the size and height of the verandah buildings built on the same road often look fairly standard. In most cases, it is the result of urban planning. Between the 1900s and late 1930s, the municipal authorities of Canton implemented a series of policies and regulations facilitating private constructions of verandah buildings along with the construction of new roads and pavements. The outcome was that rows of verandah buildings were put up along a couple of roads and streets in the Old and New cities, the West End, and on Honam Island 河南島. In spite of their similarities in size and height, the architectural and decorative details of these verandah buildings vary. You can tell how innovative the designers were trying to be vis-à-vis the standard rules and regulations imposed by the modern state. Along the Di Shi Pu Road 第十甫路, which runs parallel to Shangxia Jiu Walking trail, there are a number of historical landmarks which might help you visualize the late Qing and early Republican urban culture. Locals, if you meet any, will be proud to tell you that the Lianxiang 蓮香 and the Taotaoju 陶陶居 Tea Houses there were founded in the late Qing, and that the three characters "Tao Tao Ju" on the signboard was in the calligraphy of the celebrated late Qing and early Republican scholar Kang Youwei 康有為.

Given its complicated street layout, it is not easy to select one or two routes or to identify a few spots for comprehending the history of urban development of the West End. If you look at the 1907 map, you can see that compared with the walled city, the West End had become much more densely populated and urbanized by the first decade of the twentieth century. Here, some knowledge of historical geography is essential for identifying the right documents. If you want to read some related literature, you should realize that there were no such titles as "Guangzhou City Gazetteer" before the 1920s. Because the city of Canton was located in the territories belonging to Nanhai and Panyu counties, and the West End fell within the area of Nanhai; so you need the *Nanhai County Gazetteer* (Nanhai Xianzhi 南海縣誌). By the time the 1910 edition of the *Nanhai County Gazetteer* was compiled, the number of recorded streets and roads in the West End district amounted to more than 1,700, and registered street numbers amounted to more than 4,000!³

Hence instead of walking along certain routes, we suggest you spend some time exploring the various residential patterns and the class division they reflect while wandering in the West End (t). Parallel to the Di Shi Pu Road in the south are the Shiba Pu West Road 十八甫西路, Heping West Road 和平西路, and the Xianji 洗基 Community, where you can find a massive number of small shabby houses densely crowded with the elderly and people of meager means. By contrast, walking further westward to Enning Road 恩寧路, Duobao Road 多寶路, and Fengyuan Road 逢源路, you will find the districts there better planned, with rows of houses lying perpendicular to main roads, divided by alleys paved with strips of granite. You will also see such terms as *"yue"* (約 alliances) and *"fang"* (坊 quarters) applied here and there in this district (u). Checking the 1907 map, the 1910 edition of *Nanhai Gazetteer*, and the news reports of those years, you will realize that by the late 1890s, real estate in the West End had become well developed with investments made by local merchants. Many of these merchants would have resided in more spacious and luxurious houses located further westward around Lychee Bay (Lizhi Wan 荔枝灣). Taking a boat trip on Liwan Lake 荔灣湖 today may help you appreciate the scenery here on the water. However, you should note that Liwan was not a "lake" as it is named today. It was part of the marshy area located at the northwest end of the West End.

In the eighteenth and nineteenth centuries, you could row about the river in a pleasure boat, going along various tributaries from Lychee Bay and reach the factories district—now the site of Cultural Park. All the foreign factories were burnt down in 1856 during the Second Opium War. The location of the factories explains why the British and French Concessions built in 1859 were established on a sandbank island situated at the southernmost end of the West End. Named "Shameen" (沙面 *shamian* in mandarin, lit., sandy surface), the island, like many parts of the West End, was a result of sedimentation and reclamation (v). For years it has been the site of foreign consulates, companies, banks, and residences, as well as Catholic and Protestant Churches. In the 1990s, it was declared a protected historic area. You will find Shameen tourist-friendly, as most of the mansions have plaques providing essential information about their history.

In the pre-Opium War days, foreigners residing in Canton, but banned from entering the city, could only tour around the two islands off the West End—Fati (花地 also spelt "Fatee," Huadi in Mandarin, lit. flowery land) (z) and Honam (河南, "Henan" in Mandarin, lit., south of the river). Fati once had numerous flower gardens and nurseries where eighteenth- and nineteenth-century foreigners could have a leisurely walk and collect samples of Chinese plants to enrich their knowledge of natural history. Today you still find a huge plant and flower wholesale market there although none of the items are grown locally. But on Honam Island you will be able to find some traces of the Qing Chinese "hong merchants." Luckily, there are still regular ferry services running between the Xidi Pier (西堤碼頭 West Bund Pier) and Honam Island. After leaving Shameen, walk along the Long Bund, take a ferry at Xidi Pier to cross the river, and get off at a pier named "Haichuang Si" 海幢寺, the "Ocean Banner Monastery" (w) on Honam Island.

Honam Island

Founded in 1662, the Ocean Banner Monastery was one of the few places foreign traders could visit in Canton in the decades after 1759. Strolling around in the monastery courtyard, you could imagine yourself as a foreign merchant or missionary of the pre-Opium War days. Prohibited from entering the city and even rowing about the river in your own boat for pleasure, you could walk in the Flower Garden and the Ocean Banner Monastery only on the 8th, 18th and 28th day of each lunar month.[4] Enjoy the breeze in the shade of a banyan tree during a hot and humid Guangdong summer.

Having left the Ocean Banner Monastery via its South Gate, you are now on the Tongfu Middle Road 同福中路. Walk westward for about 200 meters and you will see a narrow lane named "Wu's Family Temple Alley" (Wu Jiaci Dao 伍家祠道) (x). This "Wu" is in fact the surname of a famous Chinese hong merchant Wu Bingjian 伍秉鑒 (1769–1843), the director of the Yihe Company 怡和行 and known by foreigners as "Howqua" (浩官, also spelt "Houqua"). Walk into the alley; the once spectacular ancestral hall, previously consisting of large folding doors of wood, a grand entrance, a high granite dais, has been left in ruins for years. Now it houses several low-income households. Just a few hundred meters westward from the Wu temple, you will find the ancestral temple of Puankhequa (Pan Qiguan 潘啟官)(y), another well-known hong merchant. It has suffered the same fate as the Wu's and is now a workshop and small warehouse.

The remains of the Wu and Pan temples may not evoke the vast wealth of the hong merchants, among the richest men in the world two to three centuries ago; yet if you wander in the quarters along the Tongfu West Road and the Nanhua West Road 南華西路, you may gain at least a sense of the space they claimed. You will find the granite-paved alleys fairly well planned, with houses built in different periods, witnessing the evolution of the area from the late Qing period to the present day. There are such place names as "Longxi Shouyue" 龍溪首約 (The First Alliance of the Dragon Stream District) and many "alliances" (約 yue) numbered one after another. Here, "Longxi" refers to the "village" built and named by Puankhequa I (1714–1788) who came from Tong'an 同安 County, Quanzhou 泉州 Prefecture, Fujian 福建 Province, probably for memorizing the village "Longxi" 龙溪乡 in Zhangzhou 漳州, Fujian, to which their distant ancestor moved in 677 AD. Howqua came from the same county in Fujian. Both of them must have found it easier to purchase land on Honam Island when land in the city became more scarce and costly by the time of their arrival. Aligned side by side, Howqua's and Puankhequa's estates were separated by a stream over which several bridges, notably the "Huanzhu" 環珠 and "Longzhu" 龍珠 bridges, were built. These names remind us that Honam Island is also called "Haizhu" 海珠, a Pearl in the Sea. Today all streams have turned into roads but you can still find the remains of the bridges. You may also notice an alley in the Pan's territory bearing the name "Julong Tongjin" 聚龍通津 inscribed on a piece of granite now quietly lying on the pavement in Longxi District. Clearly, the hong merchants have gone, and the area is no longer connected by streams, it is quite unlikely that "dragons" would assemble there. The reality you see today is quite the opposite of what the four characters "Julong Tongjin" supposedly imply.

Along Nanhua West Road 南華西路 and Hongde Road 洪德路 nearby, you will find many three-story verandah buildings similar to the ones you see on Zhongshan Road and in the West End. Most of them were built in the 1930s, at a time when this part of the Island was further integrated into the urbanization project of modernizing Canton. The rest of Honam Island, comprising a large number of village communities, is certainly worth exploring. But that will lead us to another story with a plot taking us away from our walk in the *city* of Canton.

The final ride

This is the end of the walk. It may take two to three days to finish in reality. Now you must feel quite exhausted and may want to jump onto a taxi or a ridesharing service. Such automobile tours can still be part of our "walk." You may want to talk to the drivers, pay attention to their accents, and listen to their personal stories. They might come from Henan, Hubei, or the Hakka-speaking region of Guangdong. Many would be happy to share with you why they do or do not want to stay in this city. They might also be Cantonese-speaking natives, in most cases driving their own cars providing ridesharing services, telling you in what way their family members are dispersed all over the world—in Hong Kong, Macau, Australia, New Zealand, and North America—and why they themselves chose to stay in this old city. Along your walk you may meet a variety of people while you are strolling, shopping, or dining out. Talking with people in real daily life offers something that we cannot recover by merely reading archives.

Having taken this walk, you can now sketch your own map. Even with your new mental map of the city, we believe you will find the texts more comprehensible when you go back to archives. You may want to design another walk along other themes. But we believe that the trail we recommend here is one of the best. Let us remind you again: with this walk what we try to demonstrate to you are the multiple roles of Canton. It is a capital city of imperial and modern China, a center of cultural and religious exchange, a port and a market for regional, international, and global trade. Its time is deep, and yet its space is small. This is why you can have a glimpse of its history by walking at a manageable distance from the north to the south, from ground surface to underground, from the urban to the suburban, on land and on sea. After all, Canton is an ocean city and a floating town. Its watery nature should not be overlooked while we are doing our research on foot.

Notes

1 It is therefore noteworthy that the Chinese name of Guangzhou Museum is "Guangzhou Bowuguan" and not "Guangzhou shi Bowuguan." The word *"shi"* (city) is omitted deliberately in order to accommodate objects collected in the vicinity of the city.
2 In almost all maps of the city appended to the gazetteers compiled during the Ming and the Qing, compilers would not miss drawing the Flowery Pagoda and the Smooth Pagoda with reference to their appearance and shapes, creating a comic effect on the supposedly unexciting official documents.
3 *Nanhai Xianzhi* (Xuantong edition), *juan* 6.
4 See Liang Tingnan (ed.), *Yuehaiguan Zhi* (A Chronicle of Guangdong Customs), Guangzhou : Guangdong Renmin Chubanshe, 2002, pp. 565–566.

Further Reading

Garrett, Valery. *Heaven is high, the emperor far away: Merchants and Mandarins in Old Canton*, Oxford, New York: Oxford University Press, 2002.
Guangdong Tongzhi 廣東通志 (Guangdong Provincial Gazetteer, Jiajing 嘉靖, Yongzheng 雍正 and Daoguang 道光 editions).
Guangzhoushi Wenhuaju 廣州市文化局, Guangzhoushi Difangzhi Bangongshi 廣州市地方志辦公室, Guangzhoushi wenwu kaogu yanjiusuo 廣州市文物考古研究所 (eds). 2000.

Guangzhou Wenwuzhi 廣州文物志 (Guangzhou Cultural Gazetteer), Guangzhou: Guangzhou Chubanshe.

Huang Foyi 黃佛頤. *Guangzhou Chengfangzhi* 廣州城坊志 (Gazetteer of the Walled City and Districts of Canton). Guangzhou: Guangdong renmin chubanshe, 1994 (prefaced 1948).

Liang Tingnan 梁廷楠 (ed.), Yuehaiguan Zhi 粵海關志 (A Chronicle of Guangdong Customs), Guangzhou: Guangdong Renmin Chubanshe, 2002, pp. 565–566.

Nanhai Xianzhi 南海縣志 (Nanhai County Gazetteer, Daoguang 道光 and Xuantong 宣統 editions).

14 Contextualizing ethnic classification

The case of *hemu* (合亩) among the Li of Hainan

Xi He

During the 1950s, as were many communities that came to be classified as "minority people," the Li (黎) of Hainan were subject to detailed ethnographic investigations. One of the features of some of these Li communities was a practice called *hemu* (joined acreages), a manner of communal holding of cultivated land. The Li practiced slash-and-burn farming, and the preparation of cultivation required specific ceremonies conducted under the aegis of the headman of the *hemu* known as "head of the *mu*" (*mutou* 亩头). It was recognized early in the 1950s that the *hemu* represented a primitive form of collective land ownership, even though contemporary references described the phenomenon as being in a process of dissolution. Nevertheless, *hemu* as collective land ownership came to be lodged as a fixture in the history of the Li people. I had little reason to question this received wisdom as I embarked on my own research on Wuzhishan (五指山) on Hainan.

An interview

In 2015, I met the last of the "heads of the *mu*," 78-year-old Mr. Wang. He had succeeded to his father's headmanship when he was only nine years old. He was obliged to marry in order to do so, for as headman, he was responsible for various ceremonies in which his wife must also play a part. The couple conducted ceremonies to clear the hills, to plough the land, to sow seeds, to transplant rice seedlings, and to harvest the crop. In all instances, he went in front and she followed behind. They did not stay to work in the fields, but returned home after the ceremony to lock themselves away for a day. For this ceremonial leadership, Wang obtained a share of the harvest: two bundles of grain said to be "the father and mother grain" (*daogong daomu* 稻公稻母). Wang was less specific about what happened to the rest of the harvest.

Up to that point, Mr. Wang had told me no more than what I might have learned from the ethnographic reports produced in the 1950s. But he knew much more. His father had served under Wang Zhaoyi (王昭夷), sometimes described as a big "head of the *mu*" (*da mutou* 大亩头). Wang Zhaoyi was a man of legendary reputation: he had supported the Chinese Communists in the 1920s, surrendered to the Japanese in the early 1940s, turned against the Japanese, and was arrested, imprisoned, and executed. Almost escaping my notice, Mr. Wang mentioned that, "Wang Zhaoyi was not Li, his surname wasn't Wang either." Wang Zhaoyi, he said, had come from a family of Ledong people (乐东人) who had the surname of Liu (刘). His grandfather had arrived with a brother to reclaim hill land for cultivation. In Ledong county, which stretches from the coast to half way up Wuzhishan, Han Chinese settlers had been growing rice, and so knew about building the irrigation channels needed for paddy farming. These Ledong people, possibly a combination of Han Chinese and indigenous Li who had come into contact with them, also came up the hills to work on the land for 2 yuan per *mu*, and when they had saved some money, they settled down on the hills with their families. They were successful paddy farmers not only because they knew how to build irrigation channels, but also because they knew how to deal with cobras. People who cleared the hills often came into contact with snakes. The Li people were afraid of the snakes because they had no cure for poisonous bites. They were amazed the Ledong people not only survived snake bites, but also killed snakes for food. Wang Zhaoyi's father settled into Zhaping Village which had a village headman of the Wang surname and succeeded into the headship by adoption. This same village head had helped Commander Feng Zicai 冯子材 build the road in central Hainan in 1884. In 1932, when Chen Hanguang (陈汉光) was appointed Li Pacification Commissioner (抚黎专员) by the Guangdong provincial government, Chen sent Wang Zhaoyi to Guangzhou for education.

That nutshell history of this corner of Hainan brought me to a realization. Not only had I not noticed that history in connection with Wang Zhaoyi's exploits, but recognizing it added an important nuance to my understanding of what had been described in the ethnography simply as slash-and-burn agriculture. Slash-and-burn was giving way to paddy farming at the same time as Wuzhishan was opened up to the outside world, and either people with Han Chinese connections, or the Han Chinese themselves were becoming involved in Li politics.

Fieldwork

I met Mr. Wang, the last "head of the mu," with the help of my very capable guide on Wuzhishan. She and her husband, whom I shall refer to here as Mrs. and Mr. G (short for "guide"), are ethnic Li. She belongs to the branch of the Li known as Qi 杞 and he is Meifu 美孚. I learned a great deal from them. Mrs. and Mr. G helped me locate villages, provided introductions, and, because I do not speak Li, interpreted for me when the people we spoke to did not speak Putonghua. But I learned early that even they did not speak all the mountain languages and that, although they had definite ideas of ethnic classification, sometimes ethnic terms were relative rather than absolute. For instance, Mrs. G often used as a conversation opener the distinction between the Ha 侾 and the Qi, namely that the Ha wore loincloth (that is, a single piece of cloth that went from the belly to the buttocks), but the Qi had two pieces, "a piece in front and a piece behind" as she described them. Nothing makes up for not knowing the language, but through Mr. and Mrs. G, I came to appreciate some of the differences they were guided to by their vocabulary.

An important part of that vocabulary for me had to do with the designations of social positions in ritual performances. Like many field researchers, I have been interested in ritual performances for what they tell us about social history. The Li people we now meet no longer live their traditional way of life. They have moved down from the depth of the mountain to villages located nearer the main roads. They no longer hunt or practice slash-and-burn agriculture. But memories of some such past ways of life have been preserved in rituals together with the social relationships that go into them. The *hemu* ceremonies as described to me by Mr. Wang have been preserved as his memory of such ritual.

The *hemu* ceremonies are no longer performed, but thanks to Mr. and Mrs. G, I was able to participate on one occasion in a different ceremony that had to do with hunting. In brief, the male ritualists, *geba*, were invited both at the opening of the hunt and upon the return of the hunting party to offer collective sacrifice to the ancestors, the gods of thunder, and the earth gods protecting the village. Male villagers gathered around to help with the slaughtering and cooking of a pig, a dog and a chicken, and to take part in the subsequent meal. The privileged ritual positions, however, belonged to men who had served in capacities known as *shaoguan* (哨官) and *lailao* (来唠). The term "shaoguan" (captain of the guardpost) was originally a position in the imperial government and its subsequent use can be documented from gazetteer references to the Li people. Presumably, Li people had been recruited to man guard posts. The *lailao* was said to be the *shaoguan's* assistant. Those terms were understood by the villagers when we asked about them. Interviews with villagers established that they were associated with authority, holders of such positions originally having adjudicatory roles in settling disputes, especially in cases of adultery. Nowadays, that authority is exercised only in rituals such as the hunt.

My brief visits to the Li villages also taught me much about the geography of the area. It was important, of course, to have some feel for where the villages were located and of their contact with the outside world. I had already visited villages on the coast of Hainan and knew about the salt industry in some of them. It made perfect sense, therefore, to continue learning about trade with Ledong county: people we spoke to recounted the precise routes that goods had traveled, as well as the goods traded, including salt. Likewise, we discovered a geographic basis to some reports. Many people knew about the Li people's Baisha uprising of 1943 (directed against Guomindang forces on Wuzhishan), during which headman Wang Guoxing 王国兴 sought support from the Chinese Communist Party. The Party at the time already had a branch on Hainan, but it was on the northern face of Wuzhishan, the area that had come under Wang Guoxing's control. It was in this area that people were able to tell us about the *hemu* system of agriculture. On the southern slope of the mountain, Li villagers readily spoke about Wang Zhaoyi. At Nansheng village, we were taken to the exact spot that had been Wang Zhaoyi's house, overlooking what would have been a sizable farm that he might well have been extending. As we came down on this side of the mountain, we found Fuli ("pacifying the Li") village of Qunying *xiang* in Lingshui county where Feng Zicai was said to have set up a Li Pacification Bureau (*fuli ju* 抚黎局). Villagers pointed out the overgrown site of the Li Pacification temple that his troops had built, but could not recall what deities had been enshrined there. Feng Zicai spent barely two years on Hainan. The temple was left standing after his troops had withdrawn, and that was why the local people remembered it, but clearly, it had left little impact on the local religious life.

Documentation

As a historian by training, for me, fieldwork must be related to documentation, such as government and private records. I had access to three bodies of records: Qing dynasty and Republican official papers, travelogues, and ethnographic surveys. Feng Zicai's expedition to Hainan in 1884 is well recorded and often cited by historians. Many accepted the official account that Feng had been sent to Hainan by Guangdong-Guangxi Governor General Zhang Zhidong 张之洞 to quell disorder among the Li people and that his achievement rested on his "road building," a term I initially took at face value. Nevertheless, while reports from the military commander of the area prior to Feng's arrival include mention of the occasional theft of buffaloes, they do not record incidents of unrest. In any case, Feng's men succumbed quickly to disease (probably malaria). Rather than suppressing the Li, Feng's mission in Hainan has to be understood in the broader scheme of Zhang Zhidong's interests: finding a convenient post to station Feng's victorious troops fresh from the Sino-French War in Indo-China, and gaining control of the Wuzhishan area so that the Qing government might exploit its resources in the interest of "self-strengthening." Zhang said as much in his memorials to the throne. To gain control of the region, Zhang wanted Feng to put down the traditional headmen. At the market town of Xinshi near Lingmen village, Feng set up an alliance of six districts under the authority of a Six-District Chief Battalion Committee (*Liu dong zongtuan dong* 六峒总团董) and required each district chief to build a tiled house at the market. The families of Wang Guoxing and Wang Zhaoyi both belonged to this newly appointed leadership.

Significant changes in the last years of the nineteenth century made the new Li leaders very different kinds of men from their predecessors. That account has to be juxtaposed against descriptions made of local communities and leadership in contemporary travelogues. In 1882, the American missionary B.C. Henry traveled from Lin'gao on the northern coast of Hainan, over Wuzhishan, to reach Lingshui in the southeast. In his 1886 travelogue, Henry noted that he met Chinese traders along the way, and a few Chinese people in almost every village he visited. Hu Chuan, who was sent on a fact-finding tour of the Li by Guangdong governor Wu Dacheng (吳大澂) upon Feng Zicai's departure from Hainan in 1887, was received by Li headmen, military officers and Chinese traders all along his journey. Putting the two accounts together, one can see that Feng Zicai's "road building" had little to do with the physical construction of an actual thoroughfare, and more to do with building the telegraph line and establishing a government presence up on the mountain.

Government presence brought significant changes in two apparently opposing directions, deepening a public awareness of the indigenous character of the Li, while exposing the new Li leadership to influences from the outside world. It had long been known that there were different sorts of Li, not only because some had come under the imperial realm (tame or "*shu*" 熟), while others remained outside (wild or "*sheng*" 生). Henry noticed that the Li included groups called B'lay, B'ly, S'lay, H'ay, and Moi. Hu distinguished the "mountain-crossing Li" (*guoshan* Li 过山黎) who stole buffaloes and needed suppression versus the settled Ha-Li. Taxonomy exemplified otherness, more so as it was coupled with descriptions of physique, dress, body styles, and customs. The most detailed of such descriptions was made by Hans Stubel, a German medical professor at the National Tongji University in Shanghai, who ventured into Wuzhishan in 1931 and 1932. He divided the Li into four varieties: the Bendi, the Meifu, the Qi, and the Ha, a classification that came to be used in all subsequent Li ethnographic descriptions.

Being located outside the pale of Han culture, the Li had always appeared in Chinese texts to be deficient. The new interest in ethnology fed into Republican state-building. In 1932, when Li Pacification Commissioner Chen Hanguang, a nephew of Guangdong's warlord Cheng Jitang 陈济棠, visited the Li villages, he went with a film crew to film "Guns on Wuzhishan" that was screened in the cinemas of Guangzhou. In 1933, he brought to Guangzhou a delegation of Li and Miao people from Hainan, ostensibly both to sight-see and to pay their respect to the graves of the revolutionary martyrs at Huanghua Mound (黄花岗). They did more than that, for the Li and Miao delegation remained on display in the park under media coverage, wearing their native costumes and extended earrings. The Li became a spectacle, so much so that overseas Chinese people who visited Hainan in search of investment opportunities would come to have their pictures taken with Li people outside the Li Pacification Bureau.

Yet even as the Li were deprecated as uneducated non-Han natives, some of their leaders were embracing the new-style Chinese education. One such person was Wang Zhaoyi. Huang Qiang (黄强), a military man who was appointed Hainan Development Commissioner (*Qiongya shiye zhuanyuan* 琼崖事业专员) and saw Wang Zhaoyi in 1928, described him as a graduate of the American missionary school (that is to say, the Presbyterian school at Nada, founded on land given by Feng Zicai after the missionaries had ministered to the sick among his troops). Huang had served as the head of a department in the commissioner's office and lived in a two-story Western-style house that overlooked the surrounding area. He made some films on his visit, and in an episode that showcased the part of Wuzhishan where he met Wang Zhaoyi, he presented not only an expansive tract of land under wet paddy, but also a picture of what Huang captioned as, "a gentryman's (*shenshi* 绅士) family." All the men in the picture were dressed in the modern Sun Yat-sen suit (*Zhongshan Zhuang* 中山装), while the women wore traditional Li costumes. Another visitor to the area, in 1938, 24-year-old Lin Renchao, saw Wang in his brick-and-tile house, described as somewhat like a "grand old house in Guangzhou" (*Guangzhou de gulao dawu* 广州的古老大屋). Wang was dressed in Western-style shirt and trousers, and wore a pair of black leather shoes. Lin commented that he knew that Wang had lived in Guangzhou for some time, and had received training at the Yantang Military Academy set up by warlord Chen Jitang.

In the Guangdong Provincial Library is a manuscript of a survey by Wang in 1926 of Li villages in the Lingshui region, the river valley lying at the foot of the part of Wuzhishan where Huang Qiang saw him. Several letters penned by Wang Zhaoyi preceding the survey show that he was working for the Hainan Commissioner and broadcasting essentially the Republican ideology that was taught by Sun Yat-sen. Later recollections describe his involvement in a Chinese Communist-led uprising in Lingshui city toward the end of 1927, a period of great political turmoil across China, including Guangdong. In that tumultuous year, the Guomindang turned on the Chinese Communists, not only in Shanghai and Guangzhou, but also in Haikou on Hainan. The uprising in Lingshui took place as a response to that turmoil, but Wang Zhaoyi might have also been settling a private feud. Huang Qiang alluded to that episode in Wang's life when he mentioned that nearby villagers had murdered Wang Zhaoyi's father. Therefore, when Huang visited the Li headmen, he was doing so in the aftermath of a bloody year of Chinese Communist-led resistance, a fact that he only alluded to in his travelogue.

Hemu: ethnographic studies

It is interesting that none of the travelogues, not even Stubel's ethnography or Kunio Odaka's 1942 study that devoted a chapter to property, made any mention that land was held in common. As far as I can document it, the first appearance of the term *hemu* came in an interview in 1950 that was given by Wang Guoxing, by then the acknowledged overall leader of all the Li people of Hainan. Wang presented land ownership among the Li people in some areas as a form of common ownership. As he described it,

> People of the same clan (*shizu* 氏族) farmed together, the land was commonly owned, the buffaloes were commonly owned, all able-bodied people had to farm, and all grain harvested was divided by households,

regardless of the population, one portion for one household, and, when more populous households had eaten all their grain, they could borrow from households that had it to spare, without having to repay.

Fanyang (番阳) up the mountain from Ledong county was named as an area in which "the entire *xiang*" (*quanxiang* 全乡) practiced *hemu*.

Unlike Wang Zhaoyi, before the liberation of the island in 1950, Wang Guoxing had not traveled outside Hainan. His father, Wang Zhenghe (王政和), had been the chief headman of the Six-District Chief Battalion Committee that Feng Zicai had set up. It is likely that, as his biography claims, being the chief headman, he was put under considerable pressure by Li Pacification Commissioner, Chen Hanguang, who in the 1930s pushed for a stronger government presence on Hainan, and demanded tax to finance the government offices, and able-bodied men from the chief headmen to serve as soldiers. In 1935, Wang Zhenghe was imprisoned for not paying tax and was released only shortly before he died. The story is often told that Wang Guoxing escaped into the mountains for an entire year and assumed office as village headman only in 1941 upon the urging of his fellow villagers. Meanwhile, in 1939, the Japanese had landed on Hainan, and the Guomindang-led army retreated to Wuzhishan, thus creating even greater demands on the Li villages. In those circumstances, Wang Guoxing and Wang Zhaoyi chose diametrically opposing paths. Wang Zhaoyi served variously both the Guomindang and the Japanese, leading to his execution by the Japanese in 1942. Wang Guoxing made contact with Chinese Communist guerrillas on Hainan and led the Li people in the historic Baisha uprising in 1943.

Therefore, land reform came to the Li villages well before Hainan was liberated in 1950. Under the rubric of "stamping out bandits and opposing bullies" (*qingfei fanba* 清匪反霸) in 1947 and 1948, headmen and landlords in some villages that had collaborated with the Guomindang government had their land confiscated. It was also suggested, even then, that the common practice by powerful Li people of adopting sons to work as laborers in the field could amount to exploitation. When Wang Guoxing spoke about *hemu* communal land ownership, he probably had that experience of land reform in mind.

The first post-1949 ethnographic survey of the Li people took place in 1954–1955, conducted by the South-Central College for Nationalities. It stated that its objectives included investigating and understanding "the more primitive special features of Li society" (*Lizu de shehui yuanshi chengfen jiaoduo de tezheng* 黎族社会原始成分较多的特征). The second survey was conducted as part of a much larger project initiated by the Nationalities Committee of the National People's Congress in 1956. Eight survey groups were formed to study minority nationalities all over China, including the Li. The Guangdong Province Minority Nationality History and Society Survey Group was dispatched from Beijing to Hainan, and later published two volumes on the *hemu* system. At the beginning of the Rectification Campaign of 1957, the survey teams returned once more, specifically to Fanyang and its surroundings to conduct "supplementary surveys" (*buchong diaocha* 补充调查). It is understandable that Fanyang would be the focus of the survey research because, after all, that was the area that Wang Guoxing had identified as the heartland of *hemu* agriculture.

Those studies proved to be informative sources on the history and society of the Li people. They detailed the Li people's social organization, family patterns, agriculture, hunting, industry, trade, technology, customs, religion, songs, and much else. The survey in places reached down to individual families, providing clear tabulation of how much land each family held in common with other families. They also provided greater detail than my informant Mr. Wang, the last surviving "head of the *mu*" could tell me about the ceremonies that the headman had to conduct in growing rice. For instance, on the day the seeds were put into the ground, he was to go to the field with his wife, dressed in new clothes, wearing his necklaces, hoe in hand (but not on his shoulder, in order to not disturb passing dogs whose bark might bring bad fortune). He was to dig a hole in the ground, let his sons and nephews water the earth, and not say anything until he had put into it the seeds that he had brought from home. The description went on to describe what his wife should do in the ceremony, and then what both had to do in subsequent ceremonies: transplanting seedlings, sending the buffaloes to graze in the hills, harvesting the crops, and cooking the newly harvested rice.

The surveyors had their suspicions about *hemu*, expressed in long paragraphs on the nature of adopted sons (known as "dragon sons," *longzi* 龙子), males who were attached to families that controlled land and who addressed their hosts as "fathers." They also went into detail on instances of land ownership and tenancy, on ownership and renting of buffaloes, and on the exploitation of labor. These rich details told a complicated story of economic change in Wuzhishan in the several decades before land reform. There was no question that slash-and-burn agriculture continued to be practiced even at the time of the surveys, but evidently, also, it was no longer the primary means of farming. It was recalled that hill land was also planted in rice and governed by *hemu* arrangements, that the "head of the *mu*" had a right to a share in the harvest, but that within the Republican period, such land was increasingly opened for cultivation by individual households. In Maodao *xiang* (near Fanyang) of Baoting county, after listing in detail the land holdings of each family, the 1957 surveyors noted that they had excluded all hill land (*shanlan di* 山栏地) from the tabulation, because only irrigated land could be privately owned.

It was also evident that paddy (wet rice) farming, where the control of water and the use of buffaloes for traction were essential and that neither land nor animals were really owned communally, was taking over. The strong tendency for land to be privately owned was also expressed in some rather curious reports. In the 1954 survey, in Maonong village of Ledong county, irrigated land constituted 60 percent of the land that was held in the largest *hemu* of 14 households. In 1957, at Fanyang, of which Maonong was a part, the team surveyed the area in which Wang Guoxing was headman and noted that four villages there together farmed 105.6 mu of irrigated paddy land and 653.7 mu of dry land all of which was held under *hemu* and that, again, that acreage did not include hill land. A subsequent report published in 1963 includes two detailed tables depicting individual holdings of land within every family in some villages to argue that far from being egalitarian, the *hemu* was skewed toward control of land by village heads, not only the chief headman as such, but also the headmen of villages that at different times had collaborated with the Qing and the Republican governments.

Supported by the survey results, in 1962, the doyen of the historians of ancient China, Lu Zhenyu, wrote an authoritative account agreeing with the conclusion that *hemu* land ownership was the remnant of a primitive communal form of economy (*yuanshi gongshe zhi* 原始公社制). He acknowledged that the surveys presented much data that indicated that collective ownership had been in sharp decline, but despite the skepticism, he accepted that the farther the Li settlements were from Han Chinese contact, the more likely it was for *hemu* to have continued. Despite subsequent revisionism, the idea that Li society at the time of land reform in 1947 to 1948 might have exhibited features of communal land ownership had become fixed in its history.

Conclusion

I want to make the methodological point that field and documentary work should not be, and cannot be, separated. The researcher goes about the field fully knowing that other people had done so at earlier times, and reads documents with sensitivities that only fieldwork can develop. The theoretical implications of *hemu* communal land ownership notwithstanding, my interview with the last "head of the *mu*" Mr. Wang alerted me to the history of the introduction of irrigation and paddy farming which complemented the decline of slash-and-burn agriculture and its ritual accompaniment in the role of the "head of the *mu*." The transformation of Li society, of course, belongs to a larger picture. From the fifteenth century, Li headmen on the coastal plain had taken office in the imperial state, as their clansmen adopted wet rice farming and their villages were converted from thatched to tiled-roofed houses. For centuries too, Wuzhishan was not so much impassable as remaining beyond the reach of imperial rule. The presence of Feng Zicai brought imperial presence into the mountain, and it had come not as the harbinger of economic change but in its trail. Chinese merchants had preceded him, bringing salt and iron implements that the Li did not themselves produce. But paddy farming belonged to the twentieth century. It was noted for its absence in the 1880s, was everywhere to be seen in the 1930s, and taken for granted in the surveys of the 1950s. It came as a new generation of educated Li headmen had come to be placed in charge, and they were caught up with national politics. The juxtaposition of the old and the new may be best represented by descriptions of money and of buffaloes. Buffaloes were needed for draft, but they were also representative of wealth. They made up the essential bride price, land was paid for with them, and people who had no buffaloes attached themselves as sons to persons who did. But, by the 1930s, the headmen spoke about the price of rice in money terms, and laborers might be hired for wages. Such reports make up images of a vibrant society.

But what was the rice used for? Neither the travelogues of the 1930s nor the survey reports of the 1950s suggest that rice grown on Wuzhishan was sold on the local market, or that it was transported out of it to feed the larger population of the coastal plains. By the 1920s, Wuzhishan villages exported timber, rattan, and other products such as snake skin, and headmen such as Wang Zhaoyi were interested in developing commercial crops such as coffee. Rice was stored in barns, locally consumed, and paid as tax. It must be remembered that with the increasing government presence through the 1920s to the 1940s, especially once Guomindang forces had withdrawn from the coastal plains and sheltered in the mountains, the exchange of tax in return for official appointment and recognition had become a driving force in rapid social changes. The surveyors of Li society in the 1950s probably had this description right: to understand the economy of Wuzhishan, it is necessary to relate it to the transformation of headmanship. Not the market but the political situation brought by war and revolution was the driving force for change.

15 Mud on your boots

Researching the social and environmental history of conservation in Baishui county, Shaanxi during the 1950s

Micah S. Muscolino

Environmental historians, in Donald Worster's words,

> insist that we have got to go .... down to the earth itself as an agent and presence in history ... we must now and then get out of parliamentary chambers, out of birthing rooms and factories, get out of doors altogether, and ramble into fields, woods, and the open air. It is time we bought a good set of walking shoes, and we cannot avoid getting some mud on them.

Environmental historians of China would do well to heed this call to get their boots dirty and head out into the environments that they research. Venturing out of the archive and into the field, I would add, holds even greater importance for historians, like myself, who seek to write "history from the bottom" up in two senses of the term, studying interactions between people at the foundation of social hierarchies and the biophysical world that is, to borrow the words of environmental historian John McNeill, "the real substrate of human affairs."

This chapter offers an example of what environmental historians stand to gain from employing the tools of historical anthropology. It does so through a microhistory of post-1949 water and soil conservation (水土保持 *shuitubaochi*) in Northwest China's Loess Plateau (黄土高原 *Huangtu gaoyuan*), a region covering 64,000 square kilometers that suffers from high rates of soil erosion and acute water shortages. Combining fieldwork with archival research reveals how the conjuncture of biophysical, socio-economic, and political processes generated environmental change, as well as how the rural people whose labor altered the landscape of Northwest China experienced those transformations.

Beginning in the 1950s, the government of the People's Republic of China launched large-scale water and soil conservation campaigns in Shaanxi province and other parts of the Loess Plateau region. These movements mobilized the rural populace to construct terraces, dams, embankments, and other land-management infrastructure. By combatting erosion, PRC leaders expected these conservation efforts to limit siltation on the lower reaches of the Yellow River, prolong the life of dam megaprojects, and increase agricultural yields to support the PRC's vigorous program of industrialization. Conservation measures implemented after 1949, as part of China's drive toward the interconnected goals of revolution and national economic development, struck at the most basic resources of all: land and water, and how people used them. These campaigns remade Northwest China's rural landscape, changed how people farmed, and transformed patterns of work in the countryside.

I draw on fieldwork conducted in Gounan 沟南 village in Shaanxi's Baishui 白水 county, and documents from the Shaanxi Provincial Archives and the Chinese Academy of Sciences and Ministry of Water Resources Institute of Water and Soil Conservation (中国科学院水利部水土保持研究所 *Zhongguo kexueyuan shuilibu shuitubaochi yanjiusuo*) in Yangling 杨凌, Shaanxi, to examine how mass campaigns undertaken in the name of water and soil conservation during the Mao era affected local societies and environments. I address two interrelated questions: what did state-initiated conservation campaigns mean for the rural communities in China who depended on water and soil for their livelihoods? How did rural people take part in and respond to these campaigns? Assessing the local significance of post-1949 water and soil conservation initiatives enriches our understanding of modern Chinese environmental history, while adding an ecological dimension to scholarship that reassesses the history of Maoist China in terms of the "grassroots" and everyday life. My inquiry focuses on encounters between people and the land as mediated by the state, revealing how specific ecological practices were formed through complex interactions among local knowledge and priorities, state imperatives, and dynamics of the natural landscape.

In Baishui county, as my forays out of the archive and into the village have revealed, water and soil conservation initiatives undertaken in the early PRC period actively drew upon local knowledge and experience. After 1949, agents of the PRC state identified and promoted conservation practices already in use in rural society, so as to limit erosion, control the Yellow River, and increase agricultural output. But in terms of land utilization and management in Baishui during the 1950s, a tension existed between the goals of state-initiated conservation campaigns and the priority that the rural populace placed on sustaining production and ensuring subsistence. With rural laborers called on by the central and provincial government, county leaders, and local cadres to attend to water and soil conservation measures rather than other production activities, divergent imperatives could translate into competition over how to use land and allocate labor power. Local leaders, as archival sources and oral history interviews make clear, had to engage in constant negotiations with the rural populace to resolve these contradictions. Fieldwork affords unique insight into these issues that go beyond the archival record, making it possible to comprehend what conservation meant at the local level.

Mass experience in water and soil conservation

Baishui county is geographically situated in the lower-middle reaches of the Luo River 洛河, which flows some 680 kilometers through the Loess Plateau before joining the Wei River 渭河 on central Shaanxi's Guangzhong 关中 Plain. Elevation in Baishui decreases from the northwest (1,000–1,550 meters) to the southeast (350–600 meters), with most cultivated farmland at elevations between 650 and 1,000 meters. Gullies between 100 and 220 meters in depth occupy half the county, dissecting the landscape into a maze of plateaus, ridges, and mounds. As in other parts of the Loess Plateau region, the fragile character of Baishui's loess soils combines with its fragmented topography and poor vegetation cover to make the land highly susceptible to erosion. The resulting water and soil loss hampers agricultural productivity, contributing to Baishui's relative poverty.

Baishui first came to my attention through a 1953 survey report on water and soil conservation in the Luo River watershed. Along with detailing the severity of erosion and land degradation, the survey also observed that "the masses" in this area possessed "rich experience conserving water and soil." Peasants in Baishui and surrounding counties had popular sayings related to water and soil conservation, such as the one that cautioned, "If the land does not have lips [i.e., terraces], people will starve (地没唇, 饿死人 *di meichun, esi ren*)." In the "dry plateau-gully area" in the Luo River's middle reaches, experience had proven the efficacy of constructing terraces compared to cultivating inclined land. The longstanding practice of building silt catchment dams had likewise turned the bottoms of most gullies in Baishui into fertile farmland. As the report noted, "These kinds of simple and easily implemented methods are already widely utilized by the masses in the plateau area. In terms of water and soil conservation, they perform a definite function."

In addition to checking erosion, conservation techniques targeted the acute water shortages that prevailed in Baishui and many other parts of Northwest China's Loess Plateau. Most villages in the plateau-gully area had constructed water cellars (水窖 *shuijiao*) and ponds (涝池 *laochi*) to catch rainwater, "common types of methods by which the masses store water." Plateaus had a low water table, so wells were deep, and residents had to travel long distances to obtain water. Water cellars and ponds not only alleviated the problem of acquiring drinking water, but they also conserved runoff and alleviated water and soil loss. Baishui's Gounan village, as the survey noted, had a total drainage area of 0.053 square kilometers, with 25 water cellars and one pond, which could store 3.914 cubic meters of water. If a torrential rainstorm of 100 millimeters fell and the runoff factor was 62.8 percent, water cellars and ponds could conserve rainwater, keeping it from flowing down the slopes and eroding the soil. To illustrate these conservation techniques, the survey report contained a topographical map of terraces constructed in a gully near the village to conserve soil, and a map of the water cellars and ponds that residents of Gounan had dug to conserve rainwater. These maps piqued my curiosity and I decided to take a trip to Gounan village to see the place for myself.

Gounan as a model of collective conservation

I first went to Gounan in January 2016 and climbed around in the gully that I had seen cartographically represented in the water and soil conservation survey report. My jogging shoes, Worster might be pleased to know, came away covered in Baishui's loess soil. When I met some of Gounan's residents and explained that I had come to conduct research on water and soil conservation, they eagerly took me to see Tuqiaogou 土桥沟 (Earthen Bridge Gully), the ravine south of the village, where a man called Yang Lingjun 杨凌俊 (1889–?) had gained renown during the first decade of the PRC period for building terraces. In addition to looking at a photograph of the site of Yang Lingjun's terraces taken in 1959, I interviewed the octogenarian Yang Xuxiang 杨许祥, Gounan's former cooperative accountant, brigade leader, and party-branch secretary, who gave me a copy of *Gounan wangshi* 沟南往事, the village history that he had written.

Yang Lingjun, I was told, came from an impoverished background. In his youth, he had eked out a living working as a hired laborer digging water cellars for more affluent households. After a catastrophic drought struck Shaanxi in 1929, Yang and his family sold all of their land on the plateau and moved to live in Tuqiaogou, where they set up a shed and started to cultivate around 100 *mu* 亩 of inclined land. Over several years, as Yang Xuxiang's village history records, Yang Lingjun and his nephews gradually

> filled trenches and constructed embankments (填壕邦埝 *tianhao bangnian*), made sloping land into horizontal terraces (水平梯田 *shuiping titian*), built embankments on low-lying land (埝窝地 *nianwodi*), dug fish-scale pits (鱼鳞坑 *yulinkeng*), and planted trees on empty land beside embankments to control water and soil erosion.

With these measures to control water and soil loss, grain production per *mu* on Yang Lingjun's land increased from 40–50 *jin* 斤 to over 100 *jin*. For these achievements, Yang Lingjun earned the nickname "Old Man of the Earthen Bridge" (土桥老汉 *tuqiao laohan*) from his fellow villagers.

After learning about Yang Lingjun and Tuqiaogou during my initial visit to Gounan, I went back to the Shaanxi Provincial Archives in Xi'an and uncovered a wealth of materials on the local history of water and soil conservation in the village. Unlike my local informants, archival documents stress the limitations of pre-existing conservation techniques and the necessity of state-initiated campaigns to improve them. These sources related that terraces covered only a portion of the gullies around Gounan in the early 1950s. Apart from Yang Lingjun's land, terraces had limited scope and effectiveness. Like in other parts of Baishui, erosion posed a serious threat to cultivated fields. Since the mid-nineteenth century, erosion from Tuqiaogou had formed nine branch gullies and runoff from the watershed accounted for half of annual precipitation. In a report on the management of Tuqiaogou from November 1957, Baishui's county head Li Chongshu 李崇书 noted that,

> since vegetation cover is poor, soil and water erosion conditions are relatively severe. Here people often say, "When thunder sounds, people suffer disaster. The floodwaters that come are worse than tigers and wolves." In this manner, the more the gully is washed away the deeper it gets and the more the gully gets washed away the longer it gets. Cultivated land decreases, soil gets poorer, and production decreases by the year.

Tuqiaogou lost over 16,000 cubic meters of soil due to erosion annually, washing away more than 792 tons of nitrogen, phosphorus, and potassium—equivalent to 15 times the amount of fertilizer applied to the gully each year. As a result, pre-1949 grain production in the locale averaged a meager 40–50 *jin* per *mu*. In years of dearth or drought, there was almost no harvest.

Beginning with the 1954 formation of primary agricultural cooperatives, which Yang Lingjun joined early on, Baishui's county leaders mobilized the rural populace to dig trenches, build embankments, and construct terraces on sloping land. Local cadres in Gounan, "led all of the village's cooperative members to go to war against Tuqiaogou, advancing militarily against nature, demanding productivity from barren hills and barren gullies, with everyone going all out and getting at it." Yang Lingjun's experience had provided a "foundation," as Yang Xuxiang insisted in an interview conducted during one of my later visits, but he acknowledged that the collectives managed land better than individual farmers had done previously, and the cooperative's leaders prioritized water and soil conservation.

Archival documents, however, present conservation as a top-down rather than a bottom-up initiative. Looking back from 1957, Li Chongshu's report stated that after several years of diligence conservation campaigns had "changed 'poor gullies and bad pieces [of land]' and created a fortunate situation in which 'households have water cellars, villages have ponds, all land has terraces, all gullies have dams, and there are trees beside the embankments.'" Through terracing and tree-planting, the Gounan brigade's residents ensured that "water did not run down the plateaus and soil did not wash down the slopes," thereby "forcefully assisting in the realization of the nation's great plan to fundamentally control Yellow River disasters." When 45 millimeters of precipitation fell in June 1954, conservation measures at Tuqiaogou preserved all of the storm runoff. With erosion kept in check, rainwater stayed in fields and agricultural production increased. By 1956, production per *mu* reached 150–160 *jin* and average incomes improved as well. In this manner, as Li's report emphasized, conservation furthered the PRC's larger goals of controlling the Yellow River and increasing grain output.

County leaders, as narrated in the archival documents, drew on local knowledge and techniques to lay the basis for these efforts. In this account, initiative came from agents of the PRC state as much as the local populace. Initially, Baishui's county leaders did not have adequate experience promoting water and soil conservation. "For that reason," county head Li Chongshu explained, "we deputed technical cadres deep into the field to summarize the experience of the local masses." These techniques included building trenches and embankments, constructing terraces on slopes, building dams in gullies to block silt and impede runoff, constructing terraces in gullies, digging water cellars and building ponds beside roads and villages, dispersing rainwater's flow and guiding runoff into fields, building gully-head defenses and water drops, and filling in collapses. They also included planting trees and other vegetation beside villages, on embankments, and on abandoned slopes. Afterwards, as conservation efforts at Tuqiaogou went forward, leaders "affirmed and extended" this mass experience, "which performed a definite function."

During these campaigns, Baishui county leaders extoled Yang Lingjun's success as a model for emulation. As Li Chongshu described,

> After more than twenty years of arduous labor, he [Yang Lingjun] finally made land on the two banks of a branch gully of 96 *mu* into terraces. Productivity increased over the years and in 1954 output per *mu* reached 185 *jin*, more than doubling the 90 *jin* per *mu* on most level tableland.

The best five *mu* of wheat had an average production per *mu* that reached 360 *jin*, which was twice the 180 *jin* produced on most plateau land. The 200 pepper plants and 100 pomegranate plants grown on embankments and in depressions unsuitable for grain cultivation also generated income, with the pepper plants alone bringing in over 100 *yuan* a year.

Official materials designating Yang Lingjun as an "advanced producer" (先进生产者 *xianjin shengchanzhe*) in 1958 commended him for rationally utilizing the land and "accumulating abundant water and soil conservation experience to ensure income." Under Yang Lingjun's influence, Gounan's residents mobilized to build terraces on over 680 *mu* of inclined land between 1954 and 1958. Yang also garnered acclaim for the experience he had accumulated digging more than 400 water cellars in his lifetime, and for his activism in cooperative work. Although Yang could not engage in physical labor due to his old age during the conservation campaigns of the 1950s, he personally went down into water cellars to direct young people carrying out work.

The local people I spoke with echoed the official archive by recalling the gains in agricultural production that resulted from conservation measures. But in oral history interviews they placed even greater emphasis on conservation's role in alleviating the village's severe water shortages. Yang Lingjun's skill at digging rain-saving water cellars was of especially great importance in Gounan, where the low water table (more than 120 meters underground) made it all but impossible to dig wells. Residents could collect water from a spring about one *li* away in the gully to the north of the village. But each trip to carry 40–50 *jin* of water back on shoulder poles took half an hour. Besides, water supplies obtained from the spring could barely meet the needs of the people and livestock in the village. In the dry-plateau area, as Yang Xuxiang explained during our conversations,

> Droughts couldn't be avoided. There were no water sources! .... This isn't an irrigated area. With these natural disasters, you had to rely on heaven to eat (靠天吃饭 *kao tian chifan*). There was nothing you could do about it.

Following Yang Lingjun's example and digging water cellars did not eliminate these water-scarcity problems, but it could at least alleviate them. In Gounan, people dug water cellars beside roads and anywhere else that water could be stored. In the village, as Yang Xuxiang explained, "water cellars were originally dug in basically all the fields. Some have had them for many decades or even centuries."

Because the PRC state prioritized water conservancy and agricultural production, local conservation projects garnered higher-level official support as a means of realizing national objectives. The official archive reflects these priorities. Thanks to the central government's leadership after 1949 and "under the inspiration of the 'National Comprehensive Plan to Fundamentally Control Yellow River Flood Disasters and Develop Yellow River Water Conservancy' (国家根治黄河水害和开发黄河水利综合规划 *Guojia genzhi Huanghe shuihai he kaifa Huanghe shuili zonghe guihua*)," as Li Chongshu stated, locals devoted their efforts to the PRC state's goal of "reconstructing the hilly areas (建设山区 *jianshe shanqu*)." To this end, technical personnel from the Yellow River Water Conservancy Commission's Northwest Engineering Bureau (西北工程局 *Xibei gongchengju*) came to Gounan to assist Baishui's county leaders in formulating comprehensive plans for management of Tuqiaogou. After summarizing Yang Lingjun's experience, Baishui's county government and other official agencies convened three on-the-spot meetings at Tuqiaogou in 1956 to promote the conservation measures practiced in Gounan, with more than 420 cadres from various townships and collectives coming to observe and study. Some of the most prominent provincial leaders in Shaanxi at the time, including Zhao Shoushan 赵寿山 and Zhao Boping 赵伯平, personally attended the meetings. At another water and soil conservation training class attended by 43 "backbone" (骨干 *gugan*) cadres, Yang Lingjun introduced his management techniques and demonstrated their results.

While official documents highlight the interventions of state agents, my interviews with Yang Xuxiang foreground the importance of the local knowledge held by peasants like Yang Lingjun in laying the foundation for water and soil conservation programs. As Yang Xuxiang put it,

> Of course, that old man [Yang Lingjun]'s achievements can't be obliterated. With that basis, there was already water and soil conservation and experience building terraces. But when the old man spoke he did not have any [educational] level (水平 *shuiping*) and could not speak clearly.

Rather than explaining conservation techniques, Yang Lingjun only said things like: "Work hard! Tamp down the dirt well! Don't let the water run off! Don't let the (soil) fertility run off! The land can increase production!" That simple language, according to Yang Xuxiang, served as the "basis" for water and soil conservation measures. Subsequently, "The county, district (*xiang*), and township (*zhen*) established water and soil conservation cooperatives and developed these practices, listening to the old man's experience." Specialized technical personnel translated Yang Lingjun's experience into techniques that could be replicated in a programmatic way in other locales. But in Yang Xuxiang's telling, conservation was, first and foremost, a local initiative.

Once promoted beyond Gounan, these water and soil conservation practices proved effective in terms of checking erosion and increasing productivity. Li Chongshu reported that in addition to managing 308,112 *mu* of land in 1956, which exceeded Baishui's target of 180,000 *mu* by 171 percent, these conservation initiatives "also accelerated development of terrace construction." For this reason, Li praised Tuqiaogou as a model for all of Baishui:

> We must make unceasing efforts to carry out terracing and greening (绿化 *lühua*) of all the county's gullies just as has been done in Tuqiaogou, diligently completing the water and soil conservation mission to support the realization of the Yellow River control projects and improve the people's livelihood.

In Gounan, as Yang Xuxiang proudly recalled,

> The plateau and the slopes were completely managed, so soil did not go down the plateau, water did not go out of the gully, and mud did not go out of the gully, so it was all conserved. In the gully a dam was also built—an earthen dam (土坝 *tuba*). With this management, production also increased, and we were appraised as a model (典型都评上了 *dianxing dou pingshang le*).

In large part, as detailed in Yang Xuxiang's village history, Gounan's ability to attain this model status had to do with the efforts of local leaders who built their own reputation by publicizing the village's achievements in water and soil conservation. In 1957, Gounan's party secretary Yang Yuesheng 杨岳胜 (1925–1984) represented the brigade at the Shaanxi Province Advanced Agricultural Unit Work Conference (陕西省农业先进单位工作会议 *Shaanxi sheng nongye xianjin danwei gongzuo huiyi*), where he introduced Tuqiaogou's conservation experience. At this event, Yang Yuesheng received a banner from the PRC State Council's Water and Soil Conservation Commission. The elderly Yang Lingjun could not attend the meeting due to his poor health, as Yang Xuxiang related during our interviews, so his nephew attended on his behalf. The following year, when local leaders—but not Yang Lingjun—attended the central government's Agricultural Socialist Construction Conference (农业社会主义建设会议 *Nongye shehui zhuiyi jianshe huiyi*) in Beijing, the State Council once again presented Gounan a certificate of commendation signed by Zhou Enlai 周恩来. Singled out for this praise, Gounan fit into a pattern characteristic of water and soil conservation initiatives throughout China in the 1950s, which fostered model locales selected because of favorable or special conditions for propaganda and demonstration, and comprehensive development of small watersheds like Tuqiaogou.

Landscapes of labor

For Gounan's rural populace, as oral history interviews make evident, water and soil conservation measures mainly entailed back-breaking physical labor. During the Republican period only the most well-off households in the village—the wealthy peasants and upper-middle peasants, according to Yang Xuxiang—had wheelbarrows or handcarts. After 1949 such tools remained in extremely short supply. Reliance on clumsy wooden carts, combined with the lack of roads, made moving earth for conservation projects a difficult task. As Yang Xuxiang explained:

> When you pushed those [carts], if you didn't have strength and you didn't have skill, you couldn't move them. Out in the fields you pushed that way, and if the cart didn't move you pushed it this way, pushing it along slowly. Gradually over time a road was opened up (碾开 *niankai*) by pushing them.

Moving dirt-filled wooden carts up the steep slopes surrounding Gounan proved most challenging. To keep runoff from eroding the head of Tuqiaogou, Yang Xuxiang told me, "the entire village went out to move earth. People carried it on shoulder poles, they pushed wooden carts, and shoveled it." Only after an extended period of mass mobilization did Gounan's residents move enough earth to redirect the flow of water and protect the gully head, thereby limiting erosion.

To get people to do the heavy work necessary to transform the physical landscape, local leaders in Baishui during the 1950s had to resolve what archival documents term the "temporary contradiction between water and soil conservation and agricultural production." Conservation projects had numerous components, with labor intensive work to do in all four seasons. But after cooperativization, as county head Li Chongshu pointed out, agricultural production witnessed "a new high tide" and double-cropping increased, which decreased the amount of land left fallow and created difficulties in developing field engineering projects. The crux of the issue was that land and labor could be utilized for conservation work or farming, but not for both purposes simultaneously. Crops could not be grown on land that had been dug up to build terraces, embankments, or other conservation infrastructure. "If this contradiction is not appropriately solved," Li warned, "it will influence agricultural production; or else it will squeeze out water and soil conservation." Resolving the problem was of utmost importance.

Li Chongshu's report outlined the methods Gounan and other parts of Baishui had adopted to tackle this contradiction: "Based on the needs of current farming activities, divide the contents of various water and soil conservation projects into those that are unhurried, those that are urgent, and those that must be carried out with comprehensive planning." Local cadres had to vary the timing of each kind of project to ensure that conservation work did not alter or occupy land needed for cultivation. When not tending crops in summer and autumn, they mobilized residents to construct earthen embankments and terraces; in autumn and spring, they built silt dams and other larger-scale projects. During the winter and spring, the slack agricultural season, they dug water cellars and ponds, and filled in collapses.

When implementing these arrangements, as Li Chongshu advised, one had to "flexibly initiate based on concrete circumstances." In 1956, for instance, excess rains delayed the summer harvest until the time when late-autumn crops were to be planted. In this situation, local cadres adopted the slogan "when the land is empty repair it," and "repair first and sow the land early for broom-corn millet and millet; repair afterwards and sow land later for oats and winter wheat." To make effective use of time, cadres instructed peasants to leave aside pieces of land wherever engineering projects were done. After digging up the soil, they sowed these plots with oats. As a result, Li held, "water and soil conservation did not interfere with farming season, and the masses were satisfied." When moving earth for conservation projects, technical guidance ensured that cultivators preserved the fertile topsoil to avert decreases in productivity.

At the same time, meeting conservation targets required careful adjustment of work schedules and incentives. Local cadres had to "rationally handle labor compensation" to ensure that water and soil conservation work met quality standards, and "solve [the issue of] insufficient labor power." To this end, Baishui county leaders combined "temporary assaults" (临时突击

linshi tuji) that organized the entire populace during slack farming season with year-round management. In conjunction with these "assaults," temporary work teams were organized for specific projects, while brigades allocated labor for conservation work as part of their annual plans. "Doing it this way," wrote Li, "avoided the shortcoming of cooperative members worrying that work points were not evenly distributed."

In our conversations, Yang Xuxiang repeatedly stressed the seasonal rhythms of water and soil conservation work. During the busy agricultural season, cooperative members planted crops; in the slack season, they attended to water and soil conservation, especially during winter when farmers would customarily have taken a well-deserved rest. To do conservation work, people now had to labor year-round. When not farming, everyone with the capacity to do labor—male and female, young and old—devoted their efforts to conservation projects. According to Yang Xuxiang,

> Water and soil conservation means saving water and protecting soil. Because water runs off, soil runs off and fertility runs off. When fertility runs off, productivity also suffers. The masses were organized to utilize the slack agricultural season to do it on a large scale (大搞 *dagao*), and during the busy agricultural season to do it on a small scale (小搞 *xiaogao*). Soil fertility could keep up, so productivity could keep up. When there is water, fertility can be conserved; when there is fertility, production can be conserved.

But the rural populace did not necessarily consume the increases in output that resulted from these conservation measures. They had little power to decide what and how to produce. Cooperative leaders made these decisions. With the institution of the PRC's Unified Purchase and Supply (统销统购 *tongxiao tonggou*) system in late 1953, cooperatives had to deliver any grain surpluses that resulted from water and soil conservation efforts to the state at artificially low prices. To implement conservation measures, collectives thus had to monitor work quality, adjust labor incentives and compensation via work points, and carry out ideological education and propaganda. The example of labor models like Yang Lingjun helped to convey these messages. In addition to participating "actively and responsibly" in all government campaigns, Yang Lingjun garnered praise for an instance in 1949 when he volunteered an additional 200 *jin* on top of his household's tax grain (公粮 *gongliang*) obligations. According to a 1958 document, Yang considered this his "glorious responsibility." Rural cultivators, in this didactic message, had a moral duty to hand over their grain to the state.

To convince the local populace of water and soil conservation's importance, as Li Chongshu stated, cadres had to educate peasants about the equivalence between individual and collective benefits, as well as between immediate and long-term benefit. Li advised that labor quotas set for water and soil conservation should consider each locale's "special characteristics:"

the character of the soil, the work's technical nature, people's technical proficiency, and the quotas set for other agricultural tasks. Water and soil conservation projects entailed heavy labor, so "in principle" they should count for more work points than other kinds of farm work.

Methods of compensation, as Li Chongshu explained, also differed based on how early or late projects would reap benefits and the area's "special characteristics." For example, "field engineering projects" like terraces, field embankments, and contoured gully embankments were "mostly recorded as agricultural work, with dividends distributed in the same year." In contrast, work points for projects like silt dams, gully-head defenses, ponds, and check dams, "because benefits are reaped later," were "mostly recorded as capital construction work, with the burden distributed among total labor power and dividends distributed according to periods (of 2–3 years)." After adopting these measures, Li claimed, "laborers' activism greatly increased." However, other reports state that a decision was later made to provide compensation for all conservation work in the current year, since waiting to distribute the value of work points in succeeding years negatively influenced labor effectiveness.

In our interviews, Yang Xuxiang likewise emphasized the importance of work points as the motivation and incentive for doing conservation work. In what he called the "standard system (标准制 *biaozhun zhi*)," one able-bodied adult male's "labor power (劳动力 *laodongli*)" received ten work points for one day of work. This arrangement was also called the "ten-point system." (Women, however, received only eight work points per day). Later, the cooperative shifted to promoting a piece-rate system—literally "fixed effort system (定力制 *dingli zhi*)"—for allocating work points.

As Yang Xuxiang explained, the piece-rate system meant that male laborers earned ten work points on a typical workday (工时 *gongshi*). But they could earn more work points for exceeding targets stipulated by the cooperative:

> For example, when doing water and soil conservation by digging trenches and building terraces…if you completed so many earthworks you got so many work points. If you completed a lot of earthworks, you got more and if you completed fewer earthworks you got fewer.

The standard for male laborers was ten work points, in other words, but those who were "willing to put forth effort (肯出力的 *ken chuli de*)" earned more based on their performance. Yang Xuxiang proudly told of his ability to earn work points in this manner: "I once had those kinds of results. When I was young, I wasn't tall, but I was strong….I shouldered that carrying pole and I was fast, gathering earth all in one place to earn work points." When building a dike with one his comrades, Yang Xuxiang recalled that, even though it typically took eight people to move ten *fang* 方 of earth in a day, the two of them hauled ten *fang* in a single morning, which earned each of them 25 work points. "I could turn out for work (出勤 *chuqin*) and earn over 20 or even 30 work points, earning two or three workdays' worth...If you were willing to put forth effort, you could get work points."

However, the necessity of earning work points to make a living dampened any opposition to water and soil conservation projects that may have existed among the local populace. When asked if any cooperative members in Gounan ever expressed unwillingness to do water and soil conservation work, Yang Xuxiang emphatically stated that they did not:

> To earn work points, you did not pay any attention to those matters. There were no opposing ideas. At that time, people were obedient... Peasants did farm work under the direction of the agricultural cooperative. Working for the agricultural cooperative, you couldn't do work according to your likes and dislikes. That wouldn't do.

The launch of the Great Leap Forward in 1958 ramped up the scale of water and soil conservation work all over Shaanxi. As Yang Xuxiang related, from 1958 to 1959 "going all out against Tuqiaogou" (大搞土桥沟 *dagao Tuqiaogou*) became a model for emulation throughout the entire province. But water and soil conservation campaigns soon ran into serious difficulties. Since the early 1950s, local leaders and higher-level authorities in Shaanxi had vaunted Gounan's experience digging water cellars. Starting in 1958, local leaders mobilized other locales to follow suit. Yang Shiye 杨师叶, a former labor model from a female work team in Baishui's Fumeng 扶蒙 village, currently in her early eighties, told of her experience during this conservation campaign. Cadres instructed Fumeng's residents to dig water cellars in pairs, constructing "husband and wife water cellars" (夫妻窖 *fuqi jiao*) and "sisters' water cellars" (姐妹窖 *jiemei jiao*) to collect rainwater. Yang Shiye and her husband heeded the call, but it resulted in a serious accident: "He was below digging. I was hauling up the earth. The rope snapped, and I fell in...That was 1958, when damn-near everyone dug water cellars (他妈都打过窖 *tama dou dagou jiao*)." Residents mobilized in other parts of Shaanxi to meet their water cellar targets with little regard for quality complained that: "We've dug so many 'black holes.' They occupy land, donkeys fall into them. They're useless. It's really a waste of manpower and resources."

At the height of the Great Leap Forward, fulfilling mounting conservation targets required both men and women to work at night. Rural women, for their part, had to somehow balance the exhausting work of transforming the land with their many other responsibilities. When asked who took care of cooking and other domestic labor during water and soil conservation campaigns, Yang Shiye replied that,

> We just did the housework—we weren't single men (我们这又不是单身汉 *women you bu shi danshenhan*). We made the food in advance and ate it when we came home...When we went out early in the morning we

prepared food and left it in the pot. When we came back, whether it was hot or cold, we hastily ate it and went out again. We did three shifts... At that time, you couldn't even think about eating well. In the evening there was night work (夜干 *ye gan*). When it was busy, you had to work at night for at least two or three hours.

Even archival sources note that the burden of conservation campaigns during the Great Leap weighed heavily on the rural populace. According to one document, cooperative members in Beiqian 北乾 village, which from 1956 to 1959 formed a high-level cooperative alongside Gounan,

> disliked that the retained grain standard (留粮标准 *liu liang biaozhun*) was too low and that water and soil conservation was heavy work that [made them] eat a lot, and so were not willing to go into the fields.

When drought struck in 1960 and state grain requisitioning did not relent, the threat of famine brought conservation work to a standstill. Although demographic data and oral history interviews indicate that Baishui did not witness the kind of famine-related mortality seen elsewhere in China, the county's populace certainly suffered from extreme dearth and hunger. Not until 1962–1963, when the PRC central government issued a new series of directives on water and soil conservation, did these activities regain momentum.

Conclusion

This in-depth examination of water and soil conservation in Baishui county after 1949 demonstrates how agents of the PRC state appropriated and synthesized pre-existing vernacular knowledge forms and practices, promoted them as models, and reapplied them at the local level. Village cadres in Gounan actively publicized this "peasant experience" in their efforts to gain higher-level state recognition and support. Yet conservation efforts did not garner automatic acceptance. Implementation of conservation measures required careful adjustment of farming practices and labor incentives to avoid disrupting agricultural production.

Conservation campaigns launched in Baishui during the 1950s reoriented skills and techniques that mediated human interactions with the land and its resources away from the subsistence imperatives of the rural populace, subsuming this knowledge within the state's larger-scale developmental agenda. The rural populace may have acquired new skills, but they lost the ability to deploy them as they saw fit. Water and soil conservation campaigns meant meeting targets and fulfilling state-defined goals of controlling the Yellow River and extracting agricultural resources. They had little to do with advancing the priorities of the rural populace and rarely took their needs and aspirations into account.

Methodologically, combining environmental history and historical anthropology to better appreciate the environment's role in history starts with getting outdoors and encountering the landscapes that we write about. Whenever possible, it also means talking with the people who have inhabited those environments, relied on them for their livelihoods, and transformed them through their physical labor. Rather than separating fieldwork from archival research, this chapter demonstrates the value of shuttling back and forth between the archive and the field. Reading documents gives our fieldwork direction; fieldwork makes it possible to navigate archives more effectively and interpret written materials in a more rigorously contextualized manner.

The fieldwork I have conducted in Gounan complements the archival record, at least partially corroborating official accounts from the 1950s that some might reflexively dismiss. However, these two types of sources narrate conservation campaigns from distinctly different perspectives. Reports from Baishui county leaders like Li Chongshu speak of mobilizing the masses to check water and soil loss, thereby fulfilling the national goals Yellow River water conservancy and increasing agricultural production. Top-down interventions, in this view, effectively summarized "peasant experience" and resolved the contradictions that stood in the way of plans to remake the environment. Oral histories, however, narrate water and soil conservation as a largely bottom-up initiative. Rather than higher-level party leaders or technical personnel, conservation started with model peasants like Yang Lingjun and gained recognition through the efforts of grassroots cadres.

At that same time, the significance that oral history interviews ascribe to water and soil conservation differs markedly from the meanings attached to it in the official record. Rather than the national-level objective of controlling the Yellow River, as my fieldwork has revealed, local people valued conservation for its ability to improve their livelihoods by alleviating resource scarcities. At least until the Great Leap Forward, conservation initiatives succeeded in meeting Gounan residents' most pressing needs by boosting grain output and providing access to drinking water. In contrast to the government archive, moreover, oral history interviews emphasize the sheer amount of work that went into achieving this transformation of the natural landscape. For the local populace, motivation for taking part in such backbreaking toil came from their need to earn work points, but not from a desire to meet the PRC state's centrally defined plans.

Without visiting Gounan village and getting familiar with the surrounding landscape, I would have never known what questions to ask residents about their experience with conservation and what it meant for them. Nor would I have recognized the sheer scale of this effort to transform nature and the human labor that went into it. It took getting my boots dirty to appreciate the work required to carry drinking water and move earth for conservation projects up these steep slopes. This landscape, I recognized only after visiting Gounan and speaking with elderly villagers like Yang

Xuxiang, fundamentally shaped work patterns, the quotidian rhythms of everyday life, and the meanings that conservation campaigns held for them. To appreciate the presence of the earth in history, you need to get out and walk around.

Further Reading

Brown, Jeremy and Matthew Johnson, eds., *Maoism at the Grassroots Everyday Life in China's Era of High Socialism*. Cambridge, MA: Harvard University Press, 2015.

Eyferth, Jacob, *Eating Rice from Bamboo Roots: The Social History of a Community of Artisans in Southwest China, 1920–2000*. Cambridge, MA: Harvard University Asia Center, 2009.

Hershatter, Gail, *The Gender of Memory: Rural Women and China's Collective Past*. Berkeley and Los Angeles: University of California Press, 2011.

Li, Huaiyin, *Village China Under Socialism and Reform: Micro-History, 1948–2008*. Stanford: Stanford University Press, 2009.

McNeill, John Robert, "Observations on the Nature and Culture of Environmental History," *History and Theory* 42:4 (2003), 5–43.

Muscolino, Micah S., *Fishing Wars and Environmental Change in Late Imperial and Modern China*. Cambridge, MA: Harvard University Asia Center, 2009.

———, *The Ecology of War in China: Henan Province, the Yellow River, and Beyond*. Cambridge and New York: Cambridge University Press, 2015.

Ping, Hao, "A Study of the Construction of Terraced Fields in Liulin County, Shanxi Province in the Era of Collectivization," in *Agricultural Reform and Rural Transformation in China since 1949*, ed. Thomas DuBois and Huaiyin Li, Leiden: Brill, 2016, 101–114.

Pietz, David, *The Yellow River: The Problem of Water in Modern China*. Cambridge, MA: Harvard University Press, 2015.

Schmalzer, Sigrid. *Red Revolution, Green Revolution: Scientific Farming in Socialist China*. Chicago: University of Chicago Press, 2016.

Worster, Donald, "Doing Environmental History," in *The Ends of the Earth: Perspectives on Environmental History*, Donald Worster, ed., Cambridge and New York: Cambridge University Press, 1989, 289–307.

16 Medicine, health, and disease
Among the barefoot doctors of Hangzhou

Xiaoping Fang

The history of medicine, health, and disease in the twentieth century is closely entwined with the advent of modern medicine and state-building in changing political-social contexts. During this time, the scientization, institutionalization, and professionalization of medicine and global health governance have become major issues throughout the world, including China, where they have been gradually implanted, resisted, assimilated, and accepted.

My research focuses on the histories of medicine, health, and disease in rural China after 1949. From 2002 to 2012, I researched the lives and activities of the so-called "barefoot doctors" (*chijiao yisheng* 赤脚医生) in Chinese villages during the Cultural Revolution. In contrast to much of the existing scholarship in the field, which was based largely on written texts and archival documents, the fields of medical anthropology and sociology inspired me to develop a research methodology and theoretical framework from the perspective of historical anthropology. Alongside traditional sources such as archival documents, I came to rely on oral interviews and local documents obtained from fieldwork. In this chapter, I share my fieldwork experience researching the history of medicine in Zhejiang Province by addressing the following key questions: why was fieldwork indispensable? How did I choose my fieldwork site? How did I conduct the fieldwork and overcome difficulties that arose during this process? How did my fieldwork findings contribute to current scholarship in the history of medicine, health, and disease?

The fieldwork: beyond the official and visitor narratives

Barefoot doctors were members of commune production brigades who were given brief, basic medical training so that they could provide treatment and perform public health work in their home villages. They formed the lowest level of a three-tier state medical system that comprised county, commune, and brigade levels. The concept of barefoot doctors was first introduced to the public through newspaper articles, particularly "Fostering a Revolution in Medical Education through the Growth of the Barefoot Doctors," which was published on September 14, 1968, in the Party publication, *People's Daily*.

This article described the work of barefoot doctors in Jiangzhen 江镇 Commune, Chuansha 川沙 County, Shanghai 上海 Municipality. As one of the "newly emerged things" (*xinsheng shiwu* 新生事物) that reflected the political ideologies and rural development strategies of the Cultural Revolution, the barefoot doctors rapidly spread, usually affiliated with new medical schemes called "cooperative medical service." Under this scheme, villagers paid fees to cover the costs of establishing cooperative medical stations, which would be presided over by barefoot doctors. Villagers who sought treatment at these cooperative medical stations were provided certain services and medicines free of charge. With the implementation of rural reform policies and the dismantling of the People's Commune system after 1978, the barefoot doctor program began to gradually disintegrate. Barefoot doctors who passed medical examinations and continued practicing medicine in villages were renamed "village doctors" (*xiangcun yisheng* 乡村医生). By 1983, cooperative medical services had basically ceased to function in most Chinese villages.

Since the program's inception, the Chinese government and foreign visitors (or the international community) provided two major narratives about barefoot doctors. Beginning with the 1952 Patriotic Health Campaign (爱国卫生运动), the government aimed to demonstrate its ideological superiority and to justify its rule through a series of campaigns that sought to reduce mortality rates, eradicate major endemic and epidemic diseases, and improve medicine and health conditions. In the official narrative, the barefoot doctor program reflected Chairman Mao's dicta on medicine and health in rural China and Chinese medicine, such as "Chinese medicine and pharmacology are a great treasure house" (1958) and "In medicine and health, emphasize rural areas" (1965). Barefoot doctors presented a suitable revolutionary image: young people wading undaunted through the mud of the rice paddies to provide medical services in answer to Mao's call. The doctors' main equipment was popularly described as "one silver needle and a bunch of herbs," a reference to acupuncture and Chinese herbal medicine, but their actual practice combined Chinese and Western medicine. These stereotypical narratives of barefoot doctors were repeatedly publicized and strengthened via the propaganda system nationwide.

Outside China, barefoot doctors gained an international profile. The People's Republic of China's inclusion in the United Nations in October 1971 and US president Richard Nixon's visit to China in February 1972 changed China's strategic relationship with the Western world. With specific regard to medicine and health, Western medical physicians visited China at the invitation of the Chinese government. The first medical delegation arrived in September 1971 and was composed of cardiologists Paul Dudley White and Grey Diamond, otolaryngologist Sam Rosen, and community health expert Victor Sidel, and their wives. The itinerary included visits to model hospitals and medical facilities, and talks with physicians, surgeons, and ordinary medical and health staff across China. Dr. Sidel and his wife, the psychiatric social worker Dr. Ruth Sidel, focused on rural medical care, barefoot doctors, and maternal and child healthcare. Their narratives played an important role in shaping images of barefoot doctors in the international community.

In the meantime, the Chinese government was making a great effort to publicize its medical scheme through international medical diplomacy. Inflected by (cultural) nationalism and patriotism, official narratives presented similar images of the barefoot doctor program, which has been regarded as "a low-cost solution built around easily available indigenous medicines" and a combination of Chinese and Western medicine. By the late 1970s, the Chinese system based on the barefoot doctor program was further promoted by the World Health Organization as a model for primary healthcare in developing countries. These narratives were supported by apparent evidence of improvements in basic health indicators under socialism after the founding of the People's Republic of China in 1949.

However, both official and visitor narratives neglected the dynamic relationship between Western and Chinese medicine in the barefoot doctor program. These narratives do not seem to realize that Chinese medicine still dominated the rural medical world at least to the mid-1960s. However, by the time the barefoot doctor program disintegrated in the early 1980s, Western medicine had become predominant in Chinese villages. These stereotypical narratives have cast the relationship between Chinese and Western medicine during the Cultural Revolution as static and unchanging. Furthermore, accounts based on model barefoot doctors and their programs across China were little more than repetitions of ideological discourses. Such accounts present idealized images of this nationwide campaign based on specific cases, usually ones that had benefited from substantial administrative and medical resources because they were intended as central or local models.

When I started my research in 2002, I aimed to revisit the history of barefoot doctors by examining the complex, dynamic, and flexible relationship between Chinese and Western medicine in terms of knowledge transmission, healing styles, pharmaceutical formulations, medical institutionalization and professionalization based on the case study of an ordinary rural community from a historical anthropological perspective. I hoped that oral interviews and local documents collected during fieldwork would provide new findings about barefoot doctors and further contribute to medical anthropology on these key issues.

Fieldwork sites: between the specific and the general

With these research questions in mind, I started choosing fieldwork sites for my research. From the beginning, I was determined to choose a site within Hangzhou Prefecture, Zhejiang Province, in eastern China. The main reasons for this were simple but practical: as a native of this area, I can speak the local dialect and I have access to the necessary social network to facilitate fieldwork, particularly the interviewing of barefoot doctors and ordinary villagers and the gathering of archival materials and local documents relating to the Cultural Revolution. This narrow geographic focus allowed me to analyze the actual experiences of barefoot doctors in detail. I thus felt it best to concentrate my research on a single prefecture, albeit a large one, which I could then explore in depth. Hangzhou was one of many "ordinary" prefectures in which the barefoot doctor program was implemented during the 1960s and 1970s as opposed to those model areas. A systematic analysis of this prefecture (while also paying attention to the general situation throughout the country) would reflect the trends and features of the barefoot doctor program nationwide. Within Hangzhou, I planned to choose one or two rural townships of a reasonable size as my key fieldwork sites.

From November 2003 to June 2004, I conducted my first fieldwork in Hangzhou, reading documents in local archives, conducting oral interviews, and collecting local documents at fieldwork sites. Through the generous assistance of my former middle-school classmates, I visited seven counties within Hangzhou Prefecture and interviewed former barefoot doctors, commune clinic doctors, rural cadres, ordinary villagers, and former Public Health Bureau officers. I compared and narrowed down a few prospective fieldwork sites for my research project.

At the same time, I visited Qin Xiangguan in Hubei Province and Wang Guizhen in Shanghai Municipality, and became aware of the pitfalls of concentrating on areas that had been national showcases for the barefoot doctor program during the 1970s. In September and December of 1968, these two figures had been the focus of reports on cooperative medical services and barefoot doctors in the *People's Daily* that had initiated the popularization of barefoot doctors nationwide. Qin was described as the founder of the cooperative medical service nationally. I spent one productive week interviewing Qin at his home in March 2004. Wang had been described as the first Chinese barefoot doctor and was eventually promoted to the rank of Vice Minister of Health during the Cultural Revolution. However, her family resolutely declined my interview request in June 2004 on the grounds that she did "not (wish) to recall tragic memories." Both the interview with Qin and the unsuccessful attempt to talk to Wang helped me understand the fate of model figures during political turmoil.

By the end of this first seven months of fieldwork, I decided that my main research site would be Jiang Village, which is now a suburban area under the jurisdiction of Hangzhou. From 1912 to 1961, Jiang Village was under the jurisdiction of Hang County, the most important county in Zhejiang Province because Hangzhou, the provincial capital, lay within it. In 1961, Hang County was made part of Yuhang 余杭 County, which was under the jurisdiction of Hangzhou Prefecture. Jiang Village People's Commune was established in the same year and was renamed Jiang Village Township in January 1984.

My decision to focus specifically on Jiang Village was based primarily on two reasons. My interviewees—who included pre-1949 doctors of Chinese medicine, union clinic staff, former barefoot doctors, commune clinic doctors, and ordinary villagers—were all happy to share their life histories with me and offer me assistance, even though I am not a native of their specific area. Jiang Village is located in a suburban part of Hangzhou City, and migrant workers have been flooding into the township since the early 1990s. Local residents have benefited from these workers' arrival through rapid economic development and high income from renting properties to them. For this reason, residents tend to get along well with arriving outsiders. The demographic structure of this township community means that residents can speak and understand Mandarin regardless of their age, so I was able to communicate quite easily. Moreover, the area around Jiang Village is a wetland, and before the 1950s was seriously affected by schistosomiasis, an infectious disease spread by waterborne parasites. The township had undergone all the new regime's medical and health campaigns and programs and some of the key participants in these campaigns were still alive when I started my fieldwork there. Another important factor was the size of the township, which was reasonable. The maximum distance between the town and the surrounding villages is around an hour and a half's walk, and commuting between these areas and archives and libraries located in urban areas was convenient. I would be able to make good use of my time and arrange oral interviews and archival reading. Sometimes I also allocated a few days to conduct fieldwork in villages in neighboring rural counties to obtain supplementary materials.

Subsequently, I continued to visit Jiang Village and other sites in Hangzhou Prefecture twice each year until 2011, spending two weeks to one month there on each occasion. The main thread of inquiry in my research was the development of medicine and health since the 1940s in Jiang Village, while paying close attention to evidence from seven counties in Hangzhou Prefecture. By doing so, I sought to balance the specific and the general and thus provide evidence of the actual experiences of health practitioners and patients to challenge existing preconceptions and stereotypes about healthcare in rural China.

Oral interviews, local documents: process, methods, and experiences

When I first visited Jiang Village Township in November 2003, Jiang Village was the central village and the seat of the township government. Lining the two main intersecting streets were shops, vendors, and residential buildings where locals and migrant workers lived alongside one another. The town was a microcosm of radical industrialization and urbanization in the early twenty-first century. Before my arrival, I had already contacted a friend who was teaching there. I told him that I would like to interview a few local doctors who were familiar with the history of medicine and health in the township. My friend immediately recommended I talk to Mr. Ahbao (Chen Hongting), a popular, well-respected figure in Jiang Village. After meeting my friend at the school where he worked, we went to visit Chen's home, which was only three to four minutes' walk away. Unfortunately, Chen Hongting was out visiting his brother-in-law in the city, but my friend took me to visit another local doctor known as "Mr. Cat-Dog" (Jiang Jingting), who had been in charge of anti-schistosomiasis work from the late 1950s to the mid-1990s. When I visited Chen Hongting successfully the second time, I was fascinated by his stories of family, personal life, and work. The Chen family had practiced medicine in Jiang Village for three generations—their practice stretched back to the Tongzhi reign of the Qing Dynasty (1861–1875). The family had accumulated a fortune and earned respect in the local community. Chen himself began studying medicine under his father's supervision in the 1930s. In 1952, the Communist government set up the Jiang Village Union Clinic at Chen's home, and he worked at this new union clinic (which later became the commune clinic) until his retirement in 1979. Over the course of half a century, Chen Hongting witnessed historical changes in medicine and health in Jiang Village. Chen was a "walking dictionary" and an ideal interviewee.

During the early stages of my fieldwork in Jiang Village, my interviews mainly focused on Chen Hongting and his former colleagues at what had been the union clinic in the 1950s–1960s and became the commune clinic. These interviews gave me completely fresh insight into the local nature of historical changes in medicine and health in Jiang Village. Through introductions from Chen and his colleagues, I met and started interviewing healthcare workers from the 1950s to 1960s and people who had become barefoot doctors from the late 1960s onward. The majority of these were Chen's and his colleagues' students or fellow villagers. I continued my interviews with Chen, his colleagues, healthcare workers, and barefoot doctors for as long as they were available.

Like many junior scholars conducting interviews for the first time, I had prepared a list of questions and even questionnaires for my interviewees, but these soon turned out to be unrealistic. The conversations did not follow these designated questions, and the pool of respondents to my questionnaires was too small to be meaningful. Soon I started chatting casually with my interviewees, occasionally asking questions but mostly letting them tell their own stories. When I interviewed Chen Hongting between the years 2003 and 2006, I usually went to his home and chatted with him in the morning. Sometimes he played mahjong with his old friends there, while I watched and listened to them. One of the key themes of their conversations was their work before retirement, and they often corrected one other. These older people were usually glad to have patient listeners and were very willing to introduce me to their former colleagues. The number of interviewees increased steadily in this way, extending to former county health bureau officials and their former protégé and students.

By contrast, some of the barefoot doctors I interviewed were still practicing medicine in their own village clinics during my fieldwork exercise before 2011. I went to their clinics and chatted with them. When patients came, I gave them my seat, then resumed our conversations after they had left. I tried my best to make my interviews informal and keep things light when interviewing barefoot doctors, who seemed to enjoy sharing their life histories during their working hours at the clinics. All in all, my more casual chats with them were what proved to be the most effective and productive way of conducting interviews during fieldwork. In contrast, trying to guide and intervene in conversations in order to get expected answers from interviewees proved much more problematic.

When I visited each interviewee for the first time, I would usually take a small gift, such as two bottles of wine, and inexpensive souvenirs, such as pens, with my university logo. These tokens of appreciation helped my interviewees and their families accept me more quickly as such flows of gifts are in keeping with Chinese village culture and customs. The interviewees were not concerned about the actual economic value of these presents—their symbolic value was what counted. At no point in my fieldwork did I pay my interviewees fees for talking with me. As in other areas of China, many village clinics in Hangzhou Prefecture are located in barefoot doctors' homes, and Jiang Village was no exception. If a mealtime fell during my visit, my hospitable hosts would usually invite me to have lunch or dinner with their families. These meals proved to be great opportunities for listening to the stories of barefoot doctors as told by their families. Indeed, I believe that the dining table is always one of the best fieldwork sites in Chinese society. During these relaxed, casual occasions, interviewees are usually very happy to share their work and personal experiences.

However, the matters of recording conversations and the timing of interviews raised two important issues. At the beginning, I usually took notes when I chatted with interviewees, but I soon found that this affected our conversation. It slowed things down, and I found that I often ignored some interesting content during the process. I also tried recording my interviews and then transcribing the contents, but some interviewees felt embarrassed and uncomfortable and were often sensitive about what they said. Eventually, I stopped recording during interviews and instead recalled conversations and wrote notes each night or immediately after interviews if possible. As it turned out, interesting content proved unforgettable. As for interview timing, barefoot doctors in Jiang Village usually treated patients in clinics in the morning, closed their doors at noon, and left to do other work in the afternoon. Mornings are the busiest times for them, and also for other villagers, former commune clinic doctors, and township and health bureau officials. However, things were more flexible for retirees. I usually arranged interview times with interviewees in advance and combined these visits with my research work at libraries and archives.

While oral interviews were the backbone of my fieldwork in Jiang Village, I also paid close attention to collections of local historical documents. As I mentioned above, Jiang Village is located in a suburban part of Hangzhou City. The long history and rich culture that have formed in this community over the centuries have left a wealth of local documents, and I spent a lot of time collecting and reading these. With the creation of the Xixi National Wetland Park and the run-up to the relocation of this rural community, many local historians also started collecting and compiling scattered documents. For example, Shen Qingyang, whose grandfather and father were popular heatstroke acupuncturists, compiled a brief history of the development of medicine and health since 1949. These local documents provided indispensable background knowledge, as did the specific files on Jiang Village Township from 1949 onward that was stored in the county district archives.

When I had free time, I also wandered around Jiang Village on foot and got familiar with its local customs, practices, geographical layout, and natural surroundings. This not only grounded the historical scenes my interviewees discussed but also proved to be a source of great inspiration. I walked along the banks of the Xixi Wetland and chatted with peasants who were laboring in the fields. This wetland was rife with schistosomiasis before 1949 and the battlefield for the anti-schistosomiasis campaign during the Mao era. These casual strolls greatly improved my understanding of descriptions of local doctors who had participated in this campaign. Visits to some old buildings also made a deep impression on me. For example, I visited a meeting hall in Sanshen Village which dated to the People's Commune era. As the only public space in the village, this hall had once served as a hospital ward to accommodate schistosomiasis patients from the township. This site visit helped me think further about the stratification of medical encounters and the shift in medical treatment from home bedsides to hospital wards. In Yuanjue Temple, I chatted with organizers, pilgrims, and chefs while copying inscriptions on stone tablets (which were interesting, although not directly related to my project). These visits brought historical scenes to life and shed light on changes in local religion, folk beliefs, medical practice, and ceremonies in rural communities over the twentieth century. I was very lucky that I made these visits when I did, in 2005: when I returned to visit the temple half a year later, it had been dismantled as the Xixi Wetland construction project progressed. Though these off-the-cuff walks were time-consuming, they turned out to be very fruitful for my research.

Findings and contributions

The oral interviews and local documents that I collected during my fieldwork were very significant for my research. After I returned from each fieldwork trip to Jiang Village, I was full of motivation, enthusiasm, and inspiration to start writing up what I had uncovered. I was confident that these vivid stories from barefoot doctors, villagers, commune clinic doctors, and other interviewees who had lived in villages during the Mao era would be of great interest to readers. When I started reading archival documents and newspapers that followed the party line, I read new information between the lines. More importantly, my fieldwork findings helped me re-examine my theoretical framework and thus contribute new interpretations to current scholarship. A few examples are in order.

Before the fieldwork, I had read many medical anthropological and sociological works, of which medical anthropologist Arthur Kleinman's work was the most important and inspirational for me in developing my theoretical framework. Based on his study of Taiwan Chinese society during the 1970s, Kleinman defined "medicine" as a cultural system and further proposed the theory of "plural medical systems" or "medical pluralism," which categorized all healers into professional, folk, and popular medical systems. Kleinman's theories motivated me to pay attention to the plural features of medical systems, even though the official narratives described only one top-down professional medical system.

Having interviewed Chen Hongting and his former colleagues, I was very excited to find dynamics that suggested a plural medical system during the establishment of the state medical system in rural areas after 1949. This pluralism was based on the constant differentiation of professional and folk healers according to both political ideology and practical needs by including them in or excluding them from the state medical system during the new socialist regime's continuous political campaigns. This process started with the 1952 establishment of union clinics by private practitioners of Chinese medicine and continued up to the outbreak of the Cultural Revolution, which completely reshuffled these plural medical systems. During this process, Chen Hongting's family's medical lineage, Shen Jinrong's heatstroke acupuncture and bone-setting technique, and the Yuanjue Temple represented professional, folk, and popular medical systems in Jiang Village, respectively. These systems were differentiated from one another, reorganized, and extended until 1968 when barefoot doctors emerged in the reconstructed village medical world as a national health program.

Intergenerational knowledge transmission in the medical community of Jiang Village is another example. In the social history of medicine in China up to the late imperial period, ways of transmitting medical knowledge are basically classified as either scholarly or non-scholarly. Scholarly transmission refers to the ways that the literati or Confucian physicians obtained medical knowledge. Traditionally, there were three kinds of scholarly transmission: studying under masters; training within families, clans, and lineages; and self-study. Non-scholarly transmission describes the oral transmission of folk healers' medical knowledge through medical practice within families, such as midwifery, or the healing methods of religious sects. Regardless of whether forms of learning were scholarly or non-scholarly, medical knowledge, techniques, recipes, and healing experiences were not readily shared with others. These ways of knowing continued in Jiang Village until the early 1950s, even though medical school education had existed for a few decades in Chinese urban areas.

Through my fieldwork in Jiang Village, I found how forms of medical knowledge transmission had changed since the early 1950s. I further classified local doctors and barefoot doctors into four generations: Chen Hongting and other founding members of union clinics were the first generation, Chinese medicine and pharmacology apprentices in 1958 were the second, the first batch of health workers in 1965 the third, and barefoot doctors in 1968–1969 the fourth. Under the impact of political and social campaigns, traditional and conservative methods were interwoven with open, modern education over these two decades. Despite the arrival of new methods, each generation also continued to transmit medical knowledge and lineages from the previous generation. Interestingly, folk healers, who were mobilized into the state medical system, continued to share their medical knowledge with their peers, although they also applied their medical expertise in their work as barefoot doctors. The sources of medical knowledge also gradually went beyond families and community as Western medicine steadily came to dominate the rural medical community and marginalized Chinese medicine. My findings about intergenerational knowledge transmission in the community contributed to medical anthropology and sociology in terms of knowledge, politics, and community in China's social contexts.

My fieldwork in Jiang Village also revealed the structural evolution of the rural medical system since the 1950s. The three-tiered rural medical system was regarded as the pillar of medicine and health in rural areas in Mao's China, in which barefoot doctors and cooperative medical services worked together. Previous scholarship had highlighted the functional scheme and referral system but had not interpreted this structural evolution. During my fieldwork, mentions of the establishment of Jiang Village Clinic, which was based at Chen Hongting's home, and its layout inspired me to further explore the formation of the rural medical community and the emergence of medical coordination. This led me to examine how medical stations, the proficiency hierarchy, and the referral system operated with the advent of the barefoot doctor program.

In this process, the barefoot doctor Hong Jinglin provided me with statements of Jiang Village cooperative medical service outpatient and medical fees in 1971, which recorded the number of clinic visits and average medical fees for the commune clinic headquarters, the branches of this, and village medical stations. I classified these clinics and stations into three types by geographical distance: Type I included Jiang Village Commune Clinic and its two branches in other villages; Type II referred to those neighboring villages outside Type I villages; and Type III villages lay beyond these Type II villages. This indicated that medical units at each level treated illnesses with different levels of seriousness and showed the different degrees of medical proficiency within the hierarchical medical system.

Further examination found that Type-III village medical stations attracted and treated the majority of patients, while the average cost of serious patient referrals was higher compared with clinic headquarters and branches. This meant that the medical proficiency of village medical stations started challenging that of the commune clinic and its branches, a situation which was further worsened by geographical distance as villagers sought treatment in nearby village medical stations. Finally, I analyzed the medical equipment, instruments, and expertise of commune and district clinics in Hangzhou Prefecture between 1974 and 1976. I found that commune and district clinics at the middle level of the three-tier medical system suffered serious challenges from county hospitals and barefoot doctors in treating major and minor illnesses respectively and thus lost advantages in attracting these patients. This deficiency finally contributed to the formation of a dumbbell-shaped structure for the three-tier medical system, a structure that continued into the early twenty-first century.

Future challenges

My fieldwork in Jiang Village from 2003 to 2011 was an enjoyable and unforgettable experience for me. I still miss the days I spent interviewing Chen Hongting, his colleagues, barefoot doctors, their families, villagers, former commune clinic doctors, and government officials. In addition to everything I learned from them, I also accumulated considerable experience in how to go about fieldwork. When I wrote up my findings, I incorporated texts, interviews, and theories and presented a completely new interpretation of the barefoot doctor program. This methodology has continued into my current research on the global cholera pandemic in southeast coastal China in the 1960s. Unlike my fieldwork in Jiang Village more than a decade ago, however, I have found it more difficult to find appropriate interviewees simply because many eyewitnesses are very elderly or have died. Worse still, the government has set very strict limits on access to archival documents, which poses challenges to my use of traditional methodologies for historical anthropology studies, which are based on oral interviews and archival documents. Finding a reasonable solution to these challenges is pressing and crucial for research in the future.

Further Reading

Croizier, Ralph, *Traditional Medicine in Modern China: Science, Nationalism, and the Tensions of Cultural Change*. Cambridge, MA: Harvard University Press, 1968.
Fang, Xiaoping, *Barefoot Doctors and Western Medicine in China*. Rochester, NY: University of Rochester Press, 2012.
Kleinman, Arthur, *Patients and Healers in the Context of Culture: An Exploration of the Borderland between Anthropology, Medicine, and Psychiatry*. Berkeley: University of California Press, 1980.

17 Discovering the Cultural Revolution in oral history

Guoqiang Dong

My academic path to the study of the Cultural Revolution is a long story that itself might require another lengthy article to explain, but relates to developments and changes in the Chinese academic environment since the 1980s. In this chapter, I will instead focus on how I conducted research on the Cultural Revolution in Jiangsu province and Nanjing, and on the importance of oral history to this research.

Why did I begin my research from oral history?

In early 2005, by pure chance, I got hold of a CD-ROM of the "Chinese Cultural Revolution Database" (中国文化大革命文库) edited by Song Yongyi. Although I had never done any such research on the Cultural Revolution myself, I was aware of publications by Chinese and overseas scholars. Back then, most Chinese publications on the Cultural Revolution still "looked upward" to discuss elite politics of the central Chinese Communist Party (CCP) leadership. In contrast, overseas studies had already turned their focus to local mass movements, with representative examples including the research on the Red Guards movements in Guangzhou by Lee Hong Yong and Anita Chan, Andrew Walder's research on Zhang Chunqiao and the Shanghai January Revolution, Wang Shaoguang's research on the mass movement in Wuhan, and Elizabeth Perry and Li Xun's research on workers' movements in Shanghai.

Having remained and taught in the Department of History at Nanjing University after I received my BA degree there in 1985, I had often overheard senior colleagues chatting about interesting anecdotes of recent university history and about certain faculty during the Cultural Revolution. Their recollections triggered my desire to further explore the whole story. When I had decided to focus on the Cultural Revolution as my research topic and, especially after I read Yin Hongbiao (印红标)'s research on the Cultural Revolution at Peking University and Tang Shaojie (唐少杰)'s study of the movement at Tsinghua University, a bold idea began to take shape in my mind: if the Cultural Revolution movements at Peking University and Tsinghua University can stand as individual and specific research projects, could Nanjing University be another one? This idea was actually supported by the historical fact that the so-called "Cultural Revolution" originated in the early 1960s as part of the "Socialist Education Movement" that aimed to strengthen ideological control, to eliminate all "non-proletarian" ideas, and to establish the absolute authority of Mao Zedong and his thought. Therefore, the cultural and education sectors were among the first to act. A top university under the direct supervision of the Ministry of Education, Nanjing University, occupied a pivotal position in Jiangsu's higher education sphere, making it the cradle of the Cultural Revolution in Nanjing as well as in Jiangsu province. A number of students and junior teachers from Nanjing University quickly became involved in the political conflicts on campus, and later became leaders of the major local mass organizations. From a comparative point of view, the movements at both Peking University and Tsinghua University were directly influenced by the CCP center's political struggles, while the Cultural Revolution and its local influence at Nanjing University—a provincial-level institution—was clearly of a different kind. The significance of studying the case of Nanjing University became evident. The questions I wanted to ask were: what did the CCP's call for Cultural Revolution mean to ordinary cadres and people? What were the motivations behind mass rebellion movements? Why were there fierce factional struggles in these mass movements?

With the research topic and direction decided, the biggest challenge for me was the lack of historical materials. Song Yongyi's 35-million-character "Chinese Cultural Revolution Database" primarily includes materials about national events; information on Jiangsu province and Nanjing University was too sparse and fragmentary to give a general view of the local Cultural Revolution movement. The Jiangsu provincial and Nanjing municipal archives granted no access to their post-1965 archival materials. By regulation, the Nanjing University archives did not offer services to academic researchers. Although the library had complete collections of *Xinhua Daily* and *Nanjing Daily*, these newspapers were actually the Party organ and were therefore of little use to my research. For example, apart from a few reports on the "June 2nd Incident" at Nanjing University, *Xinhua Daily* in the second half of 1966 provided little coverage of the rapid emergence of mass organizations, of the conflicts between rebel mass organizations and local authorities, or of the conflicts between rebel and conservative mass organizations. Even the sporadic reports on the "June 2nd Incident" were censored and distorted by the orthodox ideological discourse and were nowhere near the truth. Under these circumstances, I had to begin my research with interviews with my own teachers and colleagues. This approach diverged from what I had considered the normal scholarly requirements of historical studies, but I had no other option.

How do we do oral history?

Many scholars—especially younger scholars—have recognized the importance of oral history. There are, however, a few things worth paying attention to in the actual practice of it. First, we cannot assume that every interview will be successful and productive. The outcome of the interview depends on the interviewee's personal experience, their ability to objectively perceive reality as they see it, their openness in the interview, and also their storytelling ability. We will only be able to find the right people for interviews over time and often after extensive and seemingly futile interactions. Second, even after meeting a few ideal interviewees, we will only be able to get the oral history we want after spending prolonged periods of time with them. Repeated exchanges strengthen mutual trust and facilitate the interview to naturally proceed deeper. Conducting interviews is a long-term and difficult task that requires substantial investment of time and energy by the researcher. Nevertheless, as we gradually expand our contact sources and our background knowledge, interviews will become increasingly productive and we will have more and more suitable candidates to be interviewed.

The third point to keep in mind is that, even if the interview is designed with specific purposes and intentions and a list of questions drafted in advance, we cannot simply go through this question list automatically like an interrogation. If we do, the interviewee will often give simple answers of "yes" or "no," and the interview can hardly proceed further naturally and smoothly. The better way is to encourage the interviewee to tell stories that they had "personally experienced, seen, and heard" according to their own memories and concerns. We are better off raising only one or two important questions at key moments to guide the interviewee to recall a more interesting story. The greatest advantage of such "open-ended interviews" is that the person interviewed may tell a lot of things unknown to us that will then lead to more important research questions.

The fourth point is that oral history is inevitably subjective in the extreme. We therefore should be attentive to the following two points when using it: to begin, we should assess the interviewee's overall credibility by comparing what they relate with information from historical documents and other people's oral testimony; furthermore, we should try to steer away from discussions of subjective feelings and analysis, and instead focus only on objective facts—"who," "when," "on what occasion," "what was said" and "what was done."

Fifth and finally, we will meet different kinds of people in interviews and get different results. Some people's own personal experience might be ordinary and nothing special, but through their connections, we might be able to meet with more suitable interviewees or find valuable historical documents. In this sense, all interviews are meaningful. Only when we are aware of these issues and are fully prepared will we be able to get on with it productively and eventually reap repeated and often surprising rewards. None of the teachers and colleagues I interviewed was at the center of any major local Cultural Revolution events. But it was from these ordinary and "peripheral" figures that I expanded my personal network. Within about two years, I managed to get to know a number of Nanjing University alumni who were "influential" figures in the Cultural Revolution, such as Geng

Changxian (耿昌贤) and Ge Zhonglong (葛忠龙) who headed the "Good Faction" (*haopai*) in Nanjing, and Zeng Bangyuan (曾邦元), head of the opposing "Ass Faction" (*pipai*). Through their connections, I then met some of the leaders of local workers' and cadres' organizations who were deeply involved in internal factional conflicts at their own work units as well as in regional factional conflicts. These people knew well the "inside" story of the mass organizations and had frequent and substantial contact with central and local Party and military leaders. Their personal experience is an important part of local Cultural Revolution history.

In addition, from extensive interviews, I managed to get hold of my first set of valuable historical documents, including official formal documents, archives that somehow had been misplaced or lost, and such non-government historical materials as personal work notes, private correspondence, big-character poster drafts, drafts of individual confessions and appeals, grassroots newspapers and journals of mass organizations, pamphlets, and the "Great Criticism" series compiled and edited by some mass organizations. Among these, two items are of particular importance: the first is the whole set of "The August 27th Battle News" (*Ba erqi zhanbao*) produced from the end of 1966 to the spring of 1969 and collected by a former editorial team member who had studied in the Department of Politics at Nanjing University. The August 27th faction, one of the two best-known local mass organizations, was active in the Cultural Revolution for a long time and had great influence in the local community. The second item, given to me by a former cadre in the municipal Party Committee, is the *Chronicle of Events in the Cultural Revolution in Nanjing* (a draft circulated to seek opinions) 南京文化大革命大事记(征求意见稿) compiled and printed by the Nanjing Archives in 1985. This *Chronicle of Events*, of which only ten mimeographed copies were printed at the time, was initially compiled in the early 1980s in the midst of an active, national reflection on the Cultural Revolution. Although brief, missing some major incidents and contradicting certain verifiable historical facts, it is nevertheless a chronicle assembled on the basis of primary historical materials and therefore a particularly valuable reference for the movement from 1966 to 1969. In short, the "unofficial" historical documents and oral histories from influential figures in the local Cultural Revolution depicted a picture of the situation and events that was very different from the mainstream narratives on the Cultural Revolution, and this encouraged me to carry on with my research with even greater interest.

What is the significance and unique value of oral history?

I would like to further illustrate the importance and unique value of oral history with three examples. Indeed, oral histories of many ordinary people can provide completely different perspectives from official historical narratives, and thus reveal a contrasting narrative of well-known historical incidents. Let us consider first the "June 2nd Incident" at Nanjing University in 1966, which was the second major campus incident of great national political influence following the better-known "Nie Yuanzi Big-character Poster Incident" at Peking University that is associated with the beginning of the Cultural Revolution. A long report about the "June 2nd Incident" was published in *People's Daily* on June 16, 1966, together with an editorial titled "Fully mobilize the masses to crack down on the anti-revolutionary black gang." According to the news report and editorial, the "June 2nd Incident" was a political conflict caused by Kuang Yaming (匡亚明), a so-called member of the "counterrevolutionary gang," and the University Party Committee Secretary and the President of Nanjing University. Kuang was accused of brutally suppressing the "revolutionary teachers and students'" "revolutionary act" of putting up big-character posters. However, this judgment in the *People's Daily* editorial was contradicted by a document entitled "Decision to Establish the Liyang Branch Campus" issued by the Nanjing University Party Committee in 1966, as well as by the Committee's announced "Decision to Rehabilitate Kuang Yaming" in May 1978. Both of these documents were released in a 2012 publication of Nanjing University historical materials.

The obvious questions are: why are there two contradictory interpretations to the same incident? And, what actually happened in the "June 2nd Incident"? After interviewing a number of witnesses of different ages, status, and standpoints, I gradually approached an understanding of what actually occurred. In brief, it was Kuang Yaming, as head of the University Party Committee, who decided to establish the Liyang Branch Campus to experiment with the "half-farming, half-studying" (*bannong bandu*) model of education. The background to this decision was Mao Zedong's repeated criticism of the education system and his call for an "education revolution" in the early 1960s. When implemented, however, Kuang's decision encountered quite a few practical difficulties, causing irritation to some teachers and students. Yet in the conditions of that time, individual appeals putting forth differing opinions could not be expressed freely and openly. So, on learning that Mao Zedong had backed the "Nie Yuanzi Big-character Poster Incident" at Peking University, a few teachers and students at the Liyang Branch Campus also put up big-character posters, employing the strategy of radical rhetoric to voice their personal concerns and demands about the new campus and Kuang's policy. In order to protect his authority and his "politically correct" image, Kuang Yaming launched a fierce "counterattack" on the model of his previous experience of the 1957 Anti-Rightist Campaign, thereby intensifying the confrontation. This shows that the conflict actually resulted from differing opinions on one specific policy, and had nothing to do with larger ideological and political struggles. In that particular context, however, the opposing parties each adopted "revolutionary" discourse strategies and "revolutionary" means of struggle, gradually aggravating the disagreement until it burst into a fierce political confrontation. This case is particularly valuable in that it prompts us to reconsider the origins of internal political conflicts within work units and to reassess the defects of the political system and its practices in the lead up to the Cultural Revolution.

Key witness testimony in oral histories can also provide certain insider knowledge otherwise unknown that can explain seemingly un-reconcilable historical facts and facilitate our understanding of the complex interactive relationships between Party central elite politics and local mass movements. For my second example, let us recall that the official historical narratives created soon after the Cultural Revolution" claimed that the nationwide "power seizures" in early 1967 were a key factor in precipitating subsequent social chaos and had been maliciously instigated by the "Lin Biao-Jiang Qing Counterrevolutionary Gang" in concert with the political ambition of local rebel faction leaders. With this in mind, I was genuinely shocked to learn from rebel faction leaders that the "January 26th Power Seizure" in Jiangsu province was actually pursued at Zhou Enlai's direction, and that the Nanjing Military Region also knew of, and was backing it beforehand. This means two things: first, the power seizure in Jiangsu was not a spontaneous act of the rebels; and, second, the power seizure was not instigated by the "radical" faction leaders Lin Biao or Jiang Qing but by the supposedly "moderate" Zhou Enlai. This prompted me and Andrew Walder to further explore and re-explain these local seizures of power. Simply put, after Mao Zedong approved the Shanghai "January Revolution," Zhou Enlai anticipated that this incident would inevitably trigger a ripple effect throughout the country, and he actively intervened to prevent the overall situation from becoming worse.

The intervention was not limited to secretly instigating and instructing the rebels to seize power, but, more importantly, he manipulated local personnel arrangements when power was seized. Based on Zhou's judgment, the Jiangsu Provincial Party Committee Secretary Jiang Weiqing (江渭清) was not on the list of local leaders that Mao Zedong intended to purge. So, in order to secure continuity within the top-level political structure in Jiangsu, Zhou arranged for Jiang to "stand out" with a self-criticism after the mass power seizure and then, acting for the central CCP, assigned Jiang to be the main leader of the "new revolutionary regime"—the Jiangsu Provincial Revolutionary Committee. This shows Zhou Enlai's painstaking efforts to maintain stability throughout this seemingly "radical" movement. After the "Huairentang Incident" in Beijing, however, deep divisions within the central CCP reemerged, which put an end to Zhou's wishful thinking. Meanwhile, overt and covert struggles within the central CCP had intensified factional conflicts among rebel mass organizations. This in-depth study based on oral histories completely invalidates the original official explanation and, instead, highlights the disastrous consequences of the central CCP's non-institutional interventions in local mass movements.

Broadly speaking, through extensive contact with witnesses, we can collect rare, highly valuable historical materials that can help us lay a solid foundation for constructing completely new, richer and more thoroughly accurate historical narratives. For my last example I will discuss how, from oral histories and fragmentary historical documents, we could build an understanding of the process and nature of the 1974 "Criticize Lin Biao and Confucius" campaign in Jiangsu province. Because the existing materials at the time alone were not enough to produce a convincing historical study, I reached out to an important figure in the movement. Originally from a poor peasant family, this individual had already attracted the Party's attention in his school years, and, shortly after graduating from university, was named Secretary of the Suzhou Municipal Youth League Secretariat. He was a rising young cadre specifically trained by the Suzhou Municipal Party Committee in the mid-1960s. Through the complex interaction of a series of contingent factors in the early days of the Cultural Revolution, he became the leader of the rebel faction made up of Suzhou Party leadership and government functionaries. Joining the Suzhou Revolutionary Committee during the "Great Alliance" period of 1968, he was later promoted vice head of the Political Work Group of the Jiangsu Provincial Revolutionary Committee, vice head of the Organization Department of the Jiangsu Provincial Party Committee, and Secretary of the Jiangsu Provincial Youth League. This cadre's personal political path of ascent through these years challenges the "social conflict theory" explanation of the rebels' motives, and instead points to the significance of "political ambiguity" and how it led to political conflict during the Cultural Revolution. More importantly, the various leading positions he had assumed gave this cadre the opportunity to attend most of the top meetings held by the departments, committees, offices, and bureaus under the Provincial Party Committee in 1974, as well as the top meetings of such major "mass organizations" as the workers' unions, the Youth League, the peasants' associations, and the women's associations. In more than ten work notebooks, he kept detailed records of the minutes and content of each meeting, and transcribed many previously unseen central CCP documents and speeches.

Based on this collection of work notes and other historical materials, as well as his and other witnesses' oral histories, we could reconstruct systematically and completely the "Criticize Lin Biao and Confucius" campaign of 1974, and offer alternative explanations on the nature of and impetus behind the campaign. In brief, the records of central political struggles in Beijing show that the "Criticize Lin Biao and Confucius" campaign in 1973 and 1974 was carried out for two purposes—to reduce the army's influence on national politics and to reduce Zhou Enlai's political influence. This campaign in Jiangsu, however, unfolded in a different manner. By suppressing local veteran cadres, on the one hand, and cruelly purging rebel leaders, on the other, the Nanjing military leaders who took power after the "Great Alliance" in March 1968 unintentionally made two groups of formidable enemies. At the same time, the Nanjing military authorities implemented a series of social policies that aroused considerable opposition from the central government and from various local social classes. The policy that met the strongest criticism was to send down a large number of urban residents and their families to the countryside. Thus, the 1974 "Criticize Lin Biao and Confucius" campaign in Jiangsu was essentially a movement supported by the tripartite forces of local veteran cadres, former rebel leaders, and sent-down urban residents that joined together and took advantage of the central Party appeal of the campaign to oppose Nanjing's military rule. It is not difficult to see from this case that, although local mass movements were steered by central policies all along, the primary impetus behind regional political conflicts always derived from the local conditions. This explains why power struggles among the local factions never stopped, even though all parties openly pledged their loyalty to the central authority.

Some key reflections

In conclusion, I would like to make three points. First, my research on the Cultural Revolution began with interviews and collecting oral histories, and these continue to play an important role in my subsequent research. It might be worth pointing out that having oral histories that are sufficiently diverse, systematic, and comprehensive is an important prerequisite for this research paradigm. Individual and fragmentary interviews and oral histories are rarely sufficient to support this kind of study.

Second, despite its unique value and function, oral history cannot be the sole source but has to be verified and supplemented by other materials so we can assess the credibility and veracity of the interview content. The most valuable historical materials for this research consist of both official archives and unofficial documents, such as mass organizations' newspapers and journals and individuals' work notebooks; and, as long as they are as systematic and complete as possible, the unofficial materials are comparable in nature and function to official archives.

Finally, an important mission of scholarly historical research is innovation. This is not, however, something created whole in libraries simply out of deep thought or theoretical deduction; rather it is achieved gradually through the use of different research approaches and practices. The nature of academic innovation is to break through conventional ideas, methods, and concepts. From my personal experience, it is precisely because the archival materials of the Cultural Revolution are hard to access that we must try and find alternative information sources and adopt methodologies from sociology and anthropology to collect oral histories. Academic innovation is not mysterious. By continuing to experiment with seemingly impossible research topics, by looking for new methods and approaches, and by constantly adjusting research perspectives and themes, we will enter into an unknown world; and, when we systematically delineate the phenomena we observed there, academic innovation will eventually emerge.

Further Reading

Dong Guoqiang, *Shisi Wei Nanjing Daxue Shisheng Koushu Lishi* (The Oral History of Fourteen Nanjing University Teachers and Students), Cozy House Publisher, New York, 2009.

Dong Guoqiang, "The First Uprising of the Cultural Revolution at Nanjing University", *Journal of Cold War Studies*, 12, 3 (Summer 2010): pp. 30–49.

Dong Guoqiang and Andrew G. Walder, "Nanjing's 'Second Cultural Revolution' of 1974", *The China Quarterly*, 212 (December 2012): pp. 893–918.

Dong Guoqiang and Andrew G. Walder, "Nanjing's Failed 'January Revolution' of 1967", *The China Quarterly*, 203 (September 2010): pp. 675–692.

18 Walking a production chain
An interdisciplinary approach to the history of things

Thomas David DuBois

Production encompasses a large and diverse field of history, and one that can benefit immensely from fieldwork. Many of the historical sources about production—reports, records, and statistics about how and by whom things were made, shipped, sold, and purchased—are themselves firsthand accounts of fieldwork conducted generations ago. Such materials include casual and expert descriptions of crafts such as silk weaving, woodblock printing, and salt mining, studies of productive life within a locality, such as a town or village, and studies of the global circulation of one particular market commodity. Whatever the product or craft, if someone has made it, chances are good that someone else has found a reason to record how it was done.

Why a production chain?

A production chain is the sequence of steps, events, and decisions that turn raw commodities into finished goods. The term originates from a 1977 article in which Terence K. Hopkins and Immanuel Wallerstein proposed tracing the movement of specific items through "commodity chains" as a way of demonstrating integration and disaggregating patterns of development within global economic history. From this original article emerged a number of correlate ideas (e.g., value chains, commodity networks), which merged with a growing field of literature built around such theoretical concerns as the behavior of commercial firms, the value of intermediation, the relative power of buyers or producers to govern the standards of an industry. But for the historian, the conceptual utility of a production chain can be even more broad. Following this chain offers a structured way to understand production in both local and larger contexts, and to integrate the different stages of production and consumption with their many layers of meaning, what Arjun Appadurai has called the "social life of things." As a researcher, one can approach the productive sequence with the flexibility to expand or alter the scope of the project. A project might trace an entire chain or just one aspect, for example, by focusing strictly on production or pursuing related questions such as financing or competition.

Following a production chain helps a researcher adjust and shift the scale of social analysis in step with the increasing complexity of productive choices. It opens separate vantage points, for instance, on the family farm that produces a raw good, the boardroom of the company that manufactures or trades it, and finally on the real and imagined needs of consumers. Each of these stages has its own context of social networks and values, such as respect for the skills of an artisan, trust within commercial networks, or a sense of a virtual community among consumers. As distinct as these phenomena may seem from each other, they are connected by virtue of a material item that travels from one end of the chain to the other. Remaining attentive to the larger process of production is a particularly effective way to integrate different actors in a process of historical change, and to avoid the trap of fetishizing local production as being isolated or timeless.

Themes

Broadly speaking, studies of production have tended toward one of two approaches. The first, common already in the early twentieth century, examines *techniques and markets*. Aiming to pull rural China out of poverty, a generation of scholars and reformers of the early twentieth century conducted numerous local studies of agriculture and rural handicrafts, leaving us with detailed information about cropping patterns, prices of raw and processed commodities, and the role of hired and family labor in crafts such as spinning and weaving. As Linda Grove describes in her chapter, Japanese consular officials and researchers of the South Manchuria Railway (*Minami Mantetsu tetsudō* 南満洲鉄道) and the Shanghai-based East Asian Cultural Society (*Tō-A Dōbunkai* 東亜同文会) produced meticulous economic intelligence on every conceivable industry. These reports were essentially industry profiles which, like their modern cousins, were often written by and for experts in the field, and as a result are often highly technical and laden with statistics.

The second sort of scholarship focuses on the *social context* of production. These examine the way that work is structured within society and the ideas and values, such as pride in skill and local tradition, and particular social roles associated with work (e.g., "men plow and women weave") are embedded within crafts and productive practices. Social relationships also shape the way that productive resources are allocated. Land Reform campaigns of the 1940s and 1950s were based on the belief that uneven allocation of productive resources represented the deepest and most pernicious sort of class oppression. Many of the local studies conducted during that era find their way back to that foundational idea.

In practice, these two questions often combined, for example, Fei Xiaotong's 1939 study of Kaixiangong 开弦弓 village, which places equal weight on both the process and the relationships of sericulture production in a single community. Nevertheless, it is worth examining separately the logic underlying the two threads of *mechanics* and *meaning*.

Mechanics

Following the mechanics of production means observing the vital details of how and by whom things were done, how goods were bought, stored and shipped, how transactions were made, and so forth. No detail is too small to follow up on and question: *why* was a specific process done in a particular way? To avoid being swayed by any preconceptions about the most efficient or most modern methods, it is best to expect that things work the way they do for a reason. For example, many Chinese farmers of the 1920s and 1930s refused to use mechanical combines, a decision that reformers chalked up to simple ignorance of technology. But it turns out that the actual reason was much more simple: the big machines were not practical to use in small fields, and in any case, the abundant surplus labor of humans and animals was cheaper and easier to find than machine parts and fuel. Inquiring about local realities is especially important in agriculture, since differences in soil quality or the water table might be significant even over very small distances.

Fieldwork is uniquely suited to uncovering the human narrative of how things came to be. In my research on the Chinese dairy industry, I have heard many different stories of how villages and towns shifted to dairy production following the market reforms of the early 1980s. Such decisions made use of particular information or networks. When consumers in Beijing and Tianjin began to clamor for dairy, the nearby village of Xiazhuang 夏庄 began breeding dairy cows, a choice made in part because Muslim villagers were already producing their own dairy in order to keep halal. Within a few years, the Xiazhuang village cooperative was growing wealthy selling 3,000 head of cattle per year to urban dairies. At about the same time, Tuanjie 團結 village, in the far north of Inner Mongolia borrowed 130,000 yuan to increase its dairy herd and upgrade its production facilities. Their confidence was based in part on their long history as a dairy producing village and in part on knowledge that the nearby Hailar 海拉爾 Dairy was planning to significantly increase production.

Fieldwork highlights the human dimension of these decisions and their results. During the early 1990s, a few households in Quanwang 權王 Village in Hebei pooled resources to invest in a small soda bottling plant. At the time I first visited the village in 1998, this plant was doing very well, and neighbors in that and other communities looked on with admiration. Many neighboring villages had initially hoped to do something similar, but simply could not raise the resources, source the expertise, or agree on where to put their investment. When I returned some years later, the bottling plant sat derelict, reputedly done in by the incompetence of the manager, who had since returned to farming, albeit as a much diminished figure within the community. The same neighbors that had once looked on in envy at the business venture now expressed relief that they had not followed suit. These simple, human stories are the core of lived history. They are there for the asking, and yet often undetectable through any other method. Focusing on these very commonplace narratives frees us from relying solely on sweeping, structural explanations that overlook the most direct cause—inept bookkeeping, in this case—of this significant outcome.

Following a commodity from primary to finished product sets a clear sequence of "what happens next" questions for interviews. When listening to informants, the trick is to focus on those details that may initially seem too minor or obvious to investigate further. In my work on the history of the Northeast, I had ample opportunity to discuss the region's characteristic crop: soybeans. While respondents would casually relate the ways that the life of a soybean farmer had gotten better or worse, it required some persistence to examine the question in detail. Consider, for example, the transformations of the early 1980s, when farmers were newly free to sell their crop to middlemen, who, in turn, wholesaled it to a variety of industrial and other consumers. When examined closely, this seemingly straightforward process was, in fact, extremely complex, and raises a series of essential questions. Who *was* the middleman? Did the middleman operate alone or with a network of other buyers or financial backers? Did the middleman buy the beans at harvest, or offer cash on sight for the crop in the field? Which method of purchase was better for the farmer? Where were the beans warehoused, for how long, and at whose expense? How did people (at any stage of this process) cut corners, what were the consequences, and how did they get caught?

To bring out the significance of these questions, you might invite your interviewees to consider alternatives by posing counterfactuals in a "why this/not that?" formula. For example, if you learn that deliveries were made by a middleman, press the question of why the farmers did not market their crop directly. Another way is to focus on the exact moment of historical change, following the question "how long has it been this way?" with "*why* did it change?" The answer might be completely obvious to the respondent, so much so that you receive a simple, "oh, that way just makes sense." Don't leave it there, and don't be afraid to be persistent. Continue asking what are essentially the same questions in different ways (and to different people) until you get the level of detail you need, either with interview data, or written sources such as account books.

Meaning

Not every relationship is monetized, and not every good is countable. While tracing the business of production can be an effective way to examine the mechanics of historical change, fieldwork provides a way to understand the crucial, often deep and unexpected, *meanings* invested in these processes, and the non-use value of production.

Some tasks can only be understood through personal experience. Like playing a musical instrument, certain types of expertise require practice and muscle memory. Physical tasks like handcraft production are based on what folklorists have called *embodied knowledge*, physical skills that are better experienced than described. Learning such tasks as a participant allows you to understand what a doctor of Chinese medicine means by a "floating pulse," or what a chef means by "enough salt," as well as to appreciate how long different skills may take to learn, which tasks require good eyesight, manual dexterity or physical strength, and what separates good from expert craftwork. Such simulated apprenticeships also afford us ample, valuable circumstances in which to talk casually with experts, learning their life stories, the narratives of which are so often structured around the acquisition and transmission of skills.

In this volume, Stephen Jones describes his decades of experience working side-by-side with Chinese musicians. I developed a much more shallow version of this perspective by taking some months of intensive Kunqu 崑曲 opera lessons from Teacher Sun, a master in Tianjin. During these sessions, I heard stories about how Teacher Sun was trained, and how different schools of Kunqu formed and interacted, and saw the many ways that opera informs his family's ritual and medical practices. I also got a glimpse of the sheer physicality of Chinese opera: an avid runner (and at the time, a much younger one), I nevertheless fainted during my first full aria, and awoke to the sight of Teacher Sun and his family laughing and telling me that such reaction was not uncommon (and further proof that "three good martial artists can't defeat one mediocre opera singer"). Forbidden from using video or written manuscripts, I also learned something about rote memorization of long texts, a perspective that greatly informed my work on the oral scriptural tradition of village religious specialists.

Fieldwork is a particularly good way to understand the place of work within a community. Using a combination of gazetteer accounts and his own frequent trips to a group of villages near Beijing, folklorist Liu Tieliang recounts the many ways that life before 1949 in these specialized villages revolved around the weaving of willow branch baskets. The baskets were not only a source of income for the villages, but also a marker of status within the community. Many tasks were involved—cutting, carrying and boiling the heavy branches, weaving and selling the baskets—each requiring a different set of skills and abilities. Some tasks were reserved for men or women, and each carried a different ascribed social standing. Since the baskets were used primarily for carrying coal, the ability to weave a sufficiently strong basket base was considered to be the peak of the craft, and a closely guarded secret among the most experienced craftsmen, all of whom were older men.

Even after woven baskets had been replaced with cheaper plastic replicas, the memory of local craft was preserved in songs and sayings that celebrated the villages' characteristic product.

The association of work with personal, regional, ethnic, and gender identity remains discernible even on a less personal scale, at higher levels of production, commerce, and distribution. Many of the large overland trade firms of the Qing period were based in Shanxi. These firms recruited locally—often among relatives—and used these ties to hold together sprawling networks of buyers and representatives. Writing in 1928, John Stewart Burgess noted that the cattle and sheep trade in Beijing was wholly dominated by a network of Muslim buyers, slaughterers, and butchers. In 1930s Shanghai, it was controlled by Muslims from Yangzhou. Even today, much of the beef production and distribution in northern and western provinces is dominated by Hui villages and distributors, the commonly heard explanation being that even Han buyers perceive Muslims to be more clean, careful and honest when dealing with food than anyone else, but equally important is the internal coherence of the human networks behind production and distribution.

Identities associated with work constantly evolve. One large sheep concern that I visited in the Bayannur 巴彥諾爾 region of Inner Mongolia was founded by investors from the Shandong city of Liaocheng 聊城, a thousand kilometers to the southeast. When this enterprise commenced operations in 2014, its managers brought over dozens of workers from their home town. Three years later just under half of the factory's 170 workers hailed from this region. Interestingly, although Liaocheng has a long history of sheep farming, few of the imported workers had experience in the industry. If anything they knew duck farming. Yet despite professing a high opinion of the local farmers, the firm's managers and workers all agreed that it was preferable to work with "your own people," a formula that has since come to include the staffing of new ventures in Xinjiang and Henan. Farm workers and surrounding locals alike expressed confidence that the quick success of the enterprise was due to the unique commercial ability and work ethic of the Liaocheng people. When business entertainment devolved into drinking contests, as it often does, the Liaocheng accent would emerge as a mark of pride.

The final set of meanings in the production chain—those created for or by the consumer—mirror the human relationships that shape production. Consumption encompasses a wide array of values and images; advertising presents these values in an easily accessible form. Leafing through historical newspapers and magazines will show the ways that different producers tried to associate their brand with particular ideas, be that with cleanliness, prestige, family, or patriotism. But advertising shows only the "supply" side of ideas. If we wish to understand how ideas were actually received, which ones struck a chord and why, we again need to ask.

Well before I conceived of my current project on the beef trade, I developed the habit of chatting up strangers in fresh markets. Over the years, I have spoken with vendors and shoppers from Shenzhen to Harbin, asking why people prefer certain products over others. A long-held truism says that Chinese buyers prefer foreign-made foods, with places like Denmark as the perceived quality gold standard. Comparing prices on online shopping sites like Taobao shows exactly how much of a price premium these shoppers are willing to pay. But conversations reveal nuance that numbers alone cannot show; consumers comparing beef produced in China versus imports from Australia or Korea will proffer deeply held ideas about which is safer, which tastes better, and which is most appropriate for different cooking styles. These are of course merely opinions, albeit often quite strongly held ones. But regardless of whether such claims are accurate, strictly speaking, they are remarkably revealing of what people value, assume or fear about the food they consume. And far from a contemporary phenomenon, tastes and perceptions can be traced through interviews and anecdotal writings back into history.

Chains and nets

There are different ways to approach the production landscape; each new vantage point will reveal something different. The image of a *production chain* makes most sense from the perspective of a finished product. Looking backwards from this point, one can productively trace exactly what a chain represents—an unbroken, linear (vertical) series of individual actions. But things can look very different from other vantage points. Each link in a production chain is also a node, a point at which value is added, transactions are conducted, and decisions are made. Any one of these nodes also presents a series of opportunities to change course, shift to new suppliers or change markets. These (horizontal) choices also deserve attention, and when they are factored in, production begins to look less like a chain more like a *net*, with each decision leading on to new paths and possibilities.

Looking at production from these varied perspectives—both backwards and forwards along the value chain, and laterally at different points of decision—allows one to appreciate the complex network of needs and interests that go into economic activity, and prevents one from being trapped in the unique, but often limited perspective of any one producer. The importance of this distance is especially evident when focusing on farmers, handicraft producers, or factory workers: people who operate at the lower and generally more vulnerable end of the value chain. The experiences of these communities are important, and have justifiably received significant scholarly attention. But when studied in isolation, they often come down to a single narrative of victimhood. If you spoke to a Hohhot dairy farmer in 2007, you would likely have gotten a long and entirely truthful lecture about how households were being squeezed by the dual pressures of rising feed costs and low milk prices. But if you followed that same milk to the collection station, and then to the processing dairy, you would have heard something very different, about cheap foreign imports and a devastating price war within the industry. Understanding and taking into full account the reasons *why* farmgate prices have fallen (or a long-cherished craft is no longer valued, or workers' conditions have failed to improve, etc.) add depth, sophistication, and significance to the plight of those at the bottom, and may even produce some sympathy for some of the more easily villainized actors elsewhere in the chain.

So how do you start?

As a general rule, it helps to gather as much information as possible before going to a field site. Before diving into the specifics of a local study, it is vital to learn as much as you can about the larger historical context, and the mechanics of the industry itself.

One way is to read up on how this form of production developed outside of China. If the globalization of an industry was itself a historical process—as it was in the modernization of meat and dairy production—then learning the landmarks of this larger transformation will help to set a timeline of external influences. What could the history of animal production in places like South America or the American West tell me about the history of beef in China? As it turns out, quite a lot. These two trendsetting industries pioneered new technologies like railways and mechanical refrigeration, and can illuminate critical features of how production chains evolved, where value was added, and where conflicts were likely to arise. If you understand why beef production came to center on Chicago, St. Louis, and Buenos Aires, you can have a better sense of what to look for when you get to Harbin, Tianjin, or Qingdao. Of course, the best way to understand actual production is to experience it firsthand. When in doubt, I find it best to start with what you know, or at least what you can find out. Raised in the American Midwest, I know farming fairly intimately, but wanted to build up my basic knowledge of animal production by asking friends connected to the industry. Over time, I was able to make quite a few of these friends—dairy farmers in Wales, sheep farmers in New Zealand, and animal science professors at Cornell and Montana—each of whom brought a very different perspective to the question of what constitutes a well-run enterprise. Having learned a bit about how these industries operate elsewhere, I was better able to pursue specific questions about animal breeding, disease prevention, and the like. The other advantage is that I was able to share information that my respondents in China genuinely wanted to know—for example, why European farms are generally smaller than American ones—that in no way compromised my data, but did make me less an interviewer, and more a reciprocally interesting guest.

Gazetteers, most of which feature a section on native products, are generally the best first stop for diving into the specifics of a locality. New gazetteers (i.e., those compiled since the 1980s) tend also to include a brief history, culled from previous versions, summing up decades and even centuries of change. They may also lead you back to more specialized sources, such as agricultural or commercial treatises, that would otherwise be easy to overlook. Starting with these punctuated and edited contemporary sources, especially when they can be compared to such earlier compilations, is a quick way to familiarize yourself with the basic landscape, and an ideal way to begin any project.

Modern gazetteers will also be an important source of production statistics, especially for the period since 1949. Such numerical data may be useful, but should be used with caution, and supplemented with other kinds of sources, including oral accounts picked up during fieldwork. The threat of false (i.e., intentionally misleading) statistics is a serious one, but equally problematic are data that rely for meaning on the context of actual lived events. For example, food production did in fact rise throughout much of China during the 1950s, but relying solely on statistics (even accurate ones) on the dramatic expansion of grain production, it becomes dangerously easy (as simple as making a per capita graph!) to assume that consumption would have risen accordingly, when in fact much of the crop was expropriated, improperly stored, or simply left to rot. State planners published voluminous indices of official prices, but these data in no way indicate what goods were actually available. Beyond the question of truth or falsity of data, fieldwork is vital to understanding what numbers actually signify. For example, production statistics from the pastoral region of Hulunbuir 呼倫貝爾 show a vast increase in the output of beef and mutton during the 1950s. When I began fieldwork there, my first questions were about the veracity of these data. Interviews with pastoralists and slaughterhouse workers did confirm, to my satisfaction, that they were in fact correct; but that was only a start. Discussing statistics turned out to be an entry way into more substantive questions, for example, why production rose and fell in particular years, why one product was preferred over another, and how processing capacity tracked against herd growth. The answers to these questions often yielded findings of greater value than the numerical data itself.

To take a more recent example, the 2008 scandal of melamine tainting in Chinese milk was quickly followed by numerous careful studies that used statistical analysis of survey data to understand the motivations of different actors in the chain—farmers, middlemen, mega-processors, and consumers. To my reading, such studies are very good at demonstrating *correlation*, such as a positive relationship between quality standards and enterprise size, in a large sample set. But lacking a narrative, they are often less convincing at explaining the nature or *causality* of that relationship. This is the point at which fieldwork becomes invaluable. Statistical analyses of 300 farms tell us *what* happened, but a conversation with three farmers may be the best way to understand *why*.

When looking at an industry as a whole, is it necessary to talk to someone at the top? That depends on what you hope to see. Talking to someone who has experience in a large or small decision-making capacity—a production brigade leader, factory head or commune official—will bring a unique perspective, and perhaps more, such as introductions to people further down the chain. In the best case, managers might even have their original account books or will have committed many details of production (including numbers) to memory. Some of those in authority, however, may be less willing to discuss commercial information or may regard certain topics as politically sensitive. By all means respect these boundaries, and learn to recognize when a respondent wishes to end a conversation. Even if a high-level introduction initially opens doors, it is of the utmost importance not to, in any way, risk abusing the trust that this implies. Beyond the obvious question of research ethics, one may find that doors opened by trust and personal relationships can begin closing very quickly.

This sort of "insider" account compliments what we might think of as the *public face* of production, be that the perennial good news of official production figures in the press, sunny corporate statements, or the sort of images seen in consumer advertising. For the period after 1949, the pages of a state publication like *People's Daily* show this face in a fairly complete form. Reading newspaper accounts on the topic of dairy will reveal a diverse set of facts and images: state investment in dairy production rose significantly throughout the 1950s, while consumer items such as milk developed a certain iconic value as symbols of socialist progress. But just like official production statistics, even if such accounts are strictly true, they still leave significant questions unanswered. On the topic of who was actually consuming all the milk that was being made, the answer I learned from one former plant manager is that it changed: milk initially was collected to feed to calves, as part of the drive to herd recovery. Such key consumers as hospitals and nurseries were consistently a priority, but because storage and processing remained much more of a challenge than they appeared on paper, much of the milk their farm produced was consumed locally, or else went to waste.

The benefits—and for certain questions, necessity—of finding someone at the top raises the key question of how best to meet these people. Short of a personal introduction through a friend or family member, the only remedies are patience and persistence. I met one of my key contacts on a long-distance train journey—overhearing me talking with other passengers about beef industries, he introduced himself as the manager of a very large *sheep* concern, and invited me to come by. This contact not only walked me through the changes in sheep production, he also introduced me to friends in feed and other related industries. Another contact was initially a friend of a friend, introduced to me simply as someone who "knows a lot about beef." It was only after we started speaking that I learned that he had spent 15 years managing one of the largest meat processing plants in China. These relationships generally take time to develop, and there is something to be said for going straight to the source. I have found it productive to visit trade expos, which are now routinely organized all over China on an immense scale, and can be located through a simple Internet search. In a matter of days, it can be possible to gain a helicopter view of an entire industry and meet well-connected people who may be willing to further introduce you to people within their network.

Memories and perceptions

Like any historical fieldwork, there are strategies for jogging memories, and for making the process fun and meaningful for all involved. Production is very personal, and leaves very well-preserved memories. When asking questions, I find that it is always helpful to start with the smallest and most specific questions: When did the selling season end? What was the price in each year? Who did you sell to? How many times per week was there a market? When did this product become economical to produce? Were people paid in cash or work points? Because memory is grounded in context, people often remember details in terms of relevant events rather than dates. Cangzhou 滄州, a paper-flat region of southern Hebei, experienced disastrous flooding in the late 1960s. Events from that period are subsequently remembered as being "before or after the flood." This division is not merely a convention—the flooding destroyed homes, fields and infrastructure, and the world that was rebuilt in its aftermath was substantively different from the old one. Not only did entire villages change location, but the new canals that were built to prevent a repeat of flooding significantly lowered the water table, leading to all new cropping and irrigation systems. Farmers will remember this sort of change in high detail, especially if you frame the question in terms of the way that it affected them personally.

Another good way to learn about a closed production system is to ask people on the outside, particularly those who are for whatever reason *unable* to enter. For example, if production of a certain craft is or was concentrated within a few villages, people from those villages might truthfully explain the reason as being that generations of tradition has made them very good at what they do. Asking someone from outside these villages might produce a different—and equally true—answer: that the marketing network consists of the producers' own co-villagers, or that certain groups somehow managed to secure a monopoly on source materials. Whether they are strictly true or not, these alternative explanations reveal networks, production realities, and perceptions that an insider view alone will not uncover.

Challenges for the future

Production encompasses such a wide and diverse set of histories that the horizon will always beckon with challenges for new projects, and ways to incorporate perspectives from the study of production into other topics.

Two areas strike me as particularly promising for future development. The first is to make full use of the wealth of documents, and quickly fading interview opportunities for the early socialist period. Large and small collections of privately held reports, meeting notes, and account books are becoming available from the 1950 and beyond, just as the people who collected and saved these records are leaving us. The opportunity is thus one that is spiked with urgency.

The second is to use the intimate human perspective that informs local studies to further explore other aspects of business and industry history. Traditional financial guilds such as remittance houses built their business on a network of trust and an enforceable code of ethics. Historians like Luman Wang, Brett Sheehan and Elisabeth Köll (as well as the work of Kellee Tsai on the contemporary period) all highlight the importance of understanding the human side of business actors and networks. Much more can be done to understand the values, perceptions and interests that bound together producers, with financiers, investors and brokers, both locally and in the mediated networks that linked people who would never meet in person.

Further Reading

Bair, Jennifer, "Global Capitalism and Commodity Chains: Looking Back, Going Forward," *Competition & Change* 9, 2 (2005): pp. 153–180.

Belasco, Warren James, and Roger Horowitz, *Food Chains: From Farmyard to Shopping Cart*. Philadelphia: University of Pennsylvania Press, 2009.

Burgess, John Stewart, *The Guilds of Peking*. This classic work examines the city of Beijing as a collection of occupations and organized guilds. It appears in numerous reprints.

DuBois, Thomas David, "Many Roads from Pasture to Plate: A Commodity Chain Approach to China's Beef Trade, 1732–1931," *Journal of Global History* 14, 1 (2019): pp. 22–43.

DuBois, Thomas David, "China's Dairy Century: Making, Drinking and Dreaming of Milk," in Rotem Kowner, Guy Bar-Oz, Michal Biran, Meir Shahar and Gideon Shelach eds. *Animals and Human Society in Asia: Historical and Ethical Perspectives*. London: Palgrave MacMillan, (2019): pp. 179–211.

DuBois, Thomas David and Alicia E. "China Eats—Innovation, E-Commerce and Food Safety at the Hangzhou Food Forum," *Asia Pacific Journal* 17 (2019). https://apjjf.org/2019/11/DuBois.html

DuBois, Thomas David and Alisha Gao, "Big Meat: Understanding the Rise and Impact of Mega-farming in China's Beef, Sheep and Dairy Industries," *Asia Pacific Journal* 17 (2018). https://apjjf.org/2017/17/DuBois.html

Eyferth, Jacob, *Eating Rice from Bamboo Roots: The Social History of a Community of Handicraft Papermakers in Rural Sichuan, 1920–2000*. Cambridge, MA: Harvard University Press, 2009.

Hopkins, Terence K. and Wallerstein Immanuel, "Patterns of Development of the Modern World-system," *Review* 1, 2 (1977): pp. 11–145.

Japan Center for Asian Historical Records, National Archives of Japan (www.jacar.go.jp)

Liu, Tieliang, "Village Production and the Self Identification of Village Communities: The Case of Fangshan District, Beijing," *Asian Ethnology* 74, 2 (2015): 291–306. https://nirc.nanzan-u.ac.jp/nfile/4443. Explores the social context of production.

Peng, Mu. "The Doctor's Body: Embodiment and Multiplicity of Chinese Medical Knowledge," *East Asian Science, Technology, and Medicine* 25 (2006): pp. 27–46.

Xiaotong, Fei. *Peasant life in China; a Field Study of Country Life in the Yangtze Valley.* London: G. Routledge and sons [1939]. One of the first production-oriented village studies. It appears in numerous reprints.

Zelin, Madeleine, *The Merchants of Zigong: Industrial Entrepreneurship in Early Modern China.* New York: Columbia University Press, 2006.

Section 4
Finding and working with grassroots documents

19 Field research using contracts (*qiyue*)
Legal archives of late Qing and early Republican-era Longquan, Zhejiang

Zhengzhen Du

Lawsuit archives and research on contracts

The first modern academic study of Chinese contracts was Wang Guowei's *Liu sha zhui jian* (流沙墜簡) (Bamboo slips left behind in the drifting sand). Published in 1914, this work was a textual analysis of the land deeds and contracts of the Han and Wei dynasties. In the middle of the twentieth century, Fu Yiling 傅衣凌 published pioneering research on the contracts of the Ming and Qing dynasties.[1] Because contracts from this period are both large in number, and of great variety in types and regions covered, they have generated the greatest amount of research.

Previous studies of Ming and Qing contracts can be roughly divided into one of two research approaches. One is the sort of social-economic history research initiated by Fu Yiling, which uses contracts as historical materials to examine social and economic relationships in the Ming and Qing dynasties, especially the structural evolution of land ownership and lineage.[2] The other is the approach of legal history to use contracts as historical materials to "explore the private law conventions including estates and family relationships from the perspective of legal and administrative practice."[3] Comparatively speaking, the former approach pays greater attention to the specific historical context in which the contract existed, notably so in the recent scholarly project of using contract documents of an individual family, village, or region in order to systematically trace and reconstruct the long-term social-economic evolution of a particular region. Both of the two different research approaches, however, try to analyze the social-economic practice and structure from the contracts' textual documentation, or, in other words, to use the contracts as evidence to examine socio-economic phenomena or relationships.[4]

In both cases, an understanding of the contract itself is still the starting point for using contracts as historical materials. Ongoing, exhaustive examination and interpretation of numerous contracts, involving analysis of their form, language, particular characteristics, and differences across dynasties and regions, has produced admirable results in several fields;[5] yet, there is still a tendency to examine contracts in isolation, as single, static pieces of documentation. Through fieldwork investigations, however, and my own research in legal archives,[6] I began to realize that the contracts we today take as dusty historical documents once had their own fresh vitality, even life cycles. With the help of on-the-ground investigations and interviews and other relevant documents, such as family genealogies and lawsuit files from the local archive, we can re-envision the process of the making of a contract, its operation, evolution, and termination, as well as the broad social and cultural background of the time in which this entire process took place.

The significance of this re-envisioning of contracts in dynamic process is twofold. First, from the perspective of regional economic history, the increasingly common use of contracts is itself a particularly significant historical phenomenon. David Faure observed that the use of contracts in local transactions probably evolved from oral to textual agreements, a transformation that in some places likely started fairly late. In the Pearl River Delta, the use of the contract was initiated by the local establishment of the *lijia* 里甲 (rural self-administration system) registration by the Ming government. In order to calculate precisely tax liabilities, and seek official protection in land lawsuit cases, people began to write up contracts as well as to pay a contract tax. Prior to this, the personal relationships between the buyer and seller were more emphasized in transactions.[7] Recent research on the contract documents in the Qingshui River 清水江 basin also shows that the use of contracts was concurrent with the development and marketization of local forestry. Along with the increasingly common use of contracts, all of local society began to experience a dramatic change.[8]

A second point is that the written document is the product of only one stage in the entire process of the making, ratification, and use of the contract. If focusing only on interpreting the written text of the contract document, we will neglect both the negotiation details before the contract was made (including the social-historical relations between the signing parties and the possible disputes and lawsuits) and the actual use of the contract document after it was signed. It is only by tracing the contract's entire "lifecycle" that we can have a comprehensive understanding of the contract and the relevant economic activities and social relations involved. To do so, we need to find some additional pertinent historical materials. Indeed, this is why socio-economic historians particularly value the household as the unit of research on contracts (*guihu* 归户), or the "localization," of the contract. Only by viewing the contract within the historical context in which it was produced and functioned, can we discover connections between contracts and other pertinent documents such as family genealogies, ritual texts (*keyi shu* 科仪书), inscriptions, and anthologies. These kinds of documents provide us with abundant information external to the contract documents themselves, but vitally important to our understanding of the contract. For example, we rarely know for certain the nature of the relationships between the signing parties and the middlemen and clerks who signed their names on the contract. However, with the aid of family genealogies and archival lawsuit case files, we may be able to obtain this information. This will facilitate our understanding of the living social relationships in the making of the contract and bring to light non-economic factors important to these agreements.

For this research method, lawsuit case files are highly valuable historical materials. The contract itself was certainly the most important record of evidence in traditional Chinese lawsuits. The various iterations of the "Regulation on the Plaint Format" (*zhuang shi tiaoli* 状式条例) in the Qing dynasty all include the rule that "lawsuits over farmland ownership will not be accepted without the stamped contract (*yinqi* 印契) attached to the plaint."[9] The "stamped" contracts are those with the contract tax paid and the official seal. However, in order to evade contract tax and corvée, many common folk would often just use the *unstamped* contracts (*baiqi* 白契) that were not registered and verified by the local government. These unstamped contracts were also admitted as evidence in local lawsuits. As a result, we find a large number and wide range of contracts—sometimes the original and most often copies—in lawsuit case files in local archives. And in these case files, contracts can be understood in relation to the specific case and context: they are no longer isolated documents, but part of the social-economic life of a group of people, village, and lineage, as well as part of the lawsuit case. From this point, we can revisit the historical setting in which the contract was drawn up and played its role, and explore the contractual order and concept in the traditional society.

Revisiting the setting of a contract signing

Traditionally, the signing of the contract was a simple ceremony. The contracts of the sixth century contained phrases like "each has signed their names to show good faith and divided the cost of the wine" (*gezi shuming wei xin, gujiu ge ban*), which shows that people declared their good intentions to uphold the contract with a banquet and drinking alcohol—a tradition with a long history.[10] However, the emergence of a standardized text format makes it less likely that the contract document itself would reveal this sort of social context that surrounded the contract, including the negotiation process between the two parties, the oral agreement, and even the atmosphere of the signing, which are all vitally important for us if we are to understand the nature and implementation of the contract.

Let us consider the following case from the Longquan archives: in the second year of the Republic of China, Ji Guanghao's 季广昊 son Ji Qifeng 季岐峰 filed a plaint against a "dishonest tenant who over successive years failed to pay his rent grain," a man named He Xiankuan 何显宽 and others who had fallen behind his rent for years [since the 25th year of the Guangxu reign (1899)].[11] Although the original copies of the contracts presented by both parties are not present in the file, recorded testimonies attest to the fact that Ji Qifeng only submitted a land sale contract and He Shengrong's 何盛荣 (He Xiankuan's father) rental receipt in evidence after He sold the land, while He Xiankuan presented all the antecedent "old contracts" (*laoqi*

老契) on the farmland in question. Given the common practice that all old contracts had to be submitted in a land transaction, and that, given the decrees on contract tax and transfer of ownership, it is clear the plaintiff Ji Qifeng's evidence put him in a disadvantageous position. Yet, Ji related the story of the making of this land purchase contract to explain why those old contracts had not been transferred in the deal as follows:

> My father originally bought this piece of land. Our family and the He family used to be relatives, and we were initially on friendly terms at the time when we entered into this land purchase contract. In our face-to-face negotiations, it was agreed that the land was sold as a pledge for a debt, with an annual rent of twenty piculs as the interest. In anticipation of future redemption of the land, the antecedent old contracts were not submitted for inspection and the tax grain was not officially transferred; the arrangement was only in accordance with the earlier oral agreement. I did not expect that the accused had a cruel heart beneath his sugar-coated words, and would suddenly shamelessly break the agreement and refuse to pay the land rent for consecutive years. My younger sister used to live with He's family; if he had directly told me in a polite manner that the rent was used to pay for her clothes and food, I might have accepted the arrangement. It is unbearable that he even sold my sister for money. Though I always wanted to ask him for the rent, I hesitated because the two families were closely connected by marriage. My older sister was also He Xiankuan's sister-in-law (*shijie*), and, although she died young, our kinship remained. This is why the matter has been suspended. Now the rent grain has been illegally encroached upon, so I have no other option but to argue and chase after him for the rent. Who could have thought that he would find the old contracts and tell lies in his defense claiming that I had forged the contract and encroached on his land? When the commoners draw up a contract, there are witnesses and clerks present; it is impossible to forge a contract like this. The witnesses of my purchase of this land from He Shengrong are still alive; the clerk was one of his close relatives who later died, though his handwriting remains for comparison.[12]

This archival document depicts much about the scene and circumstances of the contract signing, revealing the importance of the close relationship between the two signing parties to the actual procedure of this farmland sale. The original owner of the land signed the contract to sell the land in return for a certain amount of money, but he continued to cultivate the land and agreed to pay the rent to the lender annually as interest on the debt. Therefore, the old contracts were not submitted and the ownership was not officially transferred. The distinction between "selling with recourse" (*huomai* 活卖) in land transactions and the loan on the mortgage of land was often blurred, and it is often not easy to distinguish the two merely from the written text of the contract. In fact, even the local magistrate did not decide the case solely on the basis of the contract. Rather, he summoned the witnesses listed in the contract to court, and one of them, Jiang Tusheng 蒋土生, provided the following statement:

> Originally, Ji Guanghao's family and He Shengrong's family were close relatives. The two families had drawn up this transaction contract after discussing it with each other in person. Fang Macheng 方马成 and I and some others were the witnesses and made our marks on the ready-made contract at He Mayang's 何马养 (He Shengrong's) home. At that time, because there was the matter of land that remained with the original owner (*lianye* 连业), the antecedent old contracts were not submitted but were kept by He Mayang. He Mayang then signed a rental receipt, to which Fang Macheng and I and some others were also witnesses. I confirm the above information is true and correct.[13]

Based on the witness's description of the circumstances of the contract signing, the magistrate decided that this was a sale with recourse rather than a mortgage. Yet, in accordance with the regulation that land sold with recourse is redeemable, he ordered He Xiankuang to pay 30 silver dollars to Ji Qifeng and also to manage this land.

We do not know (in fact the local magistrate probably did not make a judgment either), which side told the truth, or maybe both parties including the witness were lying. This is not, however, the key question. What we are interested in is the context in which contracts were made and these people's understandings of the contract. To begin with, it is important to recognize that the contract was very likely *not* a full account of all aspects of the deal. There may well have been many spoken agreements made at the time the contract was signed. These may have included, for example, promises as to whether the antecedent contracts should be submitted or about how the contract tax and the ownership transfer should be arranged. Indeed, although the contract text noted "clearly on this day the receipt of payment in full as per the contract without any shortchanging," it was still possible to negotiate the payment to be made by installment. The consensus between the two signing parties on these questions may not have been entirely in accordance with local "customs," but might perhaps have been reached by means of oral agreements in a mood of being on "friendly terms."

Second, the validity of clauses in the contract, including the oral agreements, was guaranteed by personal relationships in a society of acquaintances. Not only might the seller and buyer have a complicated and possibly long-lasting personal relationship, but also they and the witnesses to the contract were also members of this acquaintance society. Thus, the validity of the contract does not lie entirely on the credibility of the contract document itself, but additionally on the specific circumstances of these relationships, such as, for example, whether Ji Qifeng's brother-in-law was still alive and the treatment his widowed sister received in the He family.

Finally, as many researchers have already pointed out, the credibility of the contract depends very much on the witness's testimony, or the witness's recollection and description of the contract signing scene. In other words, the credibility of the contract is proven to a large extent by the ability to reconstruct the scene of the signing of the contract. The death of the witness will certainly weaken proof of the contract's validity. It is a technical problem to verify the authenticity of a contract drawn up a long time ago, especially those unstamped contracts that were not registered with the government and on which tax was not paid. Notably, the *Great Qing Code* (*Da Qing lüli* 大清律例) contains the provision that "old contracts and inscriptions cannot be presented as evidence or proof" in disputes over tomb hills.[14] In sum, recognizing that traditional Chinese contracts were embedded in these specific, dynamic social networks means that any interpretation we make of a contract or the roles of the historical actors involved without considering these spatially and temporally arrayed social networks will surely be problematic.

Observing the flow and use of the contract

The physical contract was usually well kept after it was made. The transfer of the contract was a necessary procedure in activities involving property transfer such as sales transactions, inheritance, and endowment. The contract could also be used as collateral on a loan or submitted as evidence in a lawsuit. In other words, in those cases the contract would be retrieved, re-read, and re-examined, passed from hand to hand, particularly in the many instances of family division, major transactions, disputes, and lawsuits.

The Longquan archives also reveal that contracts risked being destroyed, altered, or forged during these instances of their circulation among the interested parties. Evidence of their theft, concealment, fraud, and falsification is clear in a variety of disputes. For example, when "Mrs. Yin, neé Han 韩, accused Liao Yongnian 廖永年 and the others of using lawsuits to encroach on hill property in the 29th year of the Guangxu reign (1904)," the 70-year-old widow Mrs. Yin complained that the accused, Liao Yongnian and others, forged a contract for selling the hill based on a real deed that her son Yin Meijin 殷美进 had stolen from home and pawned for his gambling losses, after which Liao had sold it to the brokers.[15] In another case in which "Liu Shaofang 刘绍芳, Liu Chaogao 刘朝高, and others sued each other over a fir tree wood in the first year of the Xuantong reign," one party in the lawsuit described how the brothers and cousins in the family fell out with each other and came to blows over the physical contracts:

> They snatched away the boxes where the contracts were stored without showing any regard to whether my father was dead or alive. My father died on the twenty-third day; right after the funeral, disrespecting the fact that my father's body was scarcely cold, [they] thus invited the clan brother Shaowen to the house, brought the boxes out, and sorted and divided up the contracts. A few pages containing my share of the farmland

deeds were missing from the record of our family division, and the bundle of the land and hill deeds for Shanglai 上赖 village was also missing...[16]

The case of "Ji Xianhu 季仙护 and others accusing Ji Shengrong 季盛荣 of theft of the contract in the seventh year of the Republic of China" presents an even more striking story. Ji Qingtang 季庆堂 got hold of the old contract for the hill land that Ji Shengrong had bought, and consequently forged a contract to sell it in the 28th year of the Guangxu reign (1903). He then registered and paid tax for the two contracts at the local government. Later, Ji Xianhu obtained this old contract by taking it away from Ji Qingtang's wife, neé Mao 毛 through deception. He then exchanged it with Ji Shengrong for a contract that he wanted. In the end, Ji Qingtang and Ji Xianhu were found guilty of false accusation, contract forgery, and theft.[17]

It seems that, in these lawsuits, the contract was always critical to the exchange of property, and without it, the proof of the transaction and property rights were always in a state of uncertainty. Although the portrayal of the case documents was probably more extreme than the actual situation, it nevertheless reveals the anxiety people felt with regard to these contracts; and situations fraught with such emotions were precisely the condition in which such contracts operated. More importantly, these lawsuits also indicate that county-level judicial practice at this point was unable to eliminate the critical problems of these contract cases and could not protect the property relations they defined. For example, while cases of contract alteration and forgery are quite common in the late Qing archives of Longquan, it appears the forgers always escaped punishment.[18] The situation was not ameliorated until the Republican era when the law was improved and legal enforcement strengthened.

In fact, even a contract that had been kept safely and intact would still face the fate of being constantly re-interpreted and revised. Under the traditional system that acknowledged land property rights through a chain of contracts, it was quite common for people to have on hand antecedent "old contracts" that had been drawn up hundreds of years previously. Names and the state of the property might have changed from that time, resulting in discrepancies between different contracts and also between the contract text and the actual situation on the ground. In the case disputing "farmland property between Ji Huanwen and Ji Zhaoqi from the second year to the eighth year of the Republic of China," according to the record in the "Zhejiang High Court of Justice Civil Judgment No. 137 in the Fourth Year," the two parties in the case submitted nearly 40 different contract documents. The Civil Judgment explained that it would be very difficult to identify the transaction history and current ownership of this hillside farmland property based on these contracts:

> The measuring of hillside farmland has customarily been different from that of level land.... If we measure according to the regulations, it will

certainly not match up; this is the first difficulty... besides, the location of the land and its boundaries on all sides have to be identified and demarcated first to determine the size of the land before the measuring. This contract does not indicate the boundary on all sides, so it is impossible to measure; this is the second difficulty...The shape as well as the division of the plots can be changed artificially. The number of the thirteen plots in front of the accused Ji's house first appeared during the Kangxi reign, and after two hundred years of change, the shape of the plots are no longer reliable; this is the third difficulty.[19]

In addition, "the sizes of the various pieces of land recorded are smaller in the past and larger later; the names of the various pieces of land are imprecise in the past and specific later," This last point meant that the contracts for the same piece of land drawn up at different times might have different descriptions of the size, boundaries, and the name of the property.

In sum, the traditional system of using the land purchase contract as the primary evidence of the transaction to prove property ownership had significant problems. Although every contract clearly and precisely stipulates rights and obligations, after hundreds of years of change and transactions, divisions, and transfers, it was, indeed not easy to determine the current property ownership based on a chain of contracts. Thus, for cases of both civil mediation and lawsuits, it is necessary for us to explain what the contract meant and represented in the moment when it was presented as proof of land rights. Because such explanations had to be also accepted by consensus in rural society, when different versions of the interpretation existed, the only solution would be to re-negotiate and draw up new contracts.

The changing legal environment in which the contract functions

The Longquan lawsuit archival records reveal much about how the law, legal practice, and contracts actually related to each other in practice. The fact remains that despite the continued common use of contracts in land dispute lawsuits, judgments not made on the basis of these documents. This in part has to do with the special structure of the Chinese contract, and in part, with the characteristics of the traditional trial before the local magistrate. Hiroaki Terada observes that the contracts of the Ming and Qing dynasties cannot be understood to be reflecting a fully unfettered consensus between the two parties. Thus, there was no broadly accepted concept that a contract could only be made or cancelled willingly by the parties involved.[20] Furthermore, in what were effectively civil trials in the Qing dynasty, Terada explains that

> when handling disputes, the local magistrate did not aim to judge right and wrong between the two parties following certain objective regulations, but sought to suggest solutions to resolve the dispute and so bring about a mutual agreement and peaceful relations between the two parties.[21]

In fact, in dealing with these contractual disputes, the local magistrate was often taking the lead in negotiating a new contract for the parties for the sake of, as it was phrased, "moral and humane considerations" (*qingli* 情理).

In the early years of the Republic, this style of combined adjudication and mediation continued to be evident in the way local magistrates dealt with contractual disputes. The lineages and the local government generally tried to settle the dispute in a manner that took the particular social relationships involved into consideration, even to the point of invalidating the original contract if necessary. In the case of "Dispute over farmland between Wu Shibiao 吴时标 and Wu Kaizhen 吴开震 and the others in the fourth year of the Republic of China," Wu Kaixun [Wu Shibiao's father] sold the farmland to Wu Kaizhen and the others and drew up a contract. However, after Wu Kaixun died, Wu Kaizhen and the others were accused of forging the sale contract and encroaching on the farmland. The lineage did not check the authenticity of the sale contract. The document continues:

> regardless of whether the contract [Wu] Kaizhen and [Wu] Shiqing have is authentic or not, it is problematic that when they bought the farmland, no member from the lineage nor a male heir was present as a witness to the transaction; besides, the payment made was below market price. After mutual negotiation, a supplementary contract should be written to [Wu] Shibiao; [Wu] Shiqing should pay another fifteen silver dollars that together with the earlier balance will be fifty-seven silver dollars in total; this is restitution for the expenses [Wu] Shibiao incurred for the funeral. This is fair to both sides.

The final judgment issued by the local magistrate was essentially identical with the suggested mediation solution proposed by the clan.

We also see, however, some significant changes in these archives over time. Throughout the Beiyang Government period, although there was no systematic contract law, the Supreme Court (*dali yuan* 大理院) still ruled on the qualification of subjecthood in contracts, the statement of meaning from both parties, and the various practices of the commercial, pawn, and land property contracts and loans.[22] The approach in which the local judicial institutions dealt with contract disputes had also changed by this point. In the case of "Zhou Jinze 周金泽 accusing Zhuo Bingguang 卓炳光 of confiscating the contract and concealing the price of the redeemable property to interfere with a loan in the eleventh year of the Republic of China," Zhou Jinze complained that Zhuo Bingguang took advantage of Zhou not being at home and

> colluded with the scribe and the witnesses to cheat his father (Zhou Guangyu 周光宇, who was old and credulous, of a contract of supplementary payment (*jiazhao qi* 加找契)...while he actually paid nothing for the two payments [stated in the contracts].[23]

The *Great Qing Code* also includes two related provisions, to wit "if the payer and the payee cannot reach an agreement and if any dispute arises through use of coercion, the money that a (party) had been compelled to pay should be returned to the original owner" and "if a deal or loan is made with a real contact but the money remains unpaid, or if anyone encroaches upon another man's land or house..."[24] The language of these two legal provisions concerning the statement of meaning from the two parties in contracts is very vague and so was often used by the parties as an excuse to withdraw from a contract. However, the Supreme Court gave more detailed and practicable definitions to terms such as "fraud" and "threatening," and on how to prove if a contract was made with the consensus of both parties.[25] In this case, the civil court of Longquan county after investigation summoned the middlemen and the scribe to court who were present when the contract was signed. They confirmed that the plaintiff's father Zhou Guangyu was also been present at the time and had personally signed the contract; so the court rejected Zhou Jinze's claim.[26]

Unlike the local magistrate's previous role as a mediator in contractual disputes, the Republican era witnessed the initiation of the notion of the "freedom of contract." This idea that contracts were entered into through the personal decisions of individual subjects out of their own free will and thus had to be upheld by these individuals subsequently became the foundation of judicial mediation in contractual disputes.[27] In this manner, the contract was isolated from its external social relations and environment, and the legal officials' role also changed from one of mediation to adjudication. Of course, the transformation of contract law and legal practice in modern China, as well as its relation to the folk contractual order is a highly complex and needs much more study with these kinds of judicial archives.

Conclusion

In recent years, scholars in China and overseas have done much to advance the study of traditional contracts in China. Myron Cohen has notably reminded us that we should distinguish between the "social" and "legal" aspects. He rightly points out that traditional contracts were "far more social than they are legal" and were guaranteed not by law but by the social relationships between the signing parties.[28] Jérôme Bourgon also argues that

> when discussing the contract within the legal culture of the Qing dynasty, we should not confine ourselves only to the textual analysis of the contract document, close reading of the case files, or collecting evidence of the contract's economic and social functions; we should also examine if the legal practitioners and authors in the Qing dynasty constructed any ideas or notions within the legal culture through which they could

civilize and civicize the contract and the social relationships within which it was enmeshed.[29]

By studying the texts written by Qing jurists (judicial assistants, litigation masters, and officials from the Ministry of Justice), he arrives at an apparently negative answer. The officials generally did examine contracts during trials, but their primary concern was not with protecting property rights of people in the strict sense, but with maintaining social control.[30]

What, then, is the nature of the contract on the social level? Contracts were clearly quite common in traditional social-economic life, and even people in the most rural areas were fully aware of the importance of the contract. This is evident in the recent discoveries of large numbers of old contracts in some remote villages. These antique contracts of relatively good continuity and integrity have been carefully kept in contract boxes and preserved until today after various kinds of misfortune and revolutions. The contracts lie peaceful and organized in wooden boxes or bamboo baskets, as though they had not been disturbed since they were made. This is obviously not the case. The lawsuit archives bring us back to the actual use of a contract in society. Contracts like these were always in a state of fluid negotiation, re-interpretation, and revision; lacking any institutionalized mechanism in the so-called local "customs" for validating contracts, the documents have been dismissed as a kind of "discourse," and their negotiation and interpretation could be arbitrary and case-based. Every contract document as an antecedent contract (*shangshou qi* 上手契) has its infinite life; as long as it exists, it has the value of being used. Lawsuit archives do not show that people were unable to provide the contract as evidence in disputes, but conversely that the considerable bulk of disconnected contracts as evidence surpassed the juridical institutions' capacity to identify and judge. Taking this to the extreme, one might say that it seems that the purpose of a signed contract was to provide a document for later negotiation.

In a word, the contract is a management certificate, but it does not function by lying in the contract boxes and cabinets. In the lawsuit archives, the contract reveals its vitality and the stories it had written together with the parties involved and the judges, as well as with custom and law.

Notes

1 Zhang Chuanxi, ed., *Zhongguo lidai qiyue huibian kaoshi* [Collected Chinese land deeds with notes and transcriptions]. Beijing: Beijing daxue chubanshe, 1995: 7.
2 See, Fu Yiling, *Ming Qing nongcun shehui jingji* [Rural social economy of the Ming and Qing dynasties] Beijing: Sanlian shudian, 1961; Yang Guozhen, *Ming Qing tudi qiyue wenshu yanjiu* [Research on the land deeds of the Ming and Qing dynasties] Beijing: Zhongguo renmin daxue chubanshe, 2009; Zheng Zhenman, *Ming Qing Fujian jiazu zuzhi yu shehui bianqian* [Family structure and social

change in Fujian in the Ming and Qing dynasties] Changsha: Hunan jiaoyu chubanshe, 1992.
3 Anben Meixu [Mio Kishimoto], "Ming Qing qiyue wenshu," [Contracts of the Ming and Qing dynasties] in Zihe Xiusan [Shūzō Shiga], et al., Wang Yaxin and Liang Zhiping, eds., *Ming Qing shiqi de minshi shenpan yu minjian qiyu* [Civil trials and folk contracts in the Ming and Qing dynasties], trans. Wang Yaxin, Fan Yu, and Chen Shaofeng. Beijing: falü chubanshe, 1992: 282.
4 Madeleine Zelin, Jonathan Ocko, and Robert Gardella eds., *Contract and property in early modern China*. Stanford: Stanford University Press, 2004.
5 Zhang Chuanxi, Qiyue shi maidiquan yanjiu [(Studies on the history of contracts and tomb contracts]. Zhonghua shuju, 2008; Valerie Hansen, *Negotiating daily life in traditional China, changing gods in medieval China, 1127–1279*. New Heaven: Yale University Press, 1995; Lu Xiqi, Zhongguo gudai maidiquan yanjiu (Studies on tomb contracts in ancient China). Xiamen University Press, 2014. Some review articles supplied useful information about the research on contracts in Ming and Qing dynasties, eg. Peilin Wu, and Zeng-Zeng Li, "Liushi nianlai de Mingqing Qiyue Wenshu Zhengli yu Yanjiu," [Collection and research on Ming and Qing contract texts] *Difang dang'an yu Wenxian yanjiu* 2, Zhongguo kexue chubanshe, 2016.
6 Du Zheng-zhen, *jindai shanqu shehui de xiguan qiyue yu quanli: longquan sifa dangan de shehuishi yanjiu* (Custom, contract and right in mountain area in modern China: A social history study based on Longquan legal archives) Zhonghua Shuju, 2018.
7 David Faure, "Contractual arrangements and the emergence of a land market in the pearl River Delta, 1500–1800," in Hung Li-wan and Chen Chiu-kun, eds., *Qiyue wenshu yu shehui shenghuo (1600–1900)* [Contract documents and social life, 1600–1900]. Taipei: Zhongyang yanjiuyuan Taiwan shi yanjiusuo choubeichu, 2001: 265–283.
8 Liang Cong, *Qingdai Qingshui Jiang xiayou cunzhai shehui de qiyue guifan yu zhixu* [Contractual norms and order in the rural society on the lower reaches of the Qingshui River in the Qing dynasty]. Beijing: Renmin chubanshe 2008.
9 See, Wu Zhengqiang, Du Zhengzhen, and Zhang Kai, "Longquan sifa dang'an wan Qing suzhuang geshi yanjiu" [Study on the plaint format in the late Qing period from the Longquan lawsuit archives], *Wenshi* 4 (2011): 185–214. The explanation of "yinqi" is incorrect in this article and is rectified here.
10 Valerie Hansen, *Negotiating daily life in traditional China: How ordinary people used contracts, 600–1400*. New Haven and London: Yale University Press, 1995: 25. Madeleine Zelin's study on the business contract in Zigong in the late Qing period shows that the signing of a contract was still accompanied by grand feasts. Madeleine Zelin, "A critique of rights of property in PreWar China," in Madeleine Zelin, Jonathan Ocko, and Robert Gardella eds., *Contract and property in early modern China*. Stanford: Stanford University Press, 2004: 25.
11 The case files are stored in the Longquan Municipal Archives, file no. M003-01-1277, M003-01-4916, M003-01-15307.
12 "Civil complaint of Ji Qifeng accusing He Xiankuang of false accusation of contract forgery, on July 31, the third year of the Republic of China," Longquan Municipal Archives, file no. M003-01-1277.
13 "Statement from Jiang Tusheng who was summoned for confrontation in court on October 15 (third year of the Republic of China)," Longquan Municipal Archives, file no. M003-01-4916.
14 Xue Yunsheng, *Du Li cun yi* [Doubts from studying the Great Qing code] Taipei: Chengwen chubanshe 1970: 277.

Field research using contracts (qiyue)   251

15 Bao Weimin, ed., *Longquan sifa dang'an xuanbian (diyi ji, wan Qing bufen)* [Selected collection of the legal archives in Longquan, part 1, Late Qing period] Beijing: Zhonghua shuju, 2012: 32–81.
16 Ibid. 160.
17 The case document is stored in the Longquan Municipal Archives, file no. 003-01-314-, 003-01-5585, 003-01-5611, 003-01-9971, 003-01-11130, 003-01-14622, 003-01-17284.
18 See, Du Zhengzhen and Wu Zhengqiang, "Difang susong zhong de qiyue yingyong yu qiyue guannian—cong Longquan sifa dang'an wan Qing bufen kan guojia yu minjian de qiyue guize," [The application and concept of the contract in local lawsuits—the state and the folk contractual rules from the Longquan legal archives of the late Qing period] *Wenshi* 1 (2012): 207–225.
19 "Zhejiang High Court of Justice Civil Judgment No. 137 in the Fourth Year," Longquan Municipal Archives, file no. M003-01-13076.
20 Sitian haoming [Hiroaki Terada], "Ming Qing shiqi fa zhixu zhong 'yue' de xingzhi" [The nature of "contract" in the judicial order of the Ming and Qing dynasties], trans. Wang Yaxin, in Zihe xiusan [Shūzō Shiga], et al., Wang Yaxin and Liang Zhiping, eds., *Ming Qing shiqi de minshi shenpan yu minjian qiyue* [Civil trials and folk contracts in the Ming and Qing dynasties], trans. Wang Yaxin, Fan Yu, and Chen Shaofeng. Beijing: falü chubanshe 1992], 176.
21 Sitian haoming [Hiroaki Terada], Wang Yaxin, trans., "Quanli yu yuanyi—Qingdai tingsong he minzhong de minshifa zhixu" [Rights and bitterness—trials and the public's civil judicial order in the Qing dynasty], in ibid., 194.
22 See, Li Qian, *Minguo shiqi qiyue zhixu yanjiu* [Research on the contractual system in the Republican era] Beijing: Beijing daxue chubanshe, 2005.
23 "Civil complaint from Zhou Jinze accusing Zhuo Bingguang of cheating and contract forgery on January 9, the twelfth year of the Republic of China," Longquan Municipal Archives, file no. M003-01-17098.
24 Xue Yunsheng, *Du Li cun yi* [Doubts from studying the *Great Qing* Code] Taipei: Chengwen chubanshe, 1970: 96, 275.
25 Li Qian, *Minguo shiqi qiyue zhixu yanjiu* [Research on the contractual system in the Republican era] Beijing: Beijing daxue chubanshe, 2005: 97–98.
26 "Civil court order, the civil court of the county governor in Longquan county on March 29, the twelfth year of the Republic of China," Longquan Municipal Archives, file no. M003-01-11320.
27 See, Zhou Bofeng, *Minguo chunian "qiyue ziyou" gainian de dansheng—yi Dali Yuan de yanshuo shijian wei zhongxin* [The emergence of the concept "freedom of contract" in the early Republican years—focusing on the Supreme Court's discourse and practice] Beijing: Beijing daxue chubanshe, 2006.
28 Myron Cohen, "Writs of passage in late imperial China—The documentation of practical understandings in Minong, Taiwan," in Madeleine Zelin, Jonathan Ocko, and Robert Gardella eds., *Contract and property in early modern China*. Stanford: Stanford University Press, 2004: 88.
29 Gong Tao [Jérôme Bourgon], "Ditan shang de tu'an: shilun Qing dai falü wenhua zhong de 'xiguan' yu 'qiyue,'" [The image on the carpet: on the "customs" and "contract" in the legal culture of the Qing dynasty], trans. Huang Shih-chieh, in Chiu Peng-sheng and Chen Hsi-yuan, eds., *Ming Qing falü yunzuo zhong de quanli yu wenhua* [Power and culture in the legal practice of the Ming and Qing dyansties] Taipei: Academia Sinica; Lianjing, 2009: 239–240.
30 Ibid., 215–253.

20 Account books (*zhangben*) in local history studies

Yonghua Liu

Account books are a commonly encountered and valuable source for local history. Even in the Republican era, both Chinese and foreign scholars recognized their historical value. Since the 1980s, scholars have used them to conduct multifaceted, in-depth research, including work on price and business history, as well as social and cultural history. This chapter first introduces the current state of account book collections, their main types, and some preliminary methods for reading them. It then discusses the historical value of account books and new directions for using them as a source in economic, social, and cultural history. The final part illustrates these possibilities with the example of an account from a bookseller.

Account books as historical materials

Account books (*zhangbu* 賬簿, also known as *zhangben* 賬本, *zhangce* 賬冊, *buji* 簿記) record economic and social activity by time or category in a standardized format. Among the oldest types of written records, account books were important to administrative management, personal networks, and individual lives, and thus provide significant evidence for economic, social, and cultural historians. Account books were used frequently in both business and social life, and the number used historically must have been voluminous.

Although most have been lost, some major collections survive. The largest and most complete set of account books are those from Tai Yi 泰益, a business house in late-Qing-Republican Xiamen. Spanning 1901–1939, this set of account books altogether has 1,305 volumes; those from 1907 to 1939 have been preserved completely intact. Account books also feature in the Huizhou 徽州 documents collected in the Archives of the Department of History at Nanjing University. This collection contains almost 500 volumes, dating from the eighteenth century to 1949. This collection include various types of account books, such as property management books (*zhichan bu* 置產簿), rent collection books (*shouzu bu* 收租簿), loan society books (*hui bu* 會簿), and business account books (*shangye zhangbu* 商業賬簿).

They cover a wide range of businesses, including those involved in the trade of groceries, tea, medicine, textiles, dyes, iron, salt, as well as pawn shops, money shops, butcheries, and also shipping establishments. The multivolume publication *One Thousand Years of Huizhou Contracts and Documents* 徽州千年契約文書 contains 30–40 titles of Huizhou account books, including the *General Stocktaking Account* (盤貨店總賬簿) from the Wanli Reign (1573–1620) of the Ming dynasty, *Balance Sheet of the Cheng Family Dye House* (程氏染店查算账簿), and *General Account of Cheng Family Stocktaking, Receipts, and Expenses* (程氏盤存收支總賬) of the Kangxi Reign (1662–1722). The most complete set features almost 30 types of account books from the tea merchant and private school tutor Hu Yanqing 胡延卿 from Qimen 祁門 in the late-Qing-early Republic. The 437-volume account books (1798–1850) from Tong Tai Sheng 統泰升, a business house in North China, are held in the National Library of China and the Institute of Economy at the Chinese Academy of Social Sciences. According to my fieldwork experience, a large number of account books are still kept among the people and have yet to be collected by scholars.

Reflecting their different contents and formats, account books are often called by different names. According to their content, account books can be categorized as a household book (*jiayong bu* 家用簿), loan society book (*hui bu* 會簿), rental grains book (*zugu bu* 租谷簿), marriage and funeral book (*hunsang bu* 婚喪簿), and business account (*shangye zhang* 商業賬). According to format, there are generally two main kinds: the "flowing account" (*liushui zhang* 流水賬), that is the daily book kept in chronological order, and the "general clearing account book" (*zongqing zhang* 總清賬), which is an overall accounting of revenues and expenses for a period of time (month, quarter, or year). Business accounting was a relatively complex system. The common method of business bookkeeping in the Ming and Qing dynasties was the "three account books," these being the *rough account* (*caozhang* 草賬), the *flowing account* (*liushui zhang* 流水賬), and the *general clearing account* (*zhongqing zhang* 總清賬). This bookkeeping system came into being in the Song dynasty and reached its final form in the Ming dynasty. The *rough account*, also known as "*caoliu*" (草流, rough flowing), "*caopi*" (草批, rough commented), "*yuanliu*" (原流, original flowing), "*dizhang*" (底賬, original account), "*dibu*" (底簿, original book), or "*huazhang*" (花賬, flower account), consists of shorthand records. The *flowing account*, also known as "*riliu*" (日流, daily flowing), "*xiliu*" (細流, detailed flowing), "*qingliu*" (清流, clearing flowing), "*erliu*" (二流, second flowing), "*liushui zongdeng*" (流水總登, general flowing), "*riji yuelei*" (日積月累, daily accumulation), "*dui jin ji yu*" (堆金積玉, accumulating gold and jade), or "*tieban liushui*" (鐵板流水, iron plate flowing), is the record drawn up by the general accountant based on *rough accounts* each day at the close of business. The *general account book of clearing*, also known as "*tengqingzhang*" (謄清賬, fair copy account), "*zongbu*" (總簿, general book), or "*zongzhang*" (總賬, general account), was usually kept secret from the public and also from an enterprise's regular staff, and was therefore also called *"caishen zhang"* (財神賬, the god of wealth account) or *"kanjia zhang"* (看家賬, housekeeping account). The *general clearing account book* had three functions: classified accounting, profit and loss accounting, and as the basis for compiling the report called the "red account" (*hongzhang* 紅賬).

Running multiple business operations, the large-scale houses often kept a great variety of account books. According to Hsu Tzu-fen, account books from Tai Yi in 1907 included three major types: (1) *chronological account volumes* (i.e., daily account books): the chronological records of original transactions classified by type, including records of special daily sales 銷貨類特種日記簿, special daily purchase accounts 進貨類特種日記簿, special daily accounts of cash deposit and withdrawal 現金收支特種日記簿, and small amount cash accounts of transport and miscellaneous fees; (2) *general and classified accounts*: general accounts, and accounts sorted by category, in which each transaction was classified and organized, and the balance of each account was calculated regularly for the preparation of closing statement. This kind includes detailed ledgers for buyers and sellers, detailed sale and purchase ledgers, general account books with profit and loss statements and balance sheets; (3) *other records*, including tax books, rent books, detailed accounts of cash receipts, transport rentals, custom charges, rice imports and exports, export packaging, storage charges, bills and notes, and telegraph charges, and a book of telegraphs received and sent. These three kinds of account books together comprised a very complicated accounting system.

Although account books contain rich historical information, there are certain difficulties encountered when using them. Besides the occasional problem of illegible handwriting, many surviving account books make use of special symbols and abbreviations. For example, many sources do not use Chinese numerals, because the characters have too many strokes. Instead, they use a simple and convenient numeral system, commonly known as "Suzhou mazi" (蘇州碼子, Suzhou numerals, see Table 20.1), also known as *"caoma"* (草碼, rough numerals), *"huama"* (花碼, flower numerals), and *"chaima"* (柴碼, firewood numerals). Based on counting rod numerals, the Suzhou numeral system were used as mathematical symbols, and in account books.

Table 20.1 Comparative chart of Suzhou numerals, Chinese numerals, and Arabic numerals

Suzhou numerals	〇	〡	〢	〣	〤	〥	〦	〧	〨	〩	十
Chinese numerals	零	一	二	三	四	五	六	七	八	九	十
Arabic numerals	0	1	2	3	4	5	6	7	8	9	10

In a recent article, Jiang Qin and Cao Shuji address some of the common problems faced in reading and interpreting account books. Based on their classification and discussion, I will briefly summarize the key points.

1   *Omission of digits.* The most common problem with the Suzhou numerals is the omission of digits. Because Suzhou numerals do not employ the decimal point, the base was indicated by writing a circle over a character indicating ones, tens, hundreds, etc., in the lower line. In quick bookkeeping, however, this mark was often left out by the bookkeeper. In such cases, researchers need to determine the numerical value according to context.
2   *Mixed use of unit price and total purchase price.* There are two ways to indicate a commodity price: one is to mark only the total price and the other is to mark both the unit and total price of a batch purchase. In the latter case, it is necessary to distinguish between the unit price and the total price in order to compile the correct numbers. In research on price history, it is obvious that only unit prices should be compared. The basic method to determine unit and total prices is to look at context. For example, if total revenue and expenditure are calculated daily or monthly, prices can be deduced by checking each entry of the records.
3   *Units of measurement.* Account books throughout China often used local units of measurement, which causes difficulty for researchers attempting to read and interpret their figures. Because quantitative study requires comparable data, it is necessary to convert and unify units of measurement in account books into comparable and commonly used ones. It is thus a key step to understand the exact meaning of units of measurement used and convert them into standardized units of measurements before recording numbers to compare with those in other sources.

Having read and deciphered the text and numbers in account books, the next step is to think about how to conduct an in-depth analysis of the content from several research perspectives.

Analyzing account books in economic history

The founders of modern sociology considered accounting practices to be related to economic development (especially capital management and the emergence of the concept of profit), and therefore, early studies on account books concentrated on the relationship between bookkeeping and economic activities. Modern scholars have paid particular attention to account books because these kinds of documents were considered valuable to assessing the development of capitalism. Interest in whether double-entry bookkeeping existed in traditional Chinese bookkeeping practices or whether it had been necessary to import Western bookkeeping methods to China sparked key debates among those studying accounting in the Republican era. This context greatly shaped early research on traditional Chinese bookkeeping and accounting.

In current economic history studies, account books are mainly used in studies of changing prices and wages, rates of rental, interest, and profit, use of currency, and capital operations. This research normally involves systematic handling and statistical analysis of serial data from account books.

Among the most common information in account books are records of revenues and expenditures (including wages) indicated in monetary terms. This kind of information is useful in research on changing prices and wages, and the use of currency. For the study of price change, especially that of grain prices, a common research method is to collect grain prices from local officials' reports in the Qing Palace Archives; some scholars also systematically collect historical records on commodity prices from local gazetteers, notes, and stone tablet inscriptions. For example, Kishimoto Mio's research on price history in the Qing dynasty is heavily based on these kinds of historical materials. In an important 1987 article, Kishimoto pointed out that

> organizing long-term, high-quality historical materials about commodity prices over the span of decades even centuries into a standardized, chronological price chart is the basis for advancing research on Qing price history. The most anticipated materials for this task are account books from business houses or lineages.

When Kishimoto wrote this article, the discovery and publication of local documents was still at an early stage. This situation has since been greatly improved. Compared with grain prices in official reports and historical records in local gazetteers and notes, prices recorded in account books have a great advantage in that they were recorded in real-time and in consecutive order. If we can systematically collect grain prices from account books of different places, we should be able to verify the basic conclusions established in the price history of the Ming and Qing dynasties and at the same time advance our understanding of the reported grain price data for the Qing dynasty.

Account books are also important for reconstructing long-term wage change. Notably, Sidney Gamble published a pioneering article in 1943, in which he reconstructed wage change over nearly a century on the basis of the account books of a Beijing area fuel trading firm that recorded the cash wages paid to unskilled labors from 1807 to 1902. Sorting almost 13,000 entries from these account books, he was able to analyze the seasonal and long-term changes of cash wages.

Account books record the currency used in transactions, enabling us to observe historic change in the exchange price between silver and copper. Kishimoto's discussion of the so-called "70 percent cash" (*qizheqian* 七折錢) and the use of money in real estate transactions is a classic example.

The so-called "70 percent cash" is a form of money measurement that specifically stipulates the exchange rate between silver and copper (indicated as "70 percent" or "80 percent"). Using historical materials such as contracts, account books, and notes, Kishimoto introduces the background of the changes to the exchange rate between silver and copper and the use of currency in which the "70 percent cash" first appeared. She argues that the "70 percent cash" emerged in the mid-eighteenth century when the currency metal in circulation changed from silver to copper. Kishimoto uses a property register from which she finds that the currency used in land transaction contracts in Suzhou notably changed from silver to copper in around the year 1770.

Rent account books record payments collected over the years by landlords. They often include specific information such as the landholdings, tenant farmers' names, rental forms, and rent rates. They are therefore important documents for studying the landlord-tenant system, as is expertly demonstrated in the work of Zhang Youyi on Ming-Qing Huizhou. Demonstrating how rental change (*gai'e* 改額) is the adjustment in the absolute value of rent, while the real receipt rate is the percentage of rent actually collected, Zhang demonstrates the degree of change in the actual amounts of rent paid to a landlord. Since rental accounts usually did not indicate yields and acreages of each plot, we cannot calculate the rental rate (i.e., ratio of rent actually collected, against the actual plot yields), although Zhang sometimes deduces yields by the amount of rent received through sharecropping arrangement.

Moneylending accounts often record the amount of money and goods lent as well as the interest or repayment (sometimes also the interest rates), usually indicated as 20 percent or 30 percent (annual) interest rate (*jia'er suan* 加二算, *jiasan suan* 加三算). From these, we can directly or indirectly gather information on changing interest rates. Wang Shih-ch'ing uses moneylending records for 28 years from 1842 to 1869 kept by Guangji 廣記, a landlord holding top-soil right in late-Qing Danshui 淡水, Taiwan, to analyze the relationship between loan interest rates and rice prices. Wang also systematically analyzes grain prices in account books to discuss the causes of grain price change in mid-nineteenth-century North Taiwan.

If accounts record loan principals and receipts and expenditures of a certain period of time, then it becomes possible to calculate the interest rate. In their analysis of five account lists from lending shops in Shanxi province, for instance, Liu Qiugen and his colleagues determined from the account list records of the costs, revenues, and fees of the Shanxi money-lending business Yu Sheng Ji 玉盛吉 in 1837 a way to calculate their main business profits of the year (main business profit = main revenues minus costs and fees) and also the profit rate by dividing main business profits by costs.

The repetitive, systematic information provided by account books also includes texts which can be transferred into data for quantitative analysis. I have used this kind of information in my research on the changing livelihood of a rural family in late-Qing Huizhou. The daily accounts (*pairizhang* 排日賬) that I studied systematically recorded the account holders' daily activities, especially their participation in all kinds of economic activities. Collecting this kind of information, one can know the changing number of days of labor invested in different economic activities during a certain time period, and reconstruct the change in their livelihood model. Other kinds of information in account books can, meanwhile, support qualitative research. For example, by systematically analyzing the customer lists recorded in account books, we can reconstruct certain business networks.

Account books in social and cultural history

For social and cultural history, there are two main ways of interpreting the qualitative information provided by account books: one is to convert qualitative information into quantitative; the other is to use qualitative information on its own and systematically. The former method has long been practiced by social historians, while the latter is still not that common. Of course, the two methods are not mutually exclusive and can sometimes be combined. Since account books include abundant information on social life, they can address a wide range of topics in social and cultural history. Here, I will focus on how to conduct research on interpersonal networks and spaces of activity using account books.

A first kind of account book worth discussing in this regard is the records of gift exchange, also known as *"lidan"* (禮單, gift list), *"lizhang"* (禮賬, gift account), and *"renqing bu"* (人情簿, favor book). Yan Yunxiang's research on gift relationships in Xiajia village (下岬村) in Northeast China, for example, is based on more than 40 such local gift books. As Yan points out, the gift list is a book made of red paper and written with brush calligraphy. It is a written record of all the gifts that the host family received at the time of a ceremony. From the gift list, the host family will be able to know who attended the ceremony and the value of their gifts, and then take it as the reference to decide whether to attend others' ceremonies and the amount of cash gift to give others in the future. From this, Yan recognized that "gift lists can be seen as social maps, which record and display networks of personal connections." However, it is essential to realize that even though the gift list represents the owner's interpersonal relationships in a fairly systematic way, it does not represent all of these relationships—just the most important ones. This allows us to distinguish the closeness of relationships.

Yan Yunxiang's work exemplifies how gift lists can be drawn upon for both qualitative and quantitative information. Thus, his careful interpretation of gift lists reveals whether and how social relations such as clan relatives, in-laws, neighbors, and friends constitute an important part of a network. Also, the various ceremonial events recorded in gift lists contribute to our understanding of the main types of rituals in this society and their relation to gift-giving and interpersonal networks. For example, we can figure out which ceremonial events involve gift giving and whether there are significant differences in the interpersonal network reached in different ceremonies. Meantime, in terms of quantitative information, gift lists record the sum of cash gifts, which can be used to examine the closeness of the relatives' relationships and changes in the gift economy. Combining interviews with interpretation of gift lists, Yan established the relationship between gift-giving and relationship structure, and presented the structural layout of individual relationship networks. At the same time, he uses the rich information provided by the gift list to count the people in the different zones of an individual network and the sum of cash gifts, in order to see the importance of different zones in the individual network.

Other types of account books may also contain rich information on interpersonal relationships, as I found studying a Huizhou daily account. With a form falling somewhere between an account book and a diary, a daily account is a kind of local history document common in Wuyuan county 婺源縣. Like other account books, it contains repeated types of information that can be organized into several data sets that cover a certain period of time and it records daily economic activities which can be analyzed statistically. Records of household incomes, meanwhile, allow us to describe a household's income structure and its changes. Daily accounts, moreover, record the locations of daily operations. By systematically processing these place names, I may determine the family's activity space. The daily accounts that I have collected were kept by a rural family (the Cheng family) in Shangwan 上灣, Tuanchuan township 沱川鄉, Wuyuan county for three generations over 60 years, from 1838 to 1901. Having systematically sorted all of the place names mentioned in this set of documents, I address three key issues: distances between these places and Shangwan village where the Cheng family was located, frequency of the family's trips to these places, and the nature of their activities in these places according to the records in their daily account books. Through such spatial-relational analysis, it is possible to sketch out the approximate scope and content of the Cheng family's activity space, as well as to track significant change to these spaces over time.

Using the personal names mentioned in the daily accounts, I aim to reconstruct the Cheng family's interpersonal network and analyze its basic structure. This requires, first, sorting the individuals' or the family's interpersonal relationships into such basic categories as clan relatives, marriage ties, neighbors, friends, and business partners. Second, it is essential to sort out and classify the social groups to which the individuals or the family belong: patriarchal kinship groups (such as clans), village organizations (village organizations based on communal temples), and cross-village organizations (such as township compacts, cross-village ritual alliances). In this way, it becomes possible to identify the Cheng family's interpersonal relationships in a way through which we can determine the importance of these interpersonal relationships and social groups in their social life. My preference is to focus on functional activities of the individuals or families involved. For example, we can examine which loan societies the family joined, their exchange of labor with other families, their participation in annual and festival rituals, and the representation of different interpersonal relationships in life ceremonies of the individual or the family. Using such criteria as contact frequency, or the maintenance of a reciprocal gift relationship, we can roughly determine the importance of these relationships and groups to the individuals or families involved. We can then discuss how these relationships and groups intervene in the family-centered social lives and explore changes in these relationships and groups over a long period of time.

Finally, account books present the opportunity to establish parameters in understanding the problem of popular literacy. There is no definitive consensus on how to define literacy in Chinese history. My opinion is that it is most helpful to imagine a multiplicity of popular literacies, that is, to understand literacy as a multi-layered continuum. The highest level of literacy is the classical sort developed in preparation for the imperial civil service examination; next comes the ability to read novels, and write diaries and letters. The lowest level of literacy is bookkeeping, which requires only the ability to write a certain number of frequently repeated characters and numbers, with no need to construct full sentences, or consider logical relationships between sentences and between paragraphs. By counting the number of characters in account books, we can roughly deduce the number of words required for bookkeeping, which, in turn, provides a basic reference for the boundary between literacy and illiteracy, as well as a series of issues related to information exchange.

Interpreting a bookseller's account

Unlike the study of early modern European book history, the field of Chinese book history lacks sources on books as property that can be used to understand the circulation and reading of books in the past. Thus, we must resort to other types of documents and materials, such as records of household and property division, diaries, and catalogs of private book collections. Booksellers' account books are particularly valuable sources for understanding popular reading habits in the early Republic. I found one such account book in question in Sibao town 四堡鎮, in western Fujian. Sibao was the engraving printing and publishing center in Qing dynasty South China, and had a strong cross-regional distribution network. Through extra-textual and external evidence, I was able to conclude that this account was the record of Sibao bookstore Yingwen tang 應文堂, which sold books in Heyuan county 河源縣 in Guangdong province in the 1920s.

Written in black brush calligraphy on bamboo paper with red vertical grids, this account book has 78 intact pages showing a total of 100 sales. The main content includes the location of each sale, the names of the buyers' school, the names of the customers, and the names, quantity, and number of books or goods sold. The first step in interpreting account books is to read the characters and understand all the idiosyncratic texts and symbols (e.g., a dot under a book title represents one volume). The next step is to find out the time period of bookkeeping and locate the places where the books were sold. At this point, we can turn to examining the listed book titles, unit prices, and sales quantity. Commodities were often recorded with abbreviated names, especially of book titles. A basic amount of bibliographic knowledge thus is needed in order to read them. Researchers not only need to understand the full titles of the books sold, but also should have a sense of their general content. Unit price and quantity are also important information that is not to be ignored. In book history, the unit price is not only a focus of attention in economic history, but also an important reference in the discussion of the circulation of books, as we can roughly locate a book's target audience by comparing its price with the daily or monthly average incomes of different social and economic classes.

The bookselling account also records the names of purchasing institutions and customers. This information is particularly valuable because it provides clues to the identities of book buyers that will make possible to delve more deeply into this exploration of book history. A close reading of this text shows that most of the customers came from particular schools. Those noted as national schools, middle schools, and primary schools were presumably modern-style public schools, while those recorded as "academies" (*shushi* 書室), studies, or halls were probably the older form of private schools. By this classification, there are 45 accounts of customers from national schools and 19 from private schools, altogether accounting for more than 60 percent of total sales. Moreover, some customers' identities were indicated in account books, from which we can further determine their professions. If there is the title "xiansheng" (先生), the customer was surely a teacher, while those without titles seem to be students. Therefore, most of the customers recorded in the account book appear to have been teachers and students from different kinds of inland urban and rural public primary and secondary schools as well as private schools.

After identifying the time period of the bookkeeping, the sales regions, and the customers, the next step is to analyze the book title catalog itself. It seems that there are no definite rules for classifying books, but an effective way is to classify them by theme. I have adopted Cynthia Brokaw's method of dividing books into five categories according to themes: textbooks and supplementary materials, elementary readings and the Four Books and Five Classics, histories, practical manuals, and literature. This account records sales of 134 titles, and 647 volumes. Textbooks and various teaching materials are the bestselling of the five categories, with a total of 30 titles in 273 volumes, accounting for about 42 percent of total sales. Given the identities of most book buyers, the popularity of textbooks is easy to understand. They probably bought these books for teaching or learning needs and it may not have much to do with their own reading interests. When it comes to these book buyers' interests, the other four categories are more noteworthy because these books are generally not directly related to the buyers' own work or responsibilities. Of the other kinds of books, the best seller was elementary readings and the Four Books and Five Classics (a total of 11 titles in 130 volumes), followed by various kinds of manuals and practical readings (39 titles in 119 volumes); the third was literature such as poetry anthologies, novels, and plays (a total of 28 titles in 84 volumes), while histories come in last with the lowest sales (a total of 8 titles in 18 volumes).

In addition to classification by theme, we can also categorize the books by time period. In studies of modern history, the 1920s is regarded as an era of the wide dissemination of new ideas. Yet, I found that traditional works still comprised the majority of books. For example, except for *Furu wuzhong* 婦孺五種 (Five Books for Women and Children) that may contain some new-style, modern knowledge, elementary readings, and the Four Books and Five Classics are mostly old knowledge. With some exceptions, the manuals and practical readings have hardly any modern knowledge. Old novels, poems, and plays still dominate. There were no translated European, American, or Japanese works, and hardly any contemporary vernacular Chinese works. In histories, there were works written by contemporary authors, but they did not sell well, and there is no work on foreign history. Nor were there any books about European and American systems, cultures, or ideas.

The interpretation of this account book gives rise to a series of questions about the 1920s: what was the spatial limit of the dissemination of new ideas in the 1920s? By what means did these new ideas spread from cities to smaller towns and rural areas? Did newspapers and journals play a more important role than books? Where did "traditional" arts, knowledge, and beliefs reside?

To further the interpretation of this one account book, we can work in two directions. First, did the sales records or reading lists from other villages reflect a similar situation? Second, was there any difference in the reading habits of primary and secondary school students in bigger cities? Coincidentally, other historical materials of the same time period do provide supporting evidence. An account book of a Shanxi rural grocery that sold books, and a slightly newer catalog of books collected by a private school teacher in the New Territories, Hong Kong, both confirm the basic conclusions that I have drawn in the above catalog analysis. At the same time, several surveys of metropolitan primary and secondary school students conducted around 1930 show that students in bigger cities had quite different reading interests. In short, the interpretation of this account book provides a starting point for an examination of the circulation of books and popular ideas in rural areas in the post-May Fourth Movement era.

To sum up, the account book provides rich and interesting information on the flow of things, both as commodities and as gifts. As a record of commodities, including services, rented out, hired, or purchased, it shows the ebb and flow of the economic fortune of a family or business, and how this change is directly or indirectly connected to economic vicissitudes. As a record of gifts given and received, it reveals how social relationships were established, reproduced, and modified. As a product of mental processes, the account book also sheds light on what and how people thought about the world and themselves. Used properly, account books tell a great deal more than just accounts.

Further Reading

Gardella, Robert, "Squaring Accounts: Commercial Bookkeeping Methods and Capitalist Rationalism in Late Qing and Republican China." *Journal of Asian Studies* 51.2 (May 1992): 317–339.

Guo Daoyang, *Zhongguo kuaiji shigao* [History of Chinese Accounting]. 2 vols. Beijing: Zhongguo caizheng jingji chubanshe, 1982–1988.

Hsu Tzu-fen, *Jindai Zhongguo shangren de jingying yu zhangbu: Changqi huashang jingyingshi de yanjiu* [Modern Chinese Merchants' Business and Account Books: Study on the Business History of Chinese Merchants in Nagasaki]. Taibei: Yuanliu chuban gongsi, 2015.

Jiang Qin and Cao Shuji, "Qingdai Shicang nongjia zhangbu zhong shuzi de shidu" [Reading and Interpreting the Numbers in Peasant Family Account Books in Shicang Village of the Qing dynasty]. *Shehui kexue jikan* 5.226 (2016): 133–141.

Liu Yonghua, "Pairizhang yu 19 shiji Huizhou xiangcun shehui yanjiu—jian tan Ming Qing shehui shi yanjiu de fangfa yu shiliao" [Daily Account and Study on the Nineteenth-century Rural Society in Huizhou—With Remarks on the Methodology and Historical Materials of Studies on Ming and Qing Social History]. *Xueshu yuekan* 4 (2018): 128–141.

Mio Kishimoto [Anben meixu], *Qingdai Zhongguo de wujia yu jingji biandong* [Price and Economic Change in Qing China]. Trans. Liu Dirui. Beijing: Shehui kexue wenxian chubanshe, 2010.

Yan Yunxiang, *The Flow of Gifts, Reciprocity and Social Networks in a Chinese Village*. Stanford: Stanford University Press, 1996.

Zhang Youyi, *Ming Qing Huizhou tudi guanxi yanjiu* [Study on the Land Relationships in Ming and Qing Huizhou]. Beijing: Zhongguo shehui kexue chubanshe, 1984.

Zhang Youyi, *Jindai Huizhou zudian guanxi anli yanjiu* [Case Studies on Landlord-tenant Relationships in Modern Huizhou]. Beijing: Zhongguo shehui kexue chubanshe, 1988.

21 Land and property deeds and urban studies
A case study of deeds collected by Ms. Liu

Sujuan Huang

Over recent years, scholars of Chinese history have paid increasingly broad attention to urban history. No longer limited to major cities such as Shanghai and Beijing, the study of China's urban history has expanded to cities of secondary political and economic status such as Chengdu, Yangzhou, Changchun, Dalian, and Xiamen. In terms of research methodology, scholars have begun to emphasize perspectives from new social history, new cultural history, and microhistory to examine the daily lives of common people and analyze broader social, economic, and political phenomena. In terms of data collection and interpretation, this approach is quite demanding for researchers. While earlier studies of urban history relied on libraries, archives, museums, and other public collections as their main sources, it is now increasingly possible to incorporate oral histories and locally held documents. In 2012, I met Ms. Liu, an "old Guangzhou" who allowed me to examine her set of ancestral property deeds. This meeting greatly changed my understanding of sources that exist within society. Bringing such sources to urban studies helps to expand the scope of data collection and facilitate researchers' understanding of urban social structure, social transformation, and the larger significance of small scale change.

Contracts and deeds are indispensable sources for the study of Chinese social, economic, and legal history. In the 1940s, Fu Yiling (傅衣凌) had already noticed the significant value of land deeds dating from the Ming and Qing. With the discovery during the 1980s of a large number of folk documents in Huizhou and Fujian, Confucius family documents in Shandong, and salt industry documents in Sichuan, the collection, organization, and research of deeds have received increasing attention. Japanese and American scholars have also paid attention to deeds as a source for the study of China's economic development, legal practices, and social relationships. However, previous studies have been concerned primarily with rural land deeds and less with urban property. The reason is that urban land was far less important to the imperial state than rural land as a basis of taxation. There was neither legal provision specifically for urban land, nor any department particularly in charge of urban land administration. The deeds used in urban property transactions are very similar in form to those for the purchase and sale of rural land, including a concept of dual land ownership similar to the idea of "one field with two owners" (一田兩主 *yitian liangzhu*). With the late Qing reforms of the early 1900s (新政時期 *Xinzheng shiqi*), cities became increasingly important not only in the economic system, but also politically, as these reforms broke up the hierarchical administrative order of the "province-prefecture-county." Urban land became an important object on which the modern state government strengthened governance.

Apart from some research on title deeds in Shanghai, there is currently little research on other types of land and property deeds. Using the land and property deeds collected by Ms. Liu, this chapter discusses the relevant institutions behind these documents, and explores the ways in which historical anthropology can be better applied to urban history studies. This set of land and property deeds was originally owned by Ms. Liu's natal family, surnamed Huang. On the eve of the founding of the PRC, as they prepared to move to Hong Kong, the Huang family handed over this collection of family documents to Ms. Liu. These deeds include the "non-recourse sale deed" (斷賣屋契 *duanmai wu qi*) from the tenth year of the Tongzhi reign, the "new deed paper for the non-recourse sale" (改換斷賣新契紙 *gaihuan duanmai xinqizhi*) dated 1913, the "license for rooftop add-ons with paid tax" (補稅上蓋執照 *bushi shanggaige zhizhao*) from 1919, the "Civil Property Guarantee" (民產保證 *minchan baozheng*) from 1924, and the "receipt of temporary land tax" (征收臨時地稅單 *zhengshou linshi dishui dan*) in 1937.

The non-recourse sale deed

The earliest deed in Ms. Liu's collection is the "non-recourse sale deed," drawn up on the twentieth day of the twelfth month in the tenth year of the Tongzhi reign (1871). The deed was handwritten and recorded that Lin Fusheng *tang* 林福生堂 purchased from Ye Chengyin *tang* 葉承蔭堂, also known as Ye Xiangping 葉薌萍, an empty house-lot located in the third lane in Shiliufu 十六甫 outside Taiping Gate 太平門. As commonly seen in land leases in the Qing Dynasty, the seller and buyer traded in the name of "tang" (hall), meaning that the trading parties represent their extended families. Shiliufu is the name of a place located in Xiguan 西關 outside Taiping Gate of Guangzhou City. Xiguan was the industrial and commercial center of Guangzhou in the Qing Dynasty. Weaving factories densely lined Upper Xiguan 上西關, and business houses assembled in Lower Xiguan 下西關, attracting large numbers of merchants to purchase land and build houses in nearby neighborhoods. Located between Baohua fang 寶華坊 and Duobao Street 多寶街, Shiliufu in the late Qing Dynasty was a prosperous area inhabited by wealthy businessmen.

The document explains that the house-lot

> faces south, five *zhang* 丈 and five *chi* 尺 in length, three *zhang* five *chi* six *cun* 寸 and eight *fen* 分 wide, with the front extending to the middle of the street, back to the center of the public-owned wall, left to the center

of the public-owned wall of the Ye family's house, right to the center of the public-owned wall of the house, clearly defined in four directions.

This sentence describes the location, size, and surrounding environment of the land. It is worth noting that the length and width of the land was carefully measured, while the actual shape of the parcel is relatively vague. The "four borders" of the land—front to the middle of the street and the other three to the "public-owned walls" shared with neighbors—were clearly recorded in the deed for a more specific description of the land and clarification of the rights and obligations relationships with the neighbors. Therefore, at the end of the deed, it was also particularly mentioned that if Lin Fusheng should build a house on the spot, he "should make a supplementary payment for the public-owned wall and the street gate." According to the deed, the Ye Chengyin family "wanted to sell the land due to an emergency, so first called relatives and friends and later sold it to the Lin Fusheng family through the introduction of intermediaries." This statement of cause is also commonly seen in land transactions in the Qing Dynasty, and indicates that relatives and friends would have had the priority to purchase the land. If relatives and friends were not willing to buy, then the land could be sold freely to an outsider.

The deed then states that there was no disputed debt related to this piece of land.

> This house-lot is indeed owned by the Ye Chengyin family. It has no relation to anyone else and has not been remortgaged or repledged, nor kept for ancestral sacrifices. If there is any obscure background, or anyone arises to claim the land or any claim of pledge or mortgage, that is the business of the Ye Chengyin family, and has nothing to do with the Lin Fusheng family.

What is interesting is that, in addition to the debt-free declaration, the deed explains that "the land is originally liable to grain tax." This reminds us of the universal nature of land in the administrative structure of urban and rural areas in China during the imperial period. Even the urban land around Guangzhou city was liable to grain tax, harkening back to a time when agriculture was the foundation of production, the primary value of land was to grow crops, and the field tax was the pillar of the tax system.

In order to solve the problem of grain tax, Ye Xiangping proposed "to reclaim the ownership of the well, night soil and pier, and to pay the grain tax with its revenue." This sentence tells us two things. First, the house-lot in transaction was accompanied with the ownership of the well, night soil and pier. Second, these items could generate a certain amount of income every year, which the Ye family used to pay the grain tax on the house-lot. The price of the house-lot was 125 silver dollars, and the deed tax was 90. The deed tax represents the official recognition of the validity of this land transaction. Therefore, the deed is stamped with the Nanhai county 南海縣

magistrate's seal at the bottom, confirming that this is a "red deed" 紅契, that is, one for which official tax has been paid. At the bottom of the deed, there is also the date that the deed was drawn: "the twentieth day of the twelfth month in the tenth year of the Tongzhi reign," and seller's signature: "person to sell this house-spot without recourse: Ye Chengyin, also known as Ye Xiangping. Recorded by [Ye] Senting 葉森亭."

More than 30 years after this transaction, the land property right changed again. On the twentieth day of the seventh month in the thirty-third year of the Guangxu reign (1907), the patriarch of the Lin Fusheng family passed away and the sons divided the family (*fenjia* 分家, i.e., formally separated both ritual obligations and property of each branch). At the bottom of this deed, a sentence was added:

> on the twentieth day of the seventh month in the thirty-third year of the Guangxu reign, according to the family division instructions left by our father, the house with the street number 3 is given to the second son [Lin] Jichang tang. Recorded by [Lin] Jitao.

This shows that by this time houses had been built on the house-lot, and house numbers given. The sentence added at the bottom of the deed shows that the division of the family was agreed by the Lin brothers and that Lin Jichang had become the new owner of the property. This means that during the late Qing, it was not always necessary to write a new deed for property inheritance. As long as the parties involved agreed, the original deed would remain valid as proof of property ownership.

The "new deed for non-recourse sale"

The second deed in Ms. Liu's collection is the "new deed for the non-recourse sale" dated January 20, 1913. The "exchange of new deeds" was a measure taken by the Guangdong military government to recertify all land deeds following the Revolution of 1911. At the time of its founding, the Guangdong military government was isolated and its finances were extremely difficult. It was barely able to collect the bulk tax revenue from tariffs, land, and *lijin* taxes that had been levied by the former Qing government. To alleviate its financial difficulties, the Financial Secretary of the Guangdong Military Government, Liao Zhongkai 廖仲愷, proposed in June 1912 a measure to demand recertification of all land deeds, charging a handling fee for each transaction. On July 10, 1912, the Guangdong Military Government officially promulgated the *Regulation on Change for the New Deed Forms*. The new deed was formulated in a tripartite form. The second sheet was to be kept by the property owner, and the first and last sheets were held on record at the Financial Department and the County Government or the District Police Office. This "new deed for non-recourse sale" in Ms. Liu's collection is the second sheet of this new deed.

The deed form is divided into three columns. The right column is the *Regulation on Change for the New Deed Form* and explains procedures for changing for the new deed. There are 13 articles in the *Regulation*, which stipulates that "regarding the real estate owned by the people of Guangdong, the old deeds printed under the former Qing government will be exchanged for the new deeds issued by the Guangdong government of the Republic of China." The charge for the new deed is: "1 percent of the price in the original deeds for non-recourse deeds; 0.6 percent of the price in the original deeds for sale-with-recourse deeds." The procedures for changing the deed are that the property owner should first collect the application form in the district offices, then fill in and submit the form for examination together with the payable handling fee and deed paper fee. The owner would then receive a blank deed paper in tripartite form. They should fill in the second sheet with information such as address and price according to the original deed, write down the price as given on the original deed at the junction of the edges of two sheets, attach the original deed on the new deed, and submit all documents and payment to the district office, which will then be handed over to the Financial Department where the deed will be stamped and returned to the property owner.

The middle column of the deed paper is further divided into two parts. The property owner's basic information and amount of payment was written in the right part of the middle column. It is recorded that the property owner's name is still "Lin Fusheng tang," which is apparently copied from the original deed of the Tongzhi reign in the Qing Dynasty. The address is No. 5 of the middle subdistrict (*zhongyue* 中約) in Shiliufu. The price recorded in the original deed is 90 taels of silver, with an "added price" of 110 taels of silver, altogether 200 taels of silver, or 277 yuan and 78 cents. The "added price" (*jiajia yin* 加價銀) mentioned here is the amount for tax increase voluntarily provided by the property owner. This is because, when Sun Yat-sen vigorously campaigned for the idea of "the equalization of land rights" in Guangzhou, there was a clause for "purchasing the land by its original price" (*zhaojia shoumai* 照價收買), that is, if the government needed a piece of land, it could buy the property at the price stated in the land lease. Therefore, the property owners inside and outside the city of Guangzhou increased the land price indicated in the original deed to prevent the state from buying at the original price. Sometimes the added amount was twice as much as the original price. In other words, the value of the house listed in the deed has increased in the process of exchanging for the new deed. The value of the Lin family's house is given as 200 taels of silver, or 277 yuan and 78 cents, so they paid the handling fee of 2 yuan and 78 cents, or 1 percent of the house price. The content of the original deed was copied in the left part of the middle column. Finally, the left column contains the seal of the Financial Department and the date "January 20, second year of the Republic of China."

This "exchange for new deed form" solved the problem of confirming property rights after the change of regime. Collecting the handling fee, the government replaced the deeds of Qing-era real estate transactions with new deeds issued by the Republic of China. This fiscal measure was generally implemented by all provinces in the early years of the Republic of China. Although the primary purpose of implementing the "change for new deed form" by the Guangdong military government was to raise fiscal revenue, the new deed was in fact the government's recognition of property ownership rights. Replacing the red deed as proof of the validity of property ownership, the new deed was supported by property owners.

The "license for rooftop add-ons with paid tax"

The third deed in Ms. Liu's collection is the "license for rooftop add-ons with paid tax" dated May 20, 1919. This license is the certificate that recognizes the legality of rooftop add-ons by the Guangdong Provincial Finance Department. During this period, the military forces of the Guangxi clique warlords occupied Guangdong, and the government's fiscal revenue was extremely unstable. Like the previous document, the "license for rooftop add-ons with paid tax" was a measure to increase tax revenues. The reason for levying a tax on add-ons is that the value of a house could increase multiple times over the original purchasing price after the construction of rooftop add-ons, but often the owner would not pay additional tax. On March 9, 1918, the Finance Department issued a notice requiring the additional tax to be paid at a rate of 3 percent within three months if rooftop add-ons were built after the purchase of the house. But most owners just ignored this new regulation. After Yang Yongtai 楊永泰 assumed duty as the director of Finance Department in June 1918, he enlisted the aid of the Police Department and the Guangzhou Merchants' Association and finally carried out the collection of these overdue taxes.

The format of the "license for rooftop add-ons with paid tax" in Ms. Liu's collection is very simple. The reason for collecting "overdue tax for rooftop add-ons" was written on the right side. The property owner's name, address, original purchase price, the price of the rooftop add-ons, and the amount of tax were written in the middle. The left side contains the signature. The property owner's name is still "Lin Fusheng *tang*," and the address is still "No. 5 of the middle subdistrict in Shiliufu." It is evident that the "license for rooftop add-ons with paid tax" follows closely both the Qing Dynasty deed and the "new deed form for the non-recourse sale" issued in the early years of the Republican era. It is recorded in the license that the original purchase price was 200 taels of silver, the price of rooftop add-ons is 606 yuan, and the additional tax is 24 yuan. This means that the value of the house increased once more after rooftop add-ons were built. The conversion used here is to take 200 taels of silver simply as 200 yuan, plus the additional price of 606 yuan, which makes a total price of the house of 806 yuan to be multiplied by the tax rate of 3 percent. The license is stamped by the seal of the Guangdong Provincial Finance Department and the date is "May 20, the eighth year of the Republic of China."

The tax on rooftop add-ons was meant to solve problems of property rights and property value after house improvement. Although the property owner did not change after add-ons were built, the property value increased. As long as the tax on rooftop add-ons was paid, the government would recognize the added value. Therefore, the tax was also generally accepted by the owners. The tax on rooftop add-ons maintained as part of the municipal fiscal taxation income after the establishment of the Guangzhou municipal government in 1921. In actual implementation, the property owner would file an application to the Finance Bureau, which would verify the original red deed of the house, add the construction cost into the property price, calculate the amount of the tax, and then issue the license with the new property value.

The "Civil Property Guarantee"

The fourth deed in Ms. Liu's collection is the "Civil Property Guarantee" dated March 12, 1924. This special property right certificate appeared when there was an excessive registration of provincial and municipal properties in Guangzhou in 1924. The "Civil Property Guarantee," as its name literally suggests, is designed to guarantee civil, rather than provincial and municipal properties. At the beginning of 1923, with the help of the Yunnan and Guangxi cliques, Sun Yat-sen once again seized power in Guangzhou and established the Grand Marshal stronghold (大元帥府大本營). As a result, Guangzhou had no fewer than *four* fiscal collection agencies: the Grand Marshal stronghold, the Yunnan and Guangxi cliques, the Guangdong Provincial government, and the Guangzhou Municipal government. At the time, the Sun Yat-sen regime was surrounded by enemies, and Guangzhou with its prosperous businesses became its most important source of revenue. The Guangdong provincial government's fiscal revenue mainly depended on commercial taxation from Guangzhou, while the Guangzhou Municipal government relied primarily on claiming and selling provincial and municipal properties. The "provincial properties" (*guan chan* 官產) were those left by the former Qing government. They were taken over first by the Guangdong Military Government in the early years of the Republican era and then administered by the Finance Department of the Guangdong Provincial Government until, in 1923, the provincial properties located in the city of Guangzhou were put under the administration of the Guangzhou Municipal Government Finance Bureau. The "municipal properties" (*shi chan* 市產), as distinguished from the "provincial properties," were controlled by the provincial government. These consisted of properties that had originally belonged to the Manchu Bannermen in the city, and the land that was newly cleared as a result of municipal construction. Subsequently, the municipal government continued to expand the scope of "municipal properties" to include all the veranda land, irregular spots, deserted streets, piers, ownerless mountains, ditches and streams, rivers, and temples of shared ownership.

From May 1923 to February 1924, the municipal government raised funds for military pay by selling some of these provincial and municipal properties, which caused great public grievance as land prices in Guangzhou declined. Some people even mortgaged their own properties to foreigners for security. In October 1923, to appease the public panic caused by the excessive registration of provincial properties, the Grand Marshal stronghold ordered the establishment of the Guangdong Local Rehabilitation Commission (*shanhou weiyuan hui* 善後委員會) and proposed to ensure property rights by issuing a guarantee. The Civil Property Guarantee Bureau was established on November 30, 1923, and subsequently the Civil Property Guarantee program, in which the property owner filled in an application form, submitted deeds for inspection, and paid a 3 percent deposit fee in order to receive a "Civil Property Guarantee" certificate.

As the "Civil Property Guarantee" in Ms. Liu's collection shows, the certificate is also very simple in form. There are a few lines on the right side explaining simply the reasons for civil property guarantee. The owner's name, address, property borders in four directions, length, width, and value, of the parcel, and the amount of deposit fee are written in the middle and signature on the left side. It is worth noting that in this document the owner's name had been changed to "Huang Jifu (黃吉甫) from Lin Fusheng *tang*," which means that the property right had been transferred. Although we do not have any material that shows us the details of this property transaction between the Huang family and the Lin family, it was most likely done in a hurry during the chaotic Warlord era. The address indicated in the deed is now "No. 5, east third lane, Shiliufu, District No. 10." "District No. 10" refers to the jurisdiction unit of a police station, showing that this sort of jurisdiction had become common. The property's borders in four directions are recorded as "front to the roof tile end, back to the wall center, left and right to the wall center," which is the same as that in the original deed. It is also recorded that "the length is five *zhang* and five *cun*, the width is two *zhang* three *chi* and eight *cun*." The length is the same as before, but for reasons that are not clear, the width appears to be reduced.

The value of the house is given as 4,280 yuan, which is more than five times the value in the 1919 license. It is not possible to say for certain why the value had increased so rapidly. This change is probably related to the instability of currency value and the high inflation rate of the time. The deposit fee is 85 yuan and 60 cents, which means that it was charged at a rate of 2, not 3 percent. The stamps on the left side are from the Guangdong Civil Property Guarantee Bureau, the Guangdong Local Rehabilitation Commission, and the director of the Bureau Li Jitang 李紀堂, and the date is "March 12, the thirteenth year of the Republic of China."

The "Civil Property Guarantee" can be considered as a temporary fiscal levy measure launched by the government to raise money for the army. When the financial situation improved, the measure was immediately abolished. In September 1925, the Civil Property Guarantee Bureau was dissolved.

However, the problem of property rights that the "Civil Property Guarantee" meant to solve was one faced by all governments during the Republican era, that is, how to distinguish between "public property" (公產) and "private property." The invention of the terms "provincial property," "municipal property," and "civil property" was precisely for the purpose of clarifying the boundaries between "public" and "private" land. However, the excessive registration of provincial and municipal properties had once again blurred the already ambiguous boundary and resulted in strong mass protests. In this sense, the emergence of "Civil Property Guarantee" is a compromise between the government and the public on the boundary between public and private property rights.

The "receipt of temporary land tax levied by the Guangzhou Municipal Finance Bureau"

The fifth deed in Ms. Liu's collection is the "receipt of temporary land tax levied by the Guangzhou Municipal Finance Bureau" dated October 30, 1937. As the title suggests, this certificate indicates that the property owner has paid the temporary land tax. The collection of urban land tax depended on the urban land registration system. On July 1, 1925, the Guangzhou Municipal Government was reorganized into a commission system and announced that they would "abolish miscellaneous taxes, put provincial and municipal properties to an end, and seek municipal revenues from reasonable rents and taxes" quickly. The "reasonable rents and taxes" mean urban land tax. In January 1926, the Guangdong Provincial Government promulgated the *Regulations on Urban Land Registration and Taxation in Guangdong*. This regulation had been drafted by the German Dr. Wilhelm Ludwig Schrameyer at the invitation of Sun Yat-sen, and was the first regulation on the registration and taxation of urban land in China. The regulations applied not only to Guangzhou, but also to cities such as Shantou 汕頭, Jiangmen 江門, Foshan 佛山, Meilong 梅菉, and Beihai 北海, which had already established municipal governments.

According to the regulations, land registration was managed by the municipal land bureaus of the districts, with a registration fee of 2 percent of the land price. All land property rights including ownership and permanent tenancy, rights to pawn and pledge, rights over shop fixtures or to build add-ons, long-term leases, and mortgage rights must be registered. Once registered, these property rights were confirmed. The land tax was collected twice a year. The tax rate for an empty lot and for built land was the same 2 percent, and the tax rate for farmland was 0.5 percent. There were also regulations on land price increase tax and land transfer fee. At that time, since the Guangdong Provincial Government was still unable to implement this regulation across the province, the Guangzhou Municipal Government first set up a land bureau to put land registration in trial implementation. On August 1, 1926, the Guangzhou Municipal Land Bureau was formally established.

Land registration was finally carried out in October 1927 after the Guangdong Provincial Government promulgated the *Amendment to the Regulations on Urban Land Registration and Taxation, with Implementation Rules*. For the Municipal Government, land survey and registration were preparatory measures for land tax collection. Considering that a land survey would take a long time, the Land Bureau proposed to levy a temporary land tax, which was first collected in April 1928. By the 1930s, this temporary land tax had become one of the most important sources of fiscal revenue.

The "receipt of temporary land tax levied by the Guangzhou Municipal Finance Bureau" in Ms. Liu's collection shows that the document recorded the address of the property, the property owner's name, and the amount of assessed tax. The address in the document is "No. 5, East Third Lane, Shiliufu, Baohua Branch, Guangzhou," suggesting that the Guangzhou Police Department had already adjusted their jurisdiction areas and that Shiliufu was now under the Baohua Branch Police Station. The column for the property owner's name and information is left blank, and it is recorded that "until the second phase of the twenty-sixth year, a temporary land tax of 2 yuan and 40 cents has been paid." The rules for the taxation of temporary land tax were very complicated. The price of the property is calculated roughly based on the rental rate, minus other incidental charges. The temporary land tax was levied in two phases each year. The first was scheduled to run from March 1st to 31st and the second phase from September 1st to 30th. Yet, the date of payment recorded in the document is "October 30, the twenty-sixth year of the Republic of China," suggesting that at least some property owners failed to pay the tax on time.

The collection of urban land tax is a new form of recognition of land property rights. Using land surveys and registration, the government had first solved the problem of determining the land property rights, and then linked these rights with specific tax liabilities. In other words, private property rights were recognized and protected by the government through payment of land taxes. In this sense, the modern state government and the people had reached a new fiscal contractual relationship on land affairs. This measure also completely separated the urban land liable to land tax from the rural land liable to grain tax.

Conclusion

From the land and property deeds, we can see the difficulties of modern government management of urban land. The changes in the form of the land and property deeds in Guangzhou showed that the national power of the Republic of China constantly increased the control of urban land. However, Republican-era Guangzhou became the residence of the Guangdong military government, Guangdong provincial government, Guangzhou municipal government, etc., and the real estate of the city was one of the tax sources they all drew upon. There are obvious reasons to increase the financial revenue in the deeds. Without stable tax revenue, private property rights were hard to secure. However, for their own interests, common people did not passively accept government intervention, but constantly disputed with the government.

To many urban historians, Ms. Liu's collection of deeds might seem rather fragmented and not as complete as the land and property deeds contained in the archives. However, their value is no less than the archival collections. When Ms. Liu showed me these deeds, I could feel how much she cherished the documents. Although she did not know the full story behind each deed and could not explain the significant lack of information in some of them, she held them as evidence of the property right to the Huang family's ancestral home. In my conversation with Ms. Liu, I began to wonder for the first time, how urban residents could claim "ownership" of a certain house. Whether in an era of frequent wars and regime change or in peacetime, property rights are the foundation for people to settle down and live in peace. Any institution that involves property rights will deeply affect people's lives. Therefore, the people have a keen awareness of their property rights, and it is precisely this human emotion toward objects that deeds lying in the archives cannot convey. Only when we put these deeds back into real lives can we better understand the nature of the property right system.

Further Reading

Feng Xueqiang, *Cong chuantong dao jindai, Jiangnan chengzhen tudiquan zhidu yanjiu* [From traditional to modern, research on the rights system of urban land ownership in Jiangnan]. Shanghai: Shanghai shehui kexue chubanshe, 2004.

Huang Sujuan, *Cong shengcheng dao chengchi: Jindai Guangzhou tudiquan yu chengshi kongjian bianqian* [From provincial seat to city: Land ownership and the transformation of urban space in modern Guangzhou]. Beijing: Shehui kexue chubanshe, 2018.

Yang Guozhen, *Ming Qing tudi qiyue wenshu yanjiu* [Research on Ming-Qing land documents]. Beijing: Renmin daxue chubanshe, 2009.

Zelin, Madeleine, Jonathan K. Ocko, and Gardella Robert (eds), *Contract and property in early modern China*. Stanford, CA: Stanford University Press, 2004.

22 Genealogies and revolution in the Jiangxi Soviet

Weixin Rao

One may think that traditional family documents, such as genealogies, could not possibly have anything to do with researching the history of revolution in the Jiangxi Soviet; yet the two are in fact closely related. This connection is not only a matter of deploying a productive research method to examine this period of history, but also is manifested in the actual historical process of the revolution.

We know that the Chinese Communist Party (CCP) Soviet revolutionary movement that took place in the rural societies of southern Jiangxi province (i.e., Gannan) in the 1920s and 1930s involved both Party-led political campaigns and robust social activism. During that period, all kinds of social forces, including village-based clan organizations, the various social classes, and also thousands of ordinary people, were fully engaged in and became the historical subjects of this revolution in the Soviet zone. In order to think productively about the complex social and political issues involved in the process of revolution, it is vitally important to focus on the existing power structures and social order in the villages at the time of the arrival of the CCP in this area, and on the revolutionary experience and life encounters of the local populace with the new situation. Already many years have passed since historians first suggested that we should understand and research the history of the revolution in the rural Soviets from the perspective of social history. However, though that approach did attract increased attention, most of the actual research still relied primarily on official documents, such as published collections of Communist Party documents and memoirs. As these official documents mainly record the CCP's policy developments and its account of political and military campaigns, they afford little insight into the social history of the revolutionary process.

The genealogies that I will discuss, especially those revised and updated after the CCP's departure from Jiangxi in late 1934 (on what would become the "Long March"), represent a parochial historical record of rural patriarchal clan society. As historians have long known, genealogies recount a lineage's development, as well as such details as the birth, death, and marriage of important members. This basic information can help us understand something about the social background of the local people and their encounters with this early CCP rural revolution. Moreover, drawing on the personal and social information contained in these genealogies can help us come to a more accurate and profound interpretation of the commonly used historical materials on the Jiangxi Soviet than has been previously possible. Most importantly, local genealogies allow us to examine this early CCP effort at rural revolution from the perspective of the local society it aimed to transform. I will elaborate on these claims with a discussion of two cases.

Land ownership in the Jiangxi Soviet

The first case concerns the revolution in land ownership. It is generally held that the social revolution in the Jiangxi Soviet culminated in the transformation of traditional land ownership relations through the campaign to "beat down local bullies and redistribute the land" (打土豪, 分田地). However, the facts show that existing land ownership practices and order were not completely eliminated. In fact, land transactions and collection of rent from tenant farmers persisted in some places under the Soviet government, while some landlords managed to successfully maintain and protect their private property and its customary uses. Even landlords who fled to the Nationalist (Guomindang, KMT)-controlled areas did not always give up their land in their native places. Recently, I discovered in the Ganzhou antique market a land purchase agreement dating from the end of 1934 revealing much about a landlord named Zhang Hengzhi (張衡址). Zhang had fled a few years before from Jiangkou town (江口鎮) in Gan county (贛縣), then controlled by the Red Army, for KMT-held Ganzhou (贛州). He had sold three pieces of his land in his hometown in the Soviet area to a "Mr. Lian Yungeng" (練韻賡先生) of Ganzhou, because Mr. Zhang had used up the money he had brought with him and was having difficulty supporting his family. It was surprising to see a seller and a buyer in a KMT area carrying out a transaction of land located in a CCP-controlled area. Even though the deal was intermediated by five witnesses, it still seemed highly risky for the buyer, Lian Yungeng.

What sort of social credit mechanism, then, had made this land transaction between the seller and the buyer possible? The key lay in determining the identities of both men as well as of the five witnesses, and the nature of their relationships with each other. It was time to consult their family genealogies and conduct fieldwork in their local places. Tracking the names of the people and places mentioned in the agreement, I found the descendants of the seller, Zhang Hengzhi, and the Republican-era Zhang family genealogy in Jiangkou town. I also located the genealogies of four of the intermediaries, Xiao Shangwei (蕭尚蔚), Ma Shanzhao (馬善招), Chen Daonan (陳道南), and Lai Yanzhen (賴衍禎). The fifth intermediary, Zhang Jihua (張積譁), turned out to be Zhang Hengzhi's "clan uncle" and was noted as such in the Zhang genealogy. From my fieldwork interviews and the information on family history and lineage members, generations and relationships in the respective genealogies, I learned that the Zhang, Xiao, Ma, Chen, and Lai were all major clans in Anping village and Shantian village in the area around Jiangkou town. The five clans also had longstanding, strong connections to each other through marriage. For example, Zhang Hengzhi's wife was from the Xiao family. It became evident that Zhang, the seller, and the intermediaries in this land transaction were linked together by important connections of kinship and marriage.

Still, I had considerable difficulty tracking down the most important figure in this agreement, the buyer "Mr. Lian Yungeng." Many of my interviewees in Jiangkou town said they had never heard of this man. But they also told me that there were some people with the Lian surname living nearby in a small village called Wushixia (烏石下). Pursuing this clue, I soon found an elderly man surnamed Lian in this village. He had not heard of this Lian Yungeng and was quite sure that there was no such person from their village. Nevertheless, a Lian Family genealogy from 1993, which this old Mr. Lian had, brought further discoveries. This consolidated lineage genealogy, compiled and updated jointly by various Lian surname families descended from different ancestral lines and coming from a number of places, including Gan, Yudu, and Xingguo counties, organized the family lineage and biographical records of the multiple Lian surname family lines and groups by their places of residence. I noticed that the sections for a Lian family from Lianwu village (練屋村) in Shiyan township (石芫鄉), Gan county, listed a clan member with the generation name Lian Taikang (練泰康), also known as Ju'an (居安), and with the courtesy name Zhusheng (祝昇). The record noted he was born in the 14th year of the Guangxu reign (1888), died in 1951 and had an adopted son, named Lian Youqiu (練猷球), born in 1941. It also recorded that the senior Mr. Lian was a practicing lawyer in Ganzhou city during the Republican era.

I had the feeling that he was likely to be my "Lian Yunsheng," as a name recorded in a genealogy can often be different from a name used in daily life. Confirming my hunch, another source found in the Ganzhou municipal library and published in 1937 listed the names and brief biographies of the members of the Ganzhou Law Society of that time, including a member named Lian Zhusheng, also known as Yungeng. Later, after a few attempts and setbacks, I managed to get in touch with Mr. Lian Youqiu, who was living in the county town of Gan. He confirmed that the buyer in the agreement, "Mr. Lian Yungeng," was in fact his adoptive father, or the "Lian Tai'an" (also known as Lian Ju'an and Lian Zhusheng) in the Lian genealogy. It turns out that Lian Yungeng had graduated from the Jiangxi Public Academy of Political Science and Law before he worked as a civil court judge on the Jiangxi High Court. In the 1930s, he set up his own private law practice in the city of Ganzhou, and assumed the position of Vice President of the Ganzhou Law Society—becoming, evidently, a noted public figure in town.

Although Lian Yungeng lived mainly in Ganzhou, his major family and marriage connections were all in his hometown—Lianwu village in Shiyan township, Gan county. Shiyan township is only a little more than 10 kilometers from Jiangkou town, and was also in Jiangkou district during the 1930s. According to the Lian, Zhang, and other family genealogies, the Lian clan had equally close marriage ties with the Zhang, Xiao, and Lai families as they had with each other. For example, Lian Yungeng's father Lian Kaike (練開科) was married to a woman from the Zhang family; Lian Yungeng's paternal uncle Lian Kaiming (練開名) married first a woman from the Chen family and, later, a woman from the Xiao family; and Lian Kaiming's daughters were married into the Lai and the Zhang families. In addition, according to Lian Youqiu's recollection, his adoptive father Lian Yungeng was also a figure of considerable prominence in Jiangkou town and the surrounding areas. Zhang Hengzhi's family was considered of equally elevated status in Jiangkou: Zhang's grandfather, Zhang Zejie (張澤傑) during the late Qing and early Republican periods had held numerous prestigious local positions, including elected ward self-government councilor, manager of the local militia, and chair of the merchants association. Zhang's father Zhang Jiran (張積燃) was a licentiate (生員) under the Qing; Zhang's senior paternal uncle Zhang Jihui (張積煇) was a graduate of higher-level modern-style schools in the early Republican period; his second paternal uncle Zhang Jihuang (張積煌) was a notable business elite figure in Jiangkou town. In short, these two families, the Zhang and the Lian, were notable social elites in this place and were closely related through family and native-place ties.

Clearly, it was this longstanding relationship between the two families that could support the guarantee of such a seemingly risky land transaction between Zhang Hengzhi and Lian Yungeng. This transaction also shows that the relationships that supported the privatized and marketized land ownership trading culture could not be so easily destroyed by the CCP's land revolution. It also reveals how clan genealogies are much more than simply keys or indexes for historians to use to examine lineage and native-place relationships in relation to land ownership order; they are compilations central to the construction and maintenance of that order itself. This is probably why the CCP after 1949 launched further fierce, sustained campaigns to crack down on the major clans and why it was so set upon destroying genealogies during the more radical phase of its land revolution—the land reform movement.

Tracking the revolution's consequences for families

It is striking that the local genealogies from this area updated after 1935 were quick to record the shifting demographics of lineage members who had experienced the revolution in the Jiangxi Soviet. Analysis of these records can enhance our understanding of the impact on and the consequences of the revolutionary period for these families from a social perspective. I will demonstrate this with reference to a case study of the genealogy of the Huang family of Shuixi (水溪) township, Yudu (雩都) county.

Shuixi borders on Xingguo (興國), Ningdu (寧都), and Ruijin (瑞金) counties. It was the center of the CCP's Jiangxi Soviet base area from 1932 to 1934. The Huang family of Shuixi had first established themselves in this area in the Song dynasty and gradually, over the successive dynasties, become a locally powerful family. In 1948, more than a decade after the CCP had left southern Jiangxi, the Huang family edited and updated the twelfth edition of their genealogy. A few years ago during my fieldwork there, I managed to get hold of that edition and the thirteenth edition produced in 1993, and found the records in both to be largely the same. The recorded (male) family members who had lived as adults through the revolutionary movements of the Jiangxi Soviet period (1929–1934) had mostly been born during and since the Tongzhi reign (1862–1874) up through the early Republican years. Three distinct references in the genealogies pointed to major consequences for them and their families. The first sort of references are to those lineage members who died during the revolutionary period and particularly due to the warfare and campaign violence—killed by the "red turmoil" (赤亂), as it is phrased. An example of the specific mention of the consequences of CCP activity is Hua Yangong (華燕公) (1894–1932) of the 21st generation.

The second kind of reference is to those who were listed as "away from home" (出外) or "away in the military" (出征) as it had not been known whether they were dead or alive. Most of these men were in their early twenties during the Jiangxi Soviet period. It is clearly recorded in the 1948 edition of the genealogy when each was either forcibly conscripted by the Red Army or fled his hometown because of the "red turmoil." As the whereabouts of these men were unknown, some of their wives remarried. Adopted sons were arranged for some by the family in order to continue the family line. Interestingly, it turned out that some of these men who were noted to be "away from home" or "out for battle" had in fact not died. Some even managed to reestablish contact with their families and hometowns after 1949, sending news that they had participated in the Red Army's "Long March," had been promoted to leading cadre positions, and set up new families with wives and children in another place. As a result, when the 13th edition of the genealogy was revised in 1993, new records were added and revisions were made to these family members' biographies to include, for instance, detailed descriptions of their glorious experiences "joining the Workers' and Peasants' Red Army" or "participating in the Long March."

The third kind are references to those who had survived the revolutionary years and remained in the area. Quite a few of these people were from elite families and had subsequently become key members in the Landlords' Restitution Corps (*huanxiang tuan*) and Rural Purification Committees (*qingxiang weiyuanhui*) when the KMT retook the area. These figures also led the process of revising the genealogy in 1948. Then, after the CCP victory in 1949, some of them were punished by the new government. For example, Cai Hegong (才杆公) (1906–?) of the 22nd generation, who had held the posts of head of the township and primary school principal in Yudu county before and after the Jiangxi Soviet period, was condemned after 1949 as a "counter-revolutionary" in the Land Reform movement and sent to Heilongjiang province, eventually dying far from home.

A preliminary examination of these records shows that the number of men with the first two kinds of references is larger than that of the third kind, suggesting that, in this case, more men left the area as a result of this period than stayed behind. This indicates a very direct impact of the Jiangxi Soviet revolutionary period on the development and fate of this local lineage. This outflow and loss of young men in those years, in turn, brought about changes in family relationships and structure. This had to do with the women who were the wives of these men re-marrying, as well as the emergence of families with stepsons, and also multiple inheritance (兼祧) families, and the new families of returning native-sons who had become CCP cadres. In addition, when comparing the different records and narratives in the old and new versions of the genealogy, we find that there can be "revolutionary," "counter-revolutionary," and even "revolutionized" (*bei geming*, i.e., persecuted during the revolutionary struggle) members all in the same lineage or even in the same immediate family. These people must have lived very different lives from each other during the initial Jiangxi Soviet period, after it ended, and again after the founding of the PRC. This not only reveals people's different reactions to the revolutionary movement and their subsequent diverging fates, but also offers some insight into the deep social and discursive consequences of this early stage of the CCP's political revolution.

Conclusion

China's twentieth century witnessed many major political transformations and generated many types of historical traces. As we seek to enhance our understanding of the complex influences and consequences of these changes from the perspective of specific human actors in local societies, we may learn much from genealogies, especially with respect to reconstructing the social networks that spread across space, generations, and perceived social divisions. Not all genealogies are equally rich and detailed, and there is much that they do not say. However, when comparing these sources and finding connections with other kinds of historical materials and combining this with an in-depth understanding of a the local place through fieldwork investigation, we find much can be learned from this method using local genealogies about the structures and webs of relationships networks essential to the ordering and evolution of local society in modern times.

Further Reading

Averill, Stephen C., *Revolution in the Highlands: China's Jinggangshan Base Area.* Lanham, MD: Rowman & Littlefield, 2006.

Huang, Philip C.C., Lynda Schaefer Bell, and Kathy Lemons Walker, *Chinese Communists and Rural Society, 1927—1934.* Berkeley: University of California, Center for Chinese Studies, 1978.

Weixin, Rao, ed., *Minjian lishi wenxian luncong (di yi ji: zupu yanjiu)* [Local Historical Documents, Vol. 1, Genealogies]. Beijing: Social Sciences Academic Press, 2013.

23 Using local public security archives from the 1950s— Poyang county, Jiangxi

Shigu Liu

In recent years, the History Department of Shanghai Jiaotong University has gained access to a set of local public security archives and files dating from the 1950s to the 1970s, related to individuals in Poyang 鄱阳 county, Jiangxi province. Due to its special nature, this voluminous judicial archive has previously escaped the notice of scholars. A preliminary count shows that there are about 9,200 case files, each for one individual, each ranging in length from a few to several hundred pages.

The case records involve a wide variety of offenses, which in keeping with shifting trends over time, gradually evolve from those of mainly "political offenses" (*zhengzhi fan*) in the early years of the PRC to general criminal cases in later years. The archives from 1949 to 1952, a period that was politically centered around the "Suppression of Counterrevolutionaries" (*zhenya fangeming* 镇压反革命) campaign, deal largely with different kinds of political cases, including the labeling of individuals as "bandits," "spies," "reactionaries," "counter-revolutionaries," "lawless landlords," and, most commonly, "local bullies." The sentences handed down vary in severity from the death penalty and life imprisonment to fixed-term imprisonment, labor service (*laoyi* 劳役), surveillance (*guanzhi* 管制), and acquittal. Those charged as "bandits" or "spies" received the most severe punishments of death or life imprisonment. Together they show how the struggle against internal enemies was an integral facet of the large-scale military conflict in Korea, and the formation of the new society at home.

In 1953, China called to a close the period known as the "three years of preparation," and entered a new phase of comprehensive economic construction. During this time, political offenses, especially the "local bully" cases were joined by a growing number of criminal cases, including charges of theft, rape, manslaughter and assault, election sabotage, and arson. Later, the pattern of criminal charges would shift again. Amidst the rapid development of agricultural cooperatives, implementation of the "unified purchase and sale" (*tonggou tongxiao*) system of state monopoly, and shift to high-level cooperatives (the point at which peasants had to transfer their private productive resources like land, tools, and draft animals to collectives), charges of political crimes in Poyang county were increasingly joined by *productive* ones: tax evasion, "active counter-revolution and rumor mongering" (*xianfan zaoyao* 现反造谣), and especially theft. These types of cases, however, were still fewer in number than the many political ones that arose from successive campaigns. In fact, "political cases" continue to comprise the majority of these special individual archival case files for the whole period from throughout the 1950s to the 1970s. These findings correspond with what is known of the criminal justice system and the social-political context of this period.

In what follows, I will first introduce how we encountered and collected these archives, and discuss the opportunities and challenges involved in using them as historical materials. Finally, the chapter will point to specific research projects that might be pursued using them in conjunction with other relevant documents and fieldwork.

Collecting local documents

Over the past decade, our department has collected local archives amounting to almost six million pages from more than 50 cities and counties in Jiangsu, Zhejiang, Henan, Yunnan, Anhui, Jiangxi, Chongqing, Hunan, Shandong, and Qinghai provinces. Among these important primary sources that touch upon such a wide variety and broad range of themes for the study of Mao-era history, some are particularly rare documents, such as the files from Public Security Bureaus (PSB, *gong'an ju* 公安局), procurate (*jiancha yuan* 检察院), and people's courts. Owing to our limited access to central and provincial archives, we concentrated mainly on county-level archives. Among all the county-level documents from the 1950s collected so far, the individual case files from Poyang county stand out as an especially valuable set. This is not only because they include rarely available PSB materials, but also because their abundant, richly detailed information on many pre-1949 notable local figures bring critical social networks in the county of that time into sharp focus.

The archive came to our notice by chance. In 2010, the Poyang county government proposed constructing a website for those seeking family roots in the county and approached us to assist with scholarly support. In the course of this project, we made the acquaintance of a local police officer, and while chatting over dinner, we asked him if his bureau still kept any old documents. Coincidently, this officer actually turned out to be the archivist of the county PSB and took us to see their archives storage room. There, in this out of the way, deserted room, we saw piles and piles of individual case files scattered on racks and on the floor, covered in thick layers of dust.

As none of us could spare the time and expense to remain in this place for the length of time it would take to read and transcribe the documents, we hoped instead to photocopy or scan the documents for our own research. But our request to do so met with a nervous response and considerable hesitation. So, we went to ask the Party Secretary of Poyang County for support, and he was willing to help for the sake of the local genealogy project. Personal connections and reciprocity in relationships can play a useful part in conducting this kind of research.

It took us more than three years to digitize this set of cases. In early 2011, Professor Cao Shuji and I began to work with faculty and students from Jiangxi Normal University, and eventually finished digitizing (with digital cameras) almost 200 volumes of these Poyang archives. Teamwork was essential; it would simply have been impossible for an individual researcher to collect the nearly 10,000 volumes of case file documents. With only a week to work on our initial visit, we aimed first to digitize the thicker files, reasoning that they should contain richer, more detailed and complex information than the thinner ones. We returned that summer, this time bringing six graduate students from Shanghai to help, and worked non-stop for half a month, digitizing some 3,200 volumes of documents. On the third and final visit, we took another approach. We outsourced the digitization work to the archive staff, providing them with the necessary equipment and funding. This collaboration lasted for three years and simultaneously made it possible for us to finish collecting these sources and for these archives to launch their own digitization process.

Our fieldwork team is usually made up of about six people, including both faculty and students. In order to ensure efficient, expeditious, and reliable collection of materials, each team member brings a laptop and a digital camera with at least three external batteries and memory cards for ample storage. Our usual routine was to first skim over the full catalog before retrieving the dusty files from the storage room. Then we stood by the table and took photos of the archives page by page, usually for eight to ten hours a day, making a point of assisting the archivists in putting the files back in their original order. After dinner each day, we would get together to sort out what we had all done and to make a catalog of the photos taken that day before importing them into our master hard drive. Since we only could undertake this work during winter and summer holidays, we had to deal with some fairly uncomfortable working conditions, at times very hot or cold weather. It was essential to maintain the physical stamina and mental focus to persevere in our work.

Using early PRC local archives

As with any historical source, it is essential to treat these pubic security files as just one of many pieces of evidence to be compared and contrasted. State documents are structured by official ideology, produced by a particular group of people in an institutional unit, at a particular moment, for a particular purpose and for a targeted readership, and preserved in a particular way for particular reasons. Being attentive to the potential limitations of such documents, we need to read them alongside other local sources—histories, gazetteers, document and memoir compilations, newspapers, and folk materials, as well as interviews with those who experienced and remember past events. It is essential for us to know the geographical features of the area, and familiarize ourselves with surviving old buildings and material remnants, as well as customs and religious rituals still practiced and retaining clues to the past, and local social-cultural contexts.

These points of comparison help us to remember the political context of the time, and avoid being misled by the documents' own narrative frameworks. Remaining critical, we have to understand the limitations of the type of sources that I call "documents of results," by which I mean formal, official reporting documents characterized by their political content and highly structured style of writing. These include general summary reports and promoted model cases compiled by party cadres at various levels. They are prescriptive and didactic, describing the political forces behind their creation more than the actual social realities. The standard narrative presented in reports from the Land Reform Campaign is a good example. Such documents typically begin by listing the pre-Liberation structure of households, population, and land, according to the four rural classes: landlords, rich peasant, middle peasant, and poor peasant. This information is then followed by a report on progress made as a result of the Land Reform campaign, particularly in the transformation of land ownership. Produced according to a strict formula, not merely in style, but also in the presentation of social structure before and after the campaign, such reports state that, for instance, 10 percent of landlords owned 80 percent of the land in the village before Land Reform. Such "documents of results" supply similar patterns of information about a range of different places. They cannot be expected to provide the specific, intricate details and dynamic variation necessary to expose the complexity of local history.

By contrast, the materials I call "documents of process" more candidly address practical issues that were encountered during political movements. These documents may be found in work files at various levels, and include top-down instructions, county and district party committee meeting minutes, county party committee instructions, reports, circulars, and notifications, the situation and work reports about different stages in the process from district party committees, and the miscellaneous statistical charts for the various districts involved. Among these materials, the county- and district-level meeting reports, situation reports, and statistical charts are the essential documents through which we can examine the various institutions' and actors' perceptions, as well as their aims, strategies, methods, and other aspects of their decision-making and operations. Focused on particular problems or issues that have arisen, these documents tend to assume a pragmatic position and are only minimally concerned with performing ideological agendas. In short, despite their use of numbers and details, "documents of results" are most useful for gaining a broad sense of the political aims and outcomes of a campaign, whereas the "documents of process" reveal the micro-level practices of key processes and mechanisms of the campaigns and actual situations on the ground.

The individual case files preserved in the Poyang county archives are typical "documents of process" that record the PSB's daily operations. Based on what I have read so far, it appears that almost every case file contains one of the following five types of documents: reports and accusations from villagers or work teams; records of interrogations and testimonies; suspect confessions and self-criticisms; miscellaneous correspondence and official letters exchanged in the course of investigation; and the final verdicts. In addition, in some case files, there are also investigation materials, arrest warrants, guarantor certificates, "reform through labor" (*laogai* 劳改) registration forms, and petitions calling for severity or leniency of punishment.

Collecting and familiarizing ourselves with such materials still leaves us with the core challenge faced by all historians: we still have to ask the right questions, the ones that will shine a beam of light in the darkness, exposing the significance of findings that lay within a mountain of materials. While some scholars seek their research questions from analysis of existing scholarship, others hold that the most productive questions are those that arise directly from reading primary sources. In my limited experience, I am particularly excited to encounter historical records that seem to make little sense in relation to what is commonly believed, and discuss matters that have not been sufficiently addressed in previous research. To make the most of such opportunities, it is essential to be aware that those details that at first glance seem not to make sense can often provide the key to entirely new questions and perspectives. Most importantly, we need to be attentive to counterintuitive details, seemingly illogical phenomena, and contradictory statistics and other disruptive facts in the sources.

So far, I have completed two research projects with the Poyang individual case files. "Judicial Practices in the Land Reform Movement of 'New China'" analyses the cases of "lawless landlords" during the Land Reform movement in 1950–1952. A second project looks at the Boat Populations Democratic Reform movement from 1952 to 1953, focusing on the accusations made against boat-dwellers for being "feudalistic labor contractors" (*fengjian batou* 封建把头), "spies," "local bullies," and "bandits" during the Counterrevolutionary Suppression campaign. In the process, I have certainly found that local archives must be supplemented by higher-level documents and all the other relevant materials one can find. For instance, the high-level central government land reform documents, such as statements of policy and methods, laws and decrees, regulations, instructions, resolutions, and summary reports issued at different stages of the movement, help us see the broader developments and policy shifts in relation to which our understanding of actual local practice and process will make sense. However, for learning about the actual human actors in the Land Reform movement (beyond a few representative negative examples or propaganda models), individual case files in this PSB archive add another dimension to what we can glean from memoirs, diaries, and interviews.

These Poyang PSB case files can also shed light on much that has long been unclear about these movements in practice. For example, although it is well known that the Chinese Communist Party (CCP) government directed the incrimination and "struggle" of great numbers of landlords in the Land Reform movement, we know very little about the actual procedures of these cases. Now these case files reveal, for this county, the detailed stories of how so-called "lawless landlords" were reported, exposed, brought into the judicial process, interrogated, convicted, and punished. In addition, the rich detail contained in these documents allows us to explore the rural social structures that existed before the movement. They tell us a great deal about who these landlords were in their rural societies, what their economic situation and social status had been before, and the reasons why they were targeted by the new regime. We can also learn about the relationships between these landlords and those that accused them, and subsequently how the phenomenon of "continuous revolution" impacted the rural social structure. Most strikingly, these case files allow us to glimpse the lives of the ordinary majority as they experienced the political movements of the 1950s.

In fact, my study of the Boat Population Democratic Reform Movement had its key impetus in the other main kind of documents in the Poyang PSB archive—administrative documents, particularly relevant summaries and reports. This points to the importance of combining reading these documents with fieldwork interviews with those involved. Following up on the details provided in these reports led me to dozens of files in the bureau's business files concerning their dealings with labor contractors, boat people (*chuanmin* 船民), and boat-dwellers' groups (*shuishang chuanbang* 水上船帮). I subsequently located, visited, and interviewed the descendants of some of the labor contractors. Extensive reading of these new documents and learning from local people about local society through fieldwork opened my eyes to a new understanding of how the CCP state managed to extend its control over the boat-dwelling society on China's lakes and rivers.

Conclusion

The materials that I have discussed may seem beyond the reach of many historians, especially those overseas. It is hoped that interested scholars will eventually be able to visit and read the original documents personally in the Poyang PSB or to consult our digitized photographs in the resource room of the Department of History at Shanghai Jiaotong University. At present, access to these files remains limited, as we have not yet obtained the official authorization to make them publicly available. Someday these archives may all be accessible online, and I encourage others to seek out similar collections of value. Archival materials combined with fieldwork are, in my view, the most productive way for historians to make discoveries and find inspiration. Just as many recent advances in the study of twentieth-century Chinese history can be attributed to the opening of local archives, so too we must plan to make future progress with the construction of archival databases that cover diverse kinds of materials of different levels and regions over a long period of time. Moreover, we should devote ourselves, as researchers, to improving our abilities to effectively interpret these new historical materials and make the most of them with productive research questions. In my view, the most meaningful questions often emerge from careful field observation of the real world rather than from imported concepts and theories. This does, however, require a commitment to conducting long-term, trans-regional, and local studies in collaborative projects that will allow us overcome the inherent limitations of case studies and area studies.

Further Reading

Cao Shuji, Liu Shigu, *Chuantong Zhongguo diquan jieguo ji qi yanbian* [The Land Ownership structure and its evolution in twentieth century China]. Shanghai Jiao Tong University Press, 2015.

Liu Shigu, "Guojia, nongmin yu 'gongshang yejian dizhu:' Nanchangxian tugai zhong de 'qingsuan' douzheng" [State, peasants and 'merchant-landlords': the 'liquidation' struggle in Land Reform in Nanchang County], *Jindaishi Yanjiu*, 4, 2013: 78–93.

Liu Shigu, 'Shixu' xia de 'zhixu:' xin Zhongguo chengli chuqi tugai zhong de sifa shijian—dui Poyang xian 'bufa dizhu an' de jiedu yu fenxi' [Order under disorder: the judicial practice of Land Reform in the beginning of New China—analysis of the 'illegal landlords case' in Poyang county], *Jindaishi Yanjiu*, 6, 2015: 91–105.

24 Exploring a northern Jiangsu county Intangible Cultural Heritage archive

Jan Kiely

We were driving fast, looking for destinations that should, we thought, be easy to find in early twenty-first-century China. On this first, fieldwork foray into YY county in northern Jiangsu, my graduate-student research assistant, Miss Jia, and I had been convinced we had done our homework. Yet no paper or digital guide or map, no communication by WeChat (*weixin* 微信) or phone-call, no inquiry on the street or with our gregarious taxi-driver had yet revealed the actual location of the county library, county archives, or the Cultural Bureau (文化局) in this county town trying to grow itself into a city. It felt as if these state institutions and their promised document collections had been paved over—along with the villages dotted on our old maps—under the vast avenue that led us through a canyon of half-finished luxury apartment complexes on our way toward the new cultural zone under-construction. Then, abruptly, in the middle of nowhere, a hulking, 15-story block-tower loomed before us, revealing the imprint where a vertical line of massive characters had once read "YY County Library." Pulling in sharply, we soon confronted a grand stairway entrance with a series of narrow vertical white-board government signs naming the assortment of bureaus within, including the library, the archives and the Cultural Bureau.

Making our way inside, the euphoria of our accidental discovery quickly faded: the ostentatious yet poorly maintained entrance hall exuded emptiness. A first push on the elevator button opened reflecting-mirror doors to an enormous pile of sand. It was an inauspicious start to a long-day of registering, explaining ourselves and slow-sipping paper-cups of tea with the authorities in the hope of gaining admission. Our expectations for a first day in an archive could not have been lower, but my assistant and I had not imagined that we would both arrive independently at the same unsettling suspicion: this county may not have preserved *any* substantial materials from its past. As we ruminated, another official appeared: would we be interested in seeing the county Intangible Cultural Heritage (ICH) archive (县非物质文化遗产资料库)? Emotions and contingency play a major, unheralded part in our work. At that moment, I felt a strong sense of aversion. The boom in ICH collections came as a consequence of the largely immoderate, unreflective state-directed tradition-making project for global (represented by UNESCO) recognition. Recalling the familiar critiques of ICH as a mix of commercialized and nationalistic and regionalistic fabrications and, frankly, feeling fatigued and unsettled by the apparent vacuousness of the place, I could muster no enthusiasm for this offer. Yet thinking suddenly of my colleague John Lagerwey's advice not to overlook such "folk collections," I heard myself saying, "Okay (好吧)."

I write now, more than three years and many lengthy visits to this area later, with the assurance of hindsight and familiarity. Those county institutions we stumbled upon that first day mean something different to me now. I can afford a half-embarrassed-half-amused glance askance at my initial reactions—not least at my viscerally negative response to the ICH archive. This is a collection I now know well, as I was eventually permitted to see virtually all of it: internally published document compilations, collections in preparation for publication, filed and unfiled printed and hand-written texts and illustrated materials, extensive digitized musical recordings, photographs, and videos. Only the material objects storeroom was off-limits, though not to my research assistant, who could photograph what she wished. I finally saw many of the pieces when we were later taken on a sneak-preview tour of the new county museum. I even happened upon the official organizing documents of the project, the informants' personal files, and the periodic progress reports sent up the bureaucratic chain of command. My curiosity piqued, I subsequently interviewed a number of the key people involved in the initial collection process and the organization and management work, and so have come to know much about how this collection was assembled, ordered, and maintained.

I am not writing this to claim that all such collections, which exist in one form or another in every county, will be earth-shaking discoveries. I do, however, no longer presume ICH archives to be extraneous or necessarily problematic. Based on my experience in northern Jiangsu, I hold that these collections are worth the attention of historians interested in researching local society—surely as much so as the rest of the "*minjian*" document collections that are coming to light in great quantities all around China these days. Admittedly, reading folk culture through state-constructed projects demands of us an especially high degree of alertness and caution; but this has always been the case with interpreting all such projects in China dating at least to the *Book of Odes* (詩經). As with any other archival collection, these local ICH archive sources will only yield significant value if we decipher the institutional, conceptual, and narrative codes through which they have been sourced, organized, structured, and presented. We have to render transparent the structures of information formation and its specific relevance if we want any given document to "speak," as Marc Bloch wrote, "when it is properly questioned." This seems to me to be a matter of learning methods of reading not "against the grain," as it is commonly said, but rather, to redirect the metaphor, with an awareness of how the tree grew where it grew, came to its fullness, and was felled and had its grain exposed to us. To do this, as this volume's title emphasizes, we must, in part, go out of the archive in order to best understand and interpret the archive's content. And, it helps, as the discussion below suggests, to gain a sense not just of the concepts and policies governing the particular sourcing and arrangement of an archive, but also of the everyday human role that went into its creation.

Order and disorder in the archive

Much has been said about the distorting and contrived categorizations and ordering and valuing systems—not to mention the global politics—to ICH assessment processes around the world. The built-in tensions to the process abound. The Chinese government project competes for global recognition with ICH applications that must appeal sufficiently to UNESCO's standards of coherent significance and progressive globalist values if they are to be approved. This means they must be identifying transmitted cultural forms that are consistent with human "diversity," "creativity," "human rights," "mutual respect," and "sustainable development"—agendas that often run counter to national and local state interests. At the same time, for those involved in implementing these projects, there can be no ignoring the party-state's current standards of correct and healthy (orthodox, not heterodox) cultural practices consistent with reinforcing "stability" in local society as well as, just as commonly, the entwining of national culture propagation with the fostering of tourism for local economic development. An awareness of these competing aims and their principles and boundaries is essential for us to keep in mind as we begin to use and so evaluate how ICH collections have been ordered, and, in cases, winnowed, edited, and presented.

The next step to this end is to familiarize ourselves with the major and subcategories used by ICH collections, and, indeed, their intellectual forebearers in the formation of the folklore field, as Thomas DuBois demonstrates in *Empire and the Meaning of Religion in Northeast Asia* (2017). The key ordering categories, under which all materials had to be filed, in this archive were the standard ones for all such collections:

1. Popular literature (民间文学), 2. Traditional arts (传统美术), 3. Traditional music (传统音乐), 4. Traditional dance (传统舞蹈), 5. Traditional drama (传统戏剧), 6. Folk vocal arts (曲艺), 7. Acrobatics (杂技), 8. Traditional crafts (传统技艺), 9. Manufacturing and trade traditions (生产商贸习俗), 10. Consumption traditions (消费习俗), 11. Life customs (人生礼俗), 12. Popular beliefs (民间信仰), 13. Seasonal festivals/events (岁时节令), 14. Popular knowledge (民间知识), 15. Entertainments (游艺), and 16. Traditional sports and competitions (传统体育余竞技). Accompanying, and organized in relation to these categories, furthermore, were set guidelines for collection as well as standardized forms for summarizing information from informants that were distributed to all government staff—low-level cadres—involved in the materials collection project. With the collection apparatus thus exposed,

the scope, focus, segmentation, and ordering process and its role in differentiating, labeling, arranging, and storing the information gathered in society begins to emerge.

Examining the framework also immediately calls attention to the practical work of the local government officials and staff who implemented the project. The aspects of order and disorder to the actual process they carried out both, from the perspective of the historical researcher, turned out to have their advantages. One verifiably completed part of the orderly design of the project, for instance, produced the standardized registration of fundamental information about the hundreds of informants—their names, sex, dates of birth, educational levels, occupations over time, addresses and places they lived previously, current telephone numbers, and information about how they had learned or witnessed what they were relating. With the exception of a few obvious clerical errors, this terse information, along with always specific details provided on the locations associated with the cultural phenomenon, provided details of time and place and about the types and vantage points of the informants that could be checked, confirmed, and further contextualized with fieldwork visits to specific villages and towns.

Such traceable and verifiable information could also open several unexpected doors forward at once. Initially, I was drawn to those simplest and least coherent and elaborated reports by those with registered addresses, educations, and occupations that suggested they were very elderly (born in the 1910s–1930s) actual local villagers reporting their lived experiences. These elderly villager accounts were convincing with respect to their internal logic and the context of the time and place and in relation to what was known from other sources. In short, in keeping with the ICH project standards of evidence, we have verifiable accounts produced about specific cultural practices, narratives, art forms, customs, beliefs, and skills related by particular kinds of local people who report when, where, and under what circumstances their knowledge was acquired.

However, examining the registration information on the authors who wrote the most fluidly and with the most unrestrained elaborations proved instructive and productive in other ways. These contributions were written by figures with remarkably consistent individual profiles that could be confirmed; these people could be located and interviewed. Indeed, I have come to know and spend time with a number of them. Thus, I could eventually conclude that a substantial subset of the contributions to the county's published ICH compilation volumes (almost a quarter of the entries) were produced by these figures, all of whom were retired local cultural cadres or teachers. This local educated elite strata were nearly all trained under Maoism as propagandists, had lived in the county town or a major market town, and were experienced with previous rural culture collection projects dating to the 1960s and 1980s. Their typically effusive, overly coherent accounts tending to exaggeration, creative flourishes, displays of erudition drawing on outside sources, and often asserting implausible claims to national significance for local matters immediately invited skepticism, especially in contrast to the elderly villager accounts. However, when I took the time to sit and talk with these mostly elderly men in their 70s and 80s, I learned they had much more to share than was evident from their reports for the ICH project. Constituting, in effect, a recognized group of local chroniclers—much like those Stephen Averill discusses in his *Revolution in the Highlands*, these figures have been extraordinarily generous with their resources and insights. Dramatic and eloquent raconteurs to a man, most of them having trained at some point in local Huaihai opera, they have shown me their own historical materials and photographs, provided me with invaluable personal introductions to grassroots local history and folklore amateur enthusiasts and collectors, and have facilitated my fieldwork in many ways. Moreover, as we have spent time together over the years, they have imparted to me personal reminiscences of far greater reliability, frankness, local and personal specificity, and layered nuance than is evident in the accounts they wrote for publication or provided to the ICH project.

Nonetheless, even as I was grateful for how the orderly systematization of the ICH project opened a number of ways forward for my research, I ultimately came to have even greater appreciation for the evident disorder, even serendipity, to the project's implementation in this county. ICH projects, after all, are not the first to reveal that sources produced under the auspices of local state authorities, especially far from the metropole, can yield historians a greater diversity of voices and less varnished perspectives from and of the past than collections carefully tended near centers of state power. Above all, the strong sense of localism and the tendency to relatively disorderly, even sometimes haphazard, collection, and loose, inobtrusive management to these local projects render them, even if encumbered with as much chaff as grain, far richer in variety and intriguing incongruences than most state projects of a higher or more central level. In off-the-beaten-path counties, only a handful of local officials and staff, few with relevant specialized training as archivists, let alone as research specialists on history and folk culture, are charged with carrying out these projects; and there is only a small coterie of figures beyond this who genuinely are capable, interested, and know enough, not to mention are willing, to assist those in charge. Moreover, as I was told by multiple participants and as was evident in the project documents, the project work dynamic typically oscillated between urgent, last minute scrambling to respond to demands from higher authorities and a generally ad hoc, untrammeled style of trundling along the rest of the time. The result is an archive in which a small but substantial fraction of the collection reflects the interests of the tiny group of local chronicler figures mentioned and the rest of it results not just from the general haphazardness of collecting but also from the particular practical solutions involved in sourcing materials.

In YY county, the directives and guidelines received for the project "from above" (the provincial level) on how to carry out the project and what the local officials had to report in response on planning and compliance were as bureaucratically formal, structured, and uniform as anywhere. The principle was "Preservation as the main point, salvaging first, reasonable use, develop transmission" (保护为主, 抢救第一, 合理利用, 传承发展). The government cadres and staff involved were to be centrally concerned with "preserving representative transmitters of culture" and actively were to set about finding, enumerating, and reporting information about such people. The work method slogan in 2006, as they got started, was "aims + plan + method + hard-work + action = success." Guidelines were provided for everything from identifying cultural transmitters to preparing reports, developing "teaching centers" (传习所), and how to advertise the project to the public in the era of branding (with the example of Coca-Cola's branding success presented as an example). Capturing the imaginations of those who would participate in the production and subsequent consumption of the resulting exhibitions locally was clearly a matter of much concern to the ICH project design. Yet, more than ten years later, little imprint of the original guidelines and plans—let alone the specific plans the county reported—were in evidence. And informal interviews with those who took part and managed the effort suggested these aspects for "responding to requests from above" had never been of much relevance to the actual work in the first place.

But this was not because the local officials did not care about the project. In fact, the leading archivist over the more than decade-long period of the project seemed to me deeply committed to it and very knowledgeable. Yet, eventually, when sufficiently comfortable with us, he acknowledged that he lacked any relevant training or education for the task. It just happened, he recounted, that he had been in Nanjing, the provincial capital, at the time of the first Jiangsu provincial ICH exhibition there and, out of mild curiosity, dropped by to have a look. Six years later when YY county received the call from above to take the project in hand, he was put in charge because, as his superiors told him: "You at least have some idea what it means." He did not think he did have a solid understanding of ICH, but he went ahead nonetheless—following orders. Establishing the small project group in May 2006, the county officials ostensibly sought to follow the guidelines. They spread word of the project through local media, mobilized a reported 821 people to be involved in collection (of whom 70 were deemed "core productive members"), set up systems for reporting, filing reports, and preparing and editing texts. Informal accounts added a slightly different layer to this story: the onset of this project meant, like for a campaign, all the available local cadres around were simply called together abruptly and given these extra duties, without, it was always noted, any reduction in their existing responsibilities and without any overtime pay. No one had any experience or knew exactly what to do or even how to approach people according to the guidelines. So, they did what was most comfortable—dubbed in retrospect the "networking approach." This meant they all began to tap their personal social networks—relatives, clan-members, friends, neighbors, classmates, former colleagues—to try to locate elderly "cultural transmitters." As so many of us do in our fieldwork, this meant going through personal connections to receive introductions—which led the cadres ultimately to particular people (such as the aforementioned local chroniclers) and particular places where these cadres themselves had connections. When asked exactly what they were supposed to collect in the rural areas in this initial first two-year stage, one township-level cadre assigned to a collecting work group explained broadly as follows: there was no training or detailed guidance, so they just went around collecting anything that seemed like old or folk culture. There wasn't a question about whether they liked it or were interested in it or knew anything about it or not; they did it because they had been told to do so. The whole thing was thrown together and informal. Mostly they followed the cultural cadre at the township level who already knew some villagers, which would lead to the village entertainers and storytellers. After several years, the local government had accumulated three times the amount of material now organized in the archive and they spent years sorting it, although by their own description, nobody really had any idea what they were doing. The middle-aged or younger figures from the county town with somewhat higher education and status could not always conceal their bemusement with this assembling of so much "*tu* 土" (earthy) peasant culture, but they had done so all the same, and mostly in a rather indiscriminate manner. For this, we researchers of local history should be most grateful to the fates that be.

Assuredly, as I found, the broad, fairly arbitrary gleaning of any evidence of surviving "old culture" had jumbled together a collection much of which tells us primarily about life since the late 1980s, as well as something about what the collectors thought "tradition" was in the early twenty-first century. And yet, mixed in with all of that is ample documentation of enormous value to historians interested in the formative times from the last decades of the Qing empire to the early Reform and Opening era. We just need patience and time to sift through these collections to find the diamonds in the rough. To this purpose, it is essential to have a detailed first-hand knowledge of the specific local places mentioned in the materials. In this way, for instance, I could realize that multiple scattered accounts and materials were, in fact, all about one market-town side-street community of craftsmen that had arisen in the eighteenth century to serve the nearby mansion compounds of one of the county's most prominent, wealthiest families, and that these craft-shop enterprises had survived into the mid-twentieth century. In the process of coming to see this for what it was, it helped enormously to gain some sense of how the ICH archive was put together and what sort of information had been collected.

A few words on the collection

Having already sketched out the broad contours of what might be found in these collections, I will briefly introduce more specifically the kind of materials that seem to me the most interesting and promising for research.

Printed Materials: Among the material originally in printed form, much of it is not at all a form of culture particular to this place alone; however, it does provide evidence of a reading (including a reading out-loud for others) culture that emerged in rural areas with persistently low literacy rates from the 1930s to the 1950s. Notably, the most thorough and common such printed materials are the collections of old books found in the villages, the majority of which are pre-1949 editions of the classic novels of adventures and heroes, above all *The Three Kingdoms*, and also stories of Yue Fei and Zhu Yuanzhang primarily published in Shanghai. There are also more regionally specific northern Jiangsu printed materials, particularly from the post-1949 period. Most common among these are the mimeographed scores and librettos of local Huaihai operas from the high Maoist period of the late 1950s through the mid-1970s in the wake of the institutionalization of this folk entertainment tradition and its reorientation as a common instrument of party-state propaganda. In these, the cultural worker propagandists, including several who I have come to know in their older incarnations as local chroniclers, sought to dramatize local stories in the manner of the national-level revolutionary culture.

Hand-written Materials: Much of the collection consists of hand-written documents, a small fraction of which are included in the county's five volume initially published ICH materials compilation (资料汇编)—a collection similar in organization, if not in scale, to those published by every county ICH archive. Although the hand-written materials that have been catalogued follow the ICH categories noted above, in effect, they represent three types of sources collected locally: (1) transcriptions of stories, myths, sayings and proverbs, songs, sung or drum storytelling, and opera librettos collected both from amateur or retired entertainers (藝人) and storytellers and local collectors of folk culture. The collectors are usually school teachers and local cultural cadres, who in cases participated in local folk collecting projects or even draw from earlier collected works such as the compiled and published folk tales, by province and sub-regions, the *Collection of Stories* (《故事集成》); (2) short oral history/memoir accounts; (3) ethnographic descriptions of cultural practices based on interviews and observation. In all cases, the information presented can be determined to have become known to the informants largely between the 1920s and 1980s, even if it refers to transmission of some of this information by parents, grandparents, master teachers, or master craftsmen who, in cases, lived in the last decades of the Qing dynasty.

Having compared the five published volumes of the county ICH materials compilation (amounting to 1,400 pages) to date with some of the original hand-written versions, and having seen typed draft copies with hand-written edits for the next forthcoming edition of the county published materials compilation, it is clear that edits are made to clean up and moderate the tone of what finally appears in print. By and large, however, the editorial interventions are minimal, particularly because this task has been left to just two staff members with limited time and interest in making any substantial revisions. Any account that would require a great deal of effort is simply set aside. Most of the redactions, in any case, seem to have little to do with surface political issues or even potentially troubling matters such as revolutionary violence, some of which is graphically depicted, even for the period after 1949. Rather, the revisions tend to concentrate on moderating salty local language, sexual references, and fervent expressions of local religious beliefs or practices labeled as "superstition." In many cases, an editorial note will identify a practice discussed as a form of "local superstition" and yet provide a thorough description that can serve as highly valuable corroborating and counterpoint evidence when read alongside pre-1949 sources produced by officials, local literati, religious groups, and Christian missionaries. For instance, although it is not recognizable unless one is looking for it, there is evidence in these materials of the well-known female village *wu* (巫) shaman tradition of healers and exorcists in this region; but we need to be aware of how the editors of the compilation have adopted generalized, euphemistic language in their editing work if we are to recognize in these reports references to this *wu* tradition. The more surprising inclusions, indicative of the loose editing process, are accounts fully plagiarized from non-local sources or which present stock "peasant novelist" historical fictions about ancient, imperial era, or Communist heroes related as if they are actual local history.

Carefully examined as discussed, there is much that can be researched with these ICH materials. Let me sketch out a sense of this for this one archive:

1 **For the early 1900s to 1949:** (1) Every day local language, rhetoric, humor, variations and change. (2) Common religious practices, rituals, beliefs, including exorcistic rituals, warding off evil practices, taboos, omens, *fengshui* (geomancy), and the significant role of fengshui masters, especially relating to graves and funerary practices; family and community rituals and customs of birth, marriage, death, mourning; temple cults and the numerous festival rituals and celebrations in the calendar, and the related rural mentalities. (3) Health practices, treatments, village health practitioners, including midwives, views on the body, childbirth, illness, health threats, and epidemics (mostly relating to local religious beliefs and exorcism). (4) Views and practices relating to nature, seasons, climate, weather, natural disasters, especially flood and drought (also linked to health and religious beliefs). (5) Food culture and diet; drinking and smoking culture. (6) Clothing, hair, accessories culture. (7) Courting and marriage customs and restrictions, marriage

298 Jan Kiely

contracts, sexuality, gendered customs and practices, child-rearing practices, cultures of childhood, play, and discipline. (8) Family customs and rituals of household division, honoring ancestors. (9) Work skills, styles, cultures, methods of production, craftsmanship, including house-construction, mostly town-based trades and craftsman skills, rituals, customs, and business practices, master-apprentice relationships, trade, and business-specific ethical codes. (10) Social mediators, including matchmakers, social leaders, academies (*sishu* 私塾), village, and home-based schoolteachers and schools. (11) Community social reciprocity practices, gift-giving, sharing, mutual aid, and sources of conflict. (12) Traveling peddler culture, itinerant mendicant entertainer, and performer culture. (13) Founding and survival and reestablishment stories of clan and village. (14) Accounts of common disasters—drought, flood, famine, violence of banditry, and war. (15) The role of local people in war and revolution.

2   **For 1949 to the 1980s:** (1) Much of the *minjian* culture recalled by informants in these files—about two-thirds of the accounts—reflect memories of the period from the 1950s to the 1980s. This reveals, in part, substantial continuity of pre-1949 culture well into and beyond the Maoist era. At the same time, it provides detailed evidence of grassroots mass culture constructed under Maoism, notably the creation of Huaihai opera, storytelling groups, and literature of the masses as instruments of basic-level party-state propaganda and rural organization. (2) Information on everyday struggles of life, work, survival under socialism. (3) Information on rural education and literacy levels, health conditions and diets, and gender roles. (4) Information on changes in agricultural practices, introductions of new technologies, the rural technological and low-level marketing practices of the 1970s that predated "Reform," and became a predominant theme of the fundamental period of social and culture transformation coming only in the 1980s.

Some lessons learned

At one level, what I learned from exploring how this county ICH archive was formed that was helpful to making productive use of it was fairly straightforward. First, it was worth knowing something initially about the official guidelines and categories, though much less so than what I learned subsequently about the actual order and disorder to the project. Second, it was helpful to learn from and follow up on some of the systematic, verifiable information from the project through which I could evaluate the quality of accounts and locate highly knowledgeable informants. Third, the point about the local chroniclers and the ad hoc nature of the collection process is not merely that there was more to it all than initially met the eye. As exciting as chance discoveries are, not unlike finding the government building housing the archives, library, and Cultural Bureau in the middle of nowhere to begin with, what often matters most, finally, is deciding when—in the middle of our pressured triaging of sources—*not to turn away* too quickly from what on the surface may look unpromising. Somehow we have to summon the patience and perseverance to press on. In the middle of wading through page after page of a mish-mash of materials I had no inkling of the most interesting accounts I would find, but knowing something about the haphazard and yet wide-net approach to collecting kept alive the hunch that the search was worth it.

At another level, these lessons learned in a local archive as part of a micro-history approach, just like the fieldwork that complements it, requires and brings us into interpersonal relationships of significance rather unlike, it seems to me, what is necessary for archival, library, and online-based research. As with key informants, when communicating with these local archivists, chroniclers, project cadres, and local culture enthusiasts, we historians find ourselves in the anthropologist's realm and facing some of their conundrums. I recognize in my account here about how to use this ICH archive dilemmas of "ethnographic authority." My initial assessments of the quality of what local chroniclers wrote or the disorder of the project implementation betray hazy, uninformed assumptions about others and some kind of hierarchy of knowledge. Such views were challenged less by the anthropologist's self-reflexive turn than by the actuality of relationships in the local setting where sustained communication means knowing and taking an interest in the specificities of the individual, the place, and the multiple local meanings of past experiences and present conditions. To know something about what it means to have been a local cadre in daily life, family life, and work life, during the collection process does much to diminish any sense of particular authority in relation to that process. Such recognitions, however, have not led me to attempt any James Clifford-style "polyphonic" presentations or to blindly celebrate the local view. It seems to me that to have a genuine relationship with my local interlocutors requires my full, thoughtful and respectful but surely subjective presence. I have to keep searching for answers to my questions, just as my colleagues in that county are seeking their own.

A neglected, hand-written document I found in the ICH archive penned by one of the most prolific local chroniclers who has since passed away, Mr. Zhou, brought before me at once my strong sense of commonality with and necessary difference from my local interlocutors, especially with respect to the meanings and purpose of our work. Zhou wrote in highly personal terms of the difficulty of explaining to his informants his love of collecting local history and folk stories, relating an interview with an 88-year-old man under the shade of a village tree. When he asked the man about his experiences in the "revolutionary struggles" of the 1940s, the cantankerous, elderly villager retorted, "How much money are they giving you to do these interviews?" Zhou responded that he was doing it for the party, the nation, and the people so that the records of historical heritage would not be lost. The old man just laughed grimly, calling him an "idiot" and saying, "people just want to have clothes to wear and food to eat." As Zhou tried to defend himself, other men squatting nearby chimed in wanting to know his compensation and mocking his claims to selfless interest in them, calling it "ridiculous." Another pressed: "You've never had to struggle to make enough just to eat. Has your family lacked food to eat and clothes to wear?" Clearly moved but troubled by his informants' forthright critique, Zhou finally blurts out a concluding admission, with a common phrase making of the ridiculous something sublime. He tells them he is "sailing on dry land" (陆地行舟), that is, persevering to pursue the impossible.

Further Reading

Bloch, Marc, *The Historian's Craft*. Manchester, UK: Manchester University Press, 2012.
DuBois, Thomas David, *Empire and the Meaning of Religion in Northeast Asia: Manchuria 1900–1945*, Chapter 3. Cambridge, UK: Cambridge University Press, 2017.
Smith, Stephen Anthony, "Rethinking the History of Maoist China," *A Companion to Chinese History*, ed. Michael Szonyi. Sussex: Wiley-Blackwell, 2017, 179–190.
Wilkinson, Endymion, *Chinese History: A New Manual* (5th Edition), Chapter 67. Cambridge, MA: Harvard University Asia Center, 2018.

Index

Note: Page numbers followed by "n" denote endnotes.

account books 122; in economic history 255–8; as historical materials 252–5; interpreting bookseller's account 260–3; in social and cultural history 258–60
alcoholism 62, 63
amateur village-wide ritual group 82
Anti-Rightist Campaign 1957 219
anti-schistosomiasis campaign 211
anti-traditionalism 45
Appadurai, Arjun 224
The Art of Being Governed (Szonyi) 53, 55
"Art of the interview" 109
"Authentically Chinese" 114
Averill, Stephen 293

baibai 45
Barclay, George W.: Colonial Development and Population in Taiwan 36
Barefoot doctor program 204–7, 213, 214
Barley, Nigel 83
bazi basin society 101–4
Berezkin, Rostislav 142
Birnbaum, Raoul 126
Bloch, Marc 290
Boat Population Democratic Reform Movement 286, 287
Bourgon, Jérôme 248
British social anthropology 37
Burgess, John Stewart 229

Cai Hegong 280
Canton 159–60; axis, vertical and horizontal 163–6; Beijing Road, South End, Long Bund 166–9; Honam Island 174–5; sacred sites in secular world 169–70; shape of city and locate starting point 161–3; West End, West End! 171–4
Cao Shuji 255, 284
CBDB *see* Chinese Biographical Database (CBDB)
CCP *see* Chinese Communist Party (CCP)
Chan, Anita 215
Chen Da 11
Cheng Jitang 182
Chen Hanguang 179, 182, 184
Chen Qilu 45
Chen Youliang 54
CHGIS *see* Chinese Historical GIS (CHGIS)
Chiang Kai-Shek 44
China National Association of the Mass Education Movement 5, 16
Chinese Biographical Database (CBDB) 150, 156
Chinese Communist Party (CCP) 14, 15, 98, 142, 180, 215, 287; Soviet revolutionary movement 275
"Chinese Cultural Revolution Database" 215, 216
Chinese cultural unity 153
Chinese economy 23; field research on 25–6
Chinese Family and Marriage in Singapore (Freedman) 37
Chinese Historical GIS (CHGIS) 150, 156
Chinese intellectuals 45
Chinese Lineage and Society: Fukien and Kwangtung (Freedman) 37
Chinese merchant communities 24
Chinese musical fieldwork 83
Chinese nationalism 163
Chinese religious life 77, 125, 132

302   Index

Chinese Temple App 154
"Chinese traditional culture" 58
Chiu, Alfred Kaiming 15
Chung, Robert 39, 40
"Civil Property Guarantee" 270–2
civil service recruitment 99
class structure: from community studies to 10–17; theory of society 15
Cohen, Myron 248
collectivization 30, 38, 43
Colonial Development and Population in Taiwan (Barclay) 36
"commodity chains" 224
Communist Revolution 99
Confucian activity 149
Confucianism 15
conservation campaigns 193, 202, 203; burden of 201; diligence 192; state-initiated 189; water and soil 200
consular reports on economy and trade 24–5
Contemporary Japanese field work in China 29–31
contracts: flow and use of 244–6; functions, legal environment in 246–8; research on 239–41; signing 241–4
"cooperative medical service" 199, 205, 207, 213
Counterrevolutionary Suppression campaign 286
"Criticize Lin Biao and Confucius" campaign 221, 222
"cultural materialism" 35
Cultural Revolution 30, 37, 65, 85, 146, 156, 157, 204–7, 212, 217–22; movements 215, 216
"Cultural transmitters" 294, 295
cultural unification 152, 153
"customary law" 22, 27–31

Daoism 89–91, 93, 100
Daoist liturgical traditions 129
Daoist ritual 89, 91, 93, 109, 110; groups 88; of rituals 111; scholars of 90; traditions 146, 155
daoshi 123n1
Dean, Kenneth 52
deepening trust 65–7
Deng Zhongyuan 162
Diamond, Grey 205
Diamond, Norma 43
diligence conservation campaigns 192
dominant traditionalist mode 37
"Donghao chong" 161
Donglong Gong temple committee 130

Dream of the Red Chamber 40
DuBois, Thomas 291
"Dutch learning" 24
Dutch merchant communities 24

embodied knowledge 228
ethnic autonomous region system 99
ethnic classification: documentation 181–3; fieldwork 179–81; *hemu* 183–6; interview 178–9
"ethnographic authority" 299
"exchange for new deed form" 268

Faure, David 51, 111, 132, 152, 240; *The Structure of Rural Chinese Society* 126
Fei Xiaotong 11, 12, 14, 15, 17, 36, 44, 225
Feng Zicai 179, 181–4, 186
field engineering projects 197, 199
Flowery Pagoda 169, 170, 176n2
folk literature 4, 7–10
folklore movement 4, 7, 9, 10
Freedman, Maurice 15, 18, 36, 38, 42, 54; Chinese Family and Marriage in Singapore 37; Chinese Lineage and Society: Fukien and Kwangtung 37; Lineage Organization in Southeastern China 37
"freedom of contract" 248
Fried, Morton 11, 36, 37, 40, 42, 45
"frontier ethnic minorities" 99
frontier society 97–8, 101, 104
Fujian Folklore Society 111
fund-raising activities 127
Fu Sinian 12
Fu Yiling 239, 264

Gamble, Sidney D. 5, 6, 16, 36, 256
Ganzhou Law Society 277
Ge Hong 163
Geertz, Clifford 82
gender and ethnicity 71–9
Goh, Daniel 156
"Going to the people" 4, 7
Goossaert, Vincent 89
Gotō Shinpei 27
Gounan, model of collective conservation 191–6
Gray, John Henry: Walks in the City of Canton 171
"Great Alliance" 221
Great Qing Code 244, 248
Grootaers, William 151
"ground-truthing" correctives 151

Grove, Linda 225
Guangdong Local Rehabilitation Commission 271
"Guangzhou City Gazetteer" 173
Guangzhou Municipal Finance Bureau 272–3
Gu Jiegang 3–10, 19n12
Guojia Shiyexia de Difang 26
Guo Yuhua 87, 92

Han Chinese 44–6, 61, 62, 70, 71, 73–80, 99, 125, 179, 186
hand-written materials 296–8
Harris, Marvin 35
Hayford, Charles 16
hemu 178, 183–6
hereditary military households 55
"historical and geographic" approach 9
historical-anthropological fieldwork in Jiangnan 137–41; textual source 142–3; written sources 141–2
historical GIS in fieldwork 144–9; for Chinese temple networks across Southeast Asia 154–5; intellectual stakes 151–4; for region under study 149–51; transnational temple networks 155–7
History and Magical Power in a Chinese Community (Sangren) 43
hitchhiking 74
Holm, David 60
Hopkins, Terence K. 224
Household Responsibility system reform 98–9
Hsu Tzu-fen 254
Huang Huikun 96
Huang, Philip: Peasant Economy and Social Change in North China 28; The Peasant Family and Rural Development in the Yangzi Delta, 1350–1988 28
Huang Qiang 182, 183
Hui-Han relationship 73
Hui Muslim culture 73
Huizhou Traditional Society Series 109
Hulunbuir 61, 232
human-animal cooperation 102
Hung Chang-tai 17

ICH archive *see* Intangible Cultural Heritage (ICH) archive
"incense clubs" 3, 5
Intangible Cultural Heritage (ICH) archive 60, 83, 289, 299; hand-written materials 296–8; order and disorder in 291–5; printed materials 296
"intangible heritage" 17
intellectual environment 35
intergenerational knowledge transmission 212, 213

JACAR *see* Japan Center for Asian Historical Records (JACAR)
Jackson, Bruce 82
Japan Center for Asian Historical Records (JACAR) 32
"Japan-China Trade Institute" 25
Japanese customs service 24
Japanese field research on China: economic and business practices 24–6; *kankō chōsa* 22, 23; legal institutions and customary law 27–31; useful sources for access 31–2
Japanese research community 23
Japan Society for the Promotion of Science (JSPS) 31, 32
Jiangnan, historical-anthropological fieldwork in 137–43
Jiang Qin 220, 255
Jiangsu Provincial Revolutionary Committee 220, 221
Jiang Tusheng 243
Jiang Weiqing 220
Jiangxi Soviet 275; land ownership in 276–8; revolution's consequences for families 278–80
Jones, Stephen 228
Jordan, David 126
JSPS *see* Japan Society for the Promotion of Science (JSPS)

"Kalpic disaster" 146
kankō chōsa 22–4, 27; project 28; tradition 29–31
Kleinman, Arthur 212
Koolhaus, Rem 156
Kuang Yaming 219

Lahu village, fieldwork in 97–8
land ownership: collective 178; communal 184, 186; in Jiangxi Soviet 276–8; material for 117; private 99; rights 27; structural evolution of 239; and tenancy 185; traditional land ownership 276
Land Reform 98; campaign 225, 285; movement 278, 286, 287
"land revolution" 15, 278
landscapes of labor 196–201

Lansing, J. Stephen: *Priests and Progammers* 151
large-scale irrigation systems 152
"lawless landlords" 286, 287
lawsuit archives 239–41
Lee Hong Yong 215
Levy, Marion J. 40
Li Chongshu 192–5, 197–9, 202
Li Ji 38
Li Jinghan 4–6, 10–11, 14, 16–17
Li Ren-yuan 57
Li Yih-Yuan 38, 39, 44, 45
Liang Shuming 15
Liao Zhongkai 267
"license for rooftop add-ons with paid tax" 269–70
Li communities 178
Lineage Organization in Southeastern China (Freedman) 37
Lin Yuehua 15
Lin Zhao'en 145
Ling Chun-Sheng 38
Lingxi 61
Liu Chih-wan 127
Liu Zhiwei 152
local cultural workers 83
local Daoist ritual groups 88
local investigations, ethical problems encountered in 67–8
local political elites 99
local public security archives 282; collecting local documents 283–4; PRC local archives 284–7
local research, advantages of conducting 62–5
"local systems" approach 42
Longquan lawsuit archival records 246
"Longxi Shouyue" 175
Lu Xun 7
Lu Yao 18
Lu Zhenyu 186
Luozhou Chen 53

McNeill, John 188
"Made in Ta-Ch'i Taiwan!" 43
Malinowski, Bronislaw 12–14
Mantetsu Research Bureau 27–9, 32
Maoism 85, 92, 292, 298
Mao Zedong 38, 165, 216, 219–20
Martial Law 39
Marxist socio-economic perspective 147
Mass Education Movement 5, 16, 17
The May Fourth Movement 4, 45
"medical pluralism" 212
Miaofengshan 3–5, 10, 18

Ming dynasty 55, 103, 147, 239, 246, 256
Ming historians, fieldwork for 51–60
Ming imperial cosmology 101
Ming military colonies 55
minsu xue 3–7
Mio Kishimoto 256–7
Mitsui Bussan 26
Mulan irrigation system 152
Mule caravan transportation 102
Municipal Party Committee 218
"municipal properties" 270
Mura kara Chugoku wo yomu 30
Murray, Daniel M. 151
Musicking (Small) 82

Nakagawa Tadateru 24
National Diet Library Digital Collections 32
National Institute of Informatics (NII) 32
National Science Foundation 42
Negishi Tadashi 25
Nettl, Bruno: The Study of Ethnomusicology: Thirty-one Issues and Concepts 82
"networking approach" 295
"New Culture" project 4
"new deed for non-recourse sale" 267–9
New Life Movement 15
"new revolutionary regime" 220
NII *see* National Institute of Informatics (NII)
Nixon, Richard 205
non-agricultural economy 118
"non-proletarian" ideas 216
non-recourse sale deed 265–7
non-scholarly transmission 212
non-traditionalism 44–5

"open-ended interviews" 217
oral culture 122
oral history 89, 139, 156, 264; Cultural Revolution in 215–18; interviews 30, 189, 193, 196, 201, 202; of Maoism 92; methods 57; significance and unique value of 218–22; of social changes 97; techniques 129
Oriental Despotism (Wittfogel) 151
"Oriental Despotism" model 152
Oroqen Autonomous Banner 63, 64
"oxen assembly" 118

"pan-Chinese" festivals 120
"Panyu Xuegong" 165
Pasternak, Burton 38–9
Patriotic Health Campaign 205

Peasant Economy and Social Change in North China (Huang) 28
The Peasant Family and Rural Development in the Yangzi Delta, 1350–1988 (Huang) 28
People's Liberation Army (PLA) 36, 150
People's Republic Government 164
People's Republic of China 37
PLA *see* People's Liberation Army (PLA)
"plural medical systems" 212
"political ambiguity" 221
"political offenses" 282
Popular Culture in Late Imperial China (Johnson, Nathan and Rawski) 126
post-traditionalism 45–7
poverty relief policies 99
Practicing Kinship (Szonyi) 53
PRC 29, 37, 70, 71, 79, 164, 188–9, 191, 193, 194, 201, 202, 265, 280, 282, 284–7
pre-existing conservation techniques 191
Priests and Progammers (Lansing) 151
printed materials 296
"private law" 27
production chain 224, 232–3; chains and nets 230–1; meanings 227–30; mechanics 226–7; memories and perceptions 234; themes 225–6
Provincial Party Committee 221
"provincial properties" 270

Qiang communities 71
Qiao Qiming 14
Qin dynasty 164
Qing dynasty 14, 17, 33n10, 36, 42, 45, 103, 165, 166, 209, 239, 246, 256, 265, 266, 268, 269; gazetteers 125, 129; government 5
Qing imperial cosmology 101
Qing reforms 265

"radical" movement 220
"reasonable rents and taxes" 272
Record of Qing customs 24
Red Guards movements 215
regional economic systems 145
regional ritual alliances 152
"Regulation on the Plaint Format" 241
"residual China" 38
Reynolds, Douglas 25
ritual alliances: boundaries 150; formation of 149; regional 152; and ritual activities 153

ritual performance in changing local society: 1949 barrier 91–3; Chinese fieldworkers 84–8; "Daoist music" and participant observation 90–1; ethnography and Daoism 88–90; participant observation 91; principles of "thick description" 82; questionnaires, language, and diaries 93–5; rapport 83–4
"ritual revolution" 152
ritual specialists, basic information form for 134–6
Rosen, Sam 205
"The Rout of Custom" 37
Rui Yi-Fu 38, 44
"rural bankruptcy" 14
"rural rehabilitation" 15

Sakoku(seclusion) 24–6
"salvage anthropology" 139
Sangren, Steven 145; History and Magical Power in a Chinese Community 43
Saso, Michael 91
Sato Yoshifumi 31
Schimmelpenninck, Antoinet 83
Schipper, Kristofer 91, 144
"sectarian" traditions 141
"70 percent cash" 256, 257
shamanism 65
shangong 110
shaoguan 180
Shaoguang, Wang 215
sheji-gushe 149
Shina Keizai Zensho 33n9
Shina Shobetsu Zenshi 33n9
"Shuangmendi" 166
Silin, Robert H. 45
"single-son transmission" 114
Skinner, G. William 18, 36, 42, 144
Small, Christopher: *Musicking* 82
small-scale communities 143
Smooth Pagoda 169, 170, 176n2
social activities 97
social change in Taiwan 35
"social conflict theory" 221
Socialist Education Campaign 146
Socialist Education Movement 30, 216
"social life of things" 224
soil conservation 190–1
Song Yongyi 215, 216
"southern barbarian" accusation 115
"stamped" contracts 241
state-initiated conservation campaigns 189

306   Index

The Structure of Rural Chinese Society (Faure) 126
Stubel, Hans 182
The Study of Ethnomusicology: Thirty-one Issues and Concepts (Nettl) 82
Sun Yat-sen 7, 162, 163, 183, 268, 270, 272
Sutton, Donald S. 70
Suzhou Municipal Party Committee 221
Suzhou Revolutionary Committee 221
"syncretic ritual field" 149
Szonyi, Michael: The Art of Being Governed 53, 55; Practicing Kinship 53

Taiwan anthropology: non-traditionalism 44–5; post-traditionalism and emergence of historical anthropology 45–7; traditionalism 35–44
"Taiwan anthropology" 38
Taiwan xianzhi 127
Tang dynasty 8, 53, 147, 170
Tang Meijun 45
Tao Menghe 11, 14
"temple market festivals" 5
"ten-point system" 199
Terada, Hiroaki 246–7
"thick description" 82
three-tier medical system 214
Tian Gong Yuanshuai 149
"Tianshuixiang" 170
Tibetan monastic communities 74, 78
Tōa Dōbun Shoin 25–6
Tōyō Bunko Modern China Collection Digital Library 32
traditional Chinese culture 43
traditionalism 35–44
traditional land ownership 276
Treaty of Shimonoseki 27
Tsunoyama Sakae 33n5

Unities and Diversities in Chinese Religions (Weller) 126
unstamped contracts 241
urban land tax 272, 273

Veritable Records 52

Walder, Andrew G. 215, 220
Walks in the City of Canton (Gray) 171
Wallerstein, Immanuel 224
Wang Anshi 151
Wang Guowei 239
Wang Guoxing 180–1, 183–6

Wang Shih-ch'ing 257
Wang Zhaoyi 178–9, 181–4, 187
Wang Zhenghe 184
water conservation 190–1
Wei Hongyun 29
Weller, Robert: Unities and Diversities in Chinese Religions 126
Wen Juntian 17
Western Han dynasty 8
White, Paul Dudley 205
Wittfogel, Karl: Oriental Despotism 151
Wolf, Arthur 36
Woman Meng Jiang 8, 9
Worster, Donald 188
Wu Bingjian 174
Wu Chaoshu 163
Wu Dacheng 182
Wu Kaizhen 247
Wu Tingfang 162
Wu Wenzao 11, 13

xiangtu zhi 9
Xiao Gongquan 17
Xiao Ying 96
Xiaotong, Fei 225
Xidong polities 103
Xuxiu Taiwan xianzhi 127

Yan Yunxiang 258, 259
Yang Chengzhi 7, 15
Yang, C.K. 14
Yang Lingjun 191–6, 198, 202
Yang Shiye 200
Yang Xuxiang 191, 192, 194–6, 198–200, 202–3
Yang Yinliu 84
Yang Yongtai 269
Yang Yuesheng 196
Ye Xiangping 265–7
yingwang 127
Yushodo Shoten 26

zhangben see account books
Zhang Hengzhi 276–8
Zhang Si 30, 33n17
Zhang Youyi 257
Zhang Zhidong 169, 181
Zhao Shiyu 9, 10
Zheng Zhenman 51, 52, 145, 147, 154
Zhong Jingwen 7–11
Zhongkui 124n4
Zhou Enlai 196, 220, 221
Zhou Jinze 247, 248
Zhuo Bingguang 247
Zhu Yuanzhang 54, 147

Printed in the United States
By Bookmasters